Data Structures

for Anna University

CSE | IT Courses

Data
Structures

for Anna University

CSE | IT Courses

P Sudharsan ME
Program Manager
Infosys Ltd
Chennai

J John Manoj Kumar BE
Program Manager
Standard Chartered Bank
Chennai

CBS

CBS Publishers & Distributors Pvt Ltd

New Delhi • Bengaluru • Chennai • Kochi • Kolkata • Mumbai
Bhopal • Bhubaneswar • Hyderabad • Jharkhand • Nagpur • Patna • Pune
Uttarakhand • Dhaka (Bangladesh) • Kathmandu (Nepal)

Disclaimer

Science and technology are constantly changing fields. New research and experience broaden the scope of information and knowledge. The authors have tried their best in giving information available to them while preparing the material for this book. Although all efforts have been made to ensure optimum accuracy of the material, yet it is quite possible some errors might have been left uncorrected. The publisher, the printer and the authors will not be held responsible for any inadvertent errors or inaccuracies.

ISBN: 978-93-89688-56-6

© All rights reserved by CBS Publishers & Distributors Pvt Ltd

First Edition: 2020

This book is sold subject to the condition that it shall not, by way of trade or otherwise be lent, re-sold, hired out, or otherwise circulated without the publisher's prior consent in any form of binding or cover other than that in which it is published and without a similar condition including this condition being imposed on the subsequent purchaser.

Published by Satish Kumar Jain and produced by Varun Jain for

CBS Publishers & Distributors Pvt Ltd

4819/XI Prahlad Street, 24 Ansari Road, Daryaganj, New Delhi–110 002, India.
Ph: 23289259, 23266861, 23266867   Website: www.cbspd.com
Fax: 011-23243014   e-mail: delhi@cbspd.com; cbspubs@airtelmail.in
Corporate Office: 204 FIE, Industrial Area, Patparganj, Delhi–110 092
Ph: 4934 4934   Fax: 4934 4935
e-mail: publishing@cbspd.com; publicity@cbspd.com

Branches

- **Bengaluru:** Seema House 2975, 17th Cross, K.R. Road, Banasankari 2nd Stage, Bengaluru 560 070, Karnataka, India
  Ph: +91-80-26771678/79   Fax: +91-80-26771680   e-mail: bangalore@cbspd.com
- **Chennai:** 7, Subbaraya Street, Shenoy Nagar, Chennai 600 030, Tamil Nadu, India.
  Ph: +91-44-26680620, 26681266   Fax: +91-44-42032115   e-mail: chennai@cbspd.com
- **Kochi:** 68/1534, 35, 36 Power House Road, Opposite KSEB, Kochi-682018, Kerala, India.
  Ph: +91-484-4059061-65   Fax: +91-484-4059065   e-mail: kochi@cbspd.com
- **Kolkata:** 6/B, Ground Floor, Rameswar Shaw Road, Kolkata-700 014 (West Bengal), India.
  Ph: +91-33-2289-1126, 2289-1127, 2289-1128   e-mail: kolkata@cbspd.com
- **Mumbai:** 83-C, Dr E Moses Road, Worli, Mumbai-400018, Maharashtra, India.
  Ph: +91-22-24902340/41   Fax: +91-22-24902342   e-mail: mumbai@cbspd.com

Representatives

Bhopal	0-8319310552	Bhubaneswar	0-9911037372	Hyderabad	0-9885175004
Jharkhand	0-9811541605	Nagpur	0-9421945513	Patna	0-9334159340
Pune	0-9623451994	Uttarakhand	0-9716462459		
Dhaka (Bangladesh)	01912-003485	Kathmandu (Nepal)	977-9818742655		

Printed at Mudrak, Nodia, UP, India.

to

my father-in-law
Thiru K Karuppiah
for his love, affection and support
—P Sudharsan

my lovable wife
Sangeetha
and my charming kids
Riya and Tamizh
—John Manoj Kumar

Preface

We have immense pleasure in introducing the book *Data Structures* for the benefit of students. Although a number of textbooks are available on data structures, this text tries to be different from the rest. It aims at fulfilling the needs of those who want to be acquainted with programming in C and who want to write programs in C for the various data structures with algorithms. Algorithms in this book are presented for complicated data structures followed by complete executable C programs. These algorithms allow the reader to focus on the approach to solve a problem without concern about declaration of variables and the specifications of the programming language.

This book is organised into 5 chapters as per *Anna University 2017 regulation* for students of CSE and IT. All of the concepts in the book are illustrated by several examples, wherever required. All the programs in this text have been tested and debugged for any errors. We have strived hard to make sure that all the concepts illustrated in this text has been accompanied by worked out examples.

Although this book is written primarily for examination purposes, the practical side has been kept in view and we do hope that it will appeal to practical engineers as well as to students. This book has been written with focus on the questions and programs of various university examinations for the past 5 years. Every effort has been made to present every topic and programs from the fundamentals in an easy and expressive language for the convenience and better understanding of the readers.

This book contains more than 100+ programs and 450+ multiple choice questions. A large number and variety of illustrative examples are spread throughout the book, which would greatly help in bringing a clear picture of data structures in C programming language and the logic behind it in the readers mind.

P Sudharsan
J John Manoj Kumar

Acknowledgements

We express our whole-hearted thanks to Mr A Nagoor Kani, for all his guidance, support, motivation, encouragement and cooperation, he has extended to us for the past 20+ years. Without him, our careers as authors, would not have taken off.

We acknowledge the contributions of our technical editors, Ms C Mohana Priya, Ms K Uthra and Ms S Saranya, for editing, proofreading and typesetting of the manuscript and preparing the layout of the book.

Our sincere thanks to all reviewers, for their valuable suggestions and comments, which helped us to explore the subject to a greater depth and add to more contents with programs in this text.

We are also grateful to Mr Satish K Jain, CMD, CBS Publishers & Distributors, for his keen interest in publishing this work in CBS banner. Our sincere thanks to all team members of CBS Publishers & Distributors, for their concern and care in publishing this work.

Finally, a special note of appreciation is due to relatives, friends, students and the entire teaching community, for their overwhelming support and encouragement to our writing.

P Sudharsan
J John Manoj Kumar

Contents

Preface   *vii*

Chapter 1: Linear Data Structures—List   1.1–1.142

1.1	Introduction	1.1
1.2	Abstract Data Type	1.2
1.3	The List ADT	1.3
	1.3.1 List Operations	1.4
	1.3.2 Array Based Implementation of Lists	1.5
	1.3.3 Basic Operations in a Linear List using Arrays	1.5
1.4	Linked Lists Implementation of Lists	1.20
	1.4.1 Types of Linked Lists	1.21
1.5	Basic Operations in a Singly Linked List	1.22
	1.5.1 Creation of a List	1.22
	1.5.2 Insertion of a Node	1.24
	1.5.3 Modification of a Node	1.27
	1.5.4 Deletion of a Node	1.28
	1.5.5 Traversal of a List	1.32
	1.5.6 Count the Number of Nodes in the List	1.32
1.6	Basic Operations in a Doubly Linked List	1.46
	1.6.1 Creation of a List	1.46
	1.6.2 Insertion of a Node	1.47
	1.6.3 Modification of a Node	1.51
	1.6.4 Deletion of a Node	1.52
	1.6.5 Traversal of a List	1.56
	1.6.6 Count the Number of Nodes in the List	1.57
1.7	Basic Operations in a Circular Singly Linked List	1.71
	1.7.1 Creation of a List	1.71
	1.7.2 Insertion of a Node	1.73
	1.7.3 Modification of a Node	1.76
	1.7.4 Deletion of a Node	1.77
	1.7.5 Traversal of a List	1.82
	1.7.6 Count the Number of Nodes in the List	1.82
1.8	Basic Operation in a Circular Doubly Linked List	1.97
	1.8.1 Creation of a List	1.97
	1.8.2 Insertion of a Node	1.99
	1.8.3 Modification of a Node	1.103
	1.8.4 Deletion of a Node	1.103

	1.8.5 Traversal of a List	1.108
	1.8.6 Count the Number of Nodes in the List	1.109
1.9	Applications of Linked Lists	1.122
	1.9.1 Polynomial Manipulation	1.122
1.10	Summary	1.137
1.11	Short-answer Questions	1.138

Chapter 2: Non-Linear Data Structures—Stacks and Queues   **2.1–2.76**

2.1	Stacks	2.1
2.2	Operations of Stacks	2.2
	2.2.1 Push Operation	2.2
	2.2.2 Pop Operation	2.3
	2.2.3 Peek Operation	2.5
	2.2.4 Traversing a Stack	2.5
	2.2.5 Empty Stack	2.6
	2.2.6 Fully Occupied Stack	2.6
	2.2.7 Stack Size	2.7
2.3	Applications of Stack	2.13
	2.3.1 Towers of Hanoi	2.13
	2.3.2 Reversing a String	2.15
	2.3.3 Balanced Paranthesis	2.17
2.4	Evaluation of Arithmetic Expressions	2.21
	2.4.1 Conversions of Notations	2.22
	2.4.2 Converting Infix Expression to Postfix Form	2.28
	2.4.3 Evaluating an Expression in Postfix Notation	2.32
2.5	Queues	2.36
2.6	Types of Queues	2.37
	2.6.1 Linear Queues	2.37
	2.6.2 Circular Queues	2.37
	2.6.3 Deques	2.38
2.7	Operations of Queue	2.39
	2.7.1 Enqueue Operation	2.40
	2.7.2 Dequeue Operation	2.41
	2.7.3 Peek Operation	2.43
	2.7.4 Traversing a Queue	2.43
	2.7.5 Empty Queue	2.43
	2.7.6 Fully Occupied Queue	2.44
	2.7.7 Queue Size	2.44
2.8	Representation of Circular Queues Using Arrays	2.51
2.9	Representation of Linear Dequeues Using Arrays	2.55
	2.9.1 Enqueue Operation	2.55
	2.9.2 Dequeue Operation	2.55
	2.9.3 Empty Deque	2.56
	2.9.4 Fully Occupied Deque	2.56
2.10	Representation of Circular Deques Using Arrays	2.62
2.11	Application of Queues—Priority Queue	2.67
2.12	Summary	2.72
2.13	Short-answer Questions	2.74

Chapter 3: Non-Linear Data Structures—Trees   3.1–3.98

3.1	Introduction	3.1
3.2	Binary Tree Traversal	3.2
	3.2.1 Preorder Traversal	3.3
	3.2.2 Inorder Traversal	3.3
	3.2.3 Postorder Traversal	3.3
	3.2.4 Level Order Traversal	3.4
3.3	Binary Trees	3.13
	3.3.1 Types of Binary Trees	3.13
3.4	Representation of Binary Trees	3.14
	3.4.1 Linear Representation of Binary Trees	3.14
	3.4.2 Linked Representation of Binary Trees	3.16
3.5	Expression Trees	3.16
3.6	Applications of Trees	3.18
3.7	Binary Search Trees	3.18
	3.7.1 Basic Operations in a Binary Search Tree	3.18
3.8	Threaded Binary Trees	3.33
	3.8.1 Basic Operations in a Threaded Binary Tree	3.34
3.9	AVL Trees	3.54
3.10	Basic Operations in a AVL Tree	3.54
3.11	B– Tree	3.71
3.12	Basic Operations in a B– Tree	3.71
	3.12.1 Insertion of a Node	3.72
	3.12.2 Deletion of a Node	3.72
3.13	B+ Tree	3.90
3.14	Basic Operations in a B+ Tree	3.91
	3.14.1 Searching a Node	3.92
	3.14.2 Insertion of a Node	3.92
	3.14.3 Deletion of a Node	3.93
3.15	Binary Heaps	3.93
3.16	Applications of Heaps	3.95
3.17	Summary	3.95
3.18	Short-answer Questions	3.97

Chapter 4: Non-linear Data Structures—Graphs   4.1–4.40

4.1	Graphs	4.1
	4.1.1 Definitions in Graphs	4.1
4.2	Graph Representation and its Operations	4.3
	4.2.1 Incidence Matrix	4.3
	4.2.2 Adjacency Matrix	4.7
	4.2.3 Adjacency List	4.16
4.3	Graph Traversals	4.26
	4.3.1 Depth–First Traversal	4.26
	4.3.2 Breadth–First Traversal	4.28
4.4	Application of DFS–Topological Sorting	4.31

4.5   Application of Graphs   4.34
       4.5.1   Bi-connectivity and Cut Vertex in Graphs   4.34
       4.5.2   Euler Circuits   4.36
       4.5.3   Hamilton Circuits   4.37
4.6   Summary   4.37
4.7   Short-answer Questions   4.38

Chapter 5: Searching, Sorting and Hashing Techniques   **5.1–5.38**

5.1   Introduction   5.1
5.2   Linear Search   5.2
5.3   Binary Search   5.4
5.4   Bubble Sort   5.6
5.5   Selection Sort   5.8
5.6   Insertion Sort   5.10
5.7   Shell Sort   5.13
5.8   Radix Sort   5.16
5.9   Heap Sort   5.18
5.10   Hashing   5.23
       5.10.1   Truncation Method   5.25
       5.10.2   Folding Method   5.25
       5.10.3   Mid-square Method   5.26
       5.10.4   Division Method   5.26
5.11   Overflow Resolution Technique—Open Addressing   5.26
       5.11.1   Linear Probing   5.27
       5.11.2   Quadratic Probing   5.28
       5.11.3   Rehashing 5.29
       5.11.4   Extensible Hashing   5.30
5.12   Overflow Resolution Technique—Separate Chaining   5.31
5.13   Summary   5.32
5.14   Short-answer Questions   5.34

Technical Q & A in C   **T.1–T.54**

Appendix   **A.1–A.32**

       I.   ASCII Table   A.1
       II.   Precedence Table   A.2
       III.   Header Files   A.3
       IV.   Library Functions   A.6
       V.   Common Programming Errors   A.13
       VI.   Keys Used in C Compiler   A.19
       VII.   Glossary   A.21

Index   **I.1–I.4**

Chapter 1

Linear Data Structures —List

1.1 Introduction

Programs consist of algorithms and data structures. An ***algorithm*** is a step-by-step recipe for solving an instance of a problem. Every single procedure that a computer performs is an algorithm. An algorithm states that, the actions to be executed and the order in which the actions are to be executed. A ***data structure*** represents the logical relationship that exists between individual elements of data to carry out certain tasks. In other words, ***data structure defines a way of organising all data items that consider not only the elements stored but also stores the relationship between the elements.*** To develop a program for an algorithm, we should first decide the steps and select an appropriate data structure for that algorithm. The choice and implementation of a data structure is as important for easier manipulation of data. Therefore, algorithms and data structures are closely related to each other for developing a program.

Arrays let you access lots of data fast with the ability to access its individual elements. You can have arrays of any data type. However, you cannot make arrays bigger if your program decides it needs more space, but we can build our own set data type out of arrays to solve this problem if necessary. A data structure is an actual implementation of an array.

Primary Data Structures

Primary data structures are the basic data structures that directly operate upon the machine instructions. They have different representations on different computers. All the basic constants (integers, floating-point numbers, character constants, string constants) and pointers are considered as primary data structures.

Secondary Data Structures

Secondary data structures are more complicated data structures derived from primary data structures. They emphasize on grouping same or different data items with relationship between each data item. Secondary data structures can be broadly classified as static data structures and dynamic data structures. If a data structure is created using static memory allocation, (i.e., a data structure formed when the number of data items are known in advance) it is known as ***static data structure*** or ***fixed size data structure.*** If a data structure is created, using dynamic memory allocation (i.e., a data structure formed when the number of data items are not known in advance) is known as *dynamic data structure* or *variable size data structure.*

Dynamic data structures can be broadly classified as linear data structures and non-linear data structures. *Linear data structures*, have a linear relationship between its adjacent elements. Linked lists are examples of linear data structures. A *linked list* is a linear dynamic data structure that can grow and shrink during its execution time. Elements can be inserted and deleted from any end of the list. If the elements are inserted and deleted in the same end, then the list is referred to as a *Stack*. If the elements are inserted in one end and deleted in another end, then the list is referred to as a *Queue*. A *circular linked list* is similar to a linked list except that the first and last nodes are interconnected.

Non-linear data structures does not have a linear relationship between its adjacent elements. In a linear data structure, each node has a link which points to another node, where as in a non-linear data structure, each node may point to several other nodes. A *tree* is a non-linear dynamic data structure that may point to one or more nodes at a time. A *graph* is similar to tree except that it has no hierarchical relationship between its adjacent elements.

1.2 Abstract Data Type

A data type that is defined entirely by a set of operations is referred to as an *Abstract Data Type*, or simply ADT. These operations provide a representation-independent specification. Abstract data types are a way of seperating the specification and representation of data types. This also makes the code that implements an ADT more robust and easier to change the application code that uses the ADT.

An abstract data type can be considered as a black box, where users can only see the syntax and semantics of its operations. In general we think of an abstract data type as a type defined in terms of its behavior rather than its implementation. A set of data values and associated operations that are precisely specified independent of any particular implementation. The representation of the data structure is hidden. The only way to modify the data structure or to retrieve information from it is to call one of the operations associated with the abstract data type.

An ADT is a combination of interface and implementation. The interface defines the logical properties of the ADT and especially the signatures of its operations. The implementation defines the representation of the data structure and the algorithms that implement the operations. An ADT is realized by a package, most of the time a generic package. The specification of the package is the interface of the ADT. The data structure is declared as a structure type and the functions having at least one parameter of the type are the operations of the ADT. The part of the specification and the body of the package provide the implementation of the ADT, which also contains the representation of the data structure.

A user of an ADT need not know how the ADT is implemented. What the user really cares about is that the ADT behaves as expected or not. C supports abstract data types by allowing the user to define new data types beyond the primitive data types. An abstract data type encapsulates data and functions into a named data type. It is similar to a structure in C, but can include functions in it. The basic difference between abstract data types (ADTs) and primitive data types are, the latter allow us to look at the representation, whereas the former hide the representation from us.

In any programming language, there are several built-in data types that are available for programmers to use, such as integers, floating point numbers, strings or characters. A built-in data type consists of a set of values or elements, called its domain, and a set of operators acting on that domain. The domain may be defined either by enumeration, if finite, or by specifying a rule describing its elements. Once the domain is defined, we need to specify the operations. Two steps are involved here. First, we define operator's names, identifying what type of values they both operate on and also return. This step is referred as prescribing the syntax. Second, we need to describe the operators functionality, also referred as *semantics*. Many applications need more complicated structures of data that can be added to a program. An abstract data type consists of a collection of values and operations. It has been realized that distinct advantages can result from breaking down the data of a problem into smaller components such as abstract data types.

Benefits of Using Abstract Data Type

- Code is easier to understand

- Implementations of ADTs can be changed without requiring changes to the program that uses the ADTs.

1.3 The List ADT

A list is a dynamic collection of items or elements E_1, E_2, E_3, ... E_n, of size 'n' arranged in a linear sequence where E_i refers to the ith element in the list. A list with size zero / with no elements is referred as empty list. For any list (except an empty list), E_{i-1} precedes E_i, where i > 1 and E_{i+1} follows E_i, where i < n. In an ordered list, items are arranged based on some sort of ordering criteria (such as ascending order or in alphabetical order). In an unordered list, items are arranged in no clear fashion.

Lists serve for many useful purposes in a program, which can be used as the building blocks for many other types of abstract data types such as the STACK ADT, QUEUE ADT and so on. Elements can be inserted and deleted from any end of the list. If the elements are inserted and deleted in the same end, then the list is referred to as a *Stack*. If the elements are inserted in one end and deleted in another end, then the list is referred to as a *Queue.*

1.3.1 List Operations

The operations that can be carried on a list are listed in *Table 1.1.*

Table 1.1 : List Operations

Function	Meaning
List()	Create an un initialized list object
List(List Obj)	Create a new list and initialize it to a specified list
DestroyList()	Free previously allocated list
Assign(s,d)	Copy contents of existing list (i.e., S) into another existing list (i.e., d)
SetFirst()	First node in list is made the current node
SetLast()	Last node in list is made the current node
SetCurrent()	Node at a specified position is made the current node
SetPrev()	Node immediately preceding the current node becomes the current node
SetNext()	Node immediately following the current node becomes the current node
GetCurrent()	Returns position of current node
GetData()	Returns data stored in current node
GetCount()	Returns the number of nodes in the list
InsertBefore()	Insert a new node immediately before the current node
InsertAfter()	Insert a new node immediately after the current node
InsertFirst()	Insert a new node in the first position of the list
InsertLast()	Insert a new node in the last position of the list
DeleteBefore()	Delete a node immediately before the current node
DeleteAfter()	Delete a new node immediately after the current node
DeleteFirst()	Delete a node which is in the first position of the list
DeleteLast()	Delete a node which is in the last position of the list
DeleteCurrent()	Remove the current node from the list
Replace()	Replace the data stored in the current node with new specified data
Search()	Search the specified data in the list and return the corresponding node and make it as a current node.

Linear lists can be implemented in two ways. They are,

- Array based implementation of lists
- Linked lists implementation of lists.

1.3.2 Array Based Implementation of Lists

One of the simplest ways of representing a list is by means of arrays. Both lists and arrays are ordered collection of elements, but they are two different things. The number of elements in the array is fixed and it is not possible to change the number of elements, but the size of the list varies continuously when elements are inserted or deleted. The list is stored in a part of the array, so an array can be declared large enough to hold the maximum number of elements of the list. During execution of a program, the size of the list can be varied within the space reserved for it. One end of the array is fixed and the other end of the array is constantly changed depending upon the elements inserted or deleted in the list. Care must be taken in handling extreme cases, like not to insert an element into a fully occupied list and not to delete an element from an empty list.

Array implementation of lists is mainly used to print the list of elements in it and to find the specific element in the list. These two operations (printing the list and retrieving an element) take place in a linear running time, where as the running time for insert and delete operations, in general, is considerable large (and also the size of the array must be known in advance), due to these drawbacks arrays are not used to implement lists.

1.3.3 Basic Operations in a Linear List using Arrays

The basic operations that can be performed on linear list using arrays are,

- Creation of a list
- Insertion of a node
- Modification of a node
- Deletion of a node
- Traversal of a list.

Creation of a List

The linear list in *Program 1.1* uses an array named roll of size equal to LIST_SIZE, which is created by using the function createMemory(). Creation of linear list is carried out using the function createList(), which does the following operations,

- Initializing the top pointer by –1 (since array index starts from zero)
- Read the data to be stored in the list roll, by incrementing the top pointer by 1.

At the end of the program you should deallocate the space occupied by the list roll, (which was created dynamically by createMemory() function), by the function removeMemory().

Algorithm for CREATELIST()

CREATELIST()

Step 1 : Initialize TOP with –1

Step 2 : Print "Enter the Roll Number : "

Step 3 : Read ROLL[++TOP]

Step 4 : If you want to add another ROLL in the list proceed with **Step 2**.
Otherwise STOP.

END CREATELIST()

Insertion of a Node

The new node can be inserted in the list at three different places namely,

- Inserting as a first node in the list
- Inserting as a last node in the list
- Inserting an intermediate node in the list.

Inserting as a first node in the list

The following steps are followed to insert a new node in the start of the list.

- Check whether the list is fully occupied or not (i.e., check whether the top pointer is LIST_SIZE – 1 or not).
- If the list is full, insert operation is terminated. If the list is not full, follow the next steps.
- Right shift the existing data in the list roll by one, from its first position to the last position (pointed by the top pointer).
- Increment the top pointer by 1.
- Read the data to be stored in the first position of the list roll.

In *Program 1.1* insertFirst() function is used for inserting a new node in the first position of the list roll.

Algorithm for Inserting a Node as the First Node in the List

INSERT_FIRST()

I : INTEGER

Step 1 : If (TOP == LIST_SIZE – 1)

Print, "Linear List is Full"

Return

[End of If structure]

Step 2 : Increment TOP by 1

Step 3 : Initialize I with TOP

Step 4 : Do While (I > 0)

ROLL[I] = ROLL[I – 1]

Decrement I by 1

[End of While structure]

> **Step 5 :**   Print "Enter the Roll Number :"
>
> **Step 6 :**   Read ROLL[0]
>
> **END INSERT_FIRST()**

Inserting as a last node in the list

The following steps are followed to insert a new node in the end of the list.

- Check whether the list is fully occupied or not (i.e., check whether the top pointer is LIST_SIZE – 1 or not). If the list is full, insert operation is terminated. If the list is not full, follow the next steps.

- Increment the top pointer by 1.

- Read the data to be stored in the last position of the list roll.

In *Program 1.1* insertLast() function is used for inserting a new node in the last position of the list.

> **Algorithm for Inserting a Node as the Last Node in the List**
>
> **INSERT_LAST()**
>
> I : INTEGER
>
> **Step 1 :**   IF (TOP == LIST_SIZE – 1)
>
>   PRINT "LINEAR LIST IS FULL"
>
>   RETURN
>
>   [END OF IF STRUCTURE]
>
> **Step 2 :**   INCREMENT TOP BY 1
>
> **Step 3 :**   PRINT "ENTER THE ROLL NUMBER :"
>
> **Step 4 :**   READ ROLL[TOP]
>
> **END INSERT_LAST()**

Inserting as an intermediate node in the list

The following steps are followed to insert a new node in the middle of the list.

- Check whether the list is empty or not (i.e., check whether the top pointer is – 1 or not). If the list is empty, call the insertFirst() function. Otherwise, follow the next steps.

- Read the roll number after which the insertion is to be made.

- If the roll number read from the user is found, check whether the list is fully occupied or not (i.e., check whether the top pointer is LIST_SIZE – 1 or not). If the list is full, insert operation is terminated. If the list is not full, shift the existing data in the list roll by one, from its insert position to the last position (pointed by the top pointer) and then increment the top pointer by 1. Read the data to be stored in the insert position of the list roll.

- If the roll number read from the user is not found, insert operation is terminated.

In *Program 1.1* insertMiddle() function is used for inserting a new node in the intermediate position of the list.

Algorithm for Inserting a Node at any Intermediate Position in the List

INSERT_MIDDLE()

Step 1 :   If (TOP == – 1) Then

Print "Linear List is Empty"

CALL INSERT_FIRST()

Step 2 :   Else If (TOP == LIST_SIZE – 1) Then

Print "Linear List is Full"

Return

Step 3 :   Else

Print "Enter the node roll no after which the"

Print "insertion is to be made : "

Read INSDATA

Step 4 :   Initialize I with zero

Step 5 :   Do While (I <= TOP)

Step 6 :   If(ROLL[I] == INSDATA) Then

Step 7 :   Increment TOP by 1

Step 8 :   Initialize J with TOP

Step 9 :   Do While (J > I)

ROLL[J] == ROLL[J - 1]

Decrement J by 1

[End of **Step 9** while structure]

Step 10 :   Print, "Enter the Roll Number "

Step 11 :   Read, ROLL[I+1]

Step 12 :   Return

Step 13 :   Increment I by 1

END INSERT_MIDDLE()

Modification of a Node

A node(s) can be modified in a list, for changing its information. The following steps are followed to modify a node in the list.

- Check whether the list is empty or not (i.e., check whether the top pointer is – 1 or not). If the list is empty, modification operation terminates. Otherwise, follow the next steps.
- Search for the node to be modified.
- Change the information of the node.

In *Program 1.1* the function modifyNode() is used for modifying an existing node in the list.

Algorithm for Modifying an Existing Node

MODIFY_NODE()

I, MODDATA : INTEGER

Step 1 :   If (TOP == – 1) Then

Print "Linear List is Empty"

Return

[End of **Step 1** If structure]

Step 2 :   Print "Enter the Node Roll Number for Modification"

Read, MODDATA

Step 3 :   Initialize I with zero

Step 4 :   Do While (I < = TOP)

Step 5 :   If(ROLL[I] == MODDATA) Then

Print "Modify the Data of the Node"

Print "Enter the New Roll Number : "

Read ROLL[I]

Return

[End of **Step 5** If structure]

Step 6 :   Increment TOP by 1

Step 7 :   Print "Modify Node is Not Present"

END MODIFY_NODE()

Deletion of a Node

Another primitive operation that can be done in a linear list is the deletion of a node. A node can be deleted in the list from three different places namely,

- Deleting the first node from the list
- Deleting the last node from the list
- Deleting an intermediate node from the list.

Deleting the first node from the list

The following steps are followed, to delete a node from the start of the list.

- Check whether the list is empty or not (i.e., check whether the top pointer is -1 or not). If the list is not empty, follow the next steps.
- Left shift the existing data in the list roll by one, from its second position to the last position (pointed by the top pointer).
- Decrement the top pointer by 1.

In *Program 1.1* the function `deleteFirst()`, is used for deleting the first node in the linear list.

Algorithm for Deleting the First Node from the List

DELETE_FIRST()

I, ROLL : INTEGER

Step 1 :   If (TOP == – 1) Then

Print "Linear List is Empty"

Return

[End of **Step 1** If structure]

Step 2 :   Set TOP = TOP – 1 and Assign ROLL = ROLL[0]

Step 3 :   Initialize I with zero

Step 4 :   Do While (I <= TOP)

ROLL[I] = ROLL[I+1]

Increment TOP by 1

[End of Step 4 While structure]

Step 5 :   Print "Deleted Data is : ", ROLL

END DELETE_FIRST()

Deleting the last node from the list

The following steps are followed, to delete a node from the end of the list.

- Check whether the list is empty or not (i.e., check whether the top pointer is –1 or not). If the list is not empty, decrement the top pointer by 1.

In *Program 1.1* function `deleteLast()`, is used for deleting the last node in the list.

Algorithm for deleting the last node from the list

DELETE_LAST()

I, ROLL : INTEGER

Step 1 :   If (TOP == – 1) Then

Print "Linear List is Empty"

Return

[End of Step 1 If structure]

Step 2 :   Assign ROLL = ROLL[TOP] and Set TOP = TOP – 1

Step 3 :   Print "Deleted Data is ..."

Step 4 :   Print "Roll Number Is : ", ROLL

END DELETE_LAST()

Deleting an intermediate node from the list

The following steps are followed to delete a new node in the middle of the list.

- Check whether the list is empty or not (i.e., check whether the top pointer is – 1 or not). If the list is empty terminate the delete operation. Otherwise, follow the next steps.

- Read the roll number to be deleted.

- If the roll number read from the user is found, left shift the existing data in the list roll by one, from its delete position to the last position (pointed by the top pointer) and then decrement the top pointer by 1.

- If the roll number read from the user is not found, delete operation is terminated.

In *Program 1.1* the function `deleteMiddle()` is used for deleting an existing node from the intermediate position of the list.

Algorithm for Deleting a Node at any Intermediate Position in the List

DELETE_MIDDLE()

I, J, DELDATA : INTEGER

Step 1 :   If (TOP == – 1) Then

            Print "Linear List is Empty."

            Return

Step 2 :   Print " Enter the node roll no for deletion is to be made : "

            Read DELDATA

Step 3 :   Initialize I with zero

Step 4 :   Do While (I <= TOP)

Step 5 :   If(ROLL[I] == DELDATA] Then

Step 6 :   Print "Deleted Data is "

Step 7 :   Print "Roll Number Is : ", ROLL[I]

Step 8 :   Initialize J with I

Step 9 :   Do While (J < TOP)

            ROLL[J] = ROLL[J+1]

            Increment TOP by 1

Step 10 :   Return

Step 11 :   Print "Deleted Node is Not Found"

END DELETE_MIDDLE()

Traversal of a List

To read the information or to display the information in a linear list, you have to traverse (move) the list, from the starting position to the last position indicated by the top pointer. In *Program 1.1* `viewList()` function is used for traversing and displaying the information in the list.

Algorithm for Displaying the Contents of the List

View_LIST()

I : INTEGER

Step 1 :   If (TOP == – 1) Then

            Print "List is Empty"

            Return

            [End of Step 1 If structure]

Step 2 :   Print "Roll Number : "

Step 3 :   Initialize I with zero

Step 4 :   Do While (I <= TOP)

                    Print ROLL[I]

                    Increment TOP by 1

                [End of Step 4 While structure]

END VIEW_List()

Program 1.1 :

```
/* Program to create, insert, delete, modify and view in a linear list. */
/* linear.c */
#include<stdio.h>
#include<conio.h>
#define LIST_SIZE 30
int *roll = NULL, top = -1;
void createList();
void insertFirst();
void insertLast();
void insertMiddle();
void deleteFirst();
void deleteLast();
void deleteMiddle();
void modifyRoll();
void viewList();
void displayMenu();
void createMemory();
void removeMemory();
void main()
  {
    int ch;
    createMemory();
    displayMenu();
    while(1)
      {
        printf("\n\n ? ");
        fflush(stdin);
        scanf("%d", &ch);
        switch(ch)
          {
            case 0 :
                    displayMenu();
                    break;
```

```
                    case 1 :
                                createList();
                                break;
                    case 2 :
                                insertFirst();
                                break;
                    case 3 :
                                insertLast();
                                break;
                    case 4 :
                                insertMiddle();
                                break;
                    case 5 :
                                deleteFirst();
                                break;
                    case 6 :
                                deleteLast();
                                break;
                    case 7 :
                                deleteMiddle();
                                break;
                    case 8 :
                                modifyRoll();
                                break;
                    case 9 :
                                viewList();
                                break;
                    default:
                                removeMemory();
                                printf("\nEnd of run of your Program . . .");
                                exit(0);
                }
            }
        }
        void displayMenu()
        {
            printf("\nBasic Operations in a Linear List ...");
            printf("\n\t 0. Show Menu");
            printf("\n\t 1. Create List");
            printf("\n\t 2. Insert First");
            printf("\n\t 3. Insert Last");
            printf("\n\t 4. Insert Middle");
```

```
        printf("\n\t 5. Delete First");
        printf("\n\t 6. Delete Last");
        printf("\n\t 7. Delete Middle");
        printf("\n\t 8. Modify Roll");
        printf("\n\t 9. View List");
        printf("\n\t 10. Exit");
    }
void createList()
    {
        char ch;
        do
         {
            printf("\nEnter the Roll Number : ");
              scanf("%d", &roll[++top]);
            fflush(stdin);
            printf("Do u wish to Add Data in the List (y/n) ? ");
              scanf("%c", &ch);
         }while( (ch == 'y') || (ch == 'Y') );
    }
void insertFirst()
    {
        int i;
        if(top == LIST_SIZE - 1)
         {
            printf("\n Linear List is Full ...");
            return;
         }
        top++;
        for(i = top; i > 0; i--)
           roll[i] = roll[i-1];
        printf("\nEnter the Roll Number : ");
           scanf("%d", &roll[0]);
    }
void insertLast()
    {
        if(top == LIST_SIZE - 1)
         {
            printf("\n Linear List is Full ... ");
            return;
         }
        printf("\nEnter the Roll Number : ");
           scanf("%d", &roll[++top]);
    }
```

```c
void insertMiddle()
{
   int insdata, i, j;
   if(top == -1)
    {
      printf("List is Empty. Roll is inserted at First" );
      insertFirst();
    }
   else
    {
      printf("\n Enter the roll roll no after which the"
                                "insertion is to be made : ");
      scanf("%d", &insdata);
      for(i = 0 ; i <= top; i++)
        if(roll[i] == insdata)
          {
            if(top == LIST_SIZE - 1)
             {
               printf("\n Linear List is Full ... ");
               return;
             }
            top++;
            for(j = top; j > i; j--)
              roll[j] = roll[j-1];
            printf("\nEnter the Roll Number : ");
              scanf("%d", &roll[i+1]);
            return;
          }
    }
}
void deleteFirst()
{
   int i, deldata;
   if(top == -1)
    {
      printf("\n Linear List is Empty ... ");
      return;
    }
   top--;
   deldata = roll[0];
   for(i = 0; i <= top; i++)
     roll[i] = roll[i+1];
   printf("\n Deleted Data is ... \n");
   printf("\n Roll Number : %d", deldata);
}
```

```
    void deleteLast()
    {
       int i, roll;
       if(top == -1)
         {
           printf("\n Linear List is Empty ... ");
           return;
         }
       roll = roll[top];
       top--;
       printf("\n Deleted Data is ... \n");
       printf("\n Roll Number : %d", roll);
    }
    void deleteMiddle()
    {
       int deldata, i, j;
       if(top == -1)

         {
           printf("\n Linear List is Empty ...");
           return;
         }
       printf("\n Enter roll Roll No for deletion : ");
         scanf("%d", &deldata);
       for(i = 0; i <= top; i++)
         if(roll[i] == deldata)
           {
             printf("\n Deleted Data is ... \n");
             printf("\n Roll Number : %d", roll[i]);
             for(j = i; j < top; j++)
                roll[j] = roll[j + 1];
             top--;
             return;
           }
       printf("Delete Roll is Not Found");
    }
    void modifyRoll()
    {
       int i, moddata;
       if(top == -1)
         {
           printf("\n Linear List is Empty ... ");
           return;
         }
```

```
        printf("\n Enter roll Roll No for modification : ");
          scanf("%d", &moddata);
      for(i = 0; i <= top; i++)
        if(roll[i] == moddata)
          {
            printf("\n Modify the Data of the Roll ... \n");
            printf("\n Enter the New Roll Number : ");
              scanf("%d", &roll[i]);
            return;
          }
      printf("Modify Roll is Not Found");
  }
void viewList()
  {
    int i;
    if(top == -1)
      {
        printf("\n Linear List is Empty ... ");
        return;
      }
    printf("\n Roll Number : ");
    for(i = 0; i <= top; i++)
      printf("\n --> %d ", roll[i]);
  }
void createMemory()
  {
    roll = (int *)malloc(sizeof(int) * LIST_SIZE);
  }
void removeMemory()
  {
    free(roll);
    roll = NULL;
  }
```

The program displays the following output

```
Basic Operations in a Linear List ...
        0. Create List
        1. Insert First
        2. Insert Last
        3. Insert Middle
        4. Delete First
        5. Delete Last
        6. Delete Middle
        7. Modify Roll
```

```
            8. View List
            9. Show Menu
            10. Exit
? 4
Linear List is Empty ...
? 5
Linear List is Empty ...
? 6
Linear List is Empty ...
? 7
Linear List is Empty ...
? 8
Linear List is Empty ...
? 0
Enter the Roll Number : 1001
Do u wish to Add Data in the List (y/n) ? y
Enter the Roll Number : 1002
Do u wish to Add Data in the List (y/n) ? y
Enter the Roll Number : 1003
Do u wish to Add Data in the List (y/n) ? n
? 8
Roll Number :
--> 1001
--> 1002
--> 1003
? 1
Enter the Roll Number : 1004
? 2
Enter the Roll Number : 1005
? 3
Enter the roll roll no after which the insertion is to be made : 1002
Enter the Roll Number : 1006
? 8
Roll Number :
--> 1004
--> 1001
--> 1002
```

```
--> 1006
--> 1003
--> 1005


? 9
Basic Operations in a Linear List ...
            0. Create List
            1. Insert First
            2. Insert Last
            3. Insert Middle
            4. Delete First
            5. Delete Last
            6. Delete Middle
            7. Modify Roll
            8. View List
            9. Show Menu
            10. Exit
? 4
Deleted Data is ...
Roll Number : 1004
? 5
Deleted Data is ...
Roll Number : 1005
? 8
Roll Number :
--> 1001
--> 1002
--> 1006
--> 1003
? 6
Enter roll Roll No for deletion : 1002
Deleted Data is ...
Roll Number : 1002
? 8
Roll Number :
--> 1001
--> 1006
--> 1003
? 10
End of run of your Program . . .
```

1.4 Linked Lists Implementation of Lists

*Linked list or list is an ordered collection of elements. Each element in the list is referred as a **node**.* Each node contains two fields namely,

- Data field
- Link field.

The data field contains the actual data (i.e., value) of the element to be stored in the list and the link field also referred as the **next address field** contains the address of the next node in the list. **Fig. 1.1** helps you understand things better.

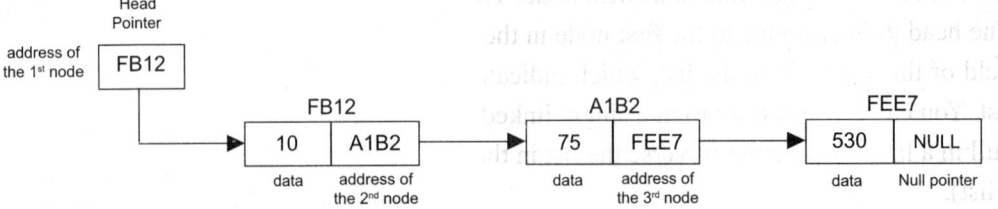

Fig. 1.1 : Representation of a linked list.

The linked list shown in **Fig. 1.1** consists of three nodes, each with a data field and a link field. A linked list contains a pointer, referred as the **head pointer**, which points to the first node in the list that stores the address of the first node of the list (i.e., FB12). The data field contains the actual information which is to be stored in the list. The data field of the first node stores the value 10. The link field of the first node contains the address of the second node (i.e., A1B2). Similarly, the second node of the list stores the value 75 in the data field and the address of the third node (i.e., FEE7) in the link field. The last node of the list contains only the information part (i.e., 530) in the data field and the address field stores the NULL pointer. This NULL pointer is used to indicate the end of a list. *Note that the nodes in a linked list are not ordered by their physical placement in memory (i.e., they may/may not be placed in contiguous memory locations) but by logical links stored as a part of the data in the node itself.*

The address stored in a linked list are divided into three types namely,

- External address
- Internal address
- Null address.

External address is the address of the first node in the list. This address is stored in the head pointer which points to the first node in the list. The entire linked list can be accessed only with the help of the head pointer. *Internal address* is the address stored in each and every node of the linked list except the last node. The content stored in the link field (also referred as next address field) is the address of the next node. *Null address* is the address stored by the NULL pointer of the last node of the list, which indicates the end of the list.

1.4.1 Types of Linked Lists

There are different types of linked lists. They can be classified as,

- Singly linked list
- Doubly linked list
- Circular linked list.

Singly Linked List

The list that we have seen so far is referred to as the singly linked list, in which each node has a single link to its next node. This list is also referred as a ***linear linked list.*** The head pointer points to the first node in the list and the null pointer is stored in the link field of the last node in the list, which indicates end of list. ***Fig. 1.1*** shows a singly linked list. You can traverse (move) in a singly linked list in only one direction (i.e., from head to null in a list). You cannot traverse the list in the reverse direction (i.e., from null to head in a list).

Doubly Linked List

For some applications, especially where it is necessary to traverse lists in both directions, doubly linked lists work much better than singly linked lists. Doubly linked list is an advanced form of a singly linked list, in which each node contains three fields namely,

- Previous address field
- Data field
- Next address field.

The previous address field of a node contains address of its previous node. This field is also referred as the ***backward link field***. The data field stores the information part of the node. The next address field contains the address of the next node in the list. This field is also referred as the ***forward link field. Fig. 1.2*** shows the structure of a doubly linked list.

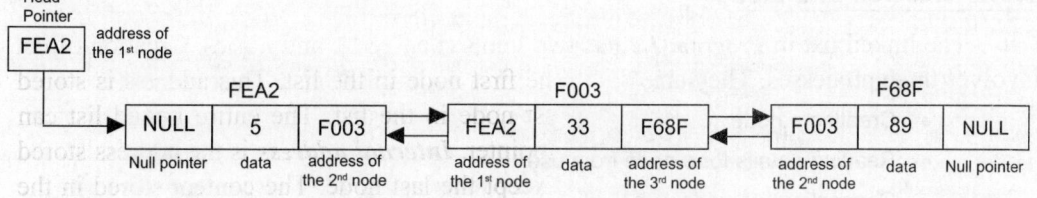

Fig. 1.2 : Doubly linked list.

Circular Linked list

Circular linked list is another form of a linked list in which the last node of the list is connected to the first node in the list. There are different types of circular linked lists. They can be classified as,

- Circular singly linked list
- Circular doubly linked list.

Note that a circular linked list looks like a cyclic list and will not have any end-of-list (i.e., there is no NULL pointer). *Fig. 1.3* shows the structure of a circular linked singly list. *Fig. 1.4* shows the structure of a circular linked doubly list.

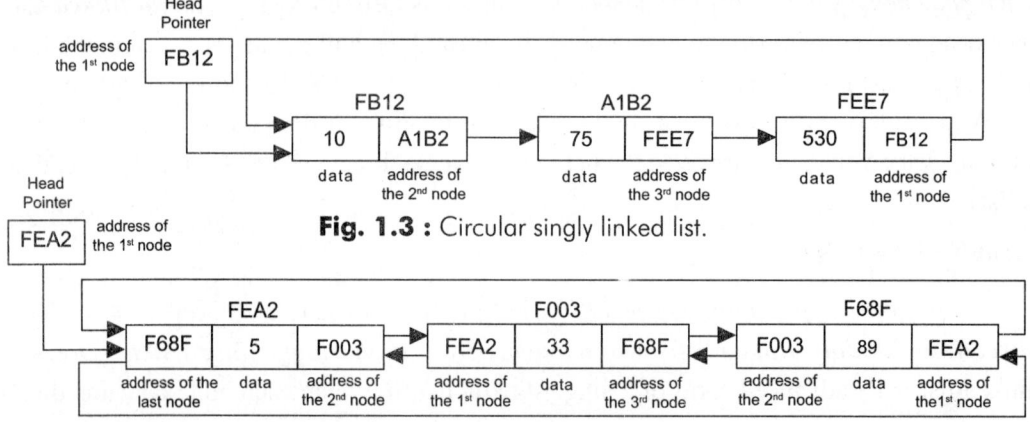

Fig. 1.3 : Circular singly linked list.

Fig. 1.4 : Circular doubly linked list.

1.5 Basic Operations in a Singly Linked List

The most commonly used linked list discussed so far is the singly linked list. The basic operations that can be performed on singly linked lists are,

- Creation of a list
- Insertion of a node
- Modification of a node
- Deletion of a node
- Traversal of a list
- Count the number of nodes.

1.5.1 Creation of a List

The linked list in *Program 1.2* has two items (i.e., roll and name). Creation of list involves three processes. They are,

- Creating a node
- Reading details for a node from user
- Connecting the node with the list.

Creating a singly linked list starts with creating a node. Sufficient memory has to be allocated for creating a node. The information is stored in the memory, allocated by using the `malloc()` function of type node. In *Program 1.2* `getNode()` function, is used to create a node.

After allocating memory for the structure, the information for the items (i.e., `roll` and `name`) has to be read from the user. In *Program 1.2* `readNode()` function is used for reading details for the node from the user.

Algorithm for Declaration of Structure NODE
Struct NODE
DATA : Data Field
LINK : Link Field (Address of next struct NODE)
End Struct

Algorithm for Allocating Memory for the New Node
GETNODE()
Step 1 : Set SIZE = get the size of the NODE
Step 2 : Set NEWNODE = Allocate space in memory for the size of SIZE and return the initial address
Step 3 : Return NEWNODE
End GETNODE()

Algorithm for Reading the Content for the New Node
READNODE(NEWNODE : NODE)
Step 1 : Read, NEWNODE -> DATA
Step 2 : Set NEWNODE -> LINK = NULL
Step 3 : Return
End READNODE()

Connecting the new node with the existing list. If the list is empty, set the head pointer of the list to the new node, other wise connect the new node in the last position of the list. In *Program 1.2* `createList()` function is used to connect the new nodes with the list.

Algorithm for CREATELIST()
CREATELIST()
Step 1 : Set NEWNODE = GETNODE()
Step 2 : CALL READNODE(NEWNODE)
Step 3 : Set HEAD = NEWNODE
Step 4 : Set LAST = NEWNODE
Step 5 : If you want to add another NODE proceed otherwise **STOP**.
Step 6 : Set NEWNODE = GETNODE()
Step 7 : CALL READNODE(NEWNODE)
Step 8 : Assign LAST -> LINK = NEWNODE
Step 9 : Assign LAST = LAST -> LINK
Step 10 : Goto **Step 5**
END CREATELIST()

1.5.2 Insertion of a Node

One of the most primitive operations that can be done in a singly linked list is the insertion of a node. Memory is to be allocated for the new node (in a similar way that is done while creating a list) before reading the data. The new node will contain empty data field and empty link field. The data field of the new node is then stored with the information read from the user. The link field of the new node is assigned to NULL.

The new node can then be inserted in the list at three different places namely,

- Inserting as a first node in the list
- Inserting as a last node in the list
- Inserting an intermediate node in the list.

Inserting as a first node in the list

The following steps are followed to insert a new node in the start of the list.

- Get the new node using GETNODE() and read the details of the node using READNODE().
- Check whether the list is empty or not (i.e., check whether the head pointer is pointing to NULL or not).
- If the list is empty, assign new node as head. If the list is not empty, follow the next steps.
- The link field of the new node is made to point the data field of the first node (i.e., head node) in the list by assigning the address of the first node.
- The head pointer is made to point the data field of the new node by assigning the address of the new node.

In *Program 1.2* insertFirst() function is used for inserting a new node in the first position of the list.

Algorithm for Inserting a Node as the First Node in the List

INSERT_FIRST(HEAD : NODE)

NEWNODE : NODE

Step 1 :   Set NEWNODE = GETNODE()

Step 2 :   CALL READNODE (NEWNODE)

Step 3 :   If (HEAD==NULL)

> Set HEAD = NEWNODE
>
> Return
>
> [End of If structure]

Step 4 :   Assign NEWNODE -> LINK = HEAD

Step 5 :   Set HEAD = NEWNODE

END INSERT_FIRST()

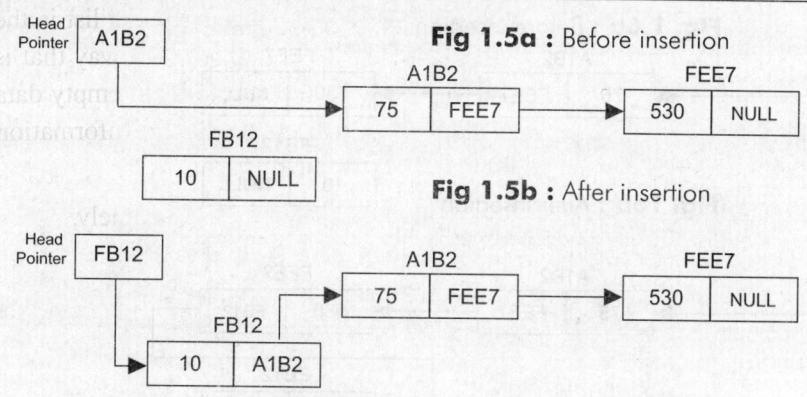

Fig 1.5a : Before insertion

Fig 1.5b : After insertion

Fig 1.5 : Inserting as a first node in the list.

Inserting as a last node in the list

The following steps are followed to insert a new node in the end of the list.

- Get the new node using GETNODE() and read the details of the node using READNODE().

- Check whether the list is empty or not (i.e., check whether the head pointer is pointing to NULL or not). If the list is empty, assign new node as head. If the list is not empty, follow the next steps.

- The link field of the last node is made to point the data field of the new node in the list by assigning the address of the new node.

- The link field of the new node is set to NULL.

In *Program 1.2* insertLast() function is used for inserting a new node in the last position of the list.

Algorithm for Inserting a Node as the Last Node in the List
INSERT_LAST(HEAD : NODE)
LAST, NEWNODE : NODE
Step 1 :   Set NEWNODE = GETNODE()
Step 2 :   CALL READNODE(NEWNODE)
Step 3 :   If (HEAD == NULL)
Set HEAD = NEWNODE
Return
[End of If structure]
Step 4 :   Set LAST = HEAD
Step 5 :   Repeat While (LAST -> LINK != NULL)
Assign LAST = LAST -> LINK
[End of While Structure]
Step 6 :   Assign LAST -> LINK = NEWNODE
END INSERT_LAST()

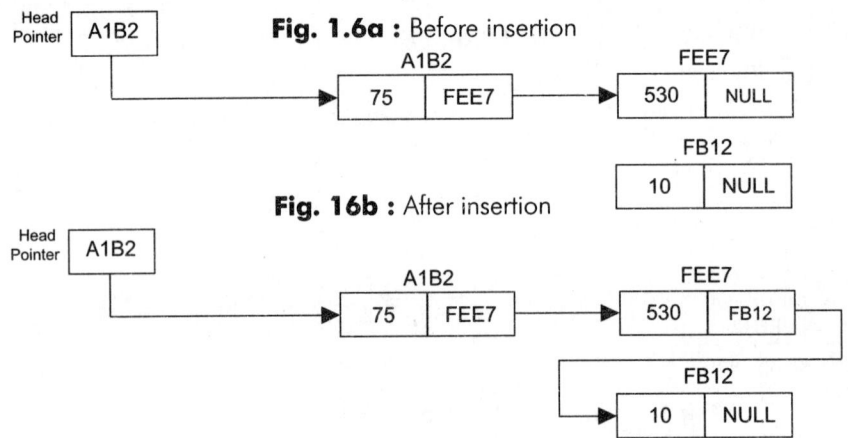

Fig. 1.6a : Before insertion

Fig. 16b : After insertion

Fig. 1.6 : Inserting as a last node in the list.

Inserting an intermediate node in the list

The following steps are followed, to insert a new node in any intermediate position in the list.

- Get the new node using GETNODE() and read the details of the node using READNODE().
- Check whether the list is empty or not (i.e., check whether the head pointer is pointing to NULL or not). If the list is empty, assign new node as head. If the list is not empty, follow the next steps.
- Get the address of the preceding node after which the new node is to be inserted.
- The link field of the new node is made to point the data field of the next node (link field of the preceding node) by assigning its address.
- The link field of the preceding node is made to point the data field of the new node by assigning the address of the new node.

In *Program 1.2* `insertMiddle()` function is used for inserting a new node in any intermediate position of the list.

Algorithm for Inserting a Node at any Intermediate Position in the List

INSERT_MIDDLE (HEAD : NODE)

LAST, NEWNODE : NODE;

CONDITION : DATA of the any one NODE in the LIST for insert

Step 1 : Set NEWNODE= GETNODE()

Step 2 : CALL READNODE(NEWNODE)

Step 3 : If (HEAD == NULL)

              Set HEAD = NEWNODE

              Return

       [End of If structure]

Step 4 : Print, "Enter the data of NODE after which the insertion is to be made"

Step 5 : READ, CONDITION

Step 6 : Set LAST = HEAD

Step 7 : Repeat While (LAST != NULL)

Step 8 : If (LAST -> DATA == CONDITION) then

        Assign NEWNODE -> LINK =LAST -> LINK

        Assign LAST - > LINK = NEWNODE

        Return

    Else

        Assign LAST = LAST -> LINK

    [End of If Structure]

Step 9 : [End of **Step 7** while structure]

Step 10 : Print, "CONDITION IS NOT AVAILABLE"

END INSERT_MIDDLE()

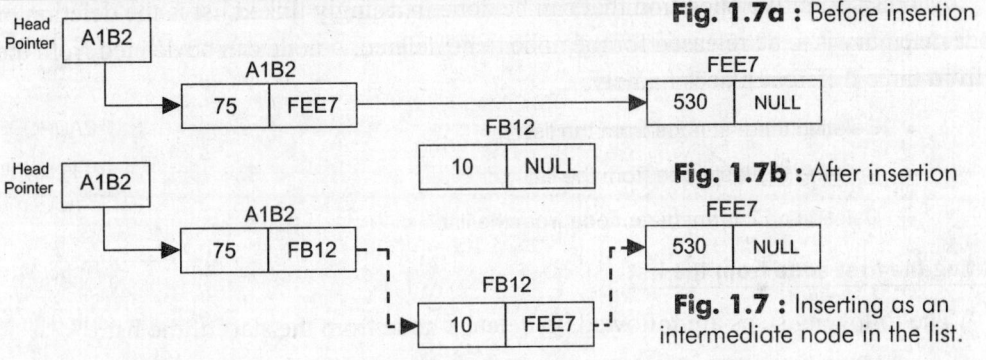

Fig. 1.7a : Before insertion

Fig. 1.7b : After insertion

Fig. 1.7 : Inserting as an intermediate node in the list.

1.5.3 Modification of a Node

A node(s) can be modified in a list, for changing its information part. The following steps are followed to modify a node in the list.

- Check whether the list is empty or not (i.e., check whether the head pointer is pointing to NULL or not). If the list is not empty, follow the next steps.

- Search for the node to be modified.

- Change the information part of the node.

In *Program 1.2* modifyNode() function is used for modifying an existing node in the list.

Algorithm for Modifying an Existing Node
MODIFY_NODE(HEAD : NODE)
Step 1 : If (HEAD == NULL)
Return
[End of If structure]
Step 2 : Print "Enter the data of NODE to be modified"
Step 3 : Read CONDITION

Step 4 :   Set LAST = HEAD

Step 5 :   Repeat While (LAST != NULL)

Step 6 :   If (LAST -> DATA == CONDITION) then

Read, LAST -> DATA

Return

Else

Assign LAST = LAST -> LINK

[End of If Structure]

Step 7 :   [End of **Step 5** while structure]

Step 8 :   Print, "CONDITION IS NOT AVAILABLE"

END MODIFY_NODE()

1.5.4 Deletion of a Node

Another primitive operation that can be done in a singly linked list is the deletion of a node. Memory is to be released for the node to be deleted. A node can be deleted from the list from three different places namely,

- Deleting the first node from the list
- Deleting the last node from the list
- Deleting an intermediate node from the list.

Deleting the first node from the list

The following steps are followed, to delete a node from the start of the list.

- Check whether the list is empty or not (i.e., check whether the head pointer is pointing to NULL or not). If the list is not empty, follow the next steps.
- Set the head pointer to the second node in the list (by assigning its address).
- Release the memory for the deleted node.

In *Program 1.2* deleteFirst() function is used for deleting the first node in the list. After deleting the node memory occupied by the deleted node is released using the releaseNode() function.

Algorithm for Releasing the Memory for the Node to be Deleted

RELEASE_NODE(NEWNODE : NODE)

Step 1 :   Deallocate the space for the NODE of NEWNODE

Step 2 :   Return

End RELEASENODE()

Algorithm for Deleting the First Node from the List

 DELETE_FIRST (HEAD : NODE)

 DELNODE : NODE

 Step 1 : If (HEAD == NULL)

     Print "List is Empty"

     Return

    [End of If structure]

 Step 2 : Set DELNODE = HEAD

 Step 3 : Assign HEAD = HEAD -> LINK

 Step 4 : Print "Deleted Data is", DELNODE -> DATA

 Step 5 : CALL RELEASENODE (DELNODE)

 END DELETE_FIRST()

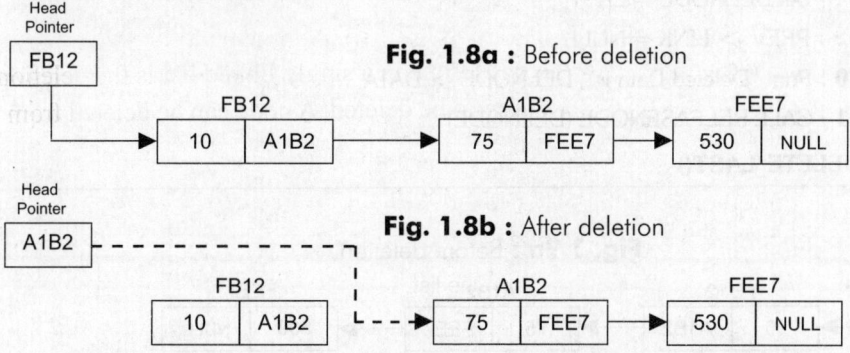

Fig. 1.8a : Before deletion

Fig. 1.8b : After deletion

Fig. 1.8 : Deleting the first node from the list.

Deleting the last node from the list

 The following steps are followed, to delete a node from the end of the list.

- Check whether the list is empty or not (i.e., check whether the head pointer is pointing to NULL or not). If the list is not empty, follow the next steps.

- The link field of the previous node (from the end of the list) is set to NULL.

- Release the memory for the deleted node.

 In **Program 1.2** deleteLast() function is used for deleting the last node in the list. After deleting the node memory occupied by the deleted node is released using the releaseNode() function.

Algorithm for Deleting the Last Node from the List

 DELETE_LAST(HEAD : NODE)

 LAST, PREV, DELNODE : NODE

 Step 1 : If (HEAD == NULL)

     Print "List is empty"

     Return

    [End of If structure]

Step 2 :   If (HEAD -> LINK == NULL) Then

Set DELNODE = HEAD

Set HEAD = NULL

Print "Deleted Data is", DELNODE -> DATA

Return

[End of If structure]

Step 3 :   Set LAST = HEAD

Step 4 :   Repeat While (LAST -> LINK != NULL)

Step 5 :   Assign PREV = LAST

Step 6 :   Assign LAST = LAST -> LINK

Step 7 :   [End of **Step 4** While loop]

Step 8 :   Set DELNODE = LAST

Step 9 :   PREV -> LINK = NULL

Step 10 : Print "Deleted Data is", DELNODE -> DATA

Step 11 : CALL RELEASENODE (DELNODE)

END DELETE_LAST()

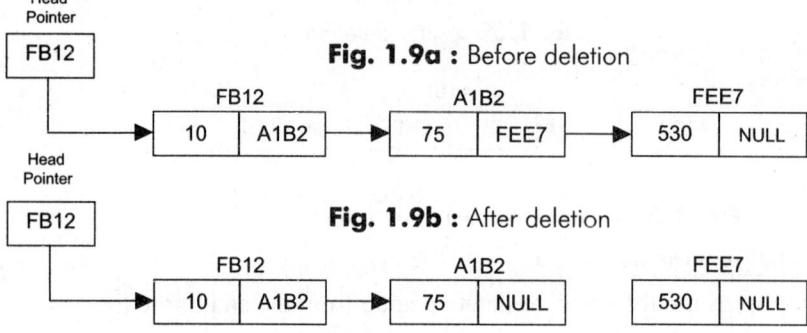

Fig. 1.9a : Before deletion

Fig. 1.9b : After deletion

Fig. 1.9 : Deleting the last node from the list.

Deleting an intermediate node from the list

The following steps are followed, to delete a node from an intermediate position in the list.

- Check whether the list is empty or not (i.e., check whether the head pointer is pointing to NULL or not). If the list is not empty, follow the next steps.
- The link field of the previous node (following the node to be deleted) is made to point the data field of the next node (before the node to be deleted), by assigning its address.
- Release the memory for the deleted node.

In *Program 1.2* deleteMiddle() function is used for deleting the intermediate node from the list. After deleting the node, memory occupied by the deleted node is released using the releaseNode() function.

Algorithm for Deleting a Node at any Intermediate Position in the List

DELETE_MIDDLE(HEAD : NODE)

    LAST, PREV, DELNODE : NODE

    DELDATA : Data of the NODE is the NODE to Delete

Step 1 :   If (HEAD == NULL)

         Print "List is Empty"

         Return

         [End of If Structure]

Step 2 :   Print "Enter the DATA of the node in the list for deletion"

Step 3 :   Read DELDATA

Step 4 :   If (HEAD -> DATA == DELDATA) Then

         Set DELNODE = HEAD

         Assign HEAD = HEAD -> LINK

         Print, "Deleted Data is", DELNODE - > DATA

         CALL RELEASENODE (DELNODE)

         Return

         [End of If Structure]

Step 5 :   Set LAST = HEAD -> LINK

Step 6 :   Set PREV = HEAD

Step 7 :   Repeat While (LAST != NULL)

Step 8 :   If (LAST -> DATA == DELDATA) Then

         Set DELNODE = LAST

         Assign PREV -> LINK = LAST -> LINK

         Print "The Deleted Data is", DELNODE -> DATA

         CALL RELEASENODE (DELNODE)

         Return

       Else

         Assign LAST = LAST -> LINK

         Assign PREV = PREV -> LINK

         [End of If structure]

Step 9 :   [End of **Step 7** While Loop]

Step 10 : Print "DELDATA is Not Available in the List"

END DELETE_MIDDLE()

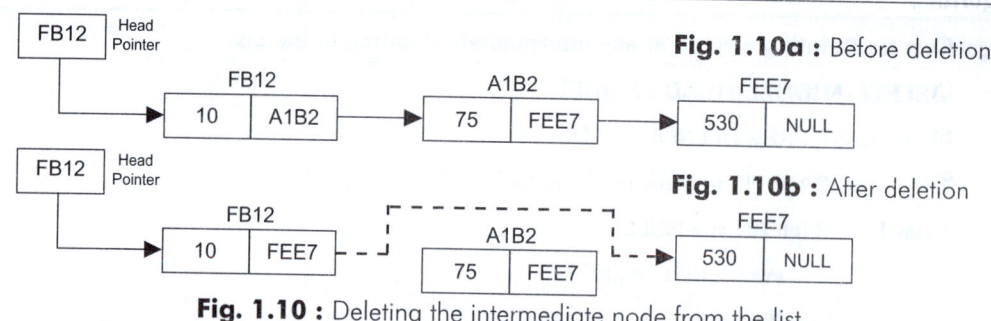

Fig. 1.10a : Before deletion

Fig. 1.10b : After deletion

Fig. 1.10 : Deleting the intermediate node from the list.

1.5.5 Traversal of a List

To read the information or to display the information in a linked list, you have to traverse (move) a linked list, node by node from the first node, until the end of the list is reached. Traversing a list involves the following steps,

- Check whether the head pointer is pointing to NULL or not. If yes, display "List is Empty" and terminate the process. Otherwise the follow the next steps.

- Display the information in the data field stored in the head pointer.

- Traverse the list from one node to another by advancing the head pointer.

In *Program 1.2* `viewList()` function is used for traversing and to display the information stored in the list.

Algorithm for Displaying the Contents of the List

VIEW_LIST(HEAD : NODE)

Step 1 : If (HEAD == NULL)

Print, "List is Empty"

Return

[End of If Structure]

Step 2 : While (HEAD != NULL)

Step 3 : Print "The data is ", HEAD –> DATA

Step 4 : HEAD = HEAD –> LINK

Step 5 : [End of **Step 2** While structure]

END VIEW_LIST()

1.5.6 Count the Number of Nodes in the List

To count the nodes in a linked list, you have to traverse (move) a linked list, node by node from the first node, until the end of the list is reached. Counting the number of nodes in the list involves the following steps,

- Initialize the count variable to zero.

- Check whether the head pointer is pointing to NULL or not. If yes, display "List is Empty" and terminate the process. Otherwise follow the next step.

- Traverse the list from one node to another by advancing the head pointer till the end of the list and increment the count variable by 1.

In *Program 1.2* `count()` function is used for counting the number of nodes in the list.

Algorithm for Counting the Number of Nodes in the List

    Count_LIST(HEAD : NODE)

COUNT : INTEGER

Step 1 : Set COUNT = 0

Step 2 : If (HEAD == NULL)

            Print, "List is Empty"

            Return COUNT

        [End of If Structure]

Step 3 : While (HEAD != NULL)

Step 4 : COUNT = COUNT + 1

Step 5 : HEAD = HEAD --> LINK

Step 6 : [End of **Step 2** While structure]

Step 7 : Return COUNT

END COUNT_LIST()

Program **1.2** :

/* **Program to create, insert, delete, modify and view in a singly linked list.** */

```c
/* SLList.c */
#include<stdio.h>
typedef struct list
 {
   int roll;
   char name[20];
   struct list *link;
 }node;
node* getNode();
void createList(node **headptr);
void insertFirst(node **headptr);
void insertLast(node **headptr);
void insertMiddle(node **headptr);
void deleteFirst(node **headptr);
void deleteLast(node **headptr);
void deleteMiddle(node **headptr);
void modifyNode(node *head);
void viewList(node *head);
void countList(node *head);
void releaseNode(node *newnode);
void displayMenu();
```

```
void main()
{
  node *head = NULL;
  int ch, count;
  displayMenu();
  while(1)
  {
    printf("\n\n ? ");
    fflush(stdin);
    scanf("%d", &ch);
    switch(ch)
    {
      case 0 :
              createList(&head);
              break;
      case 1 :
              insertFirst(&head);
              break;
      case 2 :
              insertLast(&head);
              break;
      case 3 :
              insertMiddle(&head);
              break;
      case 4 :
              deleteFirst(&head);
              break;
      case 5 :
              deleteLast(&head);
              break;
      case 6 :
              deleteMiddle(&head);
              break;
      case 7 :
              modifyNode(head);
              break;
      case 8 :
              viewList(head);
              break;
      case 9 :
              count = countList(head);
              printf("Number of nodes in the list is %d", count);
              break;
```

```
                    case 10:
                            displayMenu();
                            break;
                default:
                            printf("End of run of your program . . .");
                            exit(0);
            }
        }
    }
void displayMenu()
{
    printf("\nBasic Operations in a Singly Linked List ... ");
    printf("\n\t 0. Create List ");
    printf("\n\t 1. Insert First ");
    printf("\n\t 2. Insert Last ");
    printf("\n\t 3. Insert Middle ");
    printf("\n\t 4. Delete First ");
    printf("\n\t 5. Delete Last ");
    printf("\n\t 6. Delete Middle ");
    printf("\n\t 7. Modify Node");
    printf("\n\t 8. View List");
    printf("\n\t 9. View List");
    printf("\n\t 10. Show Menu ");
    printf("\n\t 11. Exit ");
}
node* getNode()
{
    node * newnode;
    int size = sizeof(node);
    newnode = (node *)malloc(size);
    return (newnode);
}
void readNode(node* newnode)
{
    printf("\nEnter the Roll Number : ");
        scanf("%d", &newnode->roll);
    printf("Enter the Name : ");
        scanf("%s", newnode->name);
    newnode->link = NULL;
}
void releaseNode(node *newnode)
{
    free(newnode);
}
```

```
void createList(node **headptr)
 {
    node *head = NULL, *newnode, *last;  char ch;
    do
     {
        newnode = getNode();
        readNode(newnode);
        if(head == NULL)
         {
            head = newnode;
            last = head;
         }
        else
         {
            last -> link = newnode;
            last = last -> link;
         }
       fflush(stdin);
       printf("Do u wish to Add Data in the List (y/n) ? ");
         scanf("%c", &ch);
     }while( (ch == 'y') || (ch == 'Y') );
    *headptr = head;
 }
void insertFirst(node **headptr)
 {
    node *head, *newnode;
    head = *headptr;
    newnode = getNode();
    readNode(newnode);
    if(head == NULL)
      head = newnode;
    else
     {
       newnode -> link = head;
       head = newnode;
     }
    *headptr = head;
 }
void insertLast(node **headptr)
 {
    node *head, *last, *newnode;
    head = *headptr;
```

```
        newnode = getNode();
        readNode(newnode);
        if(head == NULL)
          head = newnode;
        else
         {
           last  = head;
           while(last -> link != NULL)
             last = last -> link;
           last -> link = newnode;
         }
        *headptr = head;
  }
void insertMiddle(node **headptr)
  {
     node *head, *last, *newnode;  int insdata;
     head = *headptr;
     if(head == NULL)
       {
         printf("Singly Linked list is Empty. "
                                        "So new node is head node.");
         newnode = getNode();
         readNode(newnode);
         head = newnode;
       }
     else
       {
         printf("\n Enter the node roll no after which the"
                                " insertion is to be made : ");
          scanf("%d", &insdata);
         last  = head;
         while(last != NULL)
          {
            if(last -> roll == insdata)
              {
                  newnode = getNode();
                  readNode(newnode);
                  newnode -> link = last -> link;
                  last -> link = newnode;
                  return;
              }
          }
```

```
                else
                    last = last -> link;
            }
            printf("Insert Node is Not Found");
        }
    *headptr = head;
}
void deleteFirst(node **headptr)
{
    node *head, *delnode;
    head = *headptr;
    if(head == NULL)
    {
        printf("\n Singly Linked List is Empty ...");
        return;
    }
    delnode = head;
    head = head -> link;
    printf("\n Deleted Data is ... \n");
    printf("\n Roll Number : %d", delnode -> roll);
    printf("\n Name : %s", delnode -> name);
    releaseNode(delnode);
    *headptr = head;
}
void deleteLast(node **headptr)
{
    node *head, *delnode, *last, *prev;
    head = *headptr;
    if(head == NULL)
    {
        printf("\n Singly Linked List is Empty ...");
        return;
    }
    else if(head -> link == NULL)
    {
        delnode = head;
        head = NULL;
    }
    else
    {
        last  = head;
```

```
            while(last -> link != NULL)
             {
               prev = last;
               last = last -> link;
             }
           delnode = last;
           prev -> link = NULL;
         }
      printf("\n Deleted Data is ... \n");
      printf("\n Roll Number : %d", delnode -> roll);
      printf("\n Name : %s", delnode -> name);
      releaseNode(delnode);
      *headptr = head;
   }
void deleteMiddle(node **headptr)
   {
      node *head, *delnode, *last, *prev;
      int deldata;
      head = *headptr;
      if(head == NULL)
        {
          printf("\n Singly Linked List is Empty ...");
          return;
        }
      printf("\n Enter the node roll no to be deleted : ");
          scanf("%d", &deldata);


      if(head -> roll == deldata)
        {
          delnode = head;
          head = head -> link;
          printf("\n Deleted Data is ... \n");
          printf("\n Roll Number : %d", delnode -> roll);
          printf("\n Name : %s", delnode -> name);
          releaseNode(delnode);
          *headptr = head;
          return;
        }
      last = head -> link;
      prev = head;
```

```
      while(last != NULL)
       {
         if(last -> roll == deldata)
          {
            delnode = last;
            prev -> link = last -> link;
            printf("\n Deleted Data is ... \n");
            printf("\n Roll Number : %d", delnode -> roll);
            printf("\n Name : %s", delnode -> name);
            releaseNode(delnode);
            return;
          }
         else
          {
            last = last -> link;
            prev = prev -> link;
          }
       }
      printf("Delete Node is Not Found");
      *headptr = head;
  }
void modifyNode(node *head)
  {
      int moddata;
      if(head == NULL)
       {
          printf("\n Singly Linked List is Empty ...");
          return;
       }
      printf("\n Enter the node roll no for modification : ");
      scanf("%d", &moddata);
      while(head != NULL)
       {
         if(head -> roll == moddata)
          {
            printf("\n Modify the Data of the Node ... \n");
            printf("\n Enter the New Roll Number : ");
              scanf("%d", &head -> roll);
            printf("\n Enter the New Name : ");
              scanf("%s", head -> name);
            return;
          }
```

```
        else
         {
           head = head -> link;
         }
      }
    printf("Modify Node is Not Found");
  }
void viewList(node *head)
  {
    if(head == NULL)
     {
       printf("\nSingly Linked List is Empty ...");
       return;
     }
    for(;head != NULL; head = head -> link)
     {
       printf("\n Roll Number : %d", head -> roll);
       printf("\n Name : %s", head -> name);
     }
  }
void countList(node *head)
  {
    int count = 0;
    if(head == NULL)
     {
       printf("\nSingly Linked List is Empty ...");
       return count;
     }
    for(;head != NULL; head = head -> link)
     {
     count = count + 1;
     }
    return count;
  }
```

The program displays the following output

```
Basic Operations in a Singly Linked List ...
        0. Create List
        1. Insert First
        2. Insert Last
        3. Insert Middle
```

```
                  4. Delete First
                  5. Delete Last
                  6. Delete Middle
                  7. Modify Node
                  8. View List
                  9. Count List
                  10. Show Menu
                  11. Exit
? 4
Singly Linked List is Empty ...
? 5
Singly Linked List is Empty ...
? 6
Singly Linked List is Empty ...
? 7
Singly Linked List is Empty ...
? 8
Singly Linked List is Empty ...
? 0
Enter the Roll Number : 101
Enter the Name : Madhu
Do u wish to Add Data in the List (y/n) ? y
Enter the Roll Number : 102
Enter the Name : Priya
Do u wish to Add Data in the List (y/n) ? y
Enter the Roll Number : 103
Enter the Name : Raaji
Do u wish to Add Data in the List (y/n) ? n
? 8
Roll Number : 101
Name : Madhu
Roll Number : 102
Name : Priya
Roll Number : 103
Name : Raaji
? 9
Number of nodes in the list is 3
? 1
Enter the Roll Number : 100
Enter the Name : Sudha
```

```
? 2
Enter the Roll Number : 104
Enter the Name : Siva
? 8
Roll Number : 100
Name : Sudha
Roll Number : 101
Name : Madhu
Roll Number : 102
Name : Priya
Roll Number : 103
Name : Raaji
Roll Number : 104
Name : Siva
? 4
Deleted Data is ...
Roll Number : 100
Name : Sudha
? 5
Deleted Data is ...
Roll Number : 104
Name : Siva
? 8
Roll Number : 101
Name : Madhu
Roll Number : 102
Name : Priya
Roll Number : 103
Name : Raaji
? 9
Number of nodes in the list is 3
? 3
Enter the node roll no after which the insertion is to be made : 104
Insert Node is Not Found
? 3
Enter the node roll no after which the insertion is to be made : 102
Enter the Roll Number : 105
Enter the Name : Ramya
? 8
Roll Number : 101
```

```
Name : Madhu
Roll Number : 102
Name : Priya
Roll Number : 105
Name : Ramya
Roll Number : 103
Name : Raaji
? 6
Enter the node roll no to be deleted : 104
Delete Node is Not Found
? 6
Enter the node roll no to be deleted : 105
Deleted Data is ...
Roll Number : 105
Name : Ramya
? 8
Roll Number : 101
Name : Madhu
Roll Number : 102
Name : Priya
Roll Number : 103
Name : Raaji
? 7
Enter the node roll no for modification : 105
Modify Node is Not Found
? 7
Enter the node roll no for modification : 102
Modify the Data of the Node ...
Enter the New Roll Number : 112
Enter the New Name : Geetha
? 8
Roll Number : 101
Name : Madhu
Roll Number : 112
Name : Geetha
Roll Number : 103
Name : Raaji
? 10
```

```
Basic Operations in a Singly Linked List ...

            0. Create List

            1. Insert First

            2. Insert Last

            3. Insert Middle

            4. Delete First

            5. Delete Last

            6. Delete Middle

            7. Modify Node

            8. View List

            9. Count List

            10. Show Menu

            11. Exit
? 4
Deleted Data is ...
Roll Number : 101
Name : Madhu
? 5
Deleted Data is ...
Roll Number : 103
Name : Raaji
? 4
Deleted Data is ...
Roll Number : 102
Name : Geetha
? 3
Singly Linked list is Empty. So new node is head node.
Enter the Roll Number : 1000
Enter the Name : Vanitha
? 8
Roll Number : 1000
Name : Vanitha
? 9
Number of nodes in the list is 1
? 11
End of run of your program . . .
```

1.6 Basic Operations in a Doubly Linked List

The basic operations that can be performed on doubly linked lists are,

- Creation of a list
- Insertion of a node
- Modification of a node
- Deletion of a node
- Traversal of a list
- Count the number of nodes.

1.6.1 Creation of a List

The linked list in *Program 1.3* has two items (i.e., `roll` and `name`). Creation of list involves three processes. They are,

- Creating a node
- Reading details for a node from user
- Connect the node with the list.

Creating a doubly linked list starts with creating a node. Sufficient memory has to be allocated for creating a node. The information is stored in the memory, allocated by using the `malloc()` function of type node. In *Program 1.3* `getNode()` function is used for creating a node. After allocating memory for the structure of type `node`, the information for the items (i.e., `roll` and `name`) has to be read from the user. In *Program 1.3* `readNode()` function is used for reading details for the node from the user.

Algorithm for Declaration of Structure NODE

Struct NODE

DATA :   Data Field

FLINK :   Link Field (Address of next Struct NODE)

BLINK :   Link Field (Address of previous Struct NODE)

End Struct

Algorithm for Allocating Memory for the New Node

GETNODE()

SIZE : INTEGER

NEWNODE : NODE

Step 1 :   Set SIZE = get the size of the NODE

Step 2 :   Set NEWNODE = Allocate space in memory for the size of SIZE and

return the initial address

Step 3 :   Return NEWNODE

End GETNODE()

Algorithm for Reading the Content for the New Node

READNODE(NEWNODE : NODE)

Step 1 : Read, NEWNODE –> DATA

Step 2 : Set NEWNODE –> FLINK = NULL

Step 3 : Set NEWNODE –> BLINK = NULL

Step 4 : Return

End READNODE()

Connect the new node with the existing list. If the list is empty, set the head pointer of the list to the new node, other wise connect the new node in the last position of the list. In *Program 1.3* createList() function is used to connect the new nodes with the list.

Algorithm for CREATELIST()

CREATELIST()

HEAD, LAST, NEWNODE : NODE

Step 1 : Set NEWNODE = GETNODE()

Step 2 : CALL READNODE(NEWNODE)

Step 3 : Set HEAD = NEWNODE

Step 4 : Set LAST = NEWNODE

Step 5 : If you want to add another NODE proceed otherwise Return.

Step 6 : Set NEWNODE = GETNODE()

Step 7 : CALL READNODE(NEWNODE)

Step 8 : Assign LAST -> FLINK = NEWNODE

Step 9 : Assign NEWNODE -> BLINK = LAST

Step 10 : Assign LAST = LAST -> FLINK

Step 11 : Goto STEP 5

END CREATELIST()

1.6.2 Insertion of a Node

One of the most primitive operations that can be done in a doubly linked list is the insertion of a node. Memory is to be allocated for the new node (in a similar way that is done while creating a list) before reading the data. The new node will contain empty data field, empty forward and backward link fields. The data field of the new node is then stored with the information read from the user. Both the link fields of the new node are assigned to NULL. The new node can then be inserted in the list at three different places namely,

- Inserting as a first node in the list
- Inserting as a last node in the list
- Inserting an intermediate node in the list.

Inserting as a first node in the list

The following steps are followed to insert a new node in the start of the list.

- Get the new node using GETNODE() and read the details of the node using READNODE().
- Check whether the list is empty or not (i.e., check whether the head pointer is pointing to NULL or not). If the list is empty, assign new node as head. If the list is not empty, follow the next steps.
- The forward link field of the new node is made to point the first node (head node) in the list by assigning the address of the first node.
- The backward link field of the first node (head node) is made to point the new node, by assigning the address of the new node.
- Assign the new node as the head pointer.

In *Program 1.3* `insertFirst()` function is used for inserting a new node in the first position of the list.

Algorithm for Inserting a Node as the First Node in the List

INSERT_FIRST(HEAD : NODE)

NEWNODE : NODE

Step 1 : Set NEWNODE = GETNODE()

Step 2 : CALL READNODE (NEWNODE)

Step 3 : If (HEAD == NULL)

        Set HEAD = NEWNODE

        Return

        [End of If structure]

Step 4 : Assign NEWNODE -> FLINK = HEAD

Step 5 : Assign HEAD -> BLINK = NEWNODE

Step 6 : Assign HEAD = NEWNODE

END INSERT_FIRST()

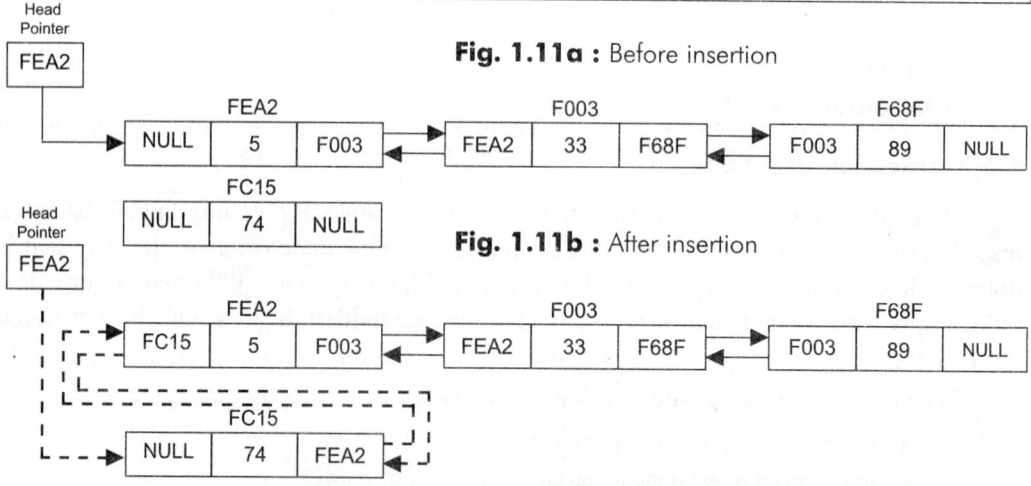

Fig. 1.11a : Before insertion

Fig. 1.11b : After insertion

Fig. 1.11 : Inserting as a first node in the list.

Inserting as a last node in the list

The following steps are followed to insert a new node at the end of the list.

- Get the new node using GETNODE(), and read the details of the node using READNODE().
- Check whether the list is empty or not (i.e., check whether the head pointer is pointing to NULL or not). If the list is empty, assign new node as a head node. If the list is not empty, follow the next steps.
- The forward link field of the last node in the list is made to point the new node, by assigning the address of the new node.
- The backward link field of the new node is made to point the last node, by assigning the address of the last node.
- The forward link field of the new node is set to NULL.

In *Program 1.3* insertLast() function is used for inserting a new node in the last position of the list.

Algorithm for inserting a node as the last node in the list

    INSERT_LAST(HEAD : NODE)

LAST, NEWNODE : NODE

Step 1 :   Set NEWNODE = GETNODE()

Step 2 :   CALL READNODE(NEWNODE)

Step 3 :   If (HEAD==NULL)

        Set HEAD = NEWNODE

        Return

        [End of If structure]

Step 4 :   Set LAST = HEAD

Step 5 :   Repeat While (LAST -> FLINK != NULL)

        Assign LAST = LAST -> FLINK

        [End of While Structure]

Step 6 :   Assign LAST -> FLINK = NEWNODE

Step 7 :   Assign NEWNODE -> BLINK = LAST

END INSERT_LAST()

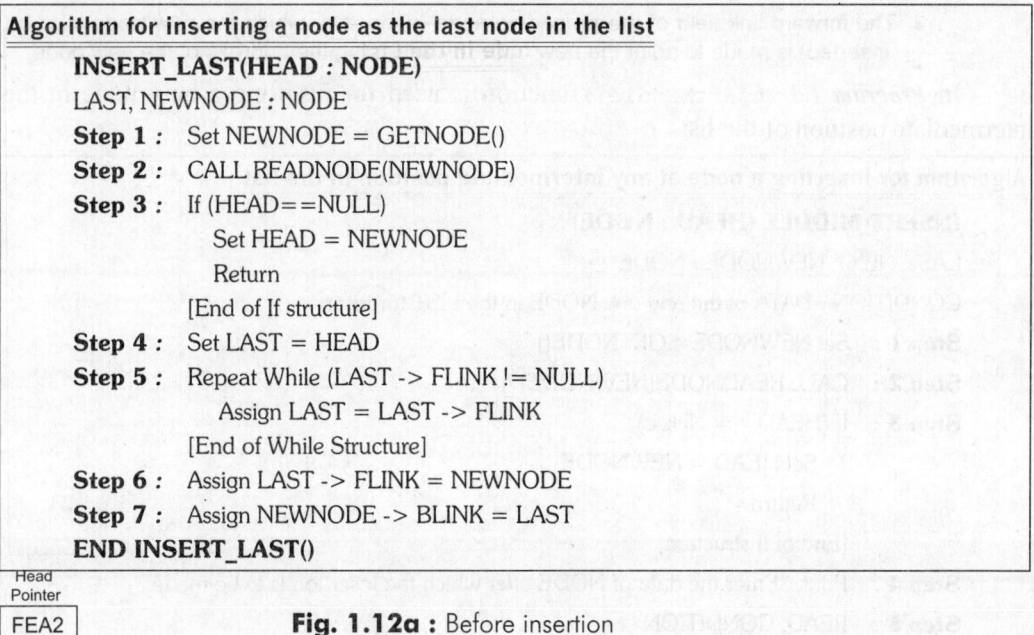

Head Pointer

FEA2

Fig. 1.12a : Before insertion

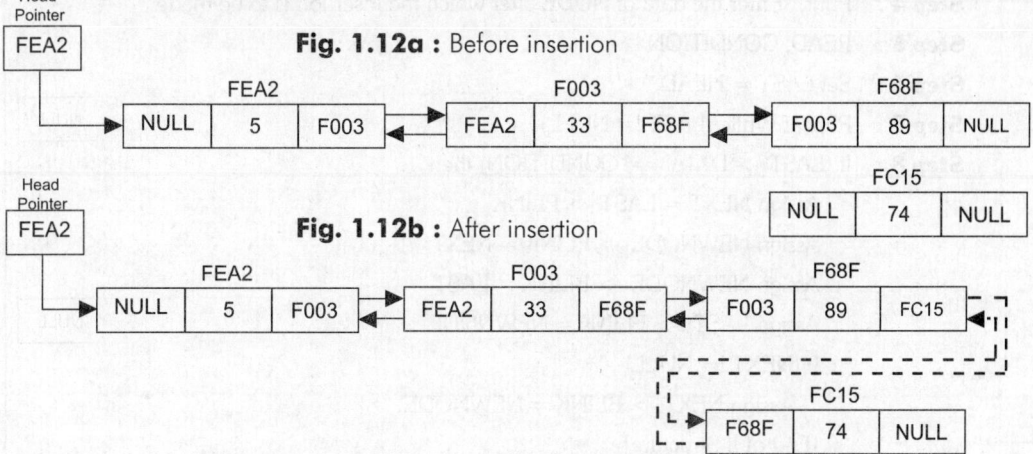

Head Pointer

FEA2

Fig. 1.12b : After insertion

Fig. 1.12 : Inserting as a last node in the list.

Inserting an intermediate node in the list

Steps to be followed, to insert a new node in any intermediate position in the list.

- Get the new node using GETNODE() and read the details of the node using READNODE().
- Check whether the list is empty or not (i.e., check whether the head pointer is pointing to NULL or not). If the list is empty, assign new node as a head node. If the list is not empty, follow the next steps.
- Get the address of the preceding node after which the new node is to be inserted.
- The forward link field of the new node is made to point the next node (forward link field of the preceding node) by assigning its address.
- The backward link field of the new node is made to point the preceding node by assigning the address of the preceding node.
- The backward link field of the next node (node before which the new node is to be inserted) is made to point the new node, by assigning the address of the new node.
- The forward link field of the preceding node (node after which the new node is to be inserted) is made to point the new node, by assigning the address of the new node.

In *Program 1.3* insertMiddle() function is used for inserting a new node in the intermediate position of the list.

Algorithm for inserting a node at any intermediate position in the list

INSERT_MIDDLE (HEAD : NODE)

LAST, NEXT, NEWNODE : NODE

CONDITION : DATA of the any one NODE in the LIST for insert

Step 1 : Set NEWNODE= GETNODE()

Step 2 : CALL READNODE(NEWNODE)

Step 3 : If (HEAD == NULL)

>   Set HEAD = NEWNODE

>   Return

> [End of If structure]

Step 4 : Print, "Enter the data of NODE after which the Insertion is to be made"

Step 5 : READ, CONDITION

Step 6 : Set LAST = HEAD

Step 7 : Repeat While (LAST != NULL)

Step 8 : If (LAST -> DATA == CONDITION) then

>   Assign NEXT = LAST -> FLINK

>   Assign NEWNODE -> FLINK = NEXT

>   Assign NEWNODE -> BLINK = LAST

>   Assign LAST - > FLINK = NEWNODE

>   If (NEXT != NULL)

>   Assign NEXT -> BLINK = NEWNODE

>   [End of If Structure]

Return

Else

Assign LAST = LAST -> FLINK

[End of If Structure]

Step 9 : [End of **Step 7** while structure]

Step 10: Print, "CONDITION IS NOT AVAILABLE"

Step 11: Return

END INSERT_MIDDLE()

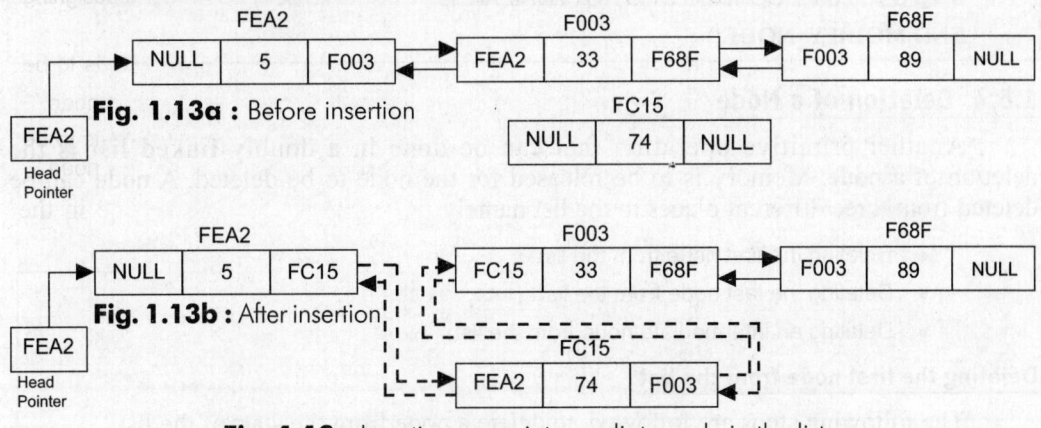

Fig. 1.13a : Before insertion

Fig. 1.13b : After insertion

Fig. 1.13 : Inserting as an intermediate node in the list.

1.6.3 Modification of a Node

A node(s) can be modified in a list, for changing its information part. The following steps are followed to modify a node in the list.

- Check whether the list is empty or not (i.e., check whether the head pointer is pointing to NULL or not). If the list is not empty, follow the next steps.
- Search for the node to be modified.
- Change the information part of the node.

In *Program 1.3* modifyNode() function is used for modifying an existing node in the list.

Algorithm for modifying an existing node
MODIFY_NODE(HEAD : NODE)
Step 1 : If (HEAD == NULL)
Return
[End of If structure]
Step 2 : Print, "Enter the data of NODE to be modified"
Step 3 : Read, CONDITION
Step 4 : Set LAST = HEAD

Step 5 : Repeat While (LAST != NULL)

Step 6 : If (LAST -> DATA == CONDITION) then

        Read, LAST -> DATA

        Return

    Else

        Assign LAST = LAST -> FLINK

    [End of If Structure]

Step 7 : [End of **Step 5** While structure]

Step 8 : Print, "CONDITION IS NOT AVAILABLE"

END MODIFY_NODE()

1.6.4 Deletion of a Node

Another primitive operation that can be done in a doubly linked list is the deletion of a node. Memory is to be released for the node to be deleted. A node can be deleted from three different places in the list namely,

- Deleting the first node from the list
- Deleting the last node from the list
- Deleting an intermediate node from the list.

Deleting the first node from the list

The following steps are followed, to delete a node from the start of the list.

- Check whether the list is empty or not (i.e., check whether the head pointer is pointing to NULL or not). If the list is not empty, follow the next steps.
- Set the head pointer to the second node in the list (by assigning its address).
- Set the backward link field of the head node in the list to NULL.
- Release the memory for the deleted node.

In *Program 1.3* deleteFirst() function is used for deleting the first node in the list. After deleting the memory occupied by the deleted node is released using releaseNode() function.

Algorithm for releasing the memory for the node to be deleted

RELEASENODE(NEWNODE : NODE)

Step 1 : Deallocate the space for the NODE of NEWNODE

Step 2 : Return

End RELEASENODE()

Algorithm for deleting the first node from the list

DELETE_FIRST (HEAD : NODE)

DELNODE : NODE

Step 1 : If (HEAD == NULL)

        Print "List is Empty"

Return

[End of If structure]

Step 2 : Set DELNODE = HEAD

Step 3 : Assign HEAD = HEAD -> FLINK

Step 4 : If (HEAD != NULL)

Assign HEAD -> BLINK = NULL

[End of If Structure]

Step 5 : Print "Deleted Data is", DELNODE -> DATA

Step 6 : CALL RELEASENODE(DELNODE)

Step 7 : Return

END DELETE_FIRST()

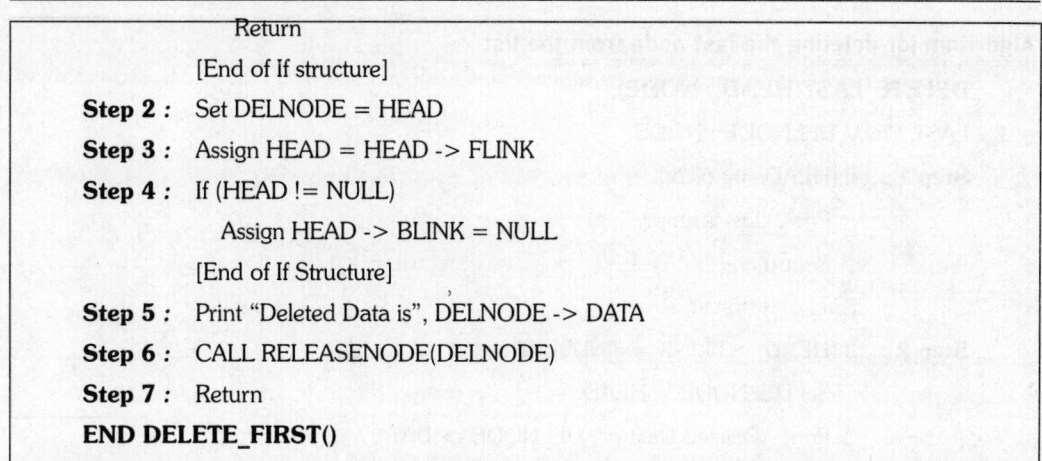

Fig. 1.14a : Before deletion

Fig. 1.14b : After deletion

Fig. 1.14 : Deleting the first node from the list.

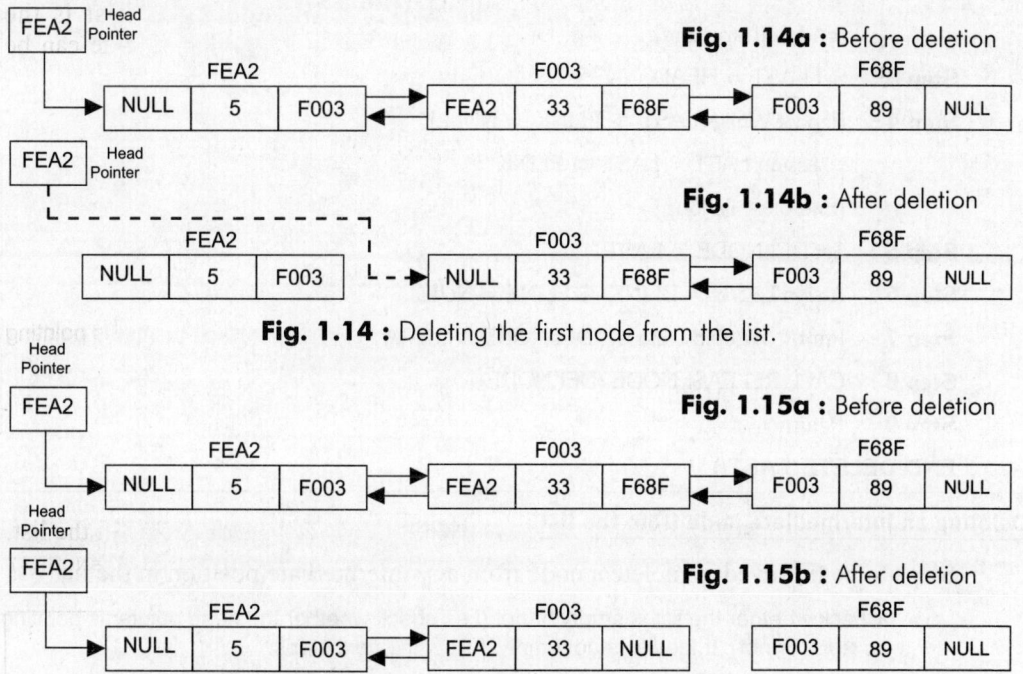

Fig. 1.15a : Before deletion

Fig. 1.15b : After deletion

Fig. 1.15 : Deleting the last node from the list.

Deleting the last node from the list

The following steps are followed, to delete a node from the end of the list.

- Check whether the list is empty or not (i.e., check whether the head pointer is pointing to NULL or not). If the list is not empty, follow the next steps.
- The forward link field of the previous node (from the end of the list) is set to NULL.
- Release the memory for the deleted node.

In *Program 1.3* deleteLast() function is used for deleting the last node in the list. After deleting the memory occupied by the deleted node is released using releaseNode() function.

Algorithm for deleting the last node from the list

DELETE_LAST(HEAD : NODE)

LAST, PREV, DELNODE : NODE

Step 1 : If (HEAD == NULL)

Print, "List is empty"

Return

[End of If structure]

Step 2 : If (HEAD -> FLINK == NULL) Then

Set DELNODE = HEAD

Print, "Deleted Data is", DELNODE -> DATA

Return

[End of If structure]

Step 3 : Set LAST = HEAD

Step 4 : Repeat While (LAST -> FLINK != NULL)

Assign LAST = LAST -> FLINK

[End of while loop]

Step 5 : Set DELNODE = LAST

Step 6 : Assign LAST -> BLINK -> FLINK = NULL

Step 7 : Print, " Deleted Data is", DELNODE -> DATA

Step 8 : CALL RELEASENODE (DELNODE)

Step 9 : Return

END DELETE_LAST()

Deleting an intermediate node from the list

Steps to be followed, to delete a node from any intermediate position in the list.

- Check whether the list is empty or not (i.e., check whether the head pointer is pointing to NULL or not). If the list is not empty, follow the next steps.

- The forward link field of the previous node (following the node to be deleted) is made to point the next node (before the node to be deleted), by assigning its address.

- The backward link field of the next node (before the node to be deleted) is made to point the previous node (following the node to be deleted), by assigning its address.

- Release the memory for the deleted node.

In *Program 1.3* deleteMiddle() function is used for deleting the intermediate node in the list. After deleting the memory occupied by the deleted node is released using releaseNode() function.

Algorithm for deleting a node at any intermediate position in the list

      DELETE_MIDDLE(HEAD : NODE)

NEXT, PREV, LAST, DELNODE : NODE

DELDATA : Data of the NODE is the List to Delete

Step 1 :   If (HEAD == NULL)

             Print "List is Empty"

             Return

            [End of If Structure]

Step 2 :   Print "Enter the DATA of the any node in the List for Delete "

Step 3 :   Read DELDATA

Step 4 :   If (HEAD -> DATA == DELDATA) Then

             Set DELNODE = HEAD

             Assign HEAD = HEAD -> FLINK

             If (HEAD != NULL)

                 Assign HEAD -> BLINK = NULL

             [End of If Structure]

                 Print, "Deleted Data is", DELNODE - > DATA

                 CALL RELEASENODE (DELNODE)

             Return

            [End of If Structure]

Step 5 :   Set LAST = HEAD -> FLINK

Step 6 :   Repeat While (LAST != NULL)

Step 7 :   If (LAST -> DATA == DELDATA) Then

             Set DELNODE = LAST

            Set PREV = LAST -> BLINK

             Set NEXT = LAST -> FLINK

             Assign PREV -> FLINK = NEXT

             If (NEXT != NULL)

                 Assign NEXT -> BLINK = PREV

             [End of If Structure]

                 Print, "The Deleted Data is ", DELNODE -> DATA

                 CALL RELEASENODE (DELNODE)

             Return

            Else

             Assign LAST = LAST -> FLINK

            [End of If structure]

Step 8 :   [End of **Step 6** While Loop]

Step 9 :   Print " DELDATA is Not Available in the List"

Step 10:   Return

END DELETE_MIDDLE()

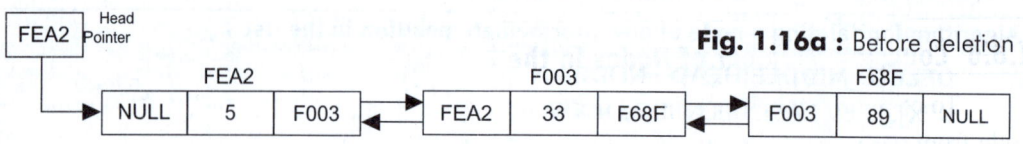

Fig. 1.16a : Before deletion

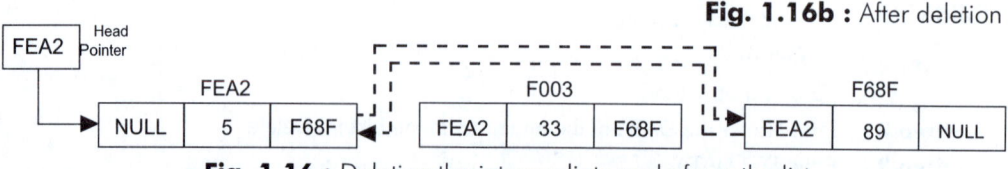

Fig. 1.16b : After deletion

Fig. 1.16 : Deleting the intermediate node from the list.

1.6.5 Traversal of a List

To read the information or to display the information in a linked list, we have to traverse (move) a linked list, node by node from the first node to the last node. Traversing a list involves the following steps,

- Check whether the head pointer is pointing to NULL or not. If yes, display "List is Empty" and terminate the process. Otherwise the follow the next steps.

- Display the information in the data field stored in the head pointer.

- Traverse the list from one node to another by advancing the head pointer, with the help of forward link (i.e., flink) till the end of the list.

In **Program 1.3** `viewList()` function is used for traversing and to display the information stored in the list.

Algorithm for displaying the contents of the list

    VIEW_LIST(HEAD : NODE)

    Step 1 : If (HEAD == NULL)

                Print, "List is Empty"

                Return

                [End of If Structure]

    Step 2 : While(HEAD != Null)

    Step 3 : Print "The data is ", HEAD -> DATA

    Step 4 : HEAD = HEAD –> FLINK

    Step 5 : [End of **Step 2** While structure]

    End View_LIST()

1.6.6 Count the Number of Nodes in the List

To count the nodes in a linked list, you have to traverse (move) a linked list, node by node from the first node to the last node. In *Program 1.3* `countList()` function is used for counting the number of nodes in the list. Counting the number of nodes in the list involves the following steps,

- Initialize the count variable to zero.

- Check whether the head pointer is pointing to NULL or not. If yes, display "List is Empty" and terminate the process. Otherwise the follow the next steps.

- Traverse the list from one node to another by advancing the head pointer, with the help of forward link (i.e., flink) till the end of the list and increment the count variable by 1.

Algorithm for counting the number of nodes in the list

Count_LIST(HEAD : NODE)

COUNT : INTEGER

Step 1 :   Set COUNT = 0

Step 2 :   If (HEAD == NULL)

Print, "List is Empty"

Return COUNT

[End of If Structure]

Step 3 :   While (HEAD != NULL)

Step 4 :   COUNT = COUNT + 1

Step 5 :   HEAD = HEAD −> FLINK

Step 6 :   [End of **Step 2** While structure]

Step 7 :   Return COUNT

END COUNT_LIST()

Program 1.3 :

```
/* Program to create, insert, delete, modify and view in a doubly linked list. */
/* dll.c */
#include <stdio.h>
typedef struct list
  {
     int roll;
     char name[20];
     struct list *flink, *blink;
  }node;
node* getNode();
void createList(node **headptr);
void insertFirst(node **headptr);
```

```
void insertLast(node **headptr);
void insertMiddle(node **headptr);
void deleteFirst(node **headptr);
void deleteLast(node **headptr);
void deleteMiddle(node **headptr);
void modifyNode(node *head);
void viewList(node *head);
void countList(node *head);
void releaseNode(node *newnode);
void displayMenu();
void main()
  {
    node *head = NULL;
    int ch, count;
    displayMenu();
    while(1)
      {
        printf("\n\n? ");
        fflush(stdin);
          scanf("%d", &ch);
        switch(ch)
          {
            case 0 :
                    createList(&head);
                    break;
            case 1 :
                    insertFirst(&head);
                    break;
            case 2 :
                    insertLast(&head);
                    break;
            case 3 :
                    insertMiddle(&head);
                    break;

            case 4 :
                    deleteFirst(&head);
                    break;
```

```
                    case 5 :
                            deleteLast(&head);
                            break;
                    case 6 :
                            deleteMiddle(&head);
                            break;
                    case 7 :
                            modifyNode(head);
                            break;
                    case 8 :
                            viewList(head);
                            break;
                    case 9 :
                            count = countList(head);
                            printf("Number of nodes in the list is %d",count);
                            break;
                    case 10:
                            displayMenu();
                            break;
                    default:
                            printf("End of run of your program . . .");
                            exit(0);
            }
        }
    }

void displayMenu()
    {
        printf("\nBasic Operations in a Doubly Linked List ... ");
        printf("\n\n\t 0. Create List ");
        printf("\n\t 1. Insert First ");
        printf("\n\t 2. Insert Last ");
        printf("\n\t 3. Insert Middle ");
        printf("\n\t 4. Delete First ");
        printf("\n\t 5. Delete Last ");
        printf("\n\t 6. Delete Middle ");
        printf("\n\t 7. Modify Node");
        printf("\n\t 8. View List");
        printf("\n\t 9. Count List");
```

```
        printf("\n\t 10. Show Menu ");

        printf("\n\t 11. Exit ");

    }

node* getNode()

    {

        int size;

        node * newnode;

        size = sizeof(node);

        newnode = (node *)malloc(size);

        return(newnode);

    }

void readNode(node* newnode)

    {

        printf("\nEnter the Roll Number : ");

            scanf("%d", &newnode->roll);

        printf("Enter the Name : ");

            scanf("%s", newnode->name);

        newnode->flink = NULL;

        newnode->blink = NULL;

    }

void releaseNode(node *newnode)

    {

        free(newnode);

    }

void createList(node **headptr)

    {

        node *head = NULL, *newnode, *last;

        char ch;

        do

        {

            newnode = getNode();

            readNode(newnode);

            if(head == NULL)

            {

                head = newnode;

                last = head;

            }
```

```
              else
                {
                   newnode -> blink = last;
                   last -> flink = newnode;
                   last = last -> flink;
                }
              fflush(stdin);
              printf("Do u wish to Add Data in the List (y/n) ? ");
                scanf("%c", &ch);
           }while( (ch == 'y') || (ch == 'Y') );
         *headptr = head;
   }
void insertFirst(node **headptr)
   {
      node *head, *newnode;
      head = *headptr;
      newnode = getNode();
      readNode(newnode);
      if(head == NULL)
         head = newnode;
      else
        {
           newnode -> flink = head;
           head -> blink = newnode;
           head = newnode;
        }
      *headptr = head;
   }
void insertLast(node **headptr)
   {
      node *newnode, *head, *last;
      head = *headptr;
      newnode = getNode();
      readNode(newnode);
      if(head == NULL)
         head = newnode;
      else
        {
           last  = head;
```

```
            while(last -> flink != NULL)
                last = last -> flink;
            newnode -> blink = last;
            last -> flink = newnode;
        }
        *headptr = head;
    }
    void insertMiddle(node **headptr)
    {
        node *newnode, *head, *last, *next;
        int insdata;
        head = *headptr;
        if(head == NULL)
        {
            printf("The Doubly Linked list is Empty. "
                                        "So new node is head node.");
            newnode = getNode();
            readNode(newnode);
            head = newnode;
        }
        else
        {
            printf("\n Enter the node roll no after which the"
                                    " insertion is to be made : ");
            scanf("%d", &insdata);
            last  = head;
            while(last != NULL)
            {
                if(last -> roll == insdata)
                {
                    newnode = getNode();
                    readNode(newnode);
                    next = last -> flink;
                    newnode -> flink = next;
                    newnode -> blink = last;
                    last -> flink = newnode;
                    if(next != NULL)
                        next -> blink = newnode;
                    return;
                }
```

```
                   else
                       last = last -> flink;
               }
           printf("Insert Condition is Not Found");
       }
     *headptr = head;
   }
void deleteFirst(node **headptr)
  {
     node *head, *delnode;
     head = *headptr;
     if(head == NULL)
       {
          printf("\n Doubly Linked List is Empty ...");
          return;
       }
     delnode = head;
     head = head -> flink;
     if(head != NULL)
        head -> blink = NULL;
     printf("\n Deleted Data is ... \n");
     printf("\n Roll Number : %d", delnode -> roll);
     printf("\n Name : %s", delnode -> name);
     releaseNode(delnode);
     *headptr = head;
  }
void deleteLast(node **headptr)
  {
     node *head, *delnode, *last, *prev;
     head = *headptr;
     if(head == NULL)
       {
          printf("\n Doubly Linked List is Empty ...");
          return;
       }
     else if(head -> flink == NULL)

       {
          delnode = head;
          head = NULL;
       }
```

```
      else
        {
          last = head;
          while(last -> flink != NULL)
            last = last -> flink;
          prev = last -> blink;
          delnode = last;
          prev -> flink = NULL;
        }
      printf("\n Deleted Data is ... \n");
      printf("\n Roll Number : %d", delnode -> roll);
      printf("\n Name : %s", delnode -> name);
      releaseNode(delnode);
      *headptr = head;
    }
void deleteMiddle(node **headptr)
  {
    node *head, *delnode, *last, *prev, *next;
    int deldata;
    head = *headptr;
    if(head == NULL)
      {
        printf("\n Doubly Linked List is Empty ... ");
        return;
      }
    printf("\nEnter the node roll no for deleteion is to be made : ");
      scanf("%d", &deldata);
    if(head -> roll == deldata)
      {
        delnode = head;
        head = head -> flink;
        if(head != NULL)
          head -> blink = NULL;
        printf("\n Deleted Data is ... \n");
        printf("\n Roll Number : %d", delnode -> roll);
        printf("\n Name : %s", delnode -> name);
        releaseNode(delnode);
        *headptr = head;
        return;
      }
```

```
            last = head -> flink;
        while(last != NULL)
         {
            if(last -> roll == deldata)
             {
                delnode = last;
                prev = last -> blink;
                next = last -> flink;
                prev -> flink = next;
                if(next != NULL)
                    next -> blink = prev;
                printf("\n Deleted Data is ... \n");
                printf("\n Roll Number : %d", delnode -> roll);
                printf("\n Name : %s", delnode -> name);
                releaseNode(delnode);
                return;
             }
            else
                last = last -> flink;
         }
        printf("Delete Node is Not Found");
            *headptr = head;
     }
void modifyNode(node *head)
     {
        int moddata;
        if(head == NULL)
         {
            printf("\n Doubly Linked List is Empty ...");
            return;
         }
        printf("\n Enter the node roll no for modification : ");
            scanf("%d", &moddata);
        while(head != NULL)
         {
            if(head -> roll == moddata)
             {
                printf("\n Modify the Data of the Node ... \n");
                printf("\n Enter the New Roll Number : ");
```

```
                scanf("%d", &head -> roll);
             printf("\n Enter the New Name : ");
                scanf("%s", head -> name);
             return;
          }
        else
          {
            head = head -> flink;
          }
      }
    printf("Modify Node is Not Found");
 }
 void viewList(node *head)
  {
    if(head == NULL)
    {
       printf("\n Doubly Linked List is Empty ...");
       return;
     }
    for(;head != NULL; head = head->flink)
     {
       printf("\n Roll Number : %d", head->roll);
       printf("\n Name : %s", head->name);
     }
  }
 void countList(node *head)
  {
    int count = 0;
    if(head == NULL)
     {
       printf("\nDoubly Linked List is Empty ...");
       return count;
     }
    for(;head != NULL; head = head -> flink)
     {
       count = count + 1;
     }
    return count;
  }
```

The program displays the following output

```
Basic Operations in a Doubly Linked List ...
        0. Create List
        1. Insert First
        2. Insert Last
        3. Insert Middle
        4. Delete First
        5. Delete Last
        6. Delete Middle
        7. Modify Node
        8. View List
        9. Count List
        10. Show Menu
        11. Exit
? 4
Doubly Linked List is Empty ...
? 5
Doubly Linked List is Empty ...
? 6
Doubly Linked List is Empty ...
? 7
Doubly Linked List is Empty ...
? 8
Doubly Linked List is Empty ...
? 0
Enter the Roll Number : 201
Enter the Name : Kannan
Do u wish to Add Data in the List (y/n) ? y
Enter the Roll Number : 202
Enter the Name : Lalitha
Do u wish to Add Data in the List (y/n) ? y
Enter the Roll Number : 203
Enter the Name : Karthik
Do u wish to Add Data in the List (y/n) ? n
? 8
Roll Number : 201
```

```
Name : Kannan
Roll Number : 202
Name : Lalitha
Roll Number : 203
Name : Karthik
? 9
Number of nodes in the list is 3
? 1
Enter the Roll Number : 200
Enter the Name : Kamal
? 2
Enter the Roll Number : 204
Enter the Name : Priya
? 8

Roll Number : 200

Name : Kamal

Roll Number : 201

Name : Kannan

Roll Number : 202

Name : Lalitha

Roll Number : 203

Name : Karthik

Roll Number : 204

Name : Priya

? 9
Number of nodes in the list is 5
? 4
Deleted Data is ...
Roll Number : 200
Name : Kamal
? 5
Deleted Data is ...
Roll Number : 204
Name : Priya
? 8
```

```
Roll Number : 201

Name : Kannan

Roll Number : 202

Name : Lalitha

Roll Number : 203

Name : Karthik

? 3

Enter the node roll no after which the insertion is to be made : 204

Insert Condition is Not Found

? 3

Enter the node roll no after which the insertion is to be made : 202

Enter the Roll Number : 205

Enter the Name : Ravi

? 8

Roll Number : 201

Name : Kannan

Roll Number : 202

Name : Lalitha

Roll Number : 205

Name : Ravi

Roll Number : 203

Name : Karthik

? 6

Enter the node roll no for deleteion is to be made : 204

Delete Node is Not Found

? 6

Enter the node roll no for deleteion is to be made : 205

Deleted Data is ...

Roll Number : 205

Name : Ravi

? 8

Roll Number : 201

Name : Kannan

Roll Number : 202

Name : Lalitha

Roll Number : 203

Name : Karthik
```

```
? 7
Enter the node roll no for modification : 205
Modify Node is Not Found
? 7
Enter the node roll no for modification : 202
Modify the Data of the Node ...
Enter the New Roll Number : 212
Enter the New Name : Lalli
? 8
Roll Number : 201
Name : Kannan
Roll Number : 212
Name : Lalli
Roll Number : 203
Name : Karthik
? 4
Deleted Data is ...
Roll Number : 201
Name : Kannan
? 5
Deleted Data is ...
Roll Number : 203
Name : Karthik
? 4
Deleted Data is ...
Roll Number : 212
Name : Lalli
? 4
Deleted Data is ...
Roll Number : 212
Name : Lalli
? 8
Doubly Linked List is Empty ...
? 9
Number of nodes in the list is 0
? 3
The Doubly Linked list is Empty. So new node is head node.
```

```
Enter the Roll Number : 2000

Enter the Name : Jeyabal

? 8

Roll Number : 2000

Name : Jeyabal

? 9

Number of nodes in the list is 1

? 10

End of run of your program . . .
```

1.7 Basic Operations in a Circular Singly Linked List

The basic operations that can be performed in circular singly linked list are similar to the singly linked list, except that the last node is made to point the first node in the list. The basic operations that can be performed on circular singly linked lists are,

- Creation of a list
- Insertion of a node
- Modification of a node
- Deletion of a node
- Traversal of a list.
- Count the number of nodes.

1.7.1 Creation of a List

The circular singly linked list in *Program 1.4* has two items (i.e., roll and name). Creation of list involves three processes.

- Creating a node
- Reading details for a node from user
- Connect the node with the list.

Creating a circular singly linked list starts with creating a node. Sufficient memory has to be allocated for creating a node. The information is stored in the memory, allocated by using the malloc() function of type node. In *Program 1.4* getNode() function is used for creating a node. After allocating memory for the structure of type node, the information for the items (i.e., roll and name) has to be read from the user. In *Program 1.4* readNode() function is used for reading details for the node from the user.

Algorithm for declaration of the structure NODE
Struct NODE DATA : Data Field LINK : Link Field (Address of next struct NODE) **End Struct**

Algorithm for allocating memory for the new node

> **GETNODE()**
>
> SIZE : INTEGER; NEWNODE : NODE
>
> **Step 1 :**   Set SIZE = get the size of the NODE
>
> **Step 2 :**   Set NEWNODE = Allocate space in memory for the size of SIZE and
>
>   return the initial address
>
> **Step 3 :**   Return NEWNODE
>
> **End GETNODE()**

Algorithm for reading the content for the new node

> **READNODE(NEWNODE : NODE)**
>
> **Step 1 :**   Read, NEWNODE -> DATA
>
> **Step 2 :**   Set NEWNODE -> LINK = NEWNODE
>
> **Step 3 :**   Return
>
> **End READNODE()**

Connect the new node with the existing list. If the list is empty, set the head pointer of the list to the new node, other wise connect the new node in the last position of the list. In *Program 1.4* createList() function is used to connect the new nodes with the list.

Algorithm for CREATELIST()

> **CREATELIST()**
>
> HEAD, LAST, NEWNODE : NODE
>
> **Step 1 :**   Assign NEWNODE = GETNODE()
>
> **Step 2 :**   CALL READNODE(NEWNODE)
>
> **Step 3 :**   Set HEAD = NEWNODE
>
> **Step 4 :**   Set LAST = NEWNODE
>
> **Step 5 :**   If you want to add another NODE proceed otherwise Return HEAD.
>
> **Step 6 :**   Set NEWNODE = GETNODE()
>
> **Step 7 :**   CALL READNODE(NEWNODE)
>
> **Step 8 :**   Assign LAST -> LINK = NEWNODE
>
> **Step 9 :**   Assign NEWNODE -> LINK = HEAD
>
> **Step 10:**   Assign LAST = LAST -> LINK
>
> **Step 11:**   Goto **Step 5**
>
> **END CREATELIST()**

1.7.2 Insertion of a Node

One of the most primitive operations that can be done in a singly linked list is the insertion of a node. Memory is to be allocated for the new node (in a similar way that is done while creating a list) before reading the data. The new node will contain empty data field and empty link field. The data field of the new node is then stored with the information read from the user. The link field of the new node is assigned to NULL. The new node can then be inserted in the list at three different places namely,

- Inserting as a first node in the list
- Inserting as a last node in the list
- Inserting as an intermediate node in the list.

Inserting as a first node in the list

The following steps are followed to insert a new node in the start of the list.

- Get the new node using GETNODE() and read the details of the node using READNODE().
- Check whether the list is empty or not (i.e., check whether the head pointer is pointing to NULL or not). If the list is empty, assign new node as head. If the list is not empty, follow the next steps.
- The link field of the new node is made to point the data field of the first node (i.e., head node) in the list by assigning the address of the first node.
- The head pointer is made to point the data field of the new node by assigning the address of the new node.

In *Program 1.4* `insertFirst()` function is used for inserting a new node in the first position of the list.

Algorithm for inserting a node as the first node in the list

INSERT_FIRST(HEAD : NODE)

NEWNODE , LAST : NODE

Step 1 :   Set NEWNODE = GETNODE()

Step 2 :   CALL READNODE (NEWNODE)

Step 3 :   If (HEAD==NULL)

        Set HEAD = NEWNODE

        Return

        [End of If structure]

Step 4 :   Set LAST = HEAD

Step 5 :   Repeat While (LAST -> LINK != HEAD)

        Assign LAST = LAST -> LINK

        [End of While Structure]

Step 6 :   Assign LAST -> LINK = NEWNODE

Step 7 :   Assign NEWNODE -> LINK = HEAD

Step 8 :   Assign HEAD = NEWNODE

END INSERT_FIRST()

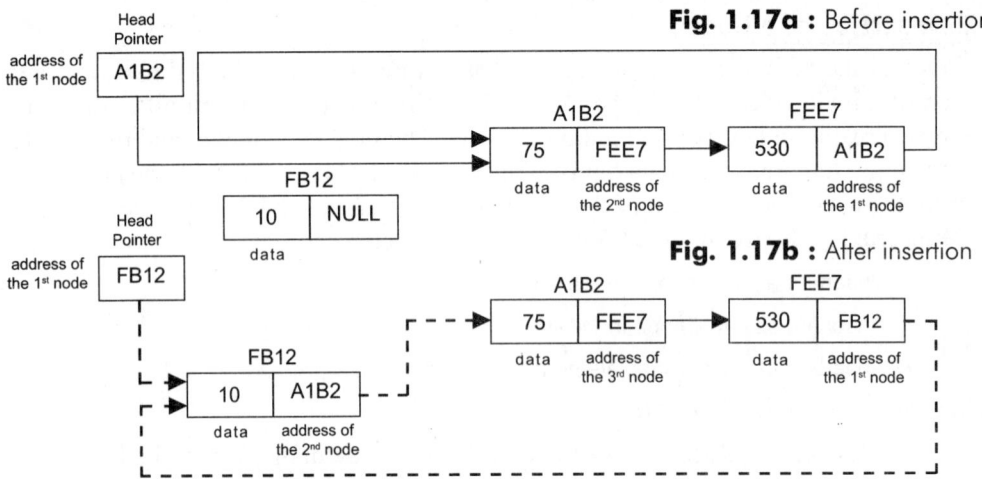

Fig. 1.17a : Before insertion

Fig. 1.17b : After insertion

Fig. 1.17 : Inserting as a first node in the list.

Inserting as a last node in the list

The following steps are followed to insert a new node in the end of the list.

- Get the new node using GETNODE() and read the details of the node using READNODE().
- Check whether the list is empty or not (i.e., check whether the head pointer is pointing to NULL or not). If the list is empty, assign new node as head. If the list is not empty, follow the next steps.
- The link field of the last node is made to point the data field of the new node in the list by assigning the address of the new node.
- The link field of the new node is set to NULL.

In **Program 1.4** `insertLast()` function is used for inserting a new node in the last position of the list.

Algorithm for inserting a node as the last node in the list
INSERT_LAST(HEAD : NODE)
LAST, NEWNODE *: NODE*
Step 1 :   Set NEWNODE = GETNODE()
Step 2 :   CALL READNODE(NEWNODE)
Step 3 :   If (HEAD==NULL)
Set HEAD = NEWNODE
Return
[End of If structure]
Step 4 :   Set LAST = HEAD
Step 5 :   Repeat While (LAST -> LINK != HEAD)
Assign LAST = LAST -> LINK
[End of While Structure]
Step 6 :   Assign LAST -> LINK = NEWNODE
Step 7 :   Assign NEWNODE -> LINK = HEAD
END INSERT_LAST()

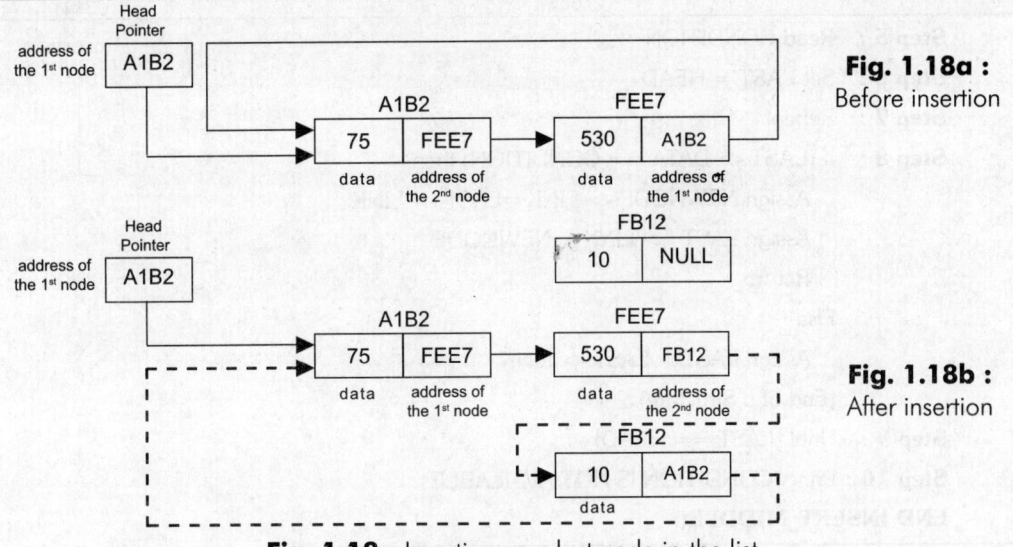

Fig. 1.18a : Before insertion

Fig. 1.18b : After insertion

Fig. 1.18 : Inserting as a last node in the list.

Inserting an intermediate node in the list

Steps to be followed, to insert a new node in any intermediate position in the list.

- Get the new node using GETNODE() and read the details of the node using READNODE().

- Check whether the list is empty or not (i.e., check whether the head pointer is pointing to NULL or not). If the list is empty, assign new node as head. If the list is not empty, follow the next steps.

- Get the address of the preceding node after which the new node is to be inserted.

- The link field of the new node is made to point the data field of the next node (link field of the preceding node) by assigning its address.

- The link field of the preceding node is made to point the data field of the new node by assigning the address of the new node.

In *Program 1.4* insertMiddle() function is used for inserting a new node in the intermediate position of the list.

Algorithm for inserting a node at any intermediate position in the list
INSERT_MIDDLE (HEAD : NODE)
LAST, NEWNODE : NODE
CONDITION : DATA of the any one NODE in the LIST for insert
Step 1 :   Set NEWNODE= GETNODE()
Step 2 :   CALL READNODE(NEWNODE)
Step 3 :   If (HEAD == NULL)
Set HEAD = NEWNODE
Return
[End of If structure]
Step 4 :   Print "Enter the data of NODE after which the insertion is to be made"

Step 5 : Read CONDITION

Step 6 : Set LAST = HEAD

Step 7 : Repeat

Step 8 : If (LAST -> DATA == CONDITION) then

Assign NEWNODE -> LINK =LAST -> LINK

Assign LAST - > LINK = NEWNODE

Return

Else

Assign LAST = LAST -> LINK

[End of If Structure]

Step 9 : Until (LAST == HEAD)

Step 10 : Print "CONDITION IS NOT AVAILABLE"

END INSERT_MIDDLE()

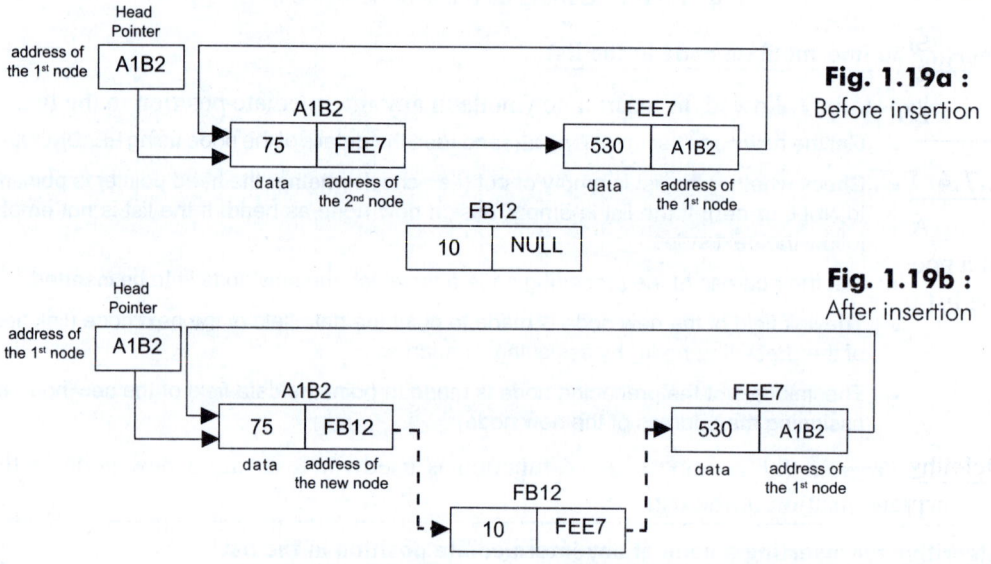

Fig. 1.19a : Before insertion

Fig. 1.19b : After insertion

Fig. 1.19 : Inserting as an intermediate node in the list.

1.7.3 Modification of a Node

A node(s) can be modified in a list, for changing its information part. The following steps are followed to modify a node in the list.

- Check whether the list is empty or not (i.e., check whether the head pointer is pointing to NULL or not). If the list is not empty, follow the next steps.

- Search for the node to be modified.

- Change the information part of the node.

In **Program 1.4** modifyNode() function is used for modifying an existing node in the list.

Algorithm for modifying an existing node

>   **MODIFY_NODE(HEAD : NODE)**
>
> **Step 1 :**   If (HEAD == NULL)
>
>   Return
>
>   [End of If structure]
>
> **Step 2 :**   Print "Enter the data of NODE to be modified"
>
> **Step 3 :**   Read CONDITION
>
> **Step 4 :**   Set LAST = HEAD
>
> **Step 5 :**   Repeat
>
> **Step 6 :**   If (LAST -> DATA == CONDITION) then
>
>   Read LAST -> DATA
>
>   Return
>
>   Else
>
>   Assign LAST = LAST -> LINK
>
>   [End of If Structure]
>
> **Step 7 :**   Until (LAST == HEAD)
>
> **Step 8 :**   Print "CONDITION IS NOT AVAILABLE"
>
> **END MODIFY_NODE()**

1.7.4 Deletion of a Node

Another primitive operation that can be done in a singly linked list is the deletion of a node. Memory is to be released for the node to be deleted. A node can be deleted from the list from three different places namely,

- Deleting the first node from the list.
- Deleting the last node from the list.
- Deleting an intermediate node from the list.

Deleting the first node from the list

The following steps are followed, to delete a node from the start of the list.

- Check whether the list is empty or not (i.e., check whether the head pointer is pointing to NULL or not). If the list is not empty, follow the next steps.
- Set the head pointer to the second node in the list (by assigning its address).
- Release the memory for the deleted node.

In *Program 1.4* deleteFirst() function is used for deleting the first node in the list. After deleting the memory occupied by the deleted node is released using releaseNode() function.

Algorithm for releasing the memory for the node to be deleted

>   **RELEASE_NODE(NEWNODE : NODE)**
>
> **Step 1 :**   Deallocate the space for the NODE of NEWNODE
>
> **Step 2 :**   Return
>
> **End RELEASENODE()**

Algorithm for deleting the first node from the list

DELETE_FIRST(HEAD : NODE)

LAST, DELNODE : NODE

Step 1 :   If (HEAD == NULL)

>   Print, "List is empty"

>   Return

>   [End of If structure]

Step 2 :   If (HEAD -> LINK == HEAD) Then

>   DELNODE = HEAD

>   Print, "Deleted Data is", DELNODE -> DATA

>   Set HEAD = NULL

>   CALL RELEASENODE(DELNODE)

>   Return

>   [End of If structure]

Step 3 :   Set LAST = HEAD

Step 4 :   Repeat

>   Assign LAST = LAST -> LINK

>   Until (LAST -> LINK == HEAD)

Step 5 :   DELNODE = HEAD

Step 6 :   HEAD = HEAD -> LINK

Step 7 :   LAST -> LINK = HEAD

Step 8 :   Print, " Deleted Data is", DELNODE -> DATA

Step 9 :   CALL RELEASENODE (DELNODE)

END DELETE_FIRST()

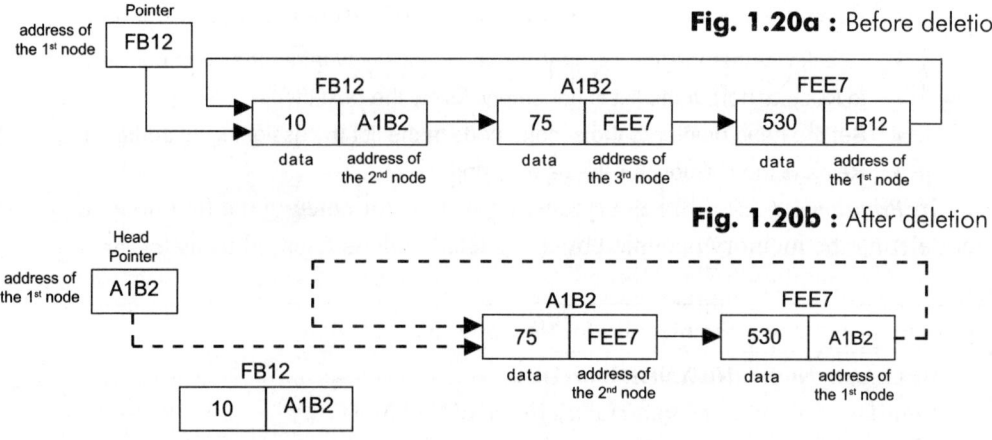

Fig. 1.20a : Before deletion

Fig. 1.20b : After deletion

Fig. 1.20 : Deleting the first node from the list.

Deleting the last node from the list

The following steps are followed, to delete a node from the end of the list.

- Check whether the list is empty or not (i.e., check whether the head pointer is pointing to NULL or not). If the list is not empty, follow the next steps.
- The link field of the previous node (from the end of the list) is set to NULL.
- Release the memory for the deleted node.

In *Program 1.4* deleteLast() function is used for deleting the last node in the list. After deleting the memory occupied by the deleted node is released using releaseNode() function.

Algorithm for deleting the last node from the list

    DELETE_LAST(HEAD : NODE)

    LAST, PREV, DELNODE : NODE

    Step 1 : If (HEAD == NULL)

            Print, "List is empty"

            Return

            [End of If structure]

    Step 2 : If (HEAD -> LINK == HEAD) Then

            Set DELNODE = HEAD

            Set HEAD = NULL

            Print, "Deleted Data is", DELNODE -> DATA

            CALL RELEASENODE(DELNODE)

            Return

            [End of If structure]

    Step 3 : Set LAST = HEAD

    Step 4 : Repeat While (LAST -> LINK != HEAD)

    Step 5 : Assign PREV = LAST

    Step 6 : Assign LAST = LAST -> LINK

    Step 7 : [End of **Step 4** While loop]

    Step 8 : Set DELNODE = LAST

    Step 9 : PREV -> LINK = HEAD

    Step 10: Print, "Deleted Data is", DELNODE -> DATA

    Step 11: CALL RELEASENODE (DELNODE)

    END DELETE_LAST()

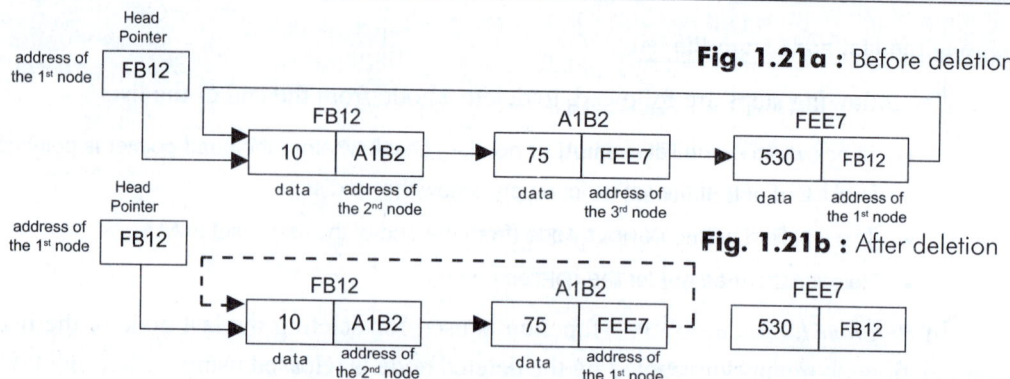

Fig. 1.21a : Before deletion

Fig. 1.21b : After deletion

Fig. 1.21 : Deleting the last node from the list.

Deleting an intermediate node from the list

Steps to be followed, to delete a node from any intermediate position in the list.

- Check whether the list is empty or not (i.e., check whether the head pointer is pointing to NULL or not). If the list is not empty, follow the next steps.
- The link field of the previous node (following the node to be deleted) is made to point the data field of the next node (before the node to be deleted), by assigning its address.
- Release the memory for the deleted node.

In *Program 1.4* deleteMiddle() function is used for deleting the intermediate node in the list and the memory occupied by the deleted node is released using releaseNode() function.

Algorithm for deleting a node at any intermediate position in the list

DELETE_MIDDLE(HEAD : NODE)

LAST, PREV, DELNODE : NODE

DELDATA : Data of the NODE is the List to Delete

Step 1 : If (HEAD == NULL)

Print, "List is Empty"

Return

[End of If Structure]

Step 2 : Print, "Enter the DATA of the any node in the List for Details "

Step 3 : Read, DELDATA

Step 4 : If (HEAD -> DATA == DELDATA) Then

DELNODE = HEAD

If (HEAD -> LINK == HEAD)

HEAD = NULL

Else

LAST = HEAD

WHILE(LAST -> LINK != HEAD)

      LAST = LAST -> LINK

      HEAD = HEAD -> LINK

      LAST -> LINK = HEAD

    [End of If Structure]

    Print, "Deleted Data is", DELNODE - > DATA

    CALL RELEASENODE (DELNODE)

    Return

    [End of If Structure]

Step 5 : Set LAST = HEAD -> LINK

Step 6 : Set PREV = HEAD

Step 7 : Repeat While (LAST != HEAD)

Step 8 : If (LAST -> DATA == DELDATA) Then

    Set DELNODE = LAST

    Assign PREV -> LINK = LAST -> LINK

    Print, "The Deleted Data is ", DELNODE -> DATA

    CALL RELEASENODE (DELNODE)

    Return

    Else

    Assign LAST = LAST -> LINK

    Assign PREV = PREV -> LINK

    [End of If structure]

Step 9 : [End of **Step 7** While Loop]

Step 10: Print, " DELDATA is Not Available in the List",

END DELETE_MIDDLE()

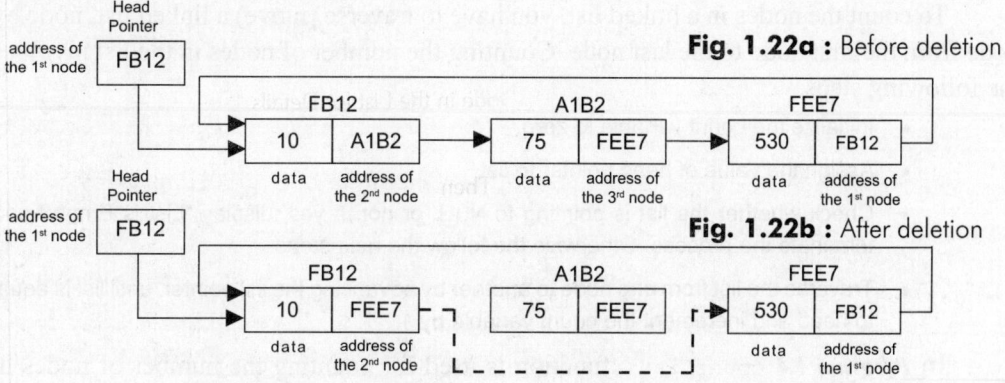

address of the 1st node   Head Pointer   FB12   **Fig. 1.22a :** Before deletion

FB12   A1B2   FEE7

10 | A1B2   75 | FEE7   530 | FB12

data | address of the 2nd node   data | address of the 3rd node   data | address of the 1st node

address of the 1st node   Head Pointer   FB12   **Fig. 1.22b :** After deletion

FB12   A1B2   FEE7

10 | FEE7   75 | FEE7   530 | FB12

data | address of the 2nd node   data | address of the 1st node

Fig. 1.22 : Deleting the intermediate node from the list.

1.7.5 Traversal of a List

To read the information or to display the information in a linked list, you have to traverse (move) through a linked list, node by node from the first node, until the end of the list is reached. Traversing a list involves the following steps,

- Check whether the head pointer is pointing to NULL or not. If yes, display "List is Empty" and terminate the process. Otherwise follow the next steps.

- Display the information in the data field stored in the head pointer.

- Traverse the list from one node to another by advancing the head pointer.

In *Program 1.4,* viewList () function is used for traversing and to display the information stored in the list.

Algorithm for displaying the contents of the list
VIEW(HEAD : NODE)
LIST : NODE
Step 1 : LIST = HEAD
Step 2 : If (LIST == NULL)
Print, "List is Empty"
Return
[End of If Structure]
Step 3 : Repeat
Step 4 : Print "The data is ", LIST -> DATA
Step 5 : LIST = LIST -> LINK
Step 6 : Until (LIST == HEAD)
End View()

1.7.6 Count the Number of Nodes in the List

To count the nodes in a linked list, you have to traverse (move) a linked list, node by node from the first node to the last node. Counting the number of nodes in the list involves the following steps,

- Initialize the count variable to zero.

- Assign the value of head pointer to list.

- Check whether the list is pointing to NULL or not. If yes, display "List is Empty" and terminate the process. Otherwise the follow the next steps.

- Traverse the list from one node to another by advancing the list pointer, until list is equal to head and increment the count variable by 1.

In *Program 1.4* countList () function is used for counting the number of nodes in the list.

Algorithm for counting the number of nodes in the list

Count_LIST(HEAD : NODE)

COUNT : INTEGER

LIST : NODE

Step 1 : Set COUNT = 0

Step 2 : LIST = HEAD

Step 3 : If (LIST == NULL)

Print, "List is Empty"

Return COUNT

[End of If Structure]

Step 4 : Repeat

Step 5 : Print "The data is ", LIST -> DATA

Step 6 : COUNT = COUNT + 1

Step 7 : LIST = LIST -> LINK

Step 8 : Until (LIST == HEAD)

Step 9 : Return COUNT

end COUNT_LIST()

Program 1.4 :

/* **Program to create, insert, delete, modify and view in circular singly linked list** */

```c
/* csll.c */
#include <stdio.h>
typedef struct list
  {
    int roll;
    char name[20];
    struct list *link;
  }node;
node* getNode();
void createList(node **headptr);
void insertFirst(node **headptr);
void insertLast(node **headptr);
void insertMiddle(node **headptr);
void deleteFirst(node **headptr);
void deleteLast(node **headptr);
void deleteMiddle(node **headptr);
void modifyNode(node *head);
void view(node *head);
```

```
    void releaseNode(node *newnode);
    void displayMenu();
    void main()
     {
        node *head = NULL;
        int ch, count;
        displayMenu();
        while(1)
         {
           printf("\n\n? ");
           fflush(stdin);
             scanf("%d", &ch);
           switch(ch)
            {
               case 0 :
                       createList(&head);
                       break;
               case 1 :
                       insertFirst(&head);
                       break;
               case 2 :
                       insertLast(&head);
                       break;
               case 3 :
                       insertMiddle(&head);
                       break;
               case 4 :
                       deleteFirst(&head);
                       break;
               case 5 :
                       deleteLast(&head);
                       break;
               case 6 :
                       deleteMiddle(&head);
                       break;
               case 7 :
                       modifyNode(head);
                       break;
```

```
              case 8 :

                      view(head);
                      break;

              case 9 :

                      count = countList(head);
                       printf("Number of nodes in the list is %d",count);
                      break;

              case 10:

                      display_menu();
                      break;

              default:

                      printf("End of run of your program ...");
                      exit(0);
          }
      }
}

void displayMenu()
{
    printf("\n Basic Operations in a Circular Singly Linked List ...");
    printf("\n\n\t 0. Create List ");
    printf("\n\t 1. Insert First ");
    printf("\n\t 2. Insert Last ");
    printf("\n\t 3. Insert Middle ");
    printf("\n\t 4. Delete First ");
    printf("\n\t 5. Delete Last ");
    printf("\n\t 6. Delete Middle ");
    printf("\n\t 7. Modify Node");
    printf("\n\t 8. View List");
    printf("\n\t 9. Count List");
    printf("\n\t 10. Show Menu ");
    printf("\n\t 11. Exit ");
}

node* getNode()
{
    int size;
    node * newnode;
    size = sizeof(node);
    newnode = (node *)malloc(size);
    return(newnode);

}
```

```c
void readNode(node* newnode)
{
    printf("\nEnter the Roll Number : ");
        scanf("%d", &newnode->roll);
    printf("Enter the Name : ");
        scanf("%s", newnode->name);
    newnode->link = newnode;
}
void releaseNode(node *newnode)
{
    free(newnode);
}
void createList(node ** headptr)
{
    node *head = NULL, *newnode, *last;
    char ch;
    do
    {
        newnode = getNode();
        readNode(newnode);
        if(head == NULL)
        {
            head = newnode;
            last = head;
        }
        else
        {
            newnode -> link = last;
            last -> link = newnode;
            last = last -> link;
        }
        fflush(stdin);
        printf("Do u wish to Add Data in the List (y/n) ? ");
            scanf("%c", &ch);
    }while( (ch == 'y') || (ch == 'Y') );
    *headptr = head;
}
```

```
    void insertFirst(node **headptr)
    {
      node *head, *newnode, *last;
      head = *headptr;
      newnode = getNode();
      readNode(newnode);
      if(head == NULL)
        head = newnode;
      else
       {
         last = head;
         while(last -> link != head)
           last = last -> link;
         last -> link = newnode;
         newnode -> link = head;
         head = newnode;
       }
      *headptr = head;
    }
    void insertLast(node **headptr)
    {
      node *head, *newnode, *last;
      head = *headptr;
      newnode = getNode();
      readNode(newnode);
      if(head == NULL)
        head = newnode;
      else
       {
         last  = head;
         while(last -> link != head) last = last -> link;
           last -> link = newnode;
         newnode -> link = head;
       }
         *headptr = head;
    }
    void insertMiddle(node **headptr)
    {
      node *head, *newnode, *last;
      int insdata;
      head = *headptr;
```

```
    if(head == NULL)
     {
        printf("The Circular Singly Linked list is Empty. "
                                    "So new node is head node.");
        newnode = getNode();
        readNode(newnode);
        head = newnode;
     }
    else
     {
        printf("\n Enter the node roll no after which the"
                            "insertion is to be made : ");
         scanf("%d", &insdata);
        last  = head;
        do
         {
            if(last -> roll == insdata)
             {
                newnode = getNode();
                readNode(newnode);
                newnode -> link = last -> link;
                last -> link = newnode;
                return;
             }
            else
                last = last -> link;
         }while(last != head);
        printf("The Insert Node is not Found");
     }
    *headptr = head;
 }
void deleteFirst(node **headptr)
 {
    node *head, *delnode, *last;
    head = *headptr;
    if(head == NULL)
     {
        printf("\n Circular Singly Linked List is Empty ...");
        return;
     }
```

```
       delnode = head;
       if(head -> link == head)
        {
          head = NULL;
        }
       else
        {
          last = head;
          while(last -> link != head)
            last = last -> link;
          head = head -> link;
          last -> link = head;
        }
    printf("\n Deleted Data is ... \n");
    printf("\n Roll Number : %d", delnode -> roll);
    printf("\n Name : %s", delnode -> name);
    releaseNode(delnode);
    *headptr = head;
  }

void deleteLast(node **headptr)
  {
    node *head, *delnode, *last, *prev;
    head = *headptr;
    if(head == NULL)
     {
       printf("\n Circular Singly Linked List is Empty ...");
       return;
     }
    if(head -> link == head)
     {
       delnode = head;
       head = NULL;
     }
    else
     {
       last  = head;
       while(last -> link != head)
```

```
            {
              prev = last;
              last = last -> link;
            }
          delnode = last;
          prev -> link = head;
        }
      printf("\n Deleted Data is ... \n");
      printf("\n Roll Number : %d", delnode -> roll);
      printf("\n Name : %s", delnode -> name);
      releaseNode(delnode);
      *headptr = head;
    }
  void deleteMiddle(node **headptr)
    {
      node *head, *delnode, *last, *prev;
      int deldata;
      head = *headptr;
      if(head == NULL)
        {
          printf("\n Circular Singly Linked List is Empty ...");
          return;
        }
      printf("\n Enter the node Roll No for deleteion is to be made : ");
        scanf("%d", &deldata);
      last = head;
      if(head -> roll == deldata)
        {
          delnode = head;
          if(head -> link == head)
            head = NULL;
          else
            {
              last = head;
              while(last -> link != head)
                last = last -> link;
              head = head -> link;
              last -> link = head;
            }
        }
```

```
      else
       {
         prev = head;
         last = head -> link;
         while(last != head)
          {
            if(last -> roll == deldata)
             {
               delnode = last;
               prev -> link = last -> link;
               break;
             }
            prev = prev -> link;
            last = last -> link;
          }
         if(last == head)
          {
            printf("Delete Node is Not Found");
            return;
          }
       }
      printf("\n Deleted Data is ... \n");
      printf("\n Roll Number : %d", delnode -> roll);
      printf("\n Name : %s", delnode -> name);
      releaseNode(delnode);
      *headptr = head;
    }
void modifyNode(node *head)
    {
      node *last;
      int moddata;
      if(head == NULL)
       {
         printf("\n Circular Singly Linked List is Empty ...");
         return;
       }
      printf("\n Enter the node roll no for modification : ");
        scanf("%d", &moddata);
      last = head;
```

```
        do
          {
             if(last -> roll == moddata)
              {
                 printf("\n Enter the new data for the Node  : \n");
                 printf("\n Enter the New Roll Number : ");
                   scanf("%d", &last -> roll);
                 printf("\n Enter the New Name : ");
                   scanf("%s", last -> name);
                 return;
              }
             else
                last = last -> link;
          }while(last != head);
        printf("Modify Node is Not Found");
    }
    void viewList(node *head)
     {
        node *last;
        if(head == NULL)
          {
             printf("\nCircular Singly Linked List is Empty ...");
             return;
          }
        last = head;
        do
          {
             printf("\n Roll Number : %d ", last->roll);
             printf("\n Name : %s", last->name);
             last = last -> link;
          }while(last != head);
      }
    void countList(node *head)
      {
        int count = 0;
        node *last;
        if(head == NULL)
          {
             printf("\nCircular Singly Linked List is Empty ...");
```

```
          return count;
      }
   last = head;
   do
     {
       count = count + 1;
       last = last -> link;
     }while(last != head);
   return count;
 }
```

The program displays the following output

```
Basic Operations in a Circular Singly Linked List ...

          0. Create List

          1. Insert First

          2. Insert Last

          3. Insert Middle

          4. Delete First

          5. Delete Last

          6. Delete Middle

          7. Modify Node

          8. View List

          9. Count List

          10. Show Menu

          11. Exit
? 4
Circular Singly Linked List is Empty ...
? 5
Circular Singly Linked List is Empty ...
? 6
Circular Singly Linked List is Empty ...
? 7
Circular Singly Linked List is Empty ...
? 8
Circular Singly Linked List is Empty ...
```

```
    ? 0

    Enter the Roll Number : 301

    Enter the Name : Raj

    Do u wish to Add Data in the List (y/n) ? y

    Enter the Roll Number : 302

    Enter the Name : Rani

    Do u wish to Add Data in the List (y/n) ? y

    Enter the Roll Number : 303

    Enter the Name : Priya

    Do u wish to Add Data in the List (y/n) ? n
    ? 8

    Roll Number : 301

    Name : Raj

    Roll Number : 302

    Name : Rani

    Roll Number : 303

    Name : Priya
    ? 1

    Enter the Roll Number : 300

    Enter the Name : Raju
    ? 2

    Enter the Roll Number : 304

    Enter the Name : Vasanth
    ? 8

    Roll Number : 300

    Name : Raju

    Roll Number : 301

    Name : Raj

    Roll Number : 302

    Name : Rani

    Roll Number : 303

    Name : Priya
```

```
Roll Number : 304

Name : Vasanth

? 4

Deleted Data is ...

Roll Number : 300

Name : Raju

? 5

Deleted Data is ...

Roll Number : 304

Name : Vasanth

? 8

Roll Number : 301

Name : Raj

Roll Number : 302

Name : Rani

Roll Number : 303

Name : Priya

? 3

Enter the node roll no after which the insertion is to be made : 304

Insert Node is Not Found

? 3

Enter the node roll no after which the insertion is to be made : 302

Enter the Roll Number : 305

Enter the Name : Jai

? 8

Roll Number : 301

Name : Raj

Roll Number : 302

Name : Rani

Roll Number : 305

Name : Jai

Roll Number : 303

Name : Priya

? 6

Enter the node roll no to be deleted : 304
```

```
Delete Node is Not Found
? 6
Enter the node roll no to be deleted : 305
Deleted Data is ...
Roll Number : 305
Name : Jai
? 8
Roll Number : 301
Name : Raj
Roll Number : 302
Name : Rani
Roll Number : 303
Name : Priya
? 7
Enter the node roll no for modification : 305
Modify Node is Not Found
? 7
Enter the node roll no for modification : 303
Modify the Data of the Node ...
Enter the New Roll Number : 313
Enter the New Name : Geetha
? 8
Roll Number : 301
Name : Raj
Roll Number : 302
Name : Rani
Roll Number : 313
Name : Geetha
? 4
Deleted Data is ...
Roll Number : 301
Name : Raj
? 5
Deleted Data is ...
Roll Number : 313
```

```
Name : Geetha

? 4

Deleted Data is ...

Roll Number : 302

Name : Rani

? 8

Circular Singly Linked List is Empty ...

? 11

End of run of your program . . .
```

1.8 Basic Operation in a Circular Doubly Linked List

The basic operations that can be performed on circular doubly linked lists are similar to the doubly linked lists, except that the last node is made to point the first node in the list. The basic operations that can be performed on circular doubly linked lists are,

- Creation of a list
- Insertion of a node
- Modification of a node

- Deletion of a node
- Traversal of a list
- Count the number of nodes

1.8.1 Creation of a List

The circular doubly linked list in *Program 1.5* has two items (i.e., roll and name). Creation of list involves three processes.

- Creating a node
- Reading details for a node from user
- Connect the node with the list.

Creating a circular doubly linked list starts with creating a node. Sufficient memory has to be allocated for creating a node. The information is stored in the memory, allocated by using the malloc() function of type node. In *Program 1.5* getNode() function is used for creating a node. After allocating memory for the structure of type node, the information for the items (i.e., roll and name) has to be read from the user. In *Program 1.5* readNode() function is used for reading details for the node from the user.

Algorithm for declaration of the structure NODE
Struct NODE
DATA : Data Field
FLINK : Link Field (Address of next Struct NODE)
BLINK : Link Field (Address of previous Struct NODE)
End Struct

Algorithm for allocating memory for the new node

GETNODE()

SIZE : INTEGER

NEWNODE : NODE

Step 1 :   Set SIZE = get the size of the NODE

Step 2 :   Set NEWNODE = Allocate space in memory for the size of SIZE and return the initial address

Step 3 :   Return NEWNODE

End GETNODE()

Algorithm for reading the content for the new node

READNODE(NEWNODE : NODE)

Step 1 :   Read, NEWNODE -> DATA

Step 2 :   Set NEWNODE -> FLINK = NEWNODE

Step 3 :   Set NEWNODE -> BLINK = NEWNODE

Step 4 :   Return

End READNODE()

Connect the new node with the existing list. If the list is empty, set the head pointer of the list to the new node, other wise connect the new node in the last position of the list. In *Program 1.5* createList() function is used to connect the new nodes with the list.

Algorithm for CREATELIST()

CREATELIST()

HEAD, LAST, NEWNODE : NODE

Step 1 :   Set NEWNODE = GETNODE()

Step 2 :   CALL READNODE(NEWNODE)

Step 3 :   Set HEAD = NEWNODE

Step 4 :   Set LAST = NEWNODE

Step 5 :   If you want to add another NODE proceed otherwise Return HEAD.

Step 6 :   Set NEWNODE = GETNODE()

Step 7 :   CALL READNODE(NEWNODE)

Step 8 :   Assign LAST -> FLINK = NEWNODE

Step 9 :   Assign NEWNODE -> FLINK = HEAD

Step 10:   Assign NEWNODE -> BLINK = LAST

Step 11:   Assign HEAD -> BLINK = NEWNODE

Step 12:   Assign LAST = LAST -> FLINK

Step 13:   Goto **Step 5**

END CREATELIST()

1.8.2 Insertion of a Node

One of the most primitive operations that can be done in a circular doubly linked list is the insertion of a node. Memory is to be allocated for the new node before reading the data. The new node will contain empty data field and empty forward and backward link fields. The data field of the new node is then stored with the information read from the user. Both the link fields of the new node are assigned to NULL. The new node can then be inserted in the list at three different places namely,

- Inserting as a first node in the list
- Inserting as a last node in the list
- Inserting an intermediate node in the list.

Inserting as a first node in the list

The following steps are followed to insert a new node in the start of the list.

- Get the new node using GETNODE() and read the details of the node using READNODE().
- Check whether the list is empty or not (i.e., check whether the head pointer is pointing to NULL or not). If the list is empty, assign new node as head. If the list is not empty, follow the next steps.
- The forward link field of the new node is made to point the first node (head node) in the list by assigning the address of the first node.
- The backward link field of the first node (head node) is made to point the new node, by assigning the address of the new node.
- Assign the new node as the head pointer.

In *Program 1.5* insertFirst() function is used for inserting a new node in the first position of the list.

Algorithm for inserting a node as the first node in the list

INSERT_FIRST(HEAD : NODE)

NEWNODE : NODE

Step 1 :   Set NEWNODE = GETNODE()

Step 2 :   CALL READNODE (NEWNODE)

Step 3 :   If (HEAD==NULL)

       Set HEAD = NEWNODE

       Return

       [End of If structure]

Step 4 :   Assign NEWNODE -> FLINK = HEAD

Step 5 :   Assign NEWNODE -> BLINK = HEAD -> BLINK

Step 6 :   Assign HEAD -> BLINK -> FLINK = NEWNODE

Step 7 :   Assign HEAD -> BLINK = NEWNODE

Step 8 :   Assign HEAD = NEWNODE

END INSERT_FIRST()

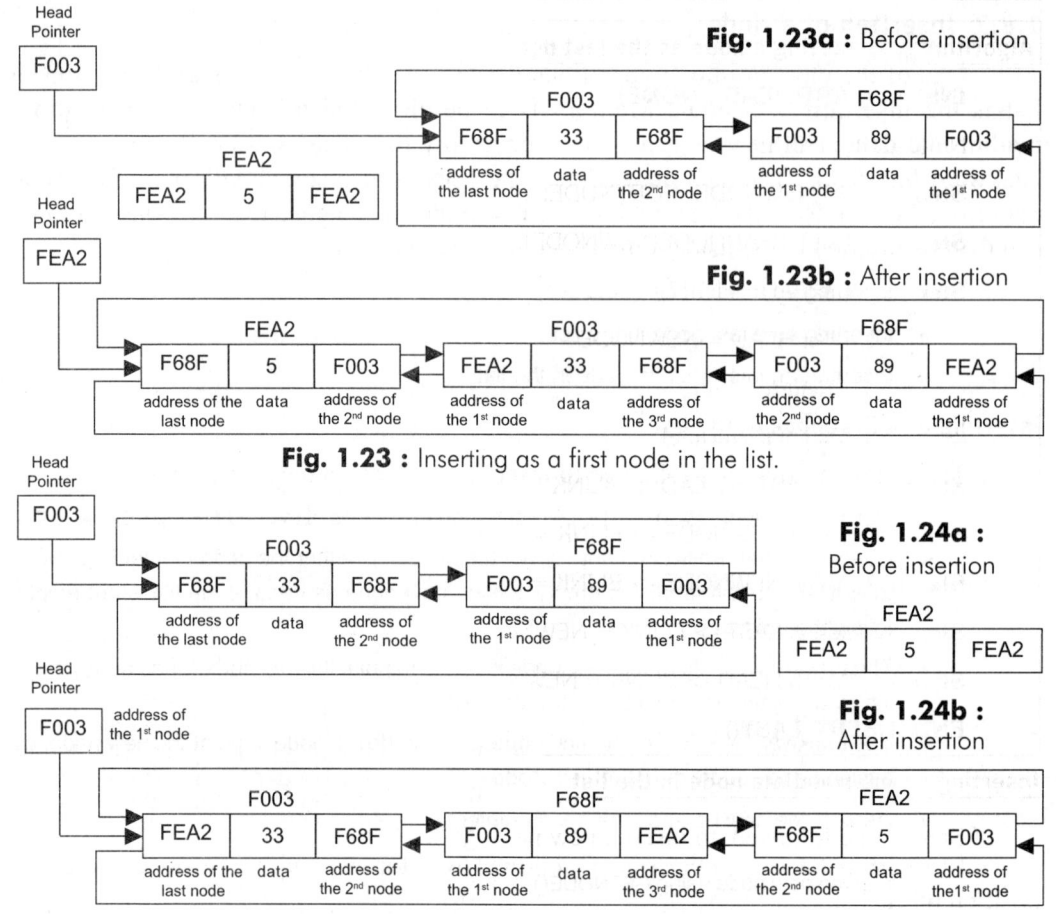

Fig. 1.23a : Before insertion

Fig. 1.23b : After insertion

Fig. 1.23 : Inserting as a first node in the list.

Fig. 1.24a : Before insertion

Fig. 1.24b : After insertion

Fig. 1.24 : Inserting as a last node in the list.

Inserting as a last node in the list

The following steps are followed to insert a new node at the end of the list.

- Get the new node using GETNODE(), and read the details of the node using READNODE().

- Check whether the list is empty or not (i.e., check whether the head pointer is pointing to NULL or not). If the list is empty, assign new node as a head node. If the list is not empty, follow the next steps.

- The forward link field of the last node in the list is made to point the new node, by assigning the address of the new node.

- The backward link field of the new node is made to point the last node, by assigning the address of the last node.

- The forward link field of the new node is set to NULL.

In *Program 1.5* insertLast() function is used for inserting a new node in the last position of the list.

Algorithm for inserting a node as the last node in the list

INSERT_LAST(HEAD : NODE)

NEWNODE : NODE

Step 1 : Set NEWNODE = GETNODE()

Step 2 : CALL READNODE(NEWNODE)

Step 3 : If (HEAD==NULL)

Set HEAD = NEWNODE

Return

[End of If structure]

Step 4 : Set LAST = HEAD -> BLINK

Step 5 : Assign NEWNODE -> FLINK = HEAD

Step 6 : Assign NEWNODE -> BLINK = LAST

Step 7 : Assign LAST -> FLINK = NEWNODE

Step 8 : Assign HEAD -> BLINK = NEWNODE

END INSERT_LAST()

Inserting an intermediate node in the list

Steps to be followed, to insert a new node in any intermediate position in the list.

- Get the new node using GETNODE(), and read the details of the node using READNODE().

- Check whether the list is empty or not (i.e., check whether the head pointer is pointing to NULL or not). If the list is empty, assign new node as a head node. If the list is not empty, follow the next steps.

- Get the address of the preceding node after which the new node is to be inserted.

- The forward link field of the new node is made to point the next node (forward link field of the preceding node) by assigning its address.

- The backward link field of the new node is made to point the preceding node by assigning the address of the preceding node.

- The backward link field of the next node (node before which the new node is to be inserted) is made to point the new node, by assigning the address of the new node.

- The forward link field of the preceding node (node after which the new node is to be inserted) is made to point the new node, by assigning the address of the new node.

In *Program 1.5* insertMiddle() function is used for inserting a new node in the intermediate position of the list.

Algorithm for inserting a node at any intermediate position in the list

INSERT_MIDDLE (HEAD : NODE)

LAST, NEXT, NEWNODE : NODE

CONDITION : DATA of the any one NODE in the LIST for insert

Step 1 : Set NEWNODE= GETNODE()

Step 2 : READNODE(NEWNODE)

Step 3 : If (HEAD == NULL)

      Set HEAD = NEWNODE

      Return

     [End of If structure]

Step 4 : Print, "Enter the data of NODE after which the Insertion is to be made"

Step 5 : READ, CONDITION

Step 6 : Set LAST = HEAD

Step 7 : Repeat

Step 8 : If (LAST -> DATA == CONDITION) then

      Assign NEWNODE -> FLINK = LAST -> FLINK

      Assign NEWNODE -> BLINK = LAST

      Assign LAST -> FLINK -> BLINK = NEWNODE

      Assign LAST -> FLINK = NEWNODE

      Return

     Else

      Assign LAST = LAST -> FLINK

     [End of If Structure]

Step 9 : Until (LAST == HEAD)

Step 10: Print, "CONDITION IS NOT AVAILABLE"

Step 11: Return

END INSERT_MIDDLE()

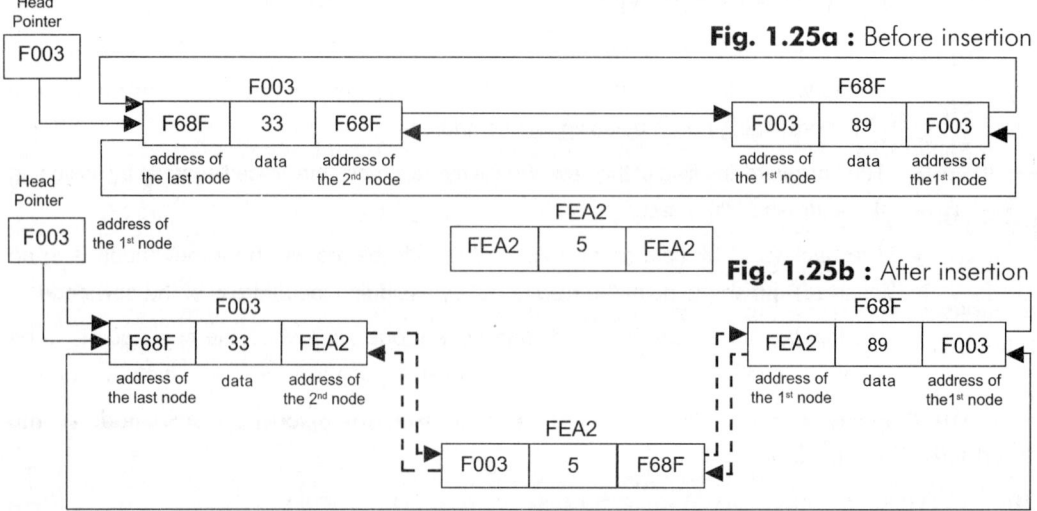

Fig. 1.25a : Before insertion

Fig. 1.25b : After insertion

Fig. 1.25 : Inserting as an intermediate node in the list.

1.8.3 Modification of a Node

A node(s) can be modified in a list, for changing its information part. The following steps are followed to modify a node in the list.

- Check whether the list is empty or not (i.e., check whether the head pointer is pointing to NULL or not). If the list is not empty, follow the next steps.
- Search for the node to be modified.
- Change the information part of the node.

In *Program 1.5* modifyNode() function is used for modifying an existing node in the list.

Algorithm for modifying an existing node

MODIFY_NODE(HEAD : NODE)

Step 1 : If (HEAD == NULL)

      Return

      [End of If structure]

Step 2 : Print, "Enter the data of NODE to be modified"

Step 3 : Read, CONDITION

Step 4 : Set LAST = HEAD

Step 5 : Repeat

Step 6 : If (LAST -> DATA == CONDITION) then

      Read, LAST -> DATA

      Return

      Else

        Assign LAST = LAST -> FLINK

      [End of If Structure]

Step 7 : Until (LAST != HEAD)

Step 8 : Print, "CONDITION IS NOT AVAILABLE"

END MODIFY_NODE()

1.8.4 Deletion of a Node

Another primitive operation that can be done in a doubly linked list is the deletion of a node. Memory is to be released for the node to be deleted. A node can be deleted from three different places in the list namely,

- Deleting the first node from the list.
- Deleting the last node from the list.
- Deleting an intermediate node from the list.

Deleting the first node from the list

The following steps are followed, to delete a node from the start of the list.

- Check whether the list is empty or not (i.e., check whether the head pointer is pointing to NULL or not). If the list is not empty, follow the next steps.
- Set the head pointer to the second node in the list (by assigning its address).
- Set the backward link field of the head node in the list to NULL.
- Release the memory for the deleted node.

In *Program 1.5* deleteFirst() function is used for deleting the first node in the list. After deleting the memory occupied by the deleted node is released using releaseNode() function.

Algorithm for releasing the memory for the node to be deleted

RELEASENODE(NEWNODE : NODE)

Step 1 : Deallocate the space for the NODE of NEWNODE

Step 2 : Return

End RELEASENODE()

Algorithm for deleting the first node from the list

DELETE_FIRST (HEAD : NODE)

DELNODE : NODE

Step 1 : If (HEAD == NULL)

        Print "List is Empty"

        Return

        [End of If structure]

Step 2 : Set DELNODE = HEAD

Step 3 : If (HEAD -> FLINK == HEAD)

        Set HEAD = NULL

        Print "Deleted Data is", DELNODE -> DATA

        CALL RELEASENODE (DELNODE)

        Return

        [End of If structure]

Step 4 : Assign HEAD -> BLINK -> FLINK = HEAD -> FLINK

Step 5 : Assign HEAD -> FLINK -> BLINK = HEAD -> BLINK

Step 6 : Assign HEAD = HEAD -> FLINK

Step 7 : Print, "Deleted Data is", DELNODE -> DATA

Step 8 : CALL RELEASENODE(DELNODE)

Step 9 : Return

END DELETE_FIRST()

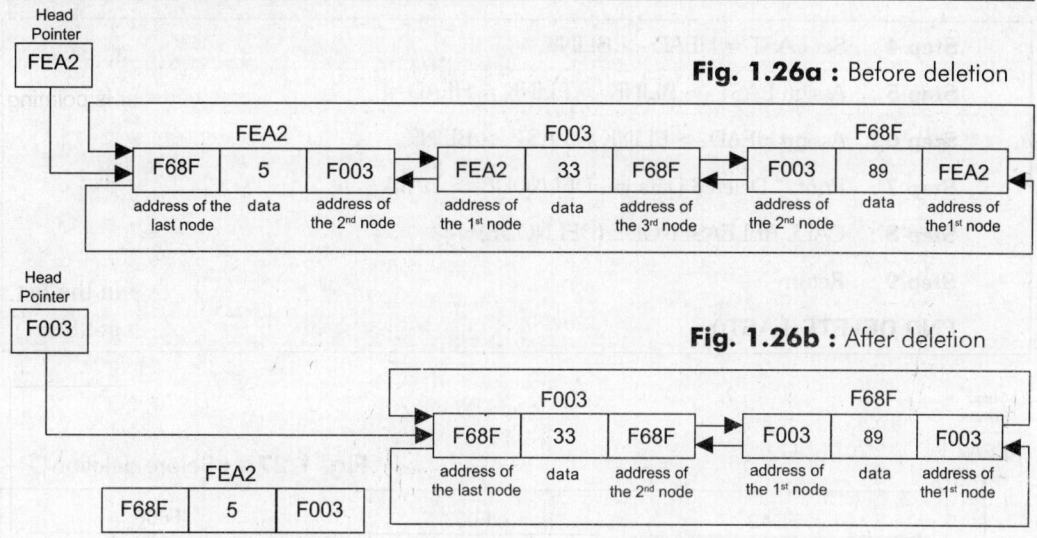

Fig. 1.26a : Before deletion

Fig. 1.26b : After deletion

Fig. 1.26 : Deleting the first node from the list.

Deleting the last node in the list

The following steps are followed, to delete a node from the end of the list.

- Check whether the list is empty or not (i.e., check whether the head pointer is pointing to NULL or not). If the list is not empty, follow the next steps.
- The forward link field of the previous node (from the end of the list) is set to NULL.
- Release the memory for the deleted node.

In *Program 1.5* deleteLast() function is used for deleting the last node in the list. After deleting the memory occupied by the deleted node is released using releaseNode() function.

Algorithm for deleting the last node from the list

DELETE_LAST(HEAD : NODE)

LAST, PREV, DELNODE : NODE

Step 1 : If (HEAD == NULL)

　　　　Print, "List is Empty"

　　　　Return

　　　　[End of If structure]

Step 2 : Set DELNODE = HEAD -> BLINK

Step 3 : If (HEAD -> FLINK == HEAD)

　　　　Set HEAD = NULL

　　　　Print, "Deleted Data is", DELNODE -> DATA

　　　　CALL RELEASENODE (DELNODE)

　　　　Return

　　　　[End of If structure]

Step 4 : Set LAST = HEAD -> BLINK

Step 5 : Assign LAST -> BLINK -> FLINK = HEAD

Step 6 : Assign HEAD -> BLINK = LAST -> BLINK

Step 7 : Print, " Deleted Data is", DELNODE -> DATA

Step 8 : CALL RELEASENODE (DELNODE)

Step 9 : Return

END DELETE_LAST()

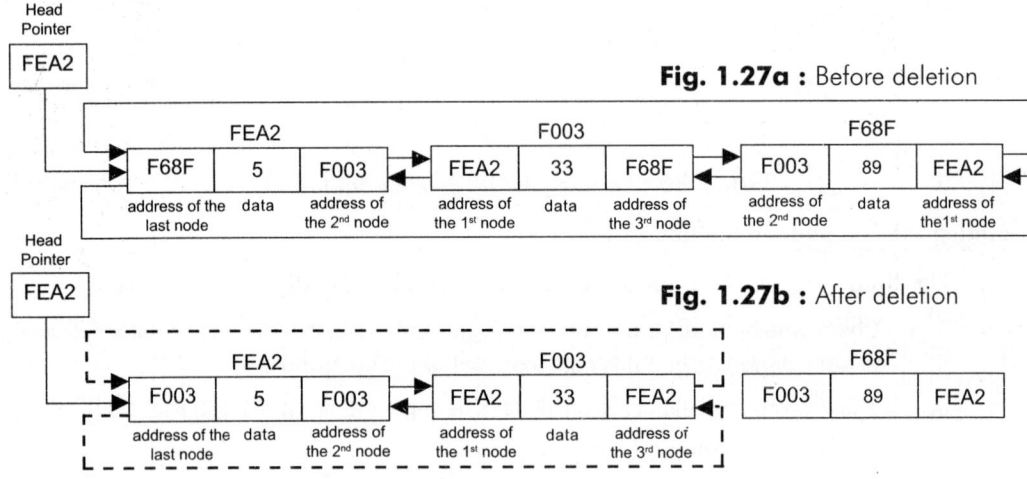

Fig. 1.27 : Deleting the last node from the list.

Deleting an intermediate node from the list

Steps are followed, to delete a node from any intermediate position in the list.

- Check whether the list is empty or not (i.e., check whether the head pointer is pointing to NULL or not). If the list is not empty, follow the next steps.

- The forward link field of the previous node (following the node to be deleted) is made to point the next node (before the node to be deleted), by assigning its address.

- The backward link field of the next node (before the node to be deleted) is made to point the previous node (following the node to be deleted), by assigning its address.

- Release the memory for the deleted node.

In *Program 1.5* deleteMiddle() function is used for deleting the intermediate node in the list and the memory occupied by the deleted node is released using releaseNode() function.

Algorithm for deleting a node at any intermediate position in the list

DELETE_MIDDLE(HEAD : NODE)

NEXT, PREV, LAST, DELNODE : NODE

DELDATA : Data of the NODE is the List to Delete

Step 1 : If (HEAD == NULL)

         Print, "List is Empty"

         Return

         [End of If Structure]

Step 2 : Print, "Enter the DATA of any node in the List for Details "

Step 3 : Read, DELDATA

Step 4 : If (HEAD -> DATA == DELDATA) Then

         Set DELNODE = HEAD

         If (HEAD -> FLINK == HEAD)

           Set HEAD = NULL

         Else

           Assign HEAD -> FLINK -> BLINK = HEAD -> BLINK

           Assign HEAD -> BLINK -> FLINK = HEAD -> FLINK

           Assign HEAD = HEAD -> FLINK

         [End of If Structure]

         Print, "Deleted Data is", DELNODE - > DATA

         CALL RELEASENODE (DELNODE)

         Return

         [End of If Structure]

Step 6 : Set LAST = HEAD -> FLINK

Step 7 : Repeat While (LAST != HEAD)

Step 8 : If (LAST -> DATA == DELDATA) Then

         Set DELNODE = LAST

         Assign LAST -> FLINK -> BLINK = LAST -> BLINK

         Assign LAST -> BLINK -> FLINK = LAST -> FLINK

         Print, "The Deleted Data is ", DELNODE -> DATA

         RELEASENODE (DELNODE)

         Return HEAD

         Else

              Assign LAST = LAST -> FLINK

         [End of If structure]

Step 8 : [End of STEP 6 While Loop]

Step 9 : Print, " DELDATA is Not Available in the List",

Step 10: Return HEAD

END DELETE_MIDDLE()

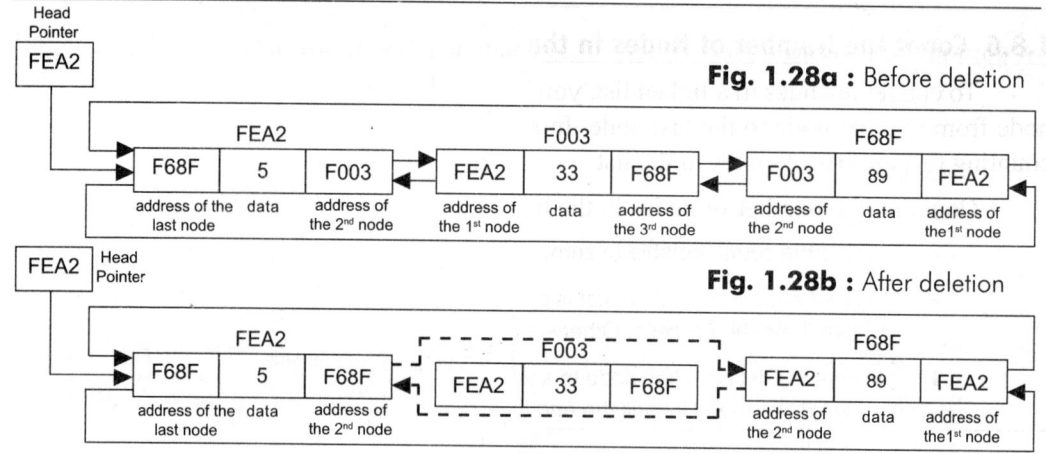

Fig. 1.28a : Before deletion

Fig. 1.28b : After deletion

Fig. 1.28 : Deleting the intermediate node from the list.

1.8.5 Traversal of a List

To read the information or to display the information in a linked list, you have to traverse (move) a linked list, node by node from the first node to the last node. Traversing a list involves the following steps,

- Check whether the head pointer is pointing to NULL or not. If yes, display "List is Empty" and terminate the process. Otherwise the follow the next steps.

- Display the information in the data field stored in the head pointer.

- Traverse the list from one node to another by advancing the head pointer, with the help of forward link (i.e., flink) till the end of the list.

In *Program 1.5* view() function is used for traversing and to display the information stored in the list.

Algorithm for displaying the contents of the list

    VIEW(HEAD : NODE)

    LIST : NODE

    Step 1 : LIST = HEAD

    Step 2 : If (LIST == NULL)

            Print, "List is Empty"

            Return

            [End of If Structure]

    Step 3 : Repeat

    Step 4 : Print "The data is ", LIST -> DATA

    Step 5 : LIST = LIST -> FLINK

    Step 6 : Until (LIST != HEAD)

    END VIEW()

1.8.6 Count the Number of Nodes in the List

To count the nodes in a linked list, you have to traverse (move) a linked list, node by node from the first node to the last node. In *Program 1.5* countList() function is used for counting the number of nodes in the list.

Counting the number of nodes in the list involves the following steps,

- Initialize the count variable to zero.
- Check whether the head pointer is pointing to NULL or not. If yes, display "List is Empty" and terminate the process. Otherwise the follow the next steps.
- Traverse the list from one node to another by advancing the head pointer, with the help of forward link (i.e., flink) till the end of the list and increment the count variable by 1.

Algorithm for counting the number of nodes in the list

    Count_LIST(HEAD : NODE)

    COUNT : INTEGER

    LIST : NODE

    Step 1 :   Set COUNT = 0

    Step 2 :   LIST = HEAD

    Step 3 :   If (LIST == NULL)

            Print "List is Empty"

            Return COUNT

            [End of If Structure]

    Step 4 :   Repeat

    Step 5 :   Print "The data is ", LIST -> DATA

    Step 6 :   COUNT = COUNT + 1

    Step 7 :   LIST = LIST -> FLINK

    Step 8 :   Until (LIST == HEAD)

    Step 9 :   Return COUNT

    end COUNT_LIST()

Program 1.5 :

/* **Program to create, insert, delete, modify and view in a Circular Doubly Linked List.** */

```c
/* cdll.c */
#include <stdio.h>
typedef struct list
  {
    int roll;
    char name[20];
    struct list *flink, *blink;
  }node;
node* getNode();
```

```c
void createList(node **headptr);

void insertFirst(node **headptr);

void insertLast(node **headptr);

void insertMiddle(node **headptr);

void deleteFirst(node **headptr);

void deleteLast(node **headptr);

void deleteMiddle(node **headptr);

void modifyNode(node *head);

void view(node *head);

void releaseNode(node *newnode);

void displayMenu();

void main()
  {
    node *head = NULL;
    int ch, count;
    displayMenu();
    while(1)
     {
       printf("\n\n? ");
       fflush(stdin);
        scanf("%d", &ch);
       switch(ch)
        {
          case 0 :
                   createList(&head);
                   break;
          case 1 :
                   insertFirst(&head);
                   break;
          case 2 :
                   insertLast(&head);
                   break;
          case 3 :
                   insertMiddle(&head);
                   break;
          case 4 :
                   deleteFirst(&head);
                   break;
          case 5 :
                   deleteLast(&head);
                   break;
```

```
                case 6 :

                        deleteMiddle(&head);

                        break;

                case 7 :

                        modifyNode(head);

                        break;

                case 8 :

                        view(head);

                        break;

                case 9 :

                        count = countList(head);

                        printf("Number of nodes in the list is %d",count);

                        break;

                case 10:

                        display_menu();

                        break;

                default:

                        printf("End of run of your program . . .");

                        exit(0);

            }

        }

    }

void displayMenu()

    {

        printf("\n Basic Operations in a Circular Doubly Linked List ...");

        printf("\n\n\t 0. Create List ");

        printf("\n\t 1. Insert First ");

        printf("\n\t 2. Insert Last ");

        printf("\n\t 3. Insert Middle ");

        printf("\n\t 4. Delete First ");

        printf("\n\t 5. Delete Last ");

        printf("\n\t 6. Delete Middle ");

        printf("\n\t 7. Modify Node");

        printf("\n\t 8. View List");

        printf("\n\t 9. Count List");

        printf("\n\t 10. Show Menu ");

        printf("\n\t 11. Exit ");

    }

node* getNode()

    {

        int size;

        node * newnode;
```

```
        size = sizeof(node);
        newnode = (node *)malloc(size);
        return(newnode);
    }
    void readNode(node* newnode)
    {
        printf("\nEnter the Roll Number : ");
            scanf("%d", &newnode->roll);
        printf("Enter the Name : ");
            scanf("%s", newnode->name);
        newnode->flink = newnode;
        newnode->blink = newnode;
    }
    void releaseNode(node *ptr)
    {
        free(ptr);
    }
    void createList(node **headptr)
    {
        node *head = NULL, *newnode, *last;
        char ch;
        do
          {
            newnode = getNode();
            readNode(newnode);
            if(head == NULL)
              {
                head = newnode;
                last = head;
              }
            else
              {
                newnode -> blink = last;
                newnode -> flink = head;
                last -> flink = newnode;
                head -> blink = newnode;
                last = last -> flink;
              }
            fflush(stdin);
            printf("Do u wish to Add Data in the List (y/n) ? ");
                scanf("%c", &ch);
```

```
        }while((ch == 'y') || (ch == 'Y'));
      *headptr = head;
   }
  void insertFirst(node **headptr)
   {
     node *head, *newnode;
     head = *headptr;
     newnode = getNode();
     readNode(newnode);
     if(head == NULL)
       head = newnode;
     else
       {
         newnode -> flink = head;
         newnode -> blink = head -> blink;
         head -> blink -> flink = newnode;
         head -> blink = newnode;
         head = newnode;
       }
     *headptr = head;
   }
  void insertLast(node **headptr)
   {
     node *head, *newnode, *last;
     head = *headptr;
     newnode = getNode();
     readNode(newnode);
     if(head == NULL)
       head = newnode;
     else
       {
         last  = head -> blink;
         newnode -> flink = head;
         newnode -> blink = last;
         last -> flink = newnode;
         head -> blink = newnode;
       }
     *headptr = head;
   }
  void insertMiddle(node **headptr)
   {
     node *head, *newnode, *last, *next;
     int insdata;
     head = *headptr;
     if(head == NULL)
```

```
    {
        printf("Circular Doubly Linked list is Empty. "
                                    "So new node is head node.");

        newnode = getNode();
        readNode(newnode);
        head = newnode;
        *headptr = head;
        return;
    }
    printf("\n Enter the node roll no after which the"
                            "insertion is to be made : ");
        scanf("%d", &insdata);
    last = head;
    do
      {
        if(last -> roll == insdata)
          {
            newnode = getNode();
            readNode(newnode);
            next = last -> flink;
            newnode -> flink = next;
            newnode -> blink = last;
            last -> flink = newnode;
            next -> blink = newnode;
            return;
          }
        else
            last = last -> flink;

      }while(last != head);
    printf("Insert Condition is Not Found");
}

void deleteFirst(node **headptr)

{
    node *head, *delnode, *last;
    head = *headptr;
    if(head == NULL)
      {
        printf("\n Circular Linked List is Empty ...");
        return;
      }
```

```
        delnode = head;
    if(head -> flink  == head)
       head = NULL;
    else
      {
        last = head -> blink;
        head = head -> flink;
        last -> flink = head;
        head -> blink = last;
      }
    printf("\n Deleted Data is ... \n");
    printf("\n Roll Number : %d", delnode -> roll);
    printf("\n Name : %s", delnode -> name);
    releaseNode(delnode);
    *headptr = head;
  }
void deleteLast(node **headptr)
  {
    node *head, *delnode, *last, *prev;
    head = *headptr;
    if(head == NULL)
      {
        printf("\n Circular Linked List is Empty ...");
        return;
      }
    if(head -> flink == head)
      {
        delnode = head;
        head = NULL;
      }
    else
      {
        last = head -> blink;
        delnode = last;
        prev = last -> blink;
        prev -> flink = head;
        head -> blink = prev;
      }
    printf("\n Deleted Data is ... \n");
    printf("\n Roll Number : %d", delnode -> roll);
    printf("\n Name : %s", delnode -> name);
```

```
        releaseNode(delnode);
      *headptr = head;
  }

void deleteMiddle(node **headptr)
  {
      node *head, *last, *prev, *next, *delnode;
      int deldata;
      head = *headptr;
      if(head == NULL)
        {
          printf("\n Circular Linked List is Empty ...");
          return;
        }
      printf("\n Enter the node roll no for deleteion is to be made : ");
        scanf("%d", &deldata);
      last = head;
      do
        {
          if(last -> roll != deldata)
            last = last -> flink;
          else
            {
              delnode = last;
              if(head -> flink == head)
                head = NULL;
              else
                {
                  prev = last -> blink;
                  next = last -> flink;
                  if(last == head)
                    head = head -> flink;
                  prev -> flink = next;
                  next -> blink = prev;
                }
              printf("\n Deleted Data is ... \n");
              printf("\n Roll Number : %d", delnode -> roll);
              printf("\n Name : %s", delnode -> name);
              releaseNode(delnode);
              *headptr = head;
              return;
            }
        }
```

```
        }while(last != head);
      printf("Delete Node is Not Found");
  }
  void modifyNode(node *head)
  {
     node *last;
     int moddata;
     if(head == NULL)
       {
         printf("\n Circular Linked List is Empty ...");
         return;
       }
     printf("\n Enter the node roll no for modification : ");
       scanf("%d", &moddata);
     last = head;
     do
       {
         if(last -> roll == moddata)
          {
            printf("\n Modify the Data of the Node ... \n");
            printf("\n Enter the New Roll Number : ");
              scanf("%d", &last -> roll);
            printf("\n Enter the New Name : ");
              scanf("%s", last -> name);
            return;
          }
         else
           last = last -> flink;
       }while(last != head);
     printf("Modify Node is Not Found");
  }
  void view(node *head)
  {
     node * list;
     list = head;
     if(list == NULL)
       {
         printf("\n Circular Doubly Linked List is Empty ...");
         return;
       }
     do
       {
         printf("\n Roll Number : %d ", list->roll);
         printf("\n Name : %s", list->name);
```

```
        list = list -> flink;
      }while(list != head);
   }
void countList(node *head)
  {
    int count = 0;
    node *last;
    if(head == NULL)
    {
        printf("\nCircular Doubly Linked List is Empty ...");
        return count;
    }
    last = head;
    do
     {
       count = count + 1;
       last = last -> link;
     }while(last != head);
    return count;
  }
```

The program displays the following output

```
Basic Operations in a Circular Doubly Linked List ...
          0. Create List
          1. Insert First
          2. Insert Last
          3. Insert Middle
          4. Delete First
          5. Delete Last
          6. Delete Middle
          7. Modify Node
          8. View List
          9. Count List
          10. Show Menu
          11. Exit
? 4
Circular Doubly Linked List is Empty ...
? 5
Circular Doubly Linked List is Empty ...
? 6
Circular Doubly Linked List is Empty ...
```

```
? 7
Circular Doubly Linked List is Empty ...
? 8
Circular Doubly Linked List is Empty ...
? 9
Circular Doubly Linked List is Empty ...
Number of nodes in the list is 0
? 0
Enter the Roll Number : 401
Enter the Name : Anusha
Do u wish to Add Data in the List (y/n) ? y
Enter the Roll Number : 402
Enter the Name : Sussela
Do u wish to Add Data in the List (y/n) ? y
Enter the Roll Number : 403
Enter the Name : Premi
Do u wish to Add Data in the List (y/n) ? n
? 8
Roll Number : 401
Name : Anusha
Roll Number : 402
Name : Sussela
Roll Number : 403
Name : Premi
? 9
Number of nodes in the list is 3
? 1
Enter the Roll Number : 400
Enter the Name : Ganesh
? 2
Enter the Roll Number : 404
Enter the Name : Sasi
? 8
Roll Number : 400
Name : Ganesh
Roll Number : 401
Name : Anusha
Roll Number : 402
Name : Sussela
Roll Number : 403
Name : Premi
```

```
Roll Number : 404
Name : Sasi
? 4
Deleted Data is ...
Roll Number : 400
Name : Ganesh
? 5
Deleted Data is ...
Roll Number : 404
Name : Sasi
? 8
Roll Number : 401
Name : Anusha
Roll Number : 402
Name : Sussela
Roll Number : 403
Name : Premi
? 3
Enter the node roll no after which the insertion is to be made : 404
Insert Node is Not Found
? 3
Enter the node roll no after which the insertion is to be made : 402
Enter the Roll Number : 405
Enter the Name : Suganya
? 8
Roll Number : 401
Name : Anusha
Roll Number : 402
Name : Sussela
Roll Number : 405
Name : Suganya
Roll Number : 403
Name : Premi
? 9
Number of nodes in the list is 4
? 6
Enter the node roll no to be deleted : 404
Delete Node is Not Found
```

```
? 6
Enter the node roll no to be deleted : 405
Deleted Data is ...
Roll Number : 405
Name : Suganya
? 8
Roll Number : 401
Name : Anusha
Roll Number : 402
Name : Sussela
Roll Number : 403
Name : Premi
? 7
Enter the node roll no for modification : 405
Modify Node is Not Found
? 7
Enter the node roll no for modification : 403
Modify the Data of the Node ...
Enter the New Roll Number : 413
Enter the New Name : Selvi
? 8
Roll Number : 401
Name : Anusha
Roll Number : 402
Name : Sussela
Roll Number : 413
Name : Selvi
? 4
Deleted Data is ...
Roll Number : 401
Name : Anusha
? 5
Deleted Data is ...
Roll Number : 413
Name : Selvi
? 4
Deleted Data is ...
Roll Number : 402
Name : Sussela
```

```
? 8

Circular Doubly Linked List is Empty ...

? 3

Circular Doubly Linked list is Empty. So new node is head node.

Enter the Roll Number : 4000

Enter the Name : Roy

? 8

Roll Number : 4000

Name : Roy

? 11

End of run of your program . . .
```

1.9 Applications of Linked Lists

Linked lists form the basis of many data structures, so it's worth looking at some applications that are implemented using linked lists. Some important applications using linked lists are

- Polynomial manipulation
- Stacks
- Queues.

1.9.1 Polynomial Manipulation

Linked list is generally used to represent and manipulate polynomials. Polynomials are expressions containing terms with non-zero co-efficients and exponents. For example,

$$P(x) = a_0 x^n + a_1 x^{n-1} + \ldots + a_{n-1} x + a_n$$

where $P(x)$ is a polynomial in x,

   $a_0, a_1, \ldots, a_{n-1}, a_n$ are constants and n is a positive integer.

In the linked list representation of polynomials, each term/element in the list is referred as a *node*. Each node contains three fields namely,

- Co-efficient field
- Exponent field
- Link field.

The co-effecient and exponent field stores the data of a polynomial. The co-efficient field holds the co-efficient value of a polynomial and the exponent field holds the exponent value of a polynomial. The link field contains the address of the next term in the polynomial. The representation of polynomial in a singly linked list is shown in *Fig. 1.29*. The representation of a polynomial using a singly linked list is shown in *Fig. 1.30*.

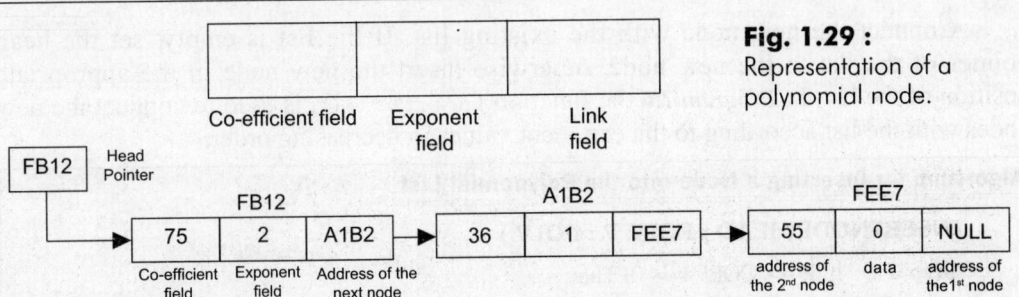

Fig. 1.29 : Representation of a polynomial node.

Fig. 1.30 : Representation of a polynomial using singly linked list.

Creating a polynomial using a singly linked list starts with creating a node. Sufficient memory has to be allocated for creating a node. The information is stored in the memory, allocated by using the `malloc()` function of type node. In **Program 1.6** the function `getNode()` is used for creating a node. After allocating memory for the structure of type `poly`, the information for the terms (i.e., `coef` and `exp`) has to be read from the user. In **Program 1.6** the function `readNode()`, is used for reading details of the node from the user.

Algorithm for Declaration of Structure Poly
Struct POLY
COEF   : FLOAT
EXP   : INTEGER
NEXT   : Link Field (Address of next Struct POLY)
End Struct
Algorithm for Allocating Memory for the New Node
GETNODE()
SIZE : INTEGER; NEWNODE : POLY
Step 1 : Set SIZE = get the size of the NODE
Step 2 : Set NEWNODE = Allocate space in memory for the size of SIZE and return the initial address
Step 3 : Return NEWNODE
End GETNODE()
Algorithm for Reading the Content for the New Node (Coefficient, Exponent)
READNODE(NEWNODE : NODE)
Step 1 : Read, NEWNODE –> COEF
Step 2 : Read, NEWNODE –> EXP
Step 3 : Set NEWNODE –> NEXT = NULL
Step 4 : Return
End READNODE()

Connect the new node with the existing list. If the list is empty, set the head pointer of the list to the new node, otherwise insert the new node in the appropriate position of the list. In *Program 1.6* the function `insertNode()`, is used to connect the new nodes with the list according to the exponent values in decreasing order.

Algorithm for Inserting a Node into the Polynomial List

INSERTNODE(HEAD : POLY, P : POLY)

Step 1 :   If (P –> COEF == 0) Then

          Return HEAD

          [End of If Structure]

Step 2 :   If (HEAD == NULL) Then

          Return P

Step 3 :   Else If (P –> EXP > HEAD –> EXP) Then

          P –> NEXT = HEAD

          Return P

Step 4 :   Else If (P –> EXP < HEAD –> EXP) Then

          HEAD –> NEXT = INSERTNODE (HEAD –> NEXT, P)

Step 5 :   Else If ((HEAD –> COEF + P –> COEF) != 0) Then

          HEAD –> COEF = HEAD –> COEF + P –> COEF

Step 6 :   Else

          Return HEAD –> NEXT

Step 7 :   [End of **Step 2** If Structure]

Step 8 :   Return HEAD

END INSERTNODE()

The `createPoly()` function is used to read the terms of the polynomial one by one in any order (of exponent / coefficient) as you wish until the exponent value is zero. Using the function `insertNode()`, insert them in their appropriate places and finally return the resultant polynomial.

Algorithm for Creating the Polynomial List

CREATEPOLY()

HEAD, P : POLY

Step 1 :   Assign HEAD = NULL

Step 2 :   Repeat

Step 3 :   P = GETNODE()

Step 4 :   READNODE(P)

Step 5 :   HEAD = INSERTNODE (HEAD, P)

Step 6 :   [End of **Step 2** Repeat Until (P –> EXP == 0)]

Step 7 :   Return HEAD

END CREATEPOLY()

To read the information or to display the information from a polynomial, you have to traverse (move) a linked list, term by term from the first term to the last term.. Traversing a polynomial is carried out by the function `viewPoly()`.

Algorithm for Displaying the Coefficients and Exponents of the Polynomial List

VIEWPOLY(HEAD : POLY)

P : POLY

Step 1 :   Assign P = HEAD

Step 2 :   While (P != NULL)

Step 3 :   Print "Coefficient is ", P –> COEF

Step 4 :   Print "Exponent is ", P –> EXP

Step 5 :   P = P –> NEXT

Step 6 :   [End of **Step 2** While Structure]

END VIEWPOLY()

The function `copyNode()` is used to make an additional copy of an existing node. Using the argument `sign`, you can change the sign of the term coefficient. The sign of the coefficient terms is changed only in case of `polySub()`.

Algorithm for Copying, by Creating a New Node

COPYNODE(P : POLY, SIGN : INTEGER)

NEWNODE : POLY

Step 1 :   NEWNODE = GETNODE()

Step 2 :   NEWNODE –> COEF = SIGN * P –> COEF

Step 3 :   NEWNODE –> EXP = P –> EXP

Step 4 :   NEWNODE –> NEXT = NULL

Step 5 :   Return NEWNODE

END COPYNODE()

The following procedure is used to add two polynomials using singly linked lists.

- Using the function createPoly() read the co-efficient and exponent terms of the first polynomial until exponent term is zero.
- Using the function createPoly() read the co-efficient and exponent terms of the second polynomial until exponent term is zero.
- Using the function polyAdd() add the two polynomials with the following comparisons.
- Copy the first polynomial using the functions copyNode() and insertNode() into the resultant polynomial.
- Traverse each term of the second polynomial and insert them into the resultant polynomial using the functions copyNode() and insertNode() until NULL value of the second polynomial is reached.
- Display the resultant polynomial.

Algorithm for Polynomial Addition

POLYADD(POLY1 : POLY, POLY2 : POLY)

HEAD : POLY

Step 1 :   Assign HEAD = NULL

Step 2 :   While (POLY1 != NULL)

Step 3 :   HEAD = INSERTNODE(HEAD, COPYNODE(POLY1, 1))

Step 4 :   POLY1 = POLY1 –> NEXT

Step 5 :   [End of **Step 2** While Structure]

Step 6 :   While (POLY2 != NULL)

Step 7 :   HEAD = INSERTNODE(HEAD, COPYNODE(POLY2, 1))

Step 8 :   POLY2 = POLY2 –> NEXT

Step 9 :   [End of **Step 6** While Structure]

Step 10 : Return HEAD

END POLYADD()

The following procedure is used to subtract two polynomials using singly linked lists.

- Using function polySub() subtract the two polynomials with the following comparisons.
- Copy the first polynomial using the functions copyNode() and insertNode() into the resultant polynomial.
- Traverse each term of second polynomial and insert them into the resultant polynomial using the functions copyNode() and insertNode() until NULL value of the second polynomial is reached. (Note: The second polynomial is inserted into the resultant polynomial by changing the sign of the coefficients using the function copyNode()).
- Display the resultant polynomial.

Algorithm for Polynomial Subtraction

POLYSUB(POLY1 : POLY, POLY2 : POLY)

HEAD : POLY

Step 1 :   Assign HEAD = NULL

Step 2 :   While (POLY1 != NULL)

Step 3 :   HEAD = INSERTNODE(HEAD, COPYNODE(POLY1, 1))

Step 4 :   POLY1 = POLY1 –> NEXT

Step 5 :   [End of **Step 2** While Structure]

Step 6 :   While (POLY2 != NULL)

Step 7 :   HEAD = INSERTNODE(HEAD, COPYNODE(POLY2, –1))

Step 8 :   POLY2 = POLY2 –> NEXT

Step 9 :   [End of **Step 6** While Structure]

Step 10 : Return HEAD

END POLYSUB()

The following procedure is used to multiply two polynomials using singly linked lists.

- Using the function polyMul() multiply two polynomials with the following comparisons.

- Traverse each term of the second polynomial and multiply with each term of the first polynomial using the function mulNode() and insert them into the resultant polynomial using the functions copyNode() and insertNode() until NULL value of the second polynomial is reached.

- Display the resultant polynomial.

Algorithm for Mulitiplying the Multiplicant Polynomial by the Multiplier Node

MULNODE(P1 : POLY, P2 : POLY)

TEMP : POLY

Step 1 :   Assign TEMP = NULL

Step 2 :   If (P1 != NULL) Then

        TEMP = GETNODE()

        TEMP –> COEF = P1 –> COEF * P2 –> COEF

        TEMP –> EXP = P1 –> EXP + P2 –> EXP

        TEMP –> NEXT = MULNODE(P1 –> NEXT, P2)

        [End of If Structure]

Step 3 :   Return TEMP

END MULNODE()

Algorithm for Polynomial Multiplication

POLYMUL(P1 : POLY, P2 : POLY)

Step 1 :   If (P2 == NULL) Then

        Return NULL

        [End of If Structure]

Step 2 :   Return POLYADD(MULNODE(P1,P2), POLYMUL(P1, P2->NEXT))

END POLYMUL()

The following procedure is used to divide two polynomials using singly linked lists.

- The function polyDiv() is used to find the quotient and remainder of the divisor (The function returns the quotient value and assigns the remainder value to the argument in the function).

- If the dividend or divisor is NULL, assign the value of the remainder as NULL and return the value of the quotient as NULL.

- If the first exponent of the dividend is greater than or equal to the first exponent of the divisor,

  - The first coefficient of the dividend is divided by the first coefficient of the divisor, & the first exponent of the dividend is subtracted from the first exponent of the divisor and the corresponding coefficient & exponent is assigned to the resultant polynomial.

- Using the function mulNode() multiply the resultant polynomial with the divisor and subtract the result with the dividend using the function polySub() to get the remainder.

- The function polyDiv() is called recursively with the remainder as the new dividend until the above condition for the division fails.

- If the above condition for the division fails, return the resultant polynomial and assign the dividend value as the remainder.

Algorithm for Polynomial Division

POLYDIV (P1 : POLY, P2 : POLY, REMR : POLY)

RES : POLY

Step 1 :   Assign RES = NULL

Step 2 :   If (P1 == NULL || P2 == NULL) Then

Set RMDR = NULL

Return NULL

[End of If Structure]

Step 3 :   If (P1 –> EXP >= P2 –> EXP) Then

RES = GETNODE()

RES –> COEF = P1 –> COEF / P2 –> COEF

RES –> EXP = P1 –> EXP – P2 –> EXP

RES –> NEXT=POLYDIV(POLYSUB(P1, MULNODE(P2,RES)), P2, RMDR)

Else

RMDR = P1

[End of If Structure]

Step 4 :   Return RES

END POLYDIV()

Program 1.6 :

/* Program to demonstrate polynomial manipulation using singly linked lists. */

```
/* polymani.c */
#include<stdio.h>
#include<conio.h>
#include<stdlib.h>
#define POSITIVE 1
#define NEGATIVE -1
typedef struct node
{
    float coef;
    int exp;
    struct node *next;
}poly;
```

```
    void viewMenu();
void readNode(poly *);
void viewPoly(poly *);
    poly *getNode();
    poly *createPoly();
    poly *copyNode(poly *, int);
    poly *insertNode(poly *, poly *);
    poly *mulNode(poly *p1, poly *p2);
    poly *polyAdd(poly *p1, poly *p2);
    poly *polySub(poly *p1, poly *p2);
    poly *polyMul(poly *p1, poly *p2);
    poly *polyDiv(poly *p1, poly *p2, poly **rmdr);
    void main()
     {
        int choice;
        poly *poly1 = NULL, *poly2 = NULL, *res = NULL;
        poly *Quotient, *Remainder = NULL;
        viewMenu();
        while(1)
         {
            printf("\n ? ");
            fflush(stdin);
              scanf("%d", &choice);
            switch(choice)
             {
                case 0 :
                        viewMenu();
                        break;
                case 1 :
                        printf("\n Enter the First Polynomial ...");
                        poly1 = createPoly();
                        printf("\n First Polynomial is : ");
                        viewPoly(poly1);
                        break;
                case 2 :
                        printf("\n Enter the Second Polynomial ...");
                        poly2 = createPoly();
                        printf("\n Second Polynomial is : ");
                        viewPoly(poly2);
                        break;
```

```
        case 3 :
                printf("\n The First Polynomial is ... \n");
                viewPoly(poly1);
                printf("\n The Second Polynomial is ... \n");
                viewPoly(poly2);
                break;
        case 4 :
                printf("\n The Resultant Polynomial after Addition
                                            is ... \n");
                res = polyAdd(poly1, poly2);
                viewPoly(res);
                break;
        case 5 :
                printf("\n The Resultant Polynomial after
                                    Subtraction is ... \n");
                res = polySub(poly1, poly2);
                viewPoly(res);
                break;
        case 6 :
                printf("\n The Resultant Polynomial after
                                Multiplication is ... \n");
                res = polyMul(poly1, poly2);
                viewPoly(res);
                break;
        case 7 :
                printf("\n The Resultant Polynomial after Division
                                            is ... \n");
                Quotient = polyDiv(poly1, poly2, &Remainder);
                printf("\n Quotient : ");
                viewPoly(Quotient);
                printf("\n Remainder : ");
                viewPoly(Remainder);
                break;
        default :
                printf("\n End of Run of your Program . . .");
                exit(0);

        }
    }
}
```

```c
void viewMenu()
{
  printf("\n Polynomial Manipulation using singly linked list ...");
  printf("\n\t 0. View the Main Menu");
  printf("\n\t 1. Create the First Polynomial");
  printf("\n\t 2. Create the Second Polynomial");
  printf("\n\t 3. View the First and Second Polynomial");
  printf("\n\t 4. Polynomial Addition");
  printf("\n\t 5. Polynomial Subtraction");
  printf("\n\t 6. Polynomial Multiplication");
  printf("\n\t 7. Polynomial Division");
  printf("\n\t 8. Exit");
}
poly *createPoly()
{
  poly *p, *head = NULL;
  do
   {
     p = getNode();
     readNode(p);
     head = insertNode(head, p);
   }while(p -> exp != 0);
  return head;
}
poly *getNode()
{
  return (poly *)malloc(sizeof(poly));
}


void readNode(poly* newnode)
{
  int exp;
  float coef;
  printf("\nEnter the Coefficient : ");
    scanf("%f", &coef);
  printf("Enter the Exponent : ");
```

```
        scanf("%d", &exp);
      newnode -> coef = coef;
      newnode -> exp = exp;
      newnode -> next = NULL;
  }
poly *insertNode(poly *head, poly *p)
  {
      if(p -> coef == 0.0f)
        return head;
      if(head == NULL)
        return p;
      else if(p->exp > head->exp)
        {
          p -> next = head;
          return p;
        }
      else if(p->exp < head->exp)
        head -> next = insertNode(head -> next, p);
      else if((head -> coef = head -> coef + p -> coef) == 0.0f)
        return head -> next;
      return head;
  }
void viewPoly(poly * ply)
  {
      if(ply == NULL)
        printf("NULL \n");
      while(ply != NULL)
        {
          printf("%.2fx^%d", ply -> coef, ply -> exp);
          printf("%s",(ply->next == NULL) ? " = 0\n" : " + ");
          ply = ply -> next;
        }
  }

poly * polyAdd(poly *poly1, poly *poly2)
  {
      poly *head = NULL;
      while(poly1 != NULL)
        {
          head  = insertNode(head, copyNode(poly1, POSITIVE));
          poly1 = poly1 -> next;
        }
```

```
        while(poly2 != NULL)
         {
            head = insertNode(head, copyNode(poly2, POSITIVE));
            poly2 = poly2 -> next;
         }
        return head;
     }
poly * polySub(poly *poly1, poly *poly2)
 {
    poly *head = NULL;
    while(poly1 != NULL)
      {
         head  = insertNode(head, copyNode(poly1, POSITIVE));
         poly1 = poly1 -> next;
      }
    while(poly2 != NULL)
      {
         head = insertNode(head, copyNode(poly2, NEGATIVE));
         poly2 = poly2 -> next;
      }
    return head;
 }
poly *polyMul(poly *poly1, poly *poly2)
 {
    if(poly2 == NULL)
      return NULL;
    else
      return polyAdd(mulNode(poly1,poly2),polyMul(poly1,poly2->next));
 }
poly * copyNode(poly * p, int sign)
 {
    poly *newnode;
    newnode = getNode();
    newnode -> coef = sign * p -> coef;
    newnode -> exp  = p -> exp;
    newnode -> next = NULL;
    return newnode;
 }
```

```
    poly *mulNode(poly *p1, poly *p2)
    {
        poly *temp = NULL;
        if(p1 != NULL)
        {
            temp = getNode();
            temp -> coef = p1 -> coef * p2 -> coef;
            temp -> exp  = p1 -> exp  + p2 -> exp;
            temp -> next = mulNode(p1->next, p2);
        }
        return temp;
    }
```

/* For Qoutient and Remainder p1 / p2 */

```
    poly *polyDiv(poly *p1, poly *p2, poly **rmdr)
    {
        poly *res = NULL;
        if(p1 == NULL || p2 == NULL)
            return (*rmdr = NULL);
        if(p1 -> exp >= p2 -> exp)
        {
            res = getNode();
            res -> coef = p1->coef / p2 -> coef;
            res -> exp  = p1->exp  - p2 -> exp;
            res -> next = polyDiv(polySub(p1,mulNode(p2,res)),p2,rmdr);
        }
        else
            *rmdr = p1;
        return res;
    }
```

The program displays the following output

```
Polynomial Manipulation using singly linked list ...

        0. View the Main Menu

        1. Create the First Polynomial

        2. Create the Second Polynomial

        3. View the First and Second Polynomial

        4. Polynomial Addition

        5. Polynomial Subtraction

        6. Polynomial Multiplication

        7. Polynomial Division
```

```
        8. Exit
? 3
The First Polynomial is ...
NULL
The Second Polynomial is ...
NULL
? 4
The Resultant Polynomial after Addition is ...
NULL
? 5
The Resultant Polynomial after Subtraction is ...
NULL
? 6
The Resultant Polynomial after Multiplication is ...
NULL
? 7
The Resultant Polynomial after Division is ...
Solution is Infinity ...
Solution is Infinity ...
Quotient : NULL
Remainder : NULL
? 1
Enter the First Polynomial . . .
Enter the Coefficient : 3
Enter the Exponent : 2
Enter the Coefficient : 2
Enter the Exponent : 1
Enter the Coefficient : 1
Enter the Exponent : 0
First Polynomial is : 3.00x^2 + 2.00x^1 + 1.00x^0 = 0
? 2
Enter the Second Polynomial . . .
Enter the Coefficient : 2
Enter the Exponent : 1
Enter the Coefficient : 3
Enter the Exponent : 1
```

```
Enter the Coefficient : 5

Enter the Exponent : 0

Second Polynomial is : 5.00x^1 + 5.00x^0 = 0

? 3

The First Polysnomial is ...

3.00x^2 + 2.00x^1 + 1.00x^0 = 0

The Second Polynomial is ...

5.00x^1 + 5.00x^0 = 0

? 4

The Resultant Polynomial after Addition is ...

3.00x^2 + 7.00x^1 + 6.00x^0 = 0

? 5

The Resultant Polynomial after Subtraction is ...

3.00x^2 + -3.00x^1 + -4.00x^0 = 0

? 6

The Resultant Polynomial after Multiplication is ...

15.00x^3 + 25.00x^2 + 15.00x^1 + 5.00x^0 = 0

? 7

The Resultant Polynomial after Division is ...

Quotient : 0.60x^1 + -0.20x^0= 0

Remainder : 2.00x^0 = 0

? 8

End of Run of your Program . . .
```

Prosgram 1.6 is capable of reading input in any sequence, and at the same time, reading input should end with an exponent value of zero. If you enter the same value of exponent again and again, it will automatically add the co-efficients of same exponent and store it in descending order. You can also change any one of the existing polynomial and manipulate (add, subtract, multiply, divide) the new polynomial with the old polynomial.

Advantages of Linked Lists

- It is not necessary to specify the number of elements in a linked list during its declaration (since memory can be allocated dynamically when a node is added to the list).
- Linked list can grow and shrink in size depending upon the insertion and deletion that occurs in the list.
- Insertions and deletions at any place in a list can be handled easily and efficiently.
- A linked list does not waste any memory space.

Disadvantages of Linked Lists

- Searching a particular element in a list is difficult and time consuming.

- A linked list will use more storage space than an array to store the same number of elements (∴ each element in a list needs additional memory space for storing the address of the next node).

1.10 Summary

✍ An array is a group of elements of same data type that share a common name and that are differentiated from one another by their positions within the array. The individual values in the array are called as elements.

✍ An algorithm is a step-by-step recipe for solving an instance of a problem. Every single procedure that a computer performs is an algorithm.

✍ A data structure represents the logical relationship that exists between individual elements of data to carry out basic tasks like insertion, deletion, searching, and so on.

✍ Primary data structures are the basic data structures that directly operate upon the machine instructions. All the integers, floating-point number, character, string constants, and pointers are considered as primary data structures.

✍ Secondary data structures emphasize on grouping same or different data items with relationship between each data item. They are broadly classified as static data structures and dynamic data structures.

✍ If a data structure is created when the number of data items is known in advance, it is known as static data structure.

✍ If a data structure is created, when the number of data items is not known in advance is known as dynamic data structure or variable size data structure. They are broadly classified as linear data structures and non- linear data structures.

✍ A data type that is defined entirely by a set of operations is referred to as an **Abstract Data Type**, or simply **ADT**.

✍ A **list** is a dynamic collection of items or elements E_1, E_2, E_3, ... E_n, of size 'n' arranged in a linear sequence where E_i refers to the ith element in the list. A list with size zero / with no elements is referred to as an **empty list**.

✍ If the elements are inserted and deleted in the same end, then the list is referred to as a Stack. If the elements are inserted in one end and deleted in another end, then the list is referred to as a Queue.

✍ Linear data structures have a linear relation ship between its adjacent elements. Linked lists are examples of linear data structures.

✍ A linked list is a linear dynamic data structure that can grow and shrink during its execution time.

✍ A circular linked list is similar to a linked list except that the first and last nodes are interconnected.

✍ Non-linear data structures don't have a linear relationship between its adjacent elements. Trees and graphs are examples of non-linear data structures.

✍ A tree is a non-linear dynamic data structure that may point to one or more nodes at a time. A graph is similar to tree except that it has no hierarchical relationship between its adjacent elements.

✍ Linked list or list is an ordered collection of elements in which each element in the list is referred as a node. Each node contains two fields namely, data field and Link field.

✍ The data field contains the actual data of the element to be stored in the list and the link field also referred as the next address field contains the address of the next node in the list.

✍ External address is the address of the first node in the list stored in the head pointer which points to the first node in the list.

✍ Internal address is the address stored in the address field of every node except the last node.

✍ Null address is the address stored by the Null pointer in the last node of the list.

✍ Singly linked list is a list in which each node as a single link to its next node.

✍ Doubly linked list is a list in which each node as two links one its next node and the other to its previous node.

✍ Circular singly linked list is a list in which each node is connected to the next node as in the case of a singly linked list except that the list has no end i.e., the last node is connected to the first node of the list.

✍ Circular doubly linked list is a list in which each node is connected to the next node as in the case of a doubly linked list except that the list has no end i.e., the last node is connected to the first node of the list.

✍ The previous address field of a node contains address of its previous node. This field is also referred as the backward link field.

✍ The next address field contains the address of the next node in the list. This field is also referred as the forward link field.

1.11 Short-answer Questions

1. *Define data structures.*

    Data structure defines a way of organising all data items that consider not only the elements stored but also stores the relationship between the elements.

2. *Define primary data structures.*

    Primary data structures are the basic data structures that directly operate upon the machine instructions. All the basic constants (i.e., integers, floating-point numbers character constants, string constants) and pointers are considered as primary data structures.

3. *Define static data structures.*

    A data structure formed when the number of data items are known in advance is referred as static data structure or fixed size data structure.

4.   *List some of the static data structures in C.*

Some of the static data structures in C refer to arrays, pointers, structures, etc.,

5.   *Define dynamic data structures.*

A data structure formed when the number of data items are not known in advance is known as dynamic data structure or variable size data structure.

6.   *List some of the dynamic data structures in C.*

Some of the dynamic data structures in C refers to linked lists, stacks, queues, trees, etc.,

7.   *Define linear data structures.*

Linear data structures are data structures having a linear relation ship between its adjacent elements. Linked lists are examples of linear data structures.

8.   *Define non-linear data structures.*

Non-Linear data structures are data structures that don't have a linear relationship between its adjacent elements but have a hierarchical relationship between the elements. Trees and graphs are examples of non-linear data structures.

9.   *State the different types of linked lists.*

The different types of linked list includes, single linked list, double linked list and circular linked list.

10.   *State the different types of circular linked lists.*

The different types of circular linked list includes circular singly linked list and circular doubly linked list.

11.   *Define abstract data types.*

A data type that is defined entirely by a set of operations is referred to as an Abstract Data Type. It provides a representation-independent specification. Abstract data types are a way of seperating the specification and representation of data types. An abstract data type can be considered as a black box, where users can only see the syntax and semantics of its operations. In general we think of an abstract data type as a type defined in terms of its behavior rather than its implementation.

12.   *List the benefits of ADT's.*

The benefits of ADT's includes,

- Code is easier to understand.
- Implementations of ADTs can be changed without requiring changes to the program that uses the ADTs.

13.   *Define a list ADT.*

A list is a dynamic collection of items or elements E_1, E_2, E_3, ... E_n, of size 'n' arranged in a linear sequence where E_i refers to the ith element in the list.

14.   *State the use of data field in a linked list.*

The data field contains the actual data (i.e., value(s)) of the element(s) to be stored in the list.

15.   State the use of link field in a linked list.

The link field also referred as the next address field contains the address of the next node in the list.

16.   State the use of head pointer in a linked list.

A linked list contains a pointer, referred as the head pointer, which points to the first node in the list that stores the address of the first node of the list. The entire linked list can be accessed only with the help of the head pointer.

17.   List the various type of addresses used in linked lists.

The addresses used in linked list includes,

- External address.
- Internal address.
- Null address.

18.   Define external address.

External address is the address of the first node in the list. This address is stored in the head pointer which points to the first node in the list.

19.   Define internal address.

Internal address is the address stored in each and every node of the linked list except the last node. The content stored in the link field (also referred as next address field) is the address of the next node.

20.   Define null address.

Null address is the address stored by the NULL pointer of the last node of the list, which indicates the end of the list.

21.   What are the three fields used in double linked lists.

The three fields used in double linked list includes,

- Previous address field.
- Data field.
- Next address field.

22.   State the use of previous address field and next address field in a linked list.

The previous address field also referred as the backward link field, of a node contains address of its previous node. The next address field also referred as the forward link field, contains the address of the next node in the list.

23.   List the basic operations carried out in a linked list.

The basic operations carried out in a linked list includes,

- Creation of a list.
- Insertion of a node.
- Deletion of a node.
- Modification of a node.
- Traversal of the list.

24.   List the other operations carried out in a linked list.

The other operations carried out in a linked list includes,

- Searching an element in a list.
- Finding the successor element of a node.
- Finding the predessor element of a node.
- Appending a linked list to another existing list.
- Splitting a linked list in to two lists.
- Arranging a linked list in ascending or descending order.

25.   List out the advantages in using a linked list.

The advantages in using a linked list are

- It is not necessary to specify the number of elements in a linked list during its declaration (since memory can be allocated dynamically when a node is added to the list).
- Linked list can grow and shrink in size depending upon the insertion and deletion that occurs in the list.
- Insertions and deletions at any place in a list can be handled easily and efficiently.
- A linked list does not waste any memory space.

26.   List out the disadvantages in using a linked list.

The disadvantages in using a linked list are

- Searching a particular element in a list is difficult and time consuming.
- A linked list will use more storage space than an array to store the same number of elements (∴ each element in a list needs additional memory space for storing the address of the next node).

27.   List out the applications of a linked list.

Some of the important applications of linked lists are, manipulation of polynomials, stacks and queues.

28.   State the difference between arrays and linked list.

Arrays	Linked lists
a) Size of any array is fixed.	a) Size of a list is variable.
b) It is necessary to specify the number of elements during declaration.	b) It is not necessary to specify the in an array number of elements in during declaration.
c) Insertion and deletions are some what difficult out easily.	c) Insertions and deletions are carried in an array.
d) It occupies less memory than a linked list for the same number of elements.	d) It occupies more memory.

29. Draw the node representation of a singly linked list.

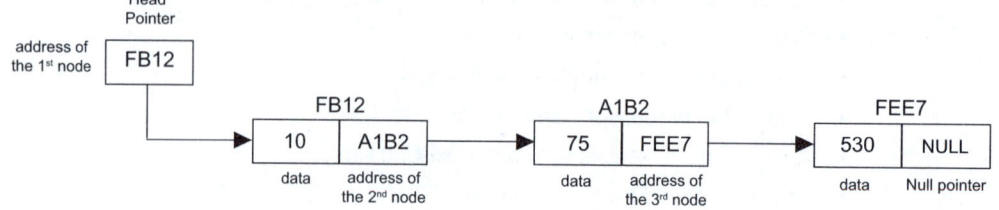

Fig : Representation of a singly linked list

30. Draw the node representation of a doubly linked list.

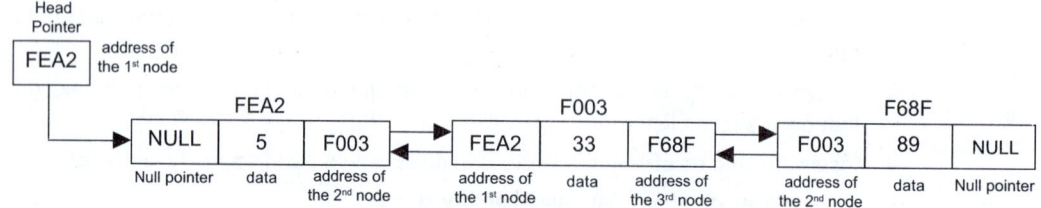

Fig : Representation of a doubly linked list.

31. Draw the node representation of a circular singly linked list.

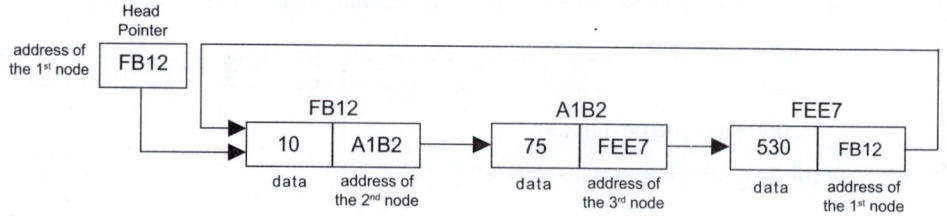

Fig : Representation of a circular singly linked list.

32. Draw the node representation of a circular doubly linked list.

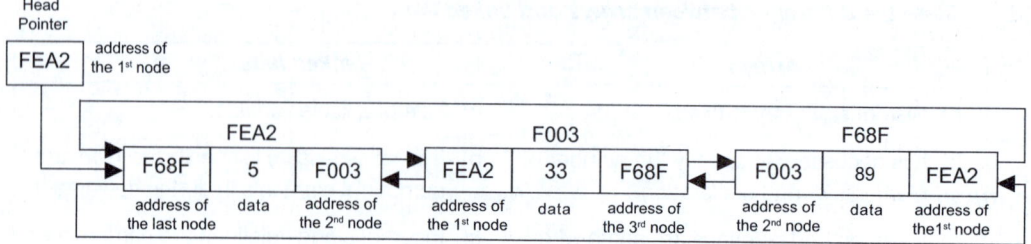

Fig : Representation of a circular doubly linked list.

Chapter 2
Non-Linear Data Structures —Stacks and Queues

2.1 Stacks

*A **stack** is an ordered collection of elements in which insertions and deletions are restricted to one end.* The end from which elements are added and/or removed is referred to as ***top*** of the stack. Stacks are also referred as "***piles***" and "***push-down lists***". The first element placed in the stack will be at the bottom of the stack. The last element placed in the stack will be at the top of the stack. The last element added to stack is the first element to be removed. Hence stacks are referred to as **Last-In-First-Out** (LIFO) lists.

Consider ***Fig. 2.1*** where five discs are placed one over the other through a shaft. If we want to insert a new disc say 6. It is possible to insert the disc on the top of disc 5. Because of the presence of shaft, it is not possible to insert the disc 6 in the middle of the discs. Similarly, if we want to remove a disc say 4, it is only possible to remove the disc 5 first and then the disc 4 and so on. Because of the presence of the shaft, it is not possible to remove the disc 4 from the middle of the discs. This similar operation is carried out in a stack.

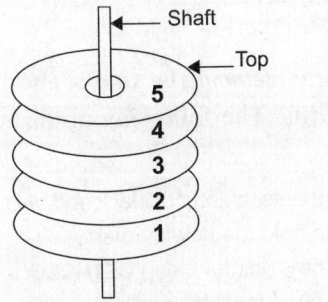

Fig. 2.1 : Shaft with five discs.

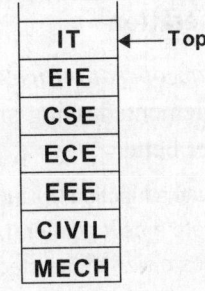

Fig. 2.2 : Stack Operation.

A stack is referenced via a pointer to the top element of the stack referred as ***top pointer***. The top pointer keeps track of the top element in the stack. Initially, when the stack is empty, the top pointer has a value zero and when the stack contains a single element, the top pointer has a value one and so on. ***Fig. 2.1*** shows the representation of a stack.

The primary operations that can be carried on a stack are insertions and deletions. These operations on a stack are referred as ***PUSH*** and ***POP*** operations respectively. A PUSH operation adds a new element to the stack. Each time a new element is inserted in the stack, the top pointer is incremented by one before the element is placed on the stack. A POP operation deletes the top most element in the stack. Each time an element is removed from the stack the top pointer is decremented by one. The stack shown in *Fig. 2.2* consists of seven elements. We know that insertions and deletions can occur only at the top of the stack, which means EIE cannot be deleted until IT is deleted, CSE cannot be deleted until IT and EIE are deleted and so on. The elements from the stack may be popped (i.e., removed/deleted) only in the reverse order in which they are pushed (i.e., inserted/added) on to the stack.

2.2 Operations of Stacks

Another way of representing a stack is by means of a singly linked list. This type of representation has more advantages than representing stacks using arrays. They are,

- It is not necessary to specify the number of elements to be stored in a stack during its declaration (since memory is allocated dynamically at run time when an element is added to the stack).
- Insertions and deletions can be handled easily and efficiently.
- Linked list representation of stacks can grow and shrink in size without wasting the memory space, depending upon the insertion and deletion that occurs in the list.
- Multiple stacks can be represented efficiently using a chain for each stack.

The basic operations that can be performed on a stack are,

- Push operation.
- Pop operation.
- Peek operation.
- View stack size.
- View stack contents.

2.2.1 Push Operation

PUSH is an operation used to add a new element the stack. The PUSH operation can also be implemented using singly linked lists. The following procedure helps you to understand things better.

- Create a function PUSH() with two arguments (pointer of stack and VALUE to be inserted).
- Create a new pointer (i.e., NEWPTR) to hold the new element.
- Allocate size of the stack node to the new pointer using GETNODE().
- The size of the stack depends on the heap memory available.
- If GETNODE() returns NULL heap memory is not available.
- Assign the VALUE to the data of new pointer.
- Assign the link of the new pointer to the head (i.e., TOP) of the stack.
- Assign the head of the stack to the new pointer.

Algorithm for Declaration of Structure Stack

Struct STACK
   DATA : Data Field
   NEXT : Link Field (Address of next Struct STACK)
End Struct

Algorithm for Allocating Memory for the New Node

GETNODE()
SIZE : INTEGER
NEWNODE : STACK
Step 1 :   Set SIZE = get the size of the STACK
Step 2 :   Set NEWNODE = Allocate space in memory for SIZE and return the initial address
Step 3 :   Return NEWNODE
End GETNODE()

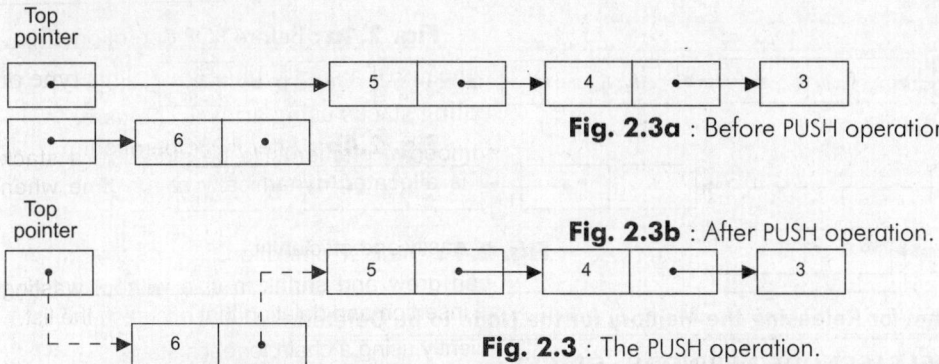

Top
pointer

Fig. 2.3a : Before PUSH operation.

Top
pointer

Fig. 2.3b : After PUSH operation.

Fig. 2.3 : The PUSH operation.

Fig. 2.3a shows stack and the new node before the PUSH operation. In *Fig. 2.3b* the TOP pointer points the NEW pointer of the new node. The element of the new node is made to point the node, which was already pointed by the TOP pointer, and the other nodes remain unchanged.

Algorithm for Inserting a Node in the Stack

PUSH(VALUE : INTEGER)
GLOBAL: TOPSTK : STACK
NEWPTR : STACK
Step 1 :   If (ISFULL() == 1)
                    Return –1
                    [End of If Structure]
Step 2 :   NEWPTR = GETNODE()
Step 3 :   NEWPTR –> DATA = VALUE
Step 4 :   NEWPTR –> NEXT = TOPSTK
Step 5 :   TOPSTK = NEWPTR
Step 6 :   Return 0
End PUSH()

2.2.2 Pop Operation

POP is an operation used to remove an element from the TOP of the stack. The POP operation of a stack can also be implemented using singly linked lists. When implementing the POP operation, underflow condition of a stack is to be checked. The user should not POP an element from an empty stack. This type of an attempt is illegal and should be avoided. The following procedure can help you to understand things better.

- Create a function POP() with two parameters that stores pointer of the stack and the address of the last element to be deleted.
- Create a temporary pointer (i.e., tempptr) to hold the removed element.
- Assign the TOP pointer to the temporary pointer.
- The TOP pointer is made to point the node after the first node and the other nodes remain unchanged.
- Free the allocated memory of the temporary pointer by using **RELEASENODE()**.

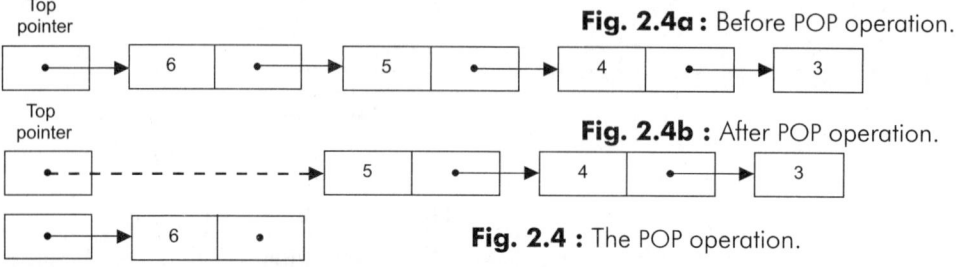

Fig. 2.4a : Before POP operation.

Fig. 2.4b : After POP operation.

Fig. 2.4 : The POP operation.

Algorithm for Releasing the Memory for the Node to be Deleted

    RELEASENODE(NEWNODE : STACK)

Step 1 :   Deallocate the space for the STACK of NEWNODE

Step 2 :   Return

End RELEASENODE()

Algorithm for Removing a Node from the Stack

    POP(VALUE : INTEGER)

GLOBAL: TOPSTK : STACK

TEMP : STACK

Step 1 :   If (ISEMPTY() == 1)

               Return –1

               [End of If Structure]

Step 2 :   TEMP = TOPSTK

Step 3 :   TOPSTK = TOPSTK –> NEXT

Step 4 :   VALUE = TEMP –> DATA

Step 5 :   RELEASENODE(TEMP)

Step 6 :   Return 0

End POP()

Fig. 2.4 illustrates the POP operation. *Fig. 2.4a* shows the stack before the POP operation. In *Fig. 2.4b* a temporary pointer (i.e., tempptr) is created and is made to point the node, which is to be removed (i.e., The node pointer by the TOP pointer). The TOP pointer is made to point the node after the first node and the other nodes remain unchanged. The memory allocated by the temporary pointer is freed. Thus, the element pointed by the TOP pointer is removed from the stack. *Note that the stacks and linked lists are represented identically. The difference between stack and ordinary linked list is that insertions and deletions may occur any where in the linked list, but only at the top node in the stack.*

2.2.3 PEEK Operation

PEEK operation is used to display the element from the TOP of the stack, pointed by the TOP pointer without actually removing it. PEEK operation of a stack is also implemented using linked lists. When implementing the PEEK operation, underflow condition of a stack is to be checked. The user should not try to PEEK an element from an empty stack. This type of an attempt is illegal and should be avoided.

Algorithm to Retrieve the Contents from the Top of the Stack

PEEK(VALUE : INTEGER)
GLOBAL: TOPSTK : STACK
TEMP : STACK
Step 1 :   If (ISEMPTY() == 1)
         Return –1
         [End of If Structure]
Step 2 :   TEMP = TOPSTK
Step 3 :   VALUE = TEMP –> DATA
Step 4 :   Return 0
End PEEK()

2.2.4 Traversing a Stack

To read the information or to display the information in a stack, you have to traverse (move) a linked list, node by node from the first node to the last node. Traversing a list involves the following steps,

- Assign the address of TOP pointer to a variable.
- Display the information in the data field.
- Traverse the list from one node to another by advancing the pointer upto NULL.

Algorithm for Displaying the Contents of the Stack

VIEW()
GLOBAL: TOPSTK : STACK
TOP : STACK
Step 1 :   If (ISEMPTY() == 1)
         Print "Stack is EMPTY"
         Return
         [End of If Structure]
Step 2 :   TOP = TOPSTK

Step 3 :   Do While(TOP != NULL)
Print "Value is", TOP -> DATA
TOP = TOP -> NEXT
[End of Step 3 While Structure]
End VIEW()

2.2.5 Empty Stack

*If a stack contains no elements, it is referred as **an empty stack.*** If an element is to be popped from a stack, you have to check whether the stack is empty or not, because elements cannot be popped from an empty stack. In a linked list, if the stack is pointing to NULL the stack is said to be an empty stack. If you want to pop an element, from an empty stack the output, "Stack is underflow" is displayed.

Algorithm for IS_EMPTY()
IS_EMPTY(VALUE : INTEGER)
GLOBAL: TOPSTK : STACK
Step 1 :   If (TOPSTK == NULL)
Return 1
Else
Return 0
[End of If Structure]
End IS_EMPTY()

2.2.6 Fully Occupied Stack

If a stack contains elements equal to its size, we say the stack is full. If an element is to be pushed into a stack, you have to check whether the stack is full or not, since elements cannot be pushed into a stack when it is fully occupied. In case of stacks, represented using linked lists, there is no limit to store the elements in the stack, since the memory required to store the elements of the stack is allocated dynamically in the example using the malloc() function. However, if the memory required for storing the elements of the stack is not available, we cannot insert elements into a stack. If the malloc() function returns NULL in a linked list it is referred as *fully occupied stack.* If you want to insert an element, in a fully occupied stack the output "Stack is overflow" is displayed.

Algorithm for IS_FULL()
IS_FULL(VALUE : INTEGER)
GLOBAL: TOPSTK : STACK
TEMP : STACK
Step 1 :   TEMP = GETNODE()
Step 2 :   If (TEMP == NULL)
Return 1

```
                Else
                      RELEASENODE(TEMP)
                      Return 0
                [End of If Structure]
      End IS_FULL()
```

2.2.7 Stack Size

In case of stacks represented using linked lists, there is no limit to store the elements, since the memory required to store the elements of the stack is allocated dynamically using the malloc() *function.* To find the size of the stack, (i.e., number of elements that has been stored), to check whether the memory required for storing the elements of the stack is available or not, use the size() function as mentioned in *Program 2.1. Note that elements cannot be stored in a stack, when the memory pointed by the linked list points to NULL.*

Algorithm to Count the Nodes in a Stack

```
      SIZE(VALUE : INTEGER)
      GLOBAL: TOPSTK : STACK
      TOP : STACK; COUNT : INTEGER
      Step 1 :   TOP = TOPSTK
      Step 2 :   COUNT = 0
      Step 3 :   Do While(TOP != NULL)
                      COUNT = COUNT + 1
                      TOP = TOP -> NEXT
                 [End of Step 3 While Structure]
      Step 4 :   Return COUNT
      End SIZE()
```

Program 2.1 :

/* Program to implement a stack using singly linked list. */

```c
/* linstack.c */
#include<stdio.h>
#include<conio.h>
#include<stdlib.h>
typedef struct node
 {
    int data;
    struct node *next;
 }stack;
int size();
void view();
int isFull();
int isEmpty();
```

```
    void displayMenu();

int push(int value);

int pop(int *value);

int peek(int *value);

stack *getNode();

void releaseNode(stack *newnode);

stack *topStk = NULL;

void main()
 {
    int data, status, choice;

    displayMenu();

    while(1)
     {
        printf("\n\n ? ");
          scanf("%d", &choice);
        switch(choice)
          {
            case 1 :
                      printf("\n Enter the element : ");
                      fflush(stdin);
                        scanf("%d", &data);
                      status = push(data);
                      if(status == -1)
                        printf("\n Memory is not available ...");
                      break;
            case 2 :
                      status = pop(&data);
                      if(status == -1)
                        printf("\n Stack underflow on POP");
                      else
                        printf("\n The popped value is %d", data);
                      break;
            case 3 :
                      status = peek(&data);
                      if(status == -1)
                        printf("\n Stack is Empty !!!");
                      else
                        printf("\n The Top most value is %d", data);
                      break;
```

```
                    case 4 :
                            printf("\n Current Stack Elements = %d", size());
                            break;
                    case 5 :
                            view();
                            break;
                    default:
                            printf("\n End of Run of your Program . . .");
                            exit(0);
            }
        }
}
void displayMenu()
{
    printf("\n Representation of stack using single linked lists ...");
    printf("\n\t 1. Push ");
    printf("\n\t 2. Pop  ");
    printf("\n\t 3. Peek ");
    printf("\n\t 4. Size ");
    printf("\n\t 5. View ");
    printf("\n\t 6. Exit ");
}
stack *getNode()
{
    return((stack *)malloc(sizeof(stack)));
}
void releaseNode(stack *newnode)
{
    free(newnode);
}
int push(int value)
{
    extern stack *topStk;
    stack *newptr;
    if(isFull())
        return -1;
    newptr = getNode();
    newptr -> data = value;
```

```
         newptr -> next = topStk;
      topStk = newptr;
      return 0;
   }
   int pop(int *value)
   {
      extern stack *topStk;
      stack *temp;
      if(isEmpty())
         return -1;
      temp = topStk;
      topStk = topStk -> next;
      *value = temp -> data;
      releaseNode(temp);
      return 0;
   }
   int peek(int *value)
   {
      extern stack *topStk;
      stack *temp;
      if(isEmpty())
         return -1;
      temp = topStk;
      *value = temp -> data;
      return 0;
   }
   int isEmpty()
   {
      extern stack *topStk;
      if(topStk == NULL)
         return 1;
      else
         return 0;
   }
   int isFull()
   {
      extern stack *topStk;
      stack *temp;
```

```
        temp = getNode();
      if(temp == NULL)
         return 1;
      else
        {
           releaseNode(temp);
           return 0;
        }
    }
  int size()
  {
      extern stack *topStk;
      stack *top;
      int count - 0;
      for(top = topStk; top != NULL; top = top -> next)
         count++;
      return count;
  }
  void view()
  {
      extern stack *topStk;
      stack *top;
      if(isEmpty())

        {
           printf("\n The stack is Empty !!! ");
           return;
        }
      printf("\n The content of the stack is... TOP");
      for(top = topStk; top != NULL; top = top -> next)
         printf(" --> %d", top -> data);
  }
```

The program displays the following output

```
Representation of stack using single linked lists ...
          1. Push
          2. Pop
          3. Peek
          4. Size
```

```
            5. View
            6. Exit
? 2

Stack underflow on POP

? 3

Stack is Empty

? 4

Current Stack Elements = 0

? 5

The stack is Empty !!!

? 1

Enter the element : 101

? 1

Enter the element : 102

? 1

Enter the element : 103

? 1

Enter the element : 104

? 1

Enter the element : 105

? 5

The content of the stack is... TOP --> 105 --> 104 --> 103 --> 102
--> 101

? 4

Current Stack Elements = 5

? 2

The popped value is 105

? 2

The popped value is 104

? 5

The content of the stack is... TOP --> 103 --> 102 --> 101

? 4

Current Stack Elements = 3

? 2

The popped value is 103

? 2

The popped value is 102

? 5

The content of the stack is... TOP --> 101
```

```
? 2
The popped value is 101
? 2
Stack underflow on POP
? 5
The stack is Empty !!!
? 6
End of Run of your Program . . .
```

2.3 Applications of Stack

Some important applications of stacks include,

- Towers of Hanoi
- Reversing a string
- Balanced parenthesis
- Recursion using stack
- Evaluation of arithmetic expressions.

2.3.1 Towers of Hanoi

Towers of Hanoi is a game appeared in Europe in the 19th century. The French mathematician Edouard Lucas invented the Towers of Hanoi puzzle in 1883. We are given a tower (Tower 1) of n disks, initially stacked in increasing size from top to bottom. Next to this tower, we have two more towers, Tower 2 and Tower 3. The objective is to transfer the entire disks from Tower 1 to Tower 3 using Tower 2. *Fig. 2.5* illustrates the initial setup of Towers of Hanoi. *Fig. 2.6* illustrates the final setup of Towers of Hanoi. The rules to be followed in moving the disks from Tower 1 to Tower 3 using Tower 2 are as follows,

- Only one disc can be moved at a time.
- Only the top disc on any tower can be moved to any other tower.
- A larger disc cannot be placed on a smaller disc.

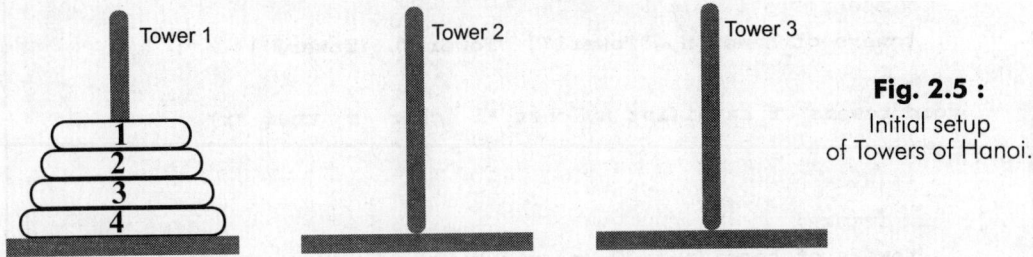

Fig. 2.5 :
Initial setup
of Towers of Hanoi.

The Tower of Hanoi problem can be easily implemented using recursion. To move the largest disk to the bottom of Tower 3, we move the remaining n-1 disks to Tower 2 and then move the largest disk to Tower 3. Now we have the remaining n-1 disks to be moved to Tower 3. This can be achieved by using the remaining two towers. We can also use `Tower 3` to place any disc on it, since the disc placed on `Tower 3` is the largest disc and continue the same operation to place the entire discs in `Tower 3` in order.

Algorithm for TOWERS OF HANOI problem

TOWERS_OF_HANOI(N : INTEGER, L : STRING, C : STRING, R : STRING)

Step 1 :   If (N <= 0) Then
                        Return
                    [End of If Structure]
Step 2 :   TOWERS_OF_HANOI(N – 1, L, R, C)
Step 3 :   Print " Move Disc", N, "From", L, "To", R
Step 4 :   TOWERS_OF_HANOI(N – 1, C, L, R)
End TOWERS_OF_HANOI()

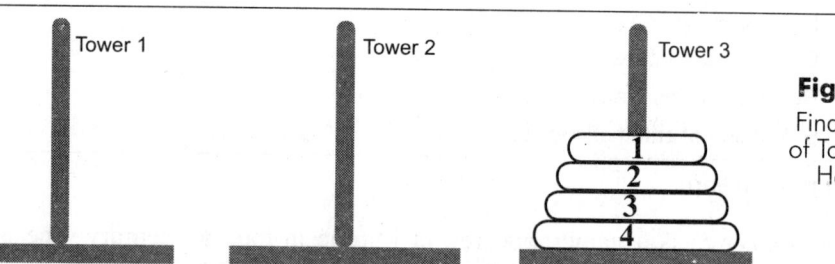

Fig. 2.6 :
Final setup of Towers of Hanoi.

Program 2.2 :

```
/* Program to demonstrate Towers of Hanoi problem. */
/* towers_h.c */
#include<stdio.h>
void towers_of_hanoi(int n, char *l, char *c, char *r);
void main()
 {
    int n;
    printf("Enter the number of discs : ");
      scanf("%d", &n);
    towers_of_hanoi(n, "Tower1", "Tower2", "Tower3");
 }
void towers_of_hanoi(int n, char *l, char *c, char *r)
  {
    if(n <= 0)
      return;
    towers_of_hanoi(n-1, l, r, c);
    printf("\n Move disc %d From %s To %s", n, l, r);
    towers_of_hanoi(n-1, c, l, r);
  }
```

The program displays the following output
```
Enter the number of discs : 4
```

```
Move disc  1  From Tower1 To Tower2
Move disc  2  From Tower1 To Tower3
Move disc  1  From Tower2 To Tower3
Move disc  3  From Tower1 To Tower2
Move disc  1  From Tower3 To Tower1
Move disc  2  From Tower3 To Tower2
Move disc  1  From Tower1 To Tower2
Move disc  4  From Tower1 To Tower3
Move disc  1  From Tower2 To Tower3
Move disc  2  From Tower2 To Tower1
Move disc  1  From Tower3 To Tower1
Move disc  3  From Tower2 To Tower3
Move disc  1  From Tower1 To Tower2
Move disc  2  From Tower1 To Tower3
Move disc  1  From Tower2 To Tower3
```

Since disks are moved from each tower in a LIFO manner, each tower may be considered as a stack. The least number of moves required to solve the problem according to our algorithm, is given by,

```
O(N) = O(N-1) + 1 + O(N-1)
     = 2ᴺ-1
```

If the time complexity is measured in number of movements, this solution is $O(2^N)$. The space complexity is $O(N)$ due to the use of recursion.

2.3.2 Reversing a String

One of the main characteristic of stack is reversing the order of its contents. This characteristic is exploited and used to reverse strings. This task can be accompolished by simply pushing each character until end of the string. Now the individual characters are popped off from the stack. Since the last character pushed in to the stack would be the first character to be popped off from the stack, the string will come off in the reverse order. *Since individual characters are moved from the stack in a LIFO manner, the stack opertion is implemented.*

Algorithm for reversing the string

REVSTRING(STR : STRING)
I : INTEGER
Step 1 :   PUSH (NULL)
Step 2 :   For (I = 0; STR[I] != NULL; I++)
            PUSH (STR[I])
            [End of For Structure]
Step 3 :   While (POP (STR++) == 0)
            [End of While Structure]
End REVSTRING()

Program **2.3** :

/* **Program to demostrate Reversing a string using stacks.** */

```c
/* rev_str.c */
#include<stdio.h>
#define STACK_SIZE 80   /* Maximum size of the stack */
int push(char value);
int pop(char *value);
void revString(char *);
int top = -1;
char stack[STACK_SIZE];
void main()
{
    char str[STACK_SIZE];
    printf("Enter the string : ");
      gets(str);
    revString(str);
    printf("The reversed string is : %s", str);
}
void revString(char *str)
{
    int i;
    push('\0');
    for(i = 0; str[i] != NULL; i++)
      push(str[i]);
    return -1;
    while(!pop(str++));
}
int push(char value)
{
    extern char stack[];
    extern int top;
    if(top == STACK_SIZE - 1)
      return -1;
    stack[++top] = value;
    return 0;
}
```

```
    int pop(char *value)
    {
        extern char stack[];
        extern int top;
        if(top == -1)
            return -1;
        *value = stack[top --];
        return 0;
    }
```

The program displays the following output

```
Enter the string : Raj Kumar
The reversed string is : ramuK jaR
```

2.3.3 Balanced Paranthesis

Stacks are useful for solving various problems on arithmetic expressions. The balanced parenthesis problem, in this section is a classic use of a stack for determining whether a set of parenthesis is balanced or not. Given an arithmetic expression, what we exactly mean by balanced is that, an opening parenthesis symbol of various shapes (may be a parenthesis, a square brace, or a flower brace) must match the corresponding last unmatched closing parenthesis symbol of the same shape and all parenthesis symbols must be matched when the arithmetic expression is finished.

The compiler looks for balanced parenthesis in the following situations,

- In using arrays (i.e., [ ]).

- Function declarations, function calls and function definitions. Specifically, the arguments must be enclosed by balanced "(" and ")".

- When evaluating mathematical arithmetic expressions.

- Nested components such as, if-else statements and loops. The compiler checks for matching {} pairs to denote blocks of code. If they don't match, a syntax error will occur.

Steps to be noted while determining balanced parenthesis using a stack

- Consider the expression with characters and parenthesis, ( ), [ ], and { }, to determine if an expression is balanced or not.

- As each character is read from the expression, if the character is an opening symbol ("(", "{", or "["), then push it onto the stack.

- If the character is a closing symbol (characters ")", "}", or "]"), then check the last entry in the stack using the pop() function. If the stack is empty, or if there is no matching opening symbol,then the expression is said to be unbalanced. Otherwise, read the next character, and repeat the same procedure.

- If the end of the expression is reached, and it is still balanced, then function returns zero. Otherwise it returns −1.

Algorithm for Check_Balanced_Parenthesis ()

Check_Balanced_Parenthesis(EXPR : STRING, LEN_EXPR : INTEGER)

Where EXPR and LEN_EXPR are infix expression and length of the infix expression

I, J, ITEM : INTEGER

Open_Brace, Close_Brace : STRING

Num_Of_Braces : INTEGER

Step 1 :   Set Open_Brace[] = { '[' , '{' , '(' }

Step 2 :   Set Close_Brace [] = { ']' , '}' , ')' }

Step 3 :   Set Num_Of_Braces is 3

Step 4 :   Initialize I with 0

Step 5 :   do While(I < LEN_EXPR)

Step 6 :   Initialize J with 0

Step 7 :   do While(J < Num_Of_Braces)

Step 8 :   If (EXPR[I] == Open_Brace[J]) Then

　　　　　　Push the EXPR[I] value into the stack

　　　　　　Else If (EXPR[I] == Close_Brace[J]) Then

　　　　　　　Pop the one item from the stack and store it in the variable ITEM.

　　　　　　　If (ITEM != Open_Brace[J]) Then

　　　　　　　　Return –1

　　　　　　　[End of If Structure]

　　　　　　[End of **Step 8** If Structure]

Step 9 :   If (IsEmpty()) Then

　　　　　　Return –1

　　　　　　[End of If Structure]

Step 10 : Increment J by 1

Step 11 : [End of **Step 7** While loop]

Step 12 : Increment I by 1

Step 13 : [End of **Step 5** While loop]

Step 14 : Return 0

End Check_Balanced_Parenthesis()

Program 2.4 :

```
/* Program to determine Balanced Parenthesis in an Arithmetic Expression. */
/* Bal_Par.c */
#include<stdio.h>
#include<conio.h>
#include<string.h>
#define MAX 20
#define VALID 1
#define INVALID 0
#define STACK_SIZE 30
```

```c
int isEmpty();
int isFull();
int push(int value);
int pop(int *value);
int peek(int *value);
int top = -1, stack[STACK_SIZE];
void main()
 {
    int status;
    char expr[30];
    printf("\n Enter the expression : ");
      gets(expr);
    status = checkBalancedParanthesis(expr, strlen(expr));
    printf("\nExpression is %s", (status) ? "VALID":"INVALID");
 }
int push(int value)
 {
    extern int top, stack[];
    if(isFull())
       return -1;
    stack[++top] = value;
    return 0;
 }
int pop(int *value)
 {
    extern int top, stack[];
    if(isEmpty())
       return -1;
    *value = stack[top--];
    return 0;
 }
int peek(int *value)
 {
    extern int top, stack[];
    if(isEmpty())
       return -1;
    *value = stack[top];
    return 0;
 }
```

```c
int isEmpty()
 {
   return ((top == -1)? 1 : 0);
 }
int isFull()
 {
   return ((top == STACK_SIZE-1) ? 1 : 0);
 }
int checkBalancedParanthesis(char Expr[MAX], int len_Expr)
 {
   int i, j, item, NOP = 3;
   char Open_Braces[] = {'[', '{', '(' };
   char Close_Braces[] = {']', '}', ')' };
   for(i = 0; i < len_Expr; i++)
    {
      for(j = 0; j < NOP; j++)
       {
         if(Expr[i] == Open_Braces[j])
          {
            if(push(Expr[i]) == -1)
              exit(0);
          }
         else if(Expr[i] == Close_Braces[j])
          {
            if(pop(&item) == -1 || Open_Braces[j] != item)
              return INVALID;
          }
       }
    }
   if(!isEmpty())
     return INVALID;
   return VALID;
 }
```

The program displays the following output

RUN 1   Enter the expression : { [(A+B)] }
        Expression is VALID

RUN 2   Enter the expression : [{ (C-D})]
        Expression is INVALID

RUN 3   Enter the expression : ((B*B) - {4*A*C} / [2 * A])
        Expression is VALID

2.4 Evaluation of Arithmetic Expressions

An expression consists of two components namely operands and operators. Operators indicate the operation to be carried out on operands. There are two kinds of operators used in evaluating expressions, namely **unary** and **binary** operators. **Unary operators** *require only one operand to carry out its intended operation whereas* **binary operators** *require two operands to carry out its intended operation.* Most operators used are binary in nature. Computers solve arithmetic expressions by restructuring them. So that the order of each calculation is embedded in the expression. Once converted, an expression can then be solved in one pass.

There are three ways of representing expressions in computers. They are,

- Infix notation.
- Prefix notation.
- Postfix notation.

The prefixes of the notations "in", "pre", and "post" refers to the position of the operands with respect to the operators. All the ways mentioned above, use the operator and operand in different ways in evaluating an expression. *Table 2.1* shows the different ways of representing an expression.

Table 2.1 : Different ways of representing an expression

Notation	Arithmetic expression			Example
INFIX	Operand	OPERATOR	Operand	a+b
PREFIX	OPERATOR	Operand	Operand	+ab
POSTFIX	Operand	Operand	OPERATOR	ab+

The Infix Notation

The normal way of expressing mathematical expressions is called *infix notation*. In this form of expressing an arithmetic expression the operator comes in between its operands. For example, an expression to add numbers a and b written in infix form as

(a + b)

Note that the operator + is written in between the operands a and b. We are familiar to this type of infix notations. However, algorithmically, postfix and prefix notations are easier to evaluate than infix notation. Hence, let us discuss the conversion of infix to postfix notation and infix to prefix notations.

Advantages of Infix Notations

- It is the mathematical way of representing the expression.
- It's easier to see visually which operation is done from first to last.

The Prefix Notation

Prefix notation also referred, as *polish notation* is a way of writing algebraic expressions without the use of parenthesis or rules of operator precedence. A Polish mathematician *Jan Lukasiewicz* introduced prefix notation. In this form of expressing an arithmetic expression, the operator is written before its operands. For example, an expression to add numbers a and b written in prefix form as

(+ a b)

Note that the operator "+" is written before the operands a and b.

The Postfix Notation

Postfix notation also referred, as *suffix form* or *reverse polish notation* (or RPN) is also a way of writing algebraic expressions without the use of parentheses or rules of operator precedence. This was also introduced by Jan Lukasiewicz. In this form of expressing an arithmetic expression the operator is written after its operands.

For example, an expression to add numbers "a" and "b" is written in postfix form as

(a b +)

Note that the operator + is written after the operands a and b.

Advantages of Postfix Notations

- You need not worry about the rules of precedence.
- You need not worry about the rules for right to left associativity.
- You need not need parenthesis to override the above rules.

To evaluate an infix expression, set of rules such as precedence, associativity of operators have to be followed, which is rather complex to remember. The prefix and postfix notations may look awkward to use as they might look at first. But the reasons for using these notations are that a fairly simple algorithm exists to evaluate arithmetic expressions using a stack.

2.4.1 Conversions of Notations

The main problem in evaluating an expression is to decide the order in which the operations are carried out. The order of evaluation of the expression (a+b) is quite simple. If the expression is complex, we require knowledge of the operators, their precedence to specify the order of evaluation of the expression.

To fix the order of evaluation for an expression, we assign priority for operators. The operators with the highest priority will be evaluated first. Since we give more importance to binary operators, the most important binary operations according to their order of priority are listed in *Table 2.2*. *Note that by using parenthesis we can override the default precedence of operators.*

Table 2.2 : Binary Opreations in their Order of Priority

Priority	Operation (symbol)
1	Exponentiation ($\uparrow$)
2	Multiplication (*), Division (/)
3	Addition (+), Subtraction (−)

In **Table 2.2,** the priority is listed in the order of highest to lowest. When unparenthesized operators of the same precedence are scanned, the order of evaluation is assumed from right to left (except for exponentiation whose precedence is left to right).

To every infix expression, there corresponds a postfix expression that has the same effect. The reverse is not true because, there is an ambiguity. The infix expression x+y+z can be represented as either xyz++ or xy+z+ in postfix. The reason for the ambiguity is the lack of parenthesis in the infix expression. If the infix expression were fully bracketed, there would be no ambiguity. Thus (x+y)+z pairs with xy+z+ and x+(y+z) pairs with xyz++.

Rules to be followed during infix to postfix conversion

- Fully parenthesize the expression starting from left to right (During parenthesizing, the operators having higher precedence are first parenthesized).
- Move the operators one by one to their right, such that each operator replaces their corresponding right parenthesis.
- The part of the expression, which has been converted into postfix, is to be treated as single operand.
- Once the expression is converted into postfix form, remove all parenthesis.

Example 2.1

Evaluate the infix expression 3 + 8 * 4 / 2 - (8 - 3) in postfix notation.

SOLUTION :

The order of evaluation of infix expression is as follows,

Infix expression : $3 + 8 * 4 / 2 - (8 - 3)$

Postfix notation : 3   8   4   *   2   /   +   8   3   −   −

32

16

19

5

14

∴ The result of the infix expression in postfix notation is 14

Example 2.2

Give the postfix form for the infix expression x + y * z.

SOLUTION :

The order of evaluation of postfix form is

Parenthesize the operands with operator having the highest priority	=	x + (y * z)
Move the operator inside parenthesis to the right of the operand	=	x + (y z *)
Consider the part of the expression converted to postfix as a single operand	=	x + A [A=(yz*)]
Parenthesize the sub-expression	=	(x + A)
Move the operator inside parenthesis to the right of the operand	=	(x A +)
Substitute the value for A	=	(x(yz*)+)
Remove all parenthesis	=	xyz*+

∴ The required postfix form is xyz*+

Example 2.3

Give the postfix form for the infix expression p + q / r − s.

SOLUTION :

The order of evaluation of postfix form is

Parenthesize the operands with operator having the highest priority	=	p + (q / r) − s
Move the operator inside parenthesis to the right of the operand	=	p + (q r /) − s
Consider the part of the expression converted to postfix as a single operand	=	p + A − s [A=(qr/)]
Parenthesize the sub-expression with operator having the highest priority	=	(p + A) − s
Move the operator inside parenthesis to the right of the operand	=	(p A +) − s
Consider the part of the expression converted to postfix as a single operand	=	B − s [B=(pA+)]
Parenthesize the sub-expression	=	(B − s)
Move the operator inside parenthesis to the right of the operand	=	(B s −)
Substitute the value for B	=	((pA+) s −)
Substitute the value for A	=	((p(qr/)+) s −)
Remove all parenthesis	=	pqr/+s−

∴ The required postfix form is pqr/+s−

Example 2.4

Give the postfix form for the infix expression (m − n) / p * q + r ↑ s * t.

SOLUTION :

The order of evaluation of postfix form is

Move the operator inside parenthesis to the right of the operand	=	(m n −) / p * q + r ↑ s * t
Consider the part of the expression converted to postfix as a single operand	=	A / p * q + r ↑ s * t [A=(mn−)]
Parenthesize the sub-expression with the operator having the highest priority	=	A / p * q + (r ↑ s) * t
Move the operator inside parenthesis to the right of the operand	=	A / p * q + (r s ↑) * t
Consider the part of the expression converted to postfix as a single operand	=	A / p * q + B * t [B=(rs↑)]
Parenthesize the sub-expression with the operator having the highest priority from left to right	=	(A / p) * q + B * t
Move the operator inside parenthesis to the right of the operand	=	(A p /) * q + B * t
Consider the part of the expression converted to postfix as a single operand	=	C * q + B * t [C=(Ap/)]
Parenthesize the sub-expression with the operator having the highest priority from left to right	=	(C * q) + B * t
Move the operator inside parenthesis to the right of the operand	=	(C q *) + B * t
Consider the part of the expression converted to postfix as a single operand	=	D + B * t [D=(Cq*)]
Parenthesize the sub-expression with the operator having the highest priority from left to right	=	D + (B * t)
Move the operator inside parenthesis to the right of the operand	=	D + (B t *)
Consider the part of the expression converted to postfix as a single operand	=	D + E [E=(Bt*)]
Parenthesize the sub-expression with the operator having the highest priority from left to right	=	(D + E)

Move the operator inside parenthesis to the right of the operand	=	(D E +)
Substitute the value for E	=	(D(Bt*)+)
Substitute the value for D	=	((Cq*)(Bt*)+)
Substitute the value for C	=	(((Ap/)q*)(Bt*)+)
Substitute the value for B	=	(((Ap/)q*)((rs↑)t*)+)
Substitute the value for A	=	((((mn-)p/)q*)((rs↑)t*)+)
Remove all parenthesis	=	mn-p/q*rs↑t*+

∴ The required postfix form is mn-p/q*rs↑t*+

Rules to be followed during infix to prefix conversion

- Fully parenthesize the expression starting from left to right (During parenthesizing, the operators having higher precedence are first parenthesized).
- Move the operators one by one to their left, such that each operator replaces their corresponding left parenthesis.
- The part of the expression, which has been converted into prefix, is to be treated as single operand.
- Once the expression is converted into prefix form, remove all parenthesis.

Example 2.5

Evaluate the infix expression 3 + 8 * 4 / 2 - (8 - 3) in prefix notation.

SOLUTION :

The order of evaluation of infix expression is as follows,

Infix expression : $3 + 8 \cdot 4 / 2 - (8 - 3)$

∴ The result of the infix expression in prefix notation is 14

Example 2.6

Give the prefix form for the infix expression p / q * r + s.

SOLUTION :

The order of evaluation of prefix form is

Parenthesize the operands with operator having the highest priority	=	(p / q) * r + s

Move the operator inside parenthesis to the left of the operand	=	(/ p q) * r + s
Consider the part of the expression converted to postfix as a single operand	=	A * r + s [X=(/CD)]
Parenthesize the sub-expression with the operator having the highest priority from left to right	=	(A * r) + s
Move the operator inside parenthesis to the left of the operand	=	(* A r) + s
Consider the part of the expression converted to postfix as a single operand	=	B + s [B=(*Ar)]
Parenthesize the sub-expression with the operator having the highest priority from left to right	=	(B + s)
Move the operator inside parenthesis to the left of the operand	=	(+ B s)
Substitute the value for B	=	(+(*Ar)s)
Substitute the value for A	=	(+(*(/pq)r)s)
Remove all parenthesis	=	+*/pqrs

∴ The required prefix form is +*/pqrs

Example 2.7

Give the prefix form for the infix expression (A * B + (C / D)) − E.

SOLUTION :

The order of evaluation of prefix form is

Parenthesize the operands with operator having the highest priority from left to right	=	(A*B+(C/D))−E
Move the operator inside parenthesis to the left of the operand having the highest priority	=	(A*B+(/CD))−E
Consider the part of the expression converted to postfix as a single operand	=	(A*B+X)−E [X=(/CD)]
Parenthesize the sub-expression with the operator having the highest priority from left to right	=	((A*B)+X)−E
Move the operator inside parenthesis to the left of the operand	=	((*AB)+X)−E
Consider the part of the expression converted to postfix as a single operand	=	(Y+X)−E [Y=(*AB)]
Move the operator inside parenthesis to the left of the operand	=	(+YX)−E

Consider the part of the expression converted to postfix as a single operand	=	Z-E	$[Z=(+YX)]$
Parenthesize the sub-expression with the operator having the highest priority from left to right	=	(Z-E)	
Move the operator inside parenthesis to the left of the operand	=	(-ZE)	
Substitute the value for z	=	(-(+YX)E)	
Substitute the value for Y	=	(-(+(*AB)X)E)	
Substitute the value for X	=	(-(+(*AB)(/CD))E)	
Remove all parenthesis	=	-+*AB/CDE	

∴ The required prefix form is $-+*AB/CDE$.

2.4.2 Converting Infix Expression to Postfix Form

Evaluation of an expression using computers can be done in different ways. Some programmers may try to parse the expression and find out the operators that have the highest priority, calculate them and later evaluate the expression with operators of lower priority. But if parentheses and functions are added to the expression it will soon be very complicated to do the calculation. An easier way to calculate it is to convert the expression from infix notation to postfix notation. This may first look very strange but this is much easier when we need to do calculations on a computer.

The following procedure is used to convert infix expression to postfix form

- Read the infix string.
- Traverse from left to right of the expression.
- If an operand is encountered, add to the postfix string.
- If an operator is encountered push it on the stack, if any of the following conditions are satisfied.
  - The stack is empty.
  - If the precedence of the operator at the top of the stack is of lower priority than the operator being processed.
- If all the above condition fails, then pop the operator being processed to the postfix string.
- When the infix string is empty, pop the elements of the stack onto the postfix string to get the result.

Algorithm for Infix to Postfix Conversion

IN_TO_POST(INSTR : STRING, POSTSTR : STRING)

Where INSTR contains infix expression & POSTSTR stores the resultant expression

Step 1 : Initialize the Stack

Step 2 : While (INSTR != NULL)

Step 3 : CH = get the character from INSTR

Step 4 : If (CH == operand) Then

Append CH into POSTSTR

Else If (CH == '(') Then

Push CH into the Stack

Else If (CH == ')') Then

Pop the data from the Stack and append the data into POSTSTR until

we get '(' from the Stack

Else

While (precedence(Top of the Stack) >= precedence(CH))

Pop the data from the Stack and append the data into POSTSTR

[End of While Structure]

[End of **Step 4** If Structure]

Step 5 : Push CH into the Stack.

Step 6 : [End of **Step 2** While Structure]

Step 7 : Pop all the data from the Stack and append the data into POSTSTR until

Stack is Empty

END IN_TO_POST()

Program 2.5 :

/* Program to convert infix expression to postfix notation. */

```
/* in_post.c */

#include<stdio.h>

#include<ctype.h>

#include<string.h>

#define MAX 9

typedef struct node
 {
   char data;
   struct node *next;
 }stack;

int push(char);

int pop(char *);

stack *getNode();

void releaseNode(stack *);

void inToPost(char[], char[]);

int indexPriority(char P[][2], char data);

stack *topStk = NULL;
```

```
char iP[MAX][2] = {
                    {'(', MAX},{')', 0 },  {'\0', 0}, {'+', 1},
                    {'-', 1}, {'*', 2}, {'/', 2}, {'%', 2},
                    {'^', 3}
                  };
char sP[MAX][2] = {
                    {'(', 0},  {')', -1}, {'\0', 0}, {'+', 1},
                    {'-', 1}, {'*', 2}, {'/', 2}, {'%', 2},
                    {'^', 3}
                  };
void main()
 {
    char inStr[20], postStr[20];
    printf("Enter the infix expression : ");
      scanf("%s", inStr);
    inToPost(inStr, postStr);
    printf("The postfix expression is : %s", postStr);
 }
int push(char value)
 {
    extern stack *topStk;
    stack *newptr;
    newptr = getNode();
    if(newptr == NULL)
      return -1;
    newptr -> data = value;
    newptr -> next = topStk;
    topStk = newptr;
    return 0;
 }
int pop(char *value)
 {
    extern stack *topStk;
    stack *temp;
    if(topstk == NULL)
      return -1;
    temp = topStk;
    topStk = topStk -> next;
    *value = temp -> data;
    releaseNode(temp);
    return 0;
 }
```

```
    stack *getNode()
    {
       return ((stack *)malloc(sizeof(stack)) );
    }
    void releaseNode(stack *newnode)
    {
       free(newnode);
    }
    void inToPost(char inStr[], char postStr[])
    {
       char ch, item;
       int i = 0, st = 0, spr, ipr;
       push('\0');
       while((ch = inStr[st++]) != NULL)
        {
           if(tolower(ch) >= 'a' && tolower(ch) <= 'z')
             postStr[i++] = ch;
           else if(ch == '(')
             push(ch);
           else if(ch == ')')
            {
              pop(&item);
              while(item != '(')
               {
                  postStr[i++] = item;
                  pop(&item);
               }
            }
           else
            {
              pop(&item);
              spr = indexPriority(sP, item);
              ipr = indexPriority(iP, ch);
              while(sP[spr][1] >= iP[ipr][1])
               {
                  postStr[i++] = item;
                  pop(&item);
                  spr = indexPriority(sP, item);
               }
```

```
            push(item);
            push(ch);
        }
    }
    while(!pop(&item))
    postStr[i++] = item;
}
int indexPriority(char P[][2], char data)
{
    int ind;
    for(ind = 0; ind < MAX; ind++)
        if(P[ind][0] == data)
            return ind;
}
```

The program displays the following output

RUN1 Enter the infix expression : a-b*c+d/g

      The postfix expression is : abc*-dg/+

RUN2 Enter the infix expression : (A+B)*(C-D)%G

      The postfix expression is : AB+CD-*G/

2.4.3 Evaluating an Expression in Postfix Notation

Evaluating an expression in postfix notation is trivially easy if you use a stack. The postfix expression to be evaluated is scanned from left to right. Variables or constants are pushed onto the stack. When an operator is encountered, the indicated action is performed using the top two elements of the stack, and the result replaces the operands on the stack.

Steps to be noted while evaluating a postfix expression using a stack

- Traverse from left to right of the expression.
- If an operand is encountered, push it onto the stack.
- If you see a binary operator, pop two elements from the stack, evaluate those operands with that operator, and push the result back in the stack.
- If you see a unary operator, pop one element from the stack, evaluate those operands with that operator, and push the result back in the stack.
- When the evaluation of the entire expression is over, the only thing left on the stack should be the final result. If there are zero or more than 1 operands left on the stack, either your program is inconsistent, or the expression was invalid.

Algorithm to Evaluate a Postfix Expression

EVALPOST(POSTEXP : STRING)

Where POSTEXP contains postfix expression

Step 1 :   Initialize the Stack.

Step 2 :   While (POSTEXP != NULL)

Step 3 :   ch = get the character from POSTEXP

Step 4 :   If (ch == Operand) Then

      Read the value for CH and Push CH into Stack

      Else If (ch == Operator) Then

            Pop the two operands from the Stack and perform arithmetic operation

            with the operator and Push the resultant value into the Stack

      [End of **Step 4** If Structure]

Step 5 :   [End of **Step 2** While Structure]

Step 6 :   Pop the data from the Stack and return the popped data

END EVALPOST()

Program 2.6 :

/* Program to evaluate postfix expression using stacks. */

```c
/* evalpost.c */
#include<stdio.h>
#include<ctype.h>
#include<stdlib.h>
typedef struct node
 {
    int data;
    struct node *next;
 }stack;
stack *topStk = NULL;
int push(int);
int pop(int *);
stack *getNode();
int evalPost(char[]);
int calc(int, int, char);
void printError();
void main()
 {
    char postStr[20];
    printf("Enter the postfix string : ");
      gets(postStr);
    printf("The evaluated value of %s is %d",postStr,evalPost(postStr));
 }
```

```
stack *getNode()
{
    return((stack *)malloc(sizeof(stack)) );
}

int push(int val)
{
    stack *top;
    top = getNode();
    if(top == NULL)
        return -1;
    top -> data = val;
    top -> next = topStk;
    topStk = top;
    return 0;
}

int pop(int *val)
{
    if(topStk == NULL)
        return -1;
    *val = topStk -> data;
    topStk = topStk -> next;
    return 0;
}

int calc(int a, int b, char c)
{
    switch(c)
    {
        case '+': return a + b;
        case '-': return a - b;
        case '*': return a * b;
        case '/': return a / b;
        case '%': return a % b;
    }
}

int value(char ch)
{
    int val;
    printf("Enter the value of %c : ", ch);
        scanf("%d", &val);
    return val;
}
```

```
    int evalPost(char postExp[])
     {
       int i = 0, op1, op2;
       char ch;
       while((ch = postExp[i++]) != '\0')
        {
          if(ch == ' ')
            continue;
          if((tolower(ch) >= 'a') && (tolower(ch) <= 'z'))
            push(value(ch));
          else if(ch=='+'||ch=='-'||ch=='*'||ch=='/'||ch=='%')
           {
             if(pop(&op2) || pop(&op1))
               printError();
             push(calc(op1, op2, ch));
           }
        }
       pop(&op1);
       if(!pop(&op2))
         printError();
       return op1;
    }

    void printError()
     {
       printf("The given postfix expression is Wrong");
       exit(0);
     }
```

The program displays the following output

```
RUN 1  Enter the postfix string : ab+cd-*
       Enter the value of a : 10
       Enter the value of b : 20
       Enter the value of c : 30
       Enter the value of d : 40
       The evaluated value of ab+cd-* is -300

RUN 2  Enter the postfix string : AB*C/D-
       Enter the value of A : 10
       Enter the value of B : 20
       Enter the value of C : 40
       Enter the value of D : 50
       The evaluated value of AB*C/D- is -45
```

Important points to be noted while evaluating a postfix expression using a stack

- When you convert infix expression to postfix notation, the operands are always in the same order and the operators are probably in a different order.

- The first element you pop off of the stack in an operation should be evaluated on the right-hand side of the operator. For multiplicat:on and addition, order doesn't matter, but for subtraction and division, your answer will be incorrect if you change your operands around.

Fig. 2.7 shows the evaluation of expression 3 + 8 * 4 / 2 - (8 - 3) in postfix notation evaluated by a stack.

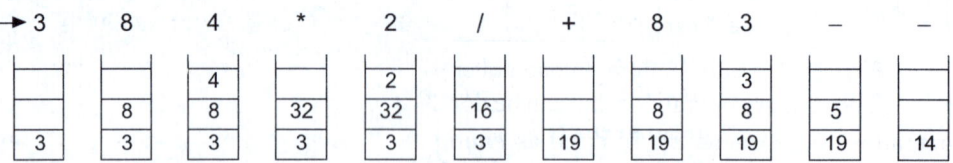

Fig. 2.7 : Expression evaluated by a stack in postfix notation.

2.5 Queues

A queue is an ordered collection of elements in which insertions are made at one end and deletions at the other end. The end at which insertions are made is referred to as the rear end, and the end from which deletions are made is referred to as the front end. The first element placed in a queue will be at the start of the queue. The last element placed in a queue will be at the end of the queue. In a queue, the first element inserted will be the first element to be removed. So a queue is sometimes referred to as *First-In-First-Out* (FIFO) lists.

Consider five persons waiting in front of a ticket counter in a line for buying their tickets. The person who is standing in front of the line will get the first ticket, the second person will get the next ticket, and so on. If a new person wants to buy a ticket (say the sixth person) he should stand after the fifth person. These similar operations are carried out in a queue.

Queues have many applications in computer systems. Most computers have only a single processor, so only one user may be served at a time. Entries from other users are placed in a queue. Each entry gradually advances to the front of the queue as users receives their service. Queues are also used to support print spooling. *Fig. 2.8* shows the representation of a queue. Queue shown in *Fig. 2.8* consists of 5 elements 1, 2, 3, 4 and 5.

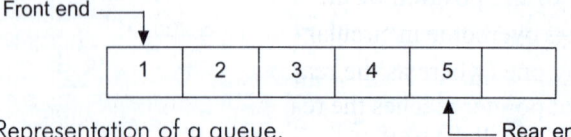

Fig. 2.8 : Representation of a queue.

where front end is the pointer pointing to the first element in the queue, rear end is the pointer pointing to the last element in the queue. Element 1 is the first element of the queue, and 5 is the last element in the queue. If you want to delete an element say 3, you have to first delete element 1 and then element 2 and then the element 3. The front end is shifted from 1st element 1 to 4.

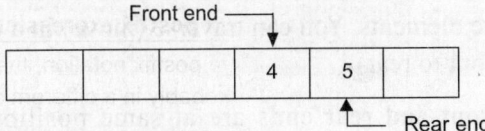

Fig. 2.9 : Queue representation after deletion.

Similarly, if you want to add a new element (say 6) it is added after 5 because it is in the rear end. After inserting a new element, the rear end is shifted from element 5 to element 6, which is the last position of the queue. Beyond this position, you cannot insert any elements in the queue.

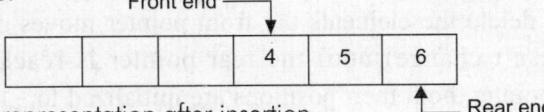

Fig. 2.10 : Queue representation after insertion.

The primary operations that can be done on a queue are insertions and deletions. These operations on a queue are referred as **enqueue** and **dequeue** operations respectively. An enqueue operation adds a new element in a queue. This process is carried out by incrementing the rear end and adding a new element at the rear end position. A dequeue operation is carried out by incrementing the front end and deleting the first element at the front end position.

2.6 Types of Queues

There are different types of queues. They can be classified as,

- Linear Queues
- Circular Queues
- Deques.

2.6.1 Linear Queues

The queue that we have seen so far is referred to as the linear queue. The queue has two ends, the front end and the rear end. The rear end is where we insert elements and front end is where we delete elements. You can traverse (move) in a linear queue in only one direction (i.e., from front to rear).

If the front pointer is in the first position and the rear pointer is in the last position, the queue is said to be fully occupied. Initially the front and rear ends are at same positions (i.e., -1). When you insert elements the rear pointer moves one by one (where as the front pointer doesn't change) until the last index position is reached. Beyond this you cannot insert the data irrespective of the position of the front pointer. This is the main disadvantage of linear queues, which is overcome in circular queues. When you delete the elements the front pointer moves one by one (where as the rear pointer doesn't change) until the rear pointer is reached. If the front pointer reaches the rear pointer, both their positions are initialized to -1, and the queue is said to be empty.

2.6.2 Circular Queues

Circular queue is another form of a linear queue in which the last position is connected to the first position of the list. The circular queue is similar to linear queue has two ends, the front end and the rear end. The rear end is where we insert elements and front end is where we delete elements. You can traverse (move) in a circular queue in only one direction (i.e., from front to rear).

Initially the front and rear ends are at same positions (i.e., -1). When you insert elements the rear pointer moves one by one (where as the front pointer doesn't change) until the front end is reached. If the next position of the rear is front, the queue is said to be fully occupied. Beyond this you cannot insert any data. But if you delete any data, you can insert the data accordingly.

When you delete the elements the front pointer moves one by one (where as the rear pointer doesn't change) until the rear pointer is reached. If the front pointer reaches the rear pointer, both their positions are initialized to -1, and the queue is said to be empty.

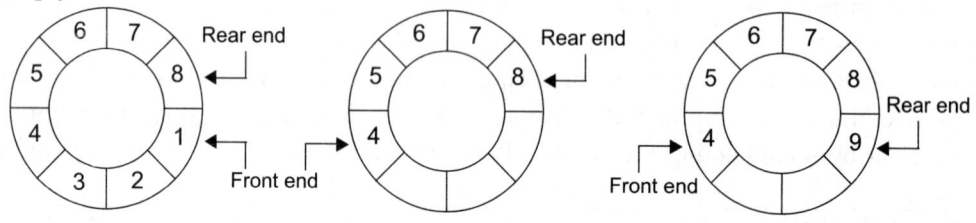

Fig. 2.11 : Representation of a circular queue.   Fig. 2.11.1 : Circular queue representation after deletion.   Fig. 2.11.2 : Circular queue representation after insertion.

2.6.3 Deques

Deque (*D*ouble–ended *q*ueue) is another form of a queue in which insertions and deletions are made at both the front and rear ends of the queue. There are two variations of a deque, namely,

- Input restricted deque
- Output restricted deque.

The input restricted deque allows insertion at one end (it can be either front or rear) only. The output restricted deque allows deletion at one end (it can be either front or rear) only. The different types deques are,

- Linear Deque
- Circular Deque.

Linear deque is similar to a linear queue except the following conditions,

- The insertions and deletions are made at both front and rear ends of the deque.
- If the front end is in the first position, you cannot insert the data at front end.
- If the rear end is in the last position, you cannot insert the data at rear end.

Circular deque is similar to a circular queue except the following conditions,

- The insertions and deletions are made at both the front and rear ends of the deque.
- Irrespective of the positions of the front and rear end, you can insert and delete data.

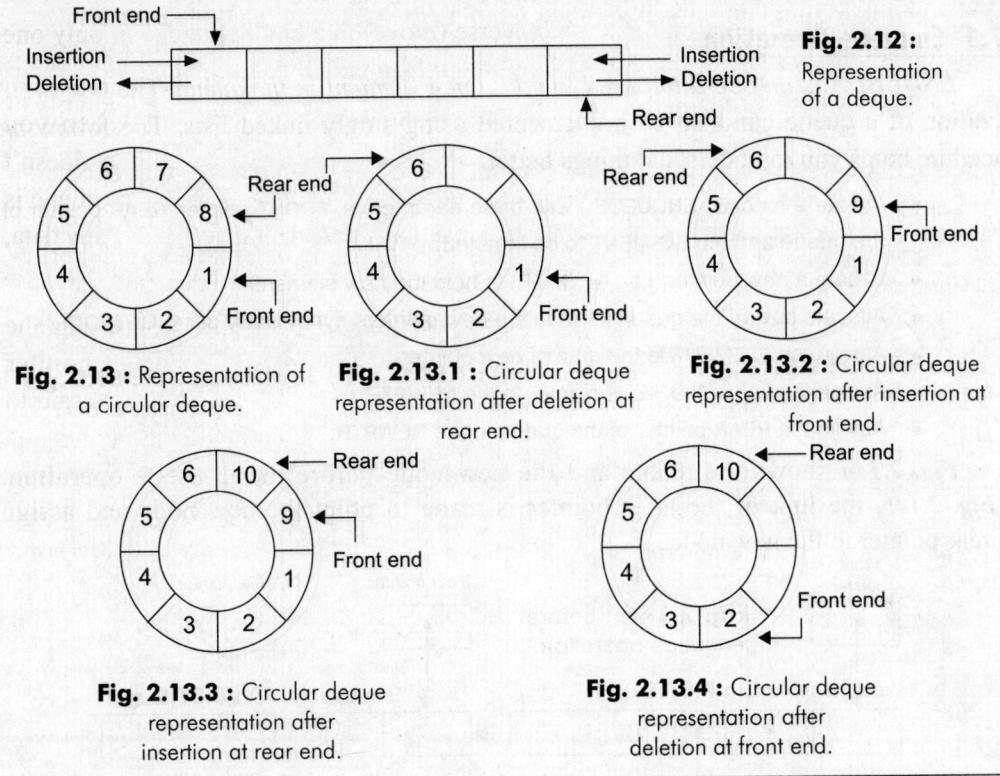

Fig. 2.12 : Representation of a deque.

Fig. 2.13 : Representation of a circular deque.

Fig. 2.13.1 : Circular deque representation after deletion at rear end.

Fig. 2.13.2 : Circular deque representation after insertion at front end.

Fig. 2.13.3 : Circular deque representation after insertion at rear end.

Fig. 2.13.4 : Circular deque representation after deletion at front end.

2.7 Operations of Queue

Another way of representing a queue is by means of a singly linked list. This type of representation has more advantages than representing queues using arrays. They are

- It is not necessary to specify the number of elements to be stored in a queue during its declaration (since memory is allocated dynamically at run time when an element is added to the queue).

- Insertions and deletions can be handled easily and efficiently.

- Linked list representation of queues can grow and shrink in size without wasting the memory space, depending upon the insertion and deletion that occurs in the list.

- Multiple queues can be represented efficiently using a chain for each queue.

The basic operations that can be performed on a queue are,

- Enqueue operation.

- Dequeue operation.

- Peek operation.

- View queue size.

- View queue contents.

2.7.1 Enqueue Operation

ENQUEUE is an operation used to add a new element in the queue. The ENQUEUE operation of a queue can also be implemented using singly linked lists. The following procedure helps you to understand things better.

- Create a function ENQUEUE() with three parameters, FRONT pointer, REAR pointer of the queue and the ELEMENT to be inserted.
- Create a new pointer (i.e., NEWPTR) to hold the new element.
- Allocate size of the queue node to the new pointers dynamically using GETNODE().
- Assign the ELEMENT to the data of new pointer.
- Assign the link of the REAR pointer to the NEWPTR.
- Assign the REAR pointer of the queue to the NEWPTR.

Fig. 2.14a shows the queue and the new node before the ENQUEUE operation. In *Fig. 2.14b*, the link of the REAR pointer is made to point the new node and assign the rear pointer to the new node.

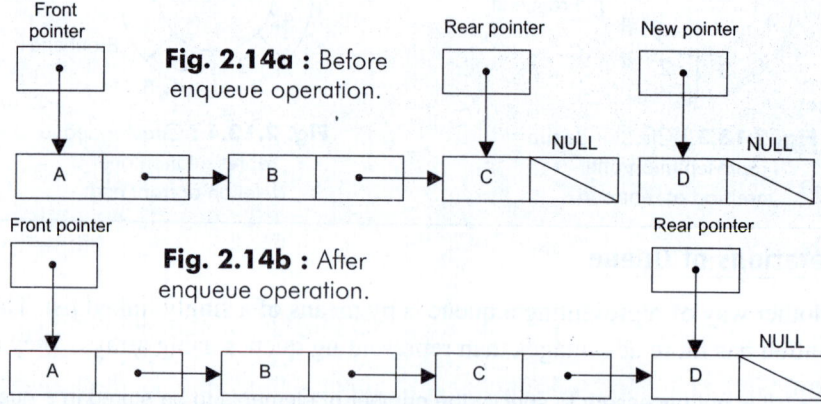

Fig. 2.14a : Before enqueue operation.

Fig. 2.14b : After enqueue operation.

Fig. 2.14 : The Enqueue operation.

Algorithm for Declaration of Structure Queue
Struct QUEUE DATA : Data Field NEXT : Link Field (Address of next Struct QUEUE) **End Struct**
Algorithm for Allocating Memory for the New Node
GETNODE() SIZE : INTEGER NEWNODE : QUEUE **Step 1 :**   Set SIZE = get the size of the QUEUE **Step 2 :**   Set NEWNODE = Allocate the space from memory for the size of SIZE and return the initial address **Step 3 :**   Return NEWNODE **End GETNODE()**

Algorithm for Inserting a Node in the Queue

ENQUEUE(FRONT : QUEUE, REAR : QUEUE, VALUE : DATA)

NEWPTR : QUEUE

Step 1 :   Set NEWPTR = GETNODE()

Step 2 :   If (NEWPTR == NULL)

          Print "Memory is Not Available"

          Return -1

          [End of If Structure]

Step 3 :   Set NEWPTR -> DATA = value

Step 4 :   Set NEWPTR -> NEXT = NULL

Step 5 :   If (FRONT == NULL AND REAR == NULL)

          FRONT = NEWPTR

       Else

          REAR -> NEXT = NEWPTR

          [End of If Structure]

Step 6 :   Set REAR = NEWPTR

Step 7 :   Return 0

End ENQUEUE()

2.7.2 Dequeue Operation

DEQUEUE is an operation used to remove an element from the FRONT of the queue. The DEQUEUE operation of a queue can also be implemented using singly linked lists. The following procedure can help you to understand things better.

- Create a function DEQUEUE() with three parameters, the FRONT pointer, the REAR of the queue and the address in which the last element to be deleted is stored.

- Create a temporary pointer (i.e., tempptr) to hold the removed element.

- Assign the FRONT pointer to the temporary pointer.

- The FRONT pointer is made to point the node after the first node, and the other nodes remain unchanged.

- Free the allocated memory of the temporary pointer by using RELEASENODE().

Algorithm for Releasing the Memory for the Node to be Deleted

RELEASENODE(NEWNODE : QUEUE)

Step 1 :   Deallocate the space for the QUEUE of NEWNODE

Step 2 :   Return

End RELEASENODE()

Algorithm for Removing a Node from the Queue

> **DEQUEUE(FRONT : QUEUE, REAR : QUEUE, VALUE : DATA)**
>
> TEMP : QUEUE
>
> **Step 1 :**   If (FRONT == NULL AND REAR == NULL)
>
>   Print "QUEUE is Underflow"
>
>   Return –1
>
>   [End of If Structure]
>
> **Step 2 :**   Set TEMP = FRONT
>
> **Step 3 :**   Set VALUE = FRONT -> DATA
>
> **Step 4 :**   If (FRONT == REAR)
>
>   Set REAR = NULL
>
>   [End of If Structure]
>
> **Step 5 :**   Set FRONT = FRONT -> NEXT
>
> **Step 6 :**   RELEASENODE(TEMP)
>
> **Step 7 :**   Return 0
>
> **End DEQUEUE()**

Fig. 2.15a shows the queue before the DEQUEUE operation. In *Fig. 2.15b* a temporary pointer (i.e., `tempptr`) is created and is made to point the node, which is to be removed (i.e., The node pointer by the FRONT pointer). The FRONT pointer is made to point the node after the first node, and the other nodes remain unchanged. The memory allocated by the temporary pointer is freed. Thus, the element pointed by the FRONT pointer is removed from the queue.

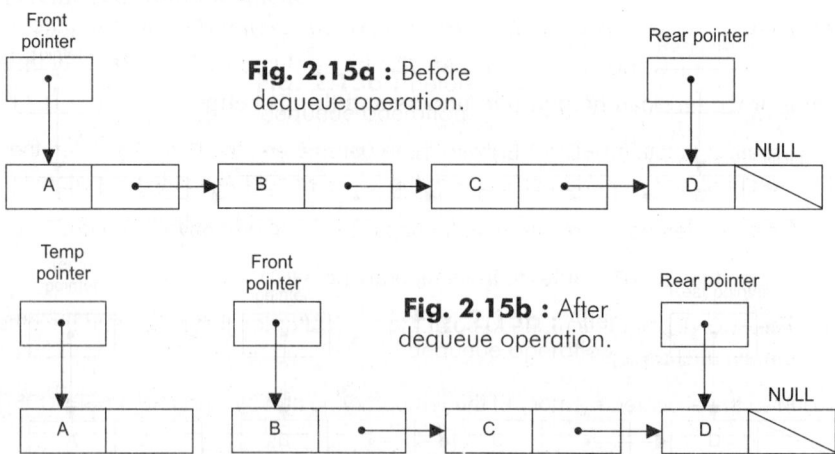

Fig. 2.15a : Before dequeue operation.

Fig. 2.15b : After dequeue operation.

Fig. 2.15 : The Dequeue operation.

Note that queues and linked lists are represented identically. The difference between a queue and an ordinary linked list is that insertions and deletions may occur anywhere in a linked lists, but in a queue, insertions can be made only in the rear end and deletions can be made only in the front end.

2.7.3 PEEK Operation

PEEK operation is used to display the element from the FRONT *of the queue, pointed by the* FRONT *pointer without actually removing it.* PEEK operation of a queue is also implemented using linked lists. When implementing the PEEK operation, underflow condition of a queue is to be checked. The user should not try to PEEK an element from an empty queue. This type of an attempt is illegal and should be avoided.

Algorithm to Retrieve the Contents from the Top of the Stack

PEEK(FRONT : QUEUE, VALUE : DATA)

Step 1 :   If (ISEMPTY(FRONT))

                Print "Queue is Empty"

                Return

                [End of If Structure]

Step 2 :   VALUE = FRONT –> DATA

End PEEK()

2.7.4 Traversing a Queue

To read the information or to display the information in a queue, you have to traverse (move) a linked list, node by node from the FRONT node, until the REAR node is reached. Traversing a list involves the following steps,

- Assign the address of FRONT pointer to a variable.
- Display the information in the data field.
- Traverse the list from one node to another by advancing the pointer upto REAR.

Algorithm for Displaying the Contents of the Queue

VIEW(FRONT : QUEUE, REAR : QUEUE)

FIRST : QUEUE

Step 1 :   FIRST = FRONT

Step 2 :   If (FIRST == NULL AND REAR == NULL)

                Print "QUEUE is Empty"

                Return

                [End of If Structure]

Step 3 :   Print FIRST -> DATA

Step 4 :   If (FIRST != REAR)

                FIRST = FIRST -> NEXT

                Goto **Step 3**

                [End of If Structure]

End VIEW()

2.7.5 Empty Queue

*If a queue contains no elements, it is referred as an **empty queue**.* If an element is to be dequeued from a queue, you have to check whether the queue is empty or not, because elements cannot be dequeued from an empty queue. If the FRONT and REAR of the queue points to NULL in a linked list, it is referred as an empty queue. If you want to dequeue an element from an empty queue the output "Queue is underflow" is displayed.

Algorithm for IS_EMPTY()

> **IS_EMPTY(FRONT : QUEUE)**
> **Step 1 :**   If (FRONT == NULL)
>   Return 1
>   Else
>   Return 0
>   [End of If Structure]
> **End IS_EMPTY()**

2.7.6 Fully Occupied Queue

If a queue contains elements equal to its size, we say that the queue is full. If an element is to be enqueued into a queue, you have to check whether the queue is full or not, since elements cannot be enqueued into a queue when it is fully occupied. In case of queues, represented using linked lists, there is no limit to store the elements in the queue, since the memory required to store the elements of the queue is allocated dynamically using the `malloc()` function. However, if the memory required for storing the elements of the queue is not available, we cannot enqueue elements into a queue. If the `malloc()` function returns NULL in a linked list it is referred as an *fully occupied queue*. If you want to enqueue an element from a fully occupied queue the output "Queue is overflow" is displayed.

Algorithm for IS_FULL()

> **IS_FULL()**
> TEMP : QUEUE
> **Step 1 :**   TEMP = GETNODE()
> **Step 2 :**   If (TEMP == NULL)
>   Return 1
>   Else
>   RELEASENODE(TEMP)
>   Return 0
>   [End of If Structure]
> **End IS_FULL()**

2.7.7 Queue Size

In case of queues represented using linked lists, there is no limit to store the elements, since the memory required to store the elements of the queue is allocated dynamically using the `malloc()` *function.* To find the size of the queue, (i.e., number of elements that have been stored) to check whether the memory required for storing the elements of the queue is available or not, use the `size()` function as mentioned in *Program 2.7. Note that elements cannot be stored in a queue, when the memory pointed by the linked list points to NULL.*

Algorithm to Count the Nodes in a Queue

    SIZE(FRONT : QUEUE)

COUNT : INTEGER

Step 1 :   COUNT = 0

Step 2 :   If (FRONT == NULL)

          Return COUNT

          [End of If Structure]

Step 3 :   Do While(FRONT != NULL)

          COUNT = COUNT + 1

          FRONT = FRONT –> LINK

          [End of **Step 3** While Structure]

Step 4 :   Return COUNT

End SIZE()

Program 2.7 :

/* **Program to implement a Queue using singly linked list.** */

```c
/* linqueue.c */
#include<stdio.h>
typedef struct node
 {
   int data;
   struct node *link;
 }queue;
queue* getNode();
void releaseNode(queue *p);
int isFull();
int isEmpty(queue *front);
void enqueue(queue **frontptr, queue **rearptr, int value);
void dequeue(queue **frontptr, queue **rearptr, int *value);
void peek(queue *front, int *value);
void view(queue *front);
int size(queue *front);
void displayMenu(void);
```

```c
    void main()
    {
       queue  *front = NULL, *rear = NULL;
       int choice, item;
       displayMenu();
       while(1)
        {
          printf("\n ? ");
            scanf("%d", &choice);
          switch(choice)
           {
             case 1 :
                      if(isFull())
                        printf("\n Queue Overflow on ENQUEUE");
                      else
                       {
                         printf("\n Enter the element : ");
                         fflush(stdin);
                         scanf("%d", &item);
                         enqueue(&front, &rear, item);
                       }
                      break;
             case 2 :
                      if(isEmpty(front))
                        printf("\n Queue Underflow on DEQUEUE");
                      else
                       {
                         dequeue(&front, &rear, &item);
                         printf("\nThe dequeued value is %d", item);
                       }
                      break;
             case 3 :
                      if(!isEmpty(front))
                       {
                         peek(front, &item);
                         printf("\n The front value is %d", item);
                       }
```

```
                        else
                        printf("\n Queue is Empty");
                        break;
                case 4 :
                        printf("\nCount of Queue Elements=%d",size(front));
                        break;
                case 5 :
                        view(front);
                        break;
                default :
                        printf("\n End of run of your program . . .");
                        exit(0);
            }
        }
}
void displayMenu()
{
    printf("\n Representation of Queue using Linked List ...");
    printf("\n\t 1. Enqueue ");
    printf("\n\t 2. Dequeue ");
    printf("\n\t 3. Peek ");
    printf("\n\t 4. Size ");
    printf("\n\t 5. View ");
    printf("\n\t 6. Exit ");
}
void releaseNode(queue *p)
{
    free(p);
}
queue* getNode()
{
    int size;
    queue * newnode;
    size = sizeof(queue);
    newnode = (queue *)malloc(size);
    return(newnode);
}
```

```
    int isEmpty(queue *front)
     {
        if(front == NULL)                    /* Check for Empty Queue */
          return 1;
        else
          return 0;
     }
    int isFull()
     {
        queue * newnode;
        newnode = getNode();
        if(newnode == NULL)      /* Check for Fully Occupied Queue */
          return 1;
        releaseNode(newnode);
        return 0;
     }
    void enqueue(queue **frontptr,queue **rearptr, int value)
     {
        queue *newnode;
        if(isFull())
         {
        printf("\n Memory not available");
        return;
         }
        newnode = getNode();
        newnode->data = value;
        newnode->link = NULL;
        if(*frontptr == NULL)
           *frontptr = newnode;
        else
           (*rearptr)->link = newnode;
        *rearptr = newnode;
     }
    void dequeue(queue **frontptr, queue **rearptr, int *value)
     {
        queue *tempnode;
        if(isEmpty(*frontptr))
          return;
```

```c
        tempnode = *frontptr;
    *frontptr = (*frontptr) -> link;
    if(*frontptr == NULL)
        *rearptr = NULL;
    *value = tempnode -> data;
    releaseNode(tempnode);
}

void peek(queue *front, int *value)
{
    if(isEmpty(front))
     {
        printf("\n The queue is empty !!!");
        return;
     }
    *value = front -> data;
 }
void view(queue *front)
 {
    if(isEmpty(front))
     {
        printf("\n The queue is empty !!!");
        return;
     }
    printf("\n Queue contains ... Front -> ");
    while(front != NULL)
     {
        printf("%d --> ", front ->data);
        front = front -> link;
     }
    printf("Rear \n");
 }
int size(queue *front)
 {
    int count = 0;
    if(front == NULL)
        return count;
    for(;front != NULL;)
```

```
      {
          count++;
          front = front -> link;
      }
      return count;
}
```

The program displays the following output

```
Representation of Queue using Linked List ...

          1. Enqueue

          2. Dequeue

          3. Peek

          4. Size

          5. View

          6. Exit
? 2
Queue Underflow on DEQUEUE
? 3
Queue is Empty !!!
? 4
Count of Queue Elements = 0
? 5
The queue is empty !!!
? 1
Enter the element : 1
? 1
Enter the element : 2
? 1
Enter the element : 3
? 1
Enter the element : 4
? 5
Queue contains ... Front -> 11 -> 22 -> 33 -> 44 -> Rear
? 4
Count of Queue Elements = 4
? 3
The front value is 11
? 2
```

```
The dequeued value is 11
? 2
The dequeued value is 22
? 4
Count of Queue Elements = 2
? 5
Queue contains ... Front -> 33 -> 44 -> Rear
? 2
The dequeued value is 33
Queue contains ... Front -> 44 -> Rear
? 2
The dequeued value is 44
The queue is empty !!!
? 2
Queue Underflow on DEQUEUE
? 4
Count of Queue Elements = 0
? 5
The queue is empty !!!
? 6
End of Run of your Program . . .
```

2.8 Representation of Circular Queues using Arrays

The implementation part of the circular queue is same as that of the linear queue, except that the last position is connected to the first position of the queue. So the front end and rear end moves circularly.

Program 2.8 :

/* Program to implement a circular queue using arrays. */

```
/* cqueue.c */
#include<stdio.h>
#define QSIZE 5                       /* Size of the queue */
void displayMenu();
int isEmpty();
int isFull();
int enqueue(int value);
int dequeue(int *value);
int peek();
```

```
    void view();
    int queue[QSIZE], front= -1, rear = -1;
    void main()
     {
        int status, choice, data;
        displayMenu();
        while(1)
         {
            printf("\n ? ");
              scanf("%d", &choice);
            switch(choice)
             {
               case 1 :
                        printf("Enter the element : ");
                        fflush(stdin);
                          scanf("%d", &data);
                        status = enqueue(data);
                        if(status == -1)
                          printf("\nQueue overflow on ENQUEUE...");
                        break;
               case 2 :
                        status = dequeue(&data);
                        if(status == -1)
                          printf("\nQueue underflow on DEQUEUE ...");
                        else
                          printf("\nThe dequeued value is %d", data);
                        break;
               case 3 :
                        status = peek(&data);
                        if(status == -1)
                          printf("\n Queue is Empty");
                        else
                          printf("\n The Front value is %d", data);
                        break;
               case 4 :
                        printf("\n Total Queue Size is = %d", QSIZE);
                        printf("\n Current Queue Elements = %d", size());
                        break;
```

```
                case 5 :
                        view();
                        break;
                default:
                        printf("\n End of Run of your Program . . .");
                        exit(0);
            }
        }
    }
void displayMenu()
{
    printf("\n Representation of Linear Queue using Arrays ...");
    printf("\n\t 1. Enqueue ");
    printf("\n\t 2. Dequeue ");
    printf("\n\t 3. Peek ");
    printf("\n\t 4. Size ");
    printf("\n\t 5. View ");
    printf("\n\t 6. Exit ");
}
int isEmpty()
{
    extern int queue[], front, rear;
    if(front == -1 && rear == -1)           /* Check for Empty Queue */
        return 1;
    else
        return 0;
}
int isFull()
{
    extern int queue[], front, rear;
    if(((rear+1) % QSIZE) == front)         /* Check for Fully Occupied Queue */
        return 1;
    else
        return 0;
}
int enqueue(int value)
{
    extern int queue[], front, rear;
    if(isEmpty())                           /* Check for Empty Queue */
        front = rear = 0;
    else if(isFull())                       /* Check for Fully Occupied Queue */
        return -1;
```

```
        else
           rear = (rear + 1) % QSIZE;
        queue[rear] = value;
        return 0;
    }
    int dequeue(int *value)
    {
        extern int queue[], front, rear;
        if(isEmpty())                      /* Check for Empty Queue */
           return -1;
        *value = queue[front];
        if(front == rear)                  /* Check for Queue contains only one element */
           front = rear = -1;
        else
           front = (front + 1) % QSIZE;
        return 0;
    }
    int peek(int *value)
    {
        extern int queue[], front, rear;
        if(isEmpty())                      /* Check for Empty Queue */
           return -1;
        *value = queue[front];
        return 0;
    }

    int size()
    {
        extern int queue[], front, rear;
        int count, f;
        if(isEmpty())
           return 0;
        for(f = front, count = 1; f != rear; f = (f + 1) % QSIZE)
           count++;
        return count;
    }
    void view()
    {
        extern int queue[], front, rear;
        int f;
        if(isEmpty())
         {
           printf("\nQueue is EMPTY !!!");
           return;
         }
```

```
        printf("\nContent of the Queue is ... \n FRONT ->");
        for(f = front; f != rear; f = (f + 1) % QSIZE)
          printf(" %d -->", queue[f]);
        printf(" %d --> REAR", queue[f]);
        if( ((rear + 1) % QSIZE) == front)
            printf("\n Queue Size : %d \n Queue is FULL", QSIZE);
    }
```

2.9 Representation of Linear Dequeues using Arrays

One of the simplest ways of representing a deque is by means of a single dimensional array. Both deques and arrays are ordered collection of elements. However, an array and a deque are two different things. The number of elements in the array is fixed and it is not possible to change the number of elements stored in the array. But the size of a deque is constantly changed when elements are enqueued and dequeued. The deque is stored in a part of the array, so an array can be declared large enough to hold the maximum number of elements of the deque. During execution of a program, the deque size can be varied within the space reserved for it. One end of the array (i.e., bottom of the deque) is referred as the rear end and the other end of the array (i.e., top of the deque) is referred as the front end is constantly changed depending upon the elements enqueued or dequeued in the deque. Care must be taken in handling extreme cases, like not to insert an element into a fully occupied deque and not to delete an element from an empty deque.

To represent a linear deque using arrays, we need,

- An array to hold the elements of a deque, which can be of any data type such as int, float or char etc.,
- An integer (i.e., FRONT) to store the position of the first element of the deque.
- Another integer (i.e., REAR) to store the position of the last element of the deque.

2.9.1 Enqueue Operation

Enqueue is an operation used to add a new element in to a deque either at the front or rear end. When implementing the enqueue operation overflow condition of the deque is to be checked. (Since we cannot insert any data if the rear end is at the last position of the deque). The following procedure helps you to understand things better.

- Create a function **enqueue_FRONT()** with an argument (i.e., the element to be added at the front end of the deque).
- Create a function **enqueue_REAR()** with an argument (i.e., the element to be added at the rear end of the deque).

2.9.2 Dequeue Operation

Dequeue is an operation used to remove an element either at the front end or at the rear end of the deque. When implementing the dequeue operation, underflow condition of a deque is to be checked (i.e., You have to check whether the deque is empty or not). The user should not delete an element from an empty deque. This type of an attempt is illegal and should be avoided. If such an attempt is made, the user should be informed of the underflow condition.

The following procedure can help you to understand things better.

- Create a function **DEQUEUE_FRONT()** with an argument, the address of the element to store the dequeued value from the front.
- Create a function with an argument, the address of the element to store the dequeued value from the rear.

2.9.3 Empty Deque

If a deque contains no elements, it is referred as an *empty deque.* If an element is to be dequeued from a deque, you have to check whether the deque is empty or not, since elements cannot be dequeued from an empty deque nor contents cannot be displayed from an empty deque. The following procedure can help you to understand things better.

- Create a function **isEmpty()** with no arguments.
- Check whether the FRONT pointer and REAR pointer is equal to -1.
- If the condition is true, it means, that the deque is empty.
  Otherwise, the deque is not empty.

2.9.4 Fully Occupied Deque

If a deque contains elements equal to its size (i.e., QSIZE), we say that the deque is full. If an element is to be inserted into a deque, you have to check whether the deque is full or not, since elements cannot be inserted into a deque when it is fully occupied. The following procedure can help you to understand things better.

- Create a function **isFull()** with no arguments.
- Check whether the REAR pointer is equal to QSIZE – 1.
- If the condition is true, it means, that the deque is full. Otherwise, the deque is not full.

Program 2.9 :

/* **Program to implement a linear deque (double ended queue) using arrays.** */

```
/* ldeque.c */
#include<stdio.h>
#include<conio.h>
#include<stdlib.h>
#define QSIZE 5              /* Size of the deque */
void displayMenu();
int isEmpty();
int isFull();
int enqueueRear(int value);
```

```
int dequeueRear(int *value);
int enqueueFront(int value);
int dequeueFront(int *value);
int size();
void view();
int queue[QSIZE], front = -1, rear = -1;
void main()
{
    int status, choice, data;
    displayMenu();
    while(1)
    {
        printf("\n ? ");
        scanf("%d", &choice);
        switch(choice)
        {
            case 0 :
                    displayMenu();
                    break;
            case 1 :
                    printf("\nEnter the element : ");
                    fflush(stdin);
                    scanf("%d", &data);
                    status = enqueueFront(data);
                    if(status == -1)
                      printf("Deque Overflow on ENQUEUE at Front...");
                    break;
            case 2 :
                    printf("\nEnter the element : ");
                    fflush(stdin);
                    scanf("%d", &data);
                    status = enqueueRear(data);
                    if(status == -1)
                      printf("Deque Overflow on ENQUEUE at Rear...");
                    break;
            case 3 :
                    status = dequeueFront(&data);
```

```
                              if(status == -1)
                                printf("Deque Underflow on DEQUEUE at Front...");
                              else
                                printf("\nThe dequeued value is %d", data);
                              break;
                  case 4 :
                              status = dequeueRear(&data);
                              if(status == -1)
                                printf("\nDeque Underflow on DEQUEUE at Rear...");
                              else
                                printf("\nThe dequeued value is %d", data);
                              break;
                  case 5 :
                              printf("Number of elements in Deque is %d", size());
                              break;
                  case 6 :
                              view();
                              break;
                  default:
                              printf("\nEnd of Run of your Program . . .");
                              exit(0);
              }
          }
      }
  void displayMenu()
  {
      printf("\n Representation of Linear Deque using arrays ...");
      printf("\n\t 0. View Menu");
      printf("\n\t 1. Enqueue at Front");
      printf("\n\t 2. Enqueue at Rear");
      printf("\n\t 3. Dequeue at Front");
      printf("\n\t 4. Dequeue at Rear");
      printf("\n\t 5. Size of the Queue ");
      printf("\n\t 6. View ");
      printf("\n\t 7. Exit ");
  }
```

```c
    int isEmpty()
    {
       extern int queue[], front, rear;
       if(front == -1 && rear == -1)          /* Check for Empty Queue */
          return 1;
       else
          return 0;
    }

    int isFull()
    {
       extern int queue[], front, rear;
       if(rear == (QSIZE - 1))                /* Check for Occupied Queue */
          return 1;
       else
          return 0;
    }

    int enqueueFront(int value)
    {
       extern int queue[], front, rear;
       if(isEmpty())                          /* Check for Empty Deque */
          front = rear = 0;
       else if(isFull())                      /* Check for Front at first position */
          return -1;
       else
          front = front - 1;
       queue[front] = value;
       return 0;
    }

    int enqueueRear(int value)
    {
       extern int queue[], front, rear;
       if(isEmpty())                          /* Check for Empty Deque */
          front = rear = 0;
       else if(isFull())                      /* Check for Rear at last position */
          return -1;
```

```
        else
            rear = rear + 1;
    queue[rear] = value;
    return 0;
}
int dequeueFront(int *value)
{
    extern int queue[], front, rear;
    if(isEmpty())                        /* Check for Empty Deque */
        return -1;
    *value = queue[front];
    if(front == rear)                    /* Check for deque contains only one element */
        front = rear = -1;
    else
        front = front + 1;
    return 0;
}
int dequeueRear(int *value)
{
    extern int queue[], front, rear;
    if(isEmpty())                        /* Check for Empty Deque */
        return -1;
    *value = queue[rear];
    if(front == rear)                    /* Check for deque contains only one element */
        front = rear = -1;
    else
        rear = rear - 1;
    return 0;
}
int size()
{
    extern int queue[], front, rear;
    if(isEmpty())
        return 0;
    return (rear - front + 1);
}
```

```
void view()
 {
    extern int queue[], front, rear;
    int f;
    if(isEmpty())
     {
        printf("\nDeque is EMPTY !!!");
        return;
     }
    printf("\nContent of the deque is ... \n FRONT ->");
    for(f = front; f != rear; f = f + 1)
       printf(" %d -->", queue[f]);
    printf(" %d -> REAR", queue[f]);
    if(isFull())
       printf("\nDeque is FULL !!!");
 }
```

The program displays the following output

```
Representation of Linear Deque using arrays ...
          0. View Menu
          1. Enqueue at Front
          2. Enqueue at Rear
          3. Dequeue at Front
          4. Dequeue at Rear
          5. Size of the Queue
          6. View
          7. Exit
? 5
Number of elements in Deque is 0
? 6
Deque is EMPTY !!!
? 1
Enter the element : 100
? 6
Content of the deque is ...
FRONT -> 100 -> REAR
? 2
Enter the element : 200
? 6
Content of the deque is ...
FRONT -> 100 -> 200 -> REAR
```

```
? 1

Enter the element : 300
? 6

Content of the deque is ...

FRONT -> 300 -> 100 -> 200 -> REAR
? 2

Enter the element : 400
? 6

Content of the deque is ...

FRONT -> 300 -> 100 -> 200 -> 400 -> REAR
? 5

Number of elements in Deque is 4
? 3

The dequeued value is 300
? 6

Content of the deque is ...

FRONT -> 100 -> 200 -> 400 -> REAR
? 4

The dequeued value is 400
? 6

Content of the deque is ...

FRONT -> 100 -> 200 -> REAR
? 3

The dequeued value is 100
? 6

Content of the deque is ...

FRONT -> 200 -> REAR
? 4

The dequeued value is 200
? 6

Deque is EMPTY !!!
? 5

Number of elements in Deque is 0
? 7

End of Run of your Program . . .
```

2.10 Representation of Circular Deques using Arrays

The implementation part of the circular deque is same as that of the linear deque, except that the last position is connected to the first position of the deque. So the front end and rear end moves circularly.

Program 2.10 :

```
/* Program to implement a circular deque (double ended queue) using arrays. */
/* cdeque.c */
#include<stdio.h>
#include<conio.h>
#include<stdlib.h>
#define QSIZE 5                    /* Size of the deque */
void displayMenu();
int isEmpty();
int isFull();
int enqueueFront(int value);
int enqueueRear(int value);
int dequeueFront(int *value);
int dequeueRear(int *value);
int size();
void view();
int queue[QSIZE], front = -1, rear = -1;
void main()
  {
    int status, choice, data;
    displayMenu();
    while(1)
     {
       printf("\n ? ");
         scanf("%d", &choice);
       switch(choice)
        {
          case 0 :
                  displayMenu();
                  break;
          case 1 :
                  printf("\nEnter the element : ");
                  fflush(stdin);
                    scanf("%d", &data);
                  status = enqueueFront(data);
                  if(status == -1)
                    printf("\nDeque Overflow on ENQUEUE at Front...");
                  break;
```

```c
        case 2 :
                printf("\nEnter the element : ");
                fflush(stdin);
                  scanf("%d", &data);
                status = enqueueRear(data);
                if(status == -1)
                  printf("\nDeque Overflow on ENQUEUE at Rear...");
                break;
        case 3 :
                status = dequeueFront(&data);
                if(status == -1)
                  printf("\nDeque Underflow on DEQUEUE at Front...");
                else
                  printf("\nThe Dequeued value is %d", data);
                break;
        case 4 :
                status = dequeueRear(&data);
                if(status == -1)
                  printf("\nDeque Underflow on DEQUEUE at Rear...");
                else
                  printf("\nThe Dequeued value is %d", data);
                break;
        case 5 :
                printf("\n Total Queue Size is = %d", QSIZE);
                printf("\n Current Queue Elements = %d", size());
                break;
        case 6 :
                view();
                break;
        default:
                printf("\n End of Run of your Program ... ");
                exit(0);
        }
      }
}

void displayMenu()
  {
    printf("\n Representation of Circular Dequeue using Arrays ...");
    printf("\n\t 0. View Menu");
    printf("\n\t 1. Enqueue at Front");
```

```
        printf("\n\t 2. Enqueue at Rear");
        printf("\n\t 3. Dequeue at Front");
        printf("\n\t 4. Dequeue at Rear");
        printf("\n\t 5. Size of the Dequeue");
        printf("\n\t 6. View ");
        printf("\n\t 7. Exit ");
}
int isEmpty()
{
    extern int queue[], front, rear;
    if(front == -1 && rear == -1)          /* Check for Empty Queue */
       return 1;
    else
       return 0;

}
int isFull()
{
    extern int queue[], front, rear;
    if(((rear+1) % QSIZE) == front)        /* Check for Occupied Queue */
       return 1;
    else
       return 0;

}
int enqueueFront(int value)
{
    extern int queue[], front, rear;
    if(isEmpty())                          /*Check for Empty Deque */
       return -1;
    else if(isFull())                      /* Check for Full Deque */
       return -1;
    else if(front == 0)                    /* Check for Front at first position */
       front = QSIZE - 1;
    else
       front = front - 1;
    queue[front] = value;
    return 0;
}
```

```
   int enqueueRear(int value)
   {
      extern int queue[], front, rear;
      if(isEmpty())                              /* Check for Empty Deque */
        front = rear = 0;
      else if(isFull())                          /* Check for Full Deque */
        return -1;
      else
        rear = (rear + 1) % QSIZE;
      queue[rear] = value;
      return 0;
   }
   int dequeueFront(int *value)
   {
      extern int queue[], front, rear;
      if(isEmpty())                              /* Check for Empty Deque */
        return -1;
      *value = queue[front];
      if(front == rear)                          /* Check for Deque contains only one element*/
        front = rear = -1;
      else
        front = (front + 1) % QSIZE;
      return 0;
   }
   int dequeueRear(int *value)
   {
      extern int queue[], front, rear;
      if(isEmpty())                              /* Check for Empty Deque */
        return -1;
      *value = queue[rear];
      if(front == rear)                          /* Check for Deque contains only one element*/
        front = rear = -1;
      else if(rear == 0)                         /* Check for Rear at first position */
        rear = QSIZE - 1;
      else
        rear = rear - 1;
      return 0;
   }
```

```
    int size()
    {
        extern int queue[], front, rear;
        int count, f;
        if(isEmpty())
            return 0;
        for(f = front, count = 1; f != rear; f = (f + 1) % QSIZE)
            count++;
        return count;
    }
    void view()
    {
        extern int queue[], front, rear;
        int f;
        if(isEmpty())
        {
            printf("\n Deque is EMPTY !!!");
            return;
        }
        printf("\nContent of the Deque is ... \n FRONT -> ");
        for(f = front; f != rear; f = (f + 1) % QSIZE)
            printf(" %d -->", queue[f]);
        printf(" %d -> REAR", queue[f]);
        if(isFull())
            printf("\n Deque Size : %d \t Deque is FULL", QSIZE);
    }
```

2.11 Application of Queues – Priority Queue

Priority queue is a collection of elements, each containing a key referred as the *priority* for that element. The operations performed in a queue are similar to the queue except that the insertion and deletion elements made in it. Elements can be inserted in any order (i.e., of alternating priority), but are arranged in order of their priority value in the queue. The elements are deleted from the queue in the order of their priority (i.e., the elements with the highest priority is deleted first). The elements with the same priority are given equal importance and processed accordingly. *Program 2.11* helps you to understand things better.

Program 2.11 :

```c
/* Program to implement a priority queue using singly linked list. */
/* priqueue.c */
#include<stdio.h>
#include<string.h>
#include<stdlib.h>
#define MIN_AGE 20
#define MAX_AGE 50
typedef struct node
  {
    char name[80];
    int age;
    struct node *next;
  }priQue;
int enqueue(priQue *v);
int dequeue(priQue **v);
void displayMenu();
void view();
void displayDequeueData(priQue *data);
priQue *getNode();
priQue *front = NULL, *rear = NULL;
void main()
  {
    int status, choice;
    priQue *p;
    displayMenu();
    while(1)
      {
        printf("\n ? ");
          scanf("%d", &choice);
        switch(choice)
          {
            case 1 :
                    fflush(stdin);
                    printf("Enter the Name : ");
                      gets(p -> name);
                    fflush(stdin);
                    printf("Enter the age [Age limit is %d to %d] : ",
                                            MIN_AGE, MAX_AGE);
```

```
                              scanf("%d", &p -> age);
                      status = enqueue(p);
                      if(status == -1)
                        printf("\n Age is out of limits or
                                        Memory is Not Available ");
                      break;
            case 2 :
                      status = dequeue(&p);
                      if(status == -1)
                        printf("Queue Underflow on DEQUEUE");
                      else
                        displayDequeueData(p);
                      break;
            case 3 :
                      view();
                      break;
            default:
                      printf("\nEnd of Run of your Program . . .");
                      exit(0);
        }
    }
}
void displayMenu()
{
    printf("\n Priority Queue operation using singly linked list ...");
    printf("\n\t 1. Enqueue ");
    printf("\n\t 2. Dequeue ");
    printf("\n\t 3. View ");
    printf("\n\t 4. Exit ");
}
int enqueue(priQue *p)
{
    extern priQue *front, *rear;
    priQue *newptr, *f;
    newptr = getNode();
    if(newptr == NULL || p -> age < MIN_AGE || p -> age > MAX_AGE)
      return -1;
```

```
       strcpy(newptr -> name, p -> name);
     newptr -> age = p -> age;
     newptr -> next = NULL;
     if(front == NULL && rear == NULL)
       front = rear = newptr;
     else if(newptr -> age < front -> age)
       {
         newptr -> next = front;
         front = newptr;
       }
     else if(newptr -> age >= rear -> age)
       {
         rear -> next = newptr;
         rear  = newptr;
       }
     else
       {

         for(f = front; (newptr -> age >= f -> next -> age); f = f -> next);
           newptr -> next = f -> next;
         f -> next = newptr;
       }
     return 0;
   }
int dequeue(priQue **pp)
   {
     extern priQue *front, *rear;
     priQue *f;
     if(front == NULL && rear == NULL)
       return -1;
     *pp = front;
     if(front -> age == rear -> age)
       front = rear = NULL;
     else
       {
         for(f = front; front -> age == f -> next -> age; f = f-> next);
           front = f -> next;
         f -> next = NULL;
       }
     return 0;
   }
```

```
priQue *getNode()
 {
    return ((priQue *)malloc(sizeof(priQue)) );
 }
void view()
 {
    extern priQue *front, *rear;
    priQue *f;
    if(front == NULL && rear == NULL)
     {
       printf("\nThe Queue is EMPTY !!!");
       return;
     }
    printf("\nContent of Queue is... \n\t FRONT");
    for(f = front; f != rear; f = f -> next)
      printf(" -> [%s | %d]", f -> name, f -> age);
    printf(" -> [%s | %d] -> REAR", f -> name, f -> age);
 }
void displayDequeueData(priQue *f)
 {
    printf("\nThe Dequeued Value is... [%s | %d]", f->name, f->age);
    if(f -> next != NULL)
       displayDequeueData(f -> next);
 }
```

The program displays the following output

```
Priority Queue operation using singly linked list ...
          1. Enqueue
          2. Dequeue
          3. View
          4. Exit
? 2
Queue Underflow on DEQUEUE

? 3
The Queue is EMPTY !!!
? 1
Enter the Name : Ramu
Enter the age [Age limit is 20 to 50] :25
? 1
```

```
    Enter the Name : Raju
    Enter the age [Age limit is 20 to 50] :30
    ? 1
    Enter the Name : Manoj
    Enter the age [Age limit is 20 to 50] :25
    ? 1
    Enter the Name : Madhu
    Enter the age [Age limit is 20 to 50] :50
    ? 3
    Content of Queue is...
    FRONT -> [Ramu | 25] -> [Manoj | 25] -> [Raju | 30] -> [Madhu | 50] -> REAR
    ? 2
    The Dequeued Value is... [Ramu | 25]
    The Dequeued Value is... [Manoj | 25]
    ? 2
    The Dequeued Value is... [Raju | 30]
    ? 2
    The Dequeued Value is... [Madhu | 50]
    ? 2
    Queue Underflow on DEQUEUE
    ? 3
    The Queue is EMPTY !!!
    ? 4
    End of Run of your Program . . .
```

2.12 Summary

✍ Some of the important applications of linked lists are, stacks and queues.

✍ Stacks can be implemented by arrays or linked lists.

✍ A stack is an ordered collection of elements in which insertions and deletions are restricted to one end. The end from which elements are added and/or removed is referred to as top of the stack.

✍ Stacks are referred to as Last-In-First-Out (LIFO) lists or **piles** or **push-down lists**.

✍ The primitive operations that can be carried out in a stack are push, pop and peek operations.

✍ Push is an operation used to add a new element into a stack.

✍ Pop is an operation used to remove the top most elements from the stack.

- ✍ Peek is an operation used to display the top most element from the stack.

- ✍ In array representation of stacks, if a stack contains no elements, it is referred to as an empty stack.

- ✍ In array representation of stacks, if a stack contains elements equal to its size, it is referred to as an fully occupied stack.

- ✍ In a linked list, if the stack is pointing to NULL the stack is said to be an empty stack.

- ✍ If the malloc function returns NULL in a linked list it is referred as an fully occupied stack.

- ✍ Some of the important applications of stacks inlude tower of hanoi, reversing a string, checking for balanced parenthesis and evaluation of arithmetic expressions.

- ✍ Towers of Hanoi is a game in which we are given a tower of n disks, initially stacked in increasing size from top to bottom. Next to this tower, we have two more towers. The objective is to transfer the entire disks from Tower 1 to entire Tower 3 using Tower 2.

- ✍ Given an arithmetic expression, what we exactly mean by balanced is that, an opening parenthesis of various shapes (parenthesis, a square brace, or a flower brace) must match the corresponding last unmatched closing parenthesis symbol of the same shape and all parenthesis symbols must be matched when the arithmetic expression is finished.

- ✍ The different notations for representing arithmetic expressions are infix, prefix and postfix notations.

- ✍ The normal way of expressing mathematical expressions is called as infix notation.

- ✍ Prefix notation also referred, as polish notation is a way of writing algebraic expressions without the use of parenthesis or rules of operator precedence.

- ✍ Postfix notation also referred, as suffix form or reverse polish notation (or RPN) is also a way of writing algebraic expressions without the use of parentheses or rules of operator precedence.

- ✍ A queue is an ordered collection of elements in which insertions are made at one end and deletion are made at the other end. The end at which insertions are made is referred to as the rear end, and the end from which deletions are made is referred to as the front end.

- ✍ The primitive operations that can be carried out in a queue are enqueue and dequeue operations.

✍ Enqueue is an operation used to add a new element into the rear end of a queue.

✍ Dequeue is an operation used to remove an element from the front end of a queue.

✍ Circular queue is another form of a linear queue in which the last node is connected to the first node of the list.

✍ Deque (Double–ended queue) is another form of a queue in which insertions and deletions are made at both the front and rear ends of the queue.

✍ There are two variations of a deque, namely input restricted deque and output restricted deque. The input restricted deque allows insertion at one end (it can be either front or rear) only. The output restricted deque allows deletion at one end (it can be either front or rear) only.

✍ The implementation part of the circular queue is same as that of the linear queue, except that the last position is connected to the first position of the queue. So the front end and rear end moves circularly.

✍ The implementation part of the circular deque is same as that of the linear deque, except that the last position is connected to the first position of the deque. So the front end and rear end moves circularly.

2.13 Short-answer Questions

1. *Mention some of the application of linked lists.*

Some of the appliations of linked lists are,
- Polynomial Manipulation
- Stacks
- Queues.

2. *Draw node of a polynomial & its representation using a singly linked list.*

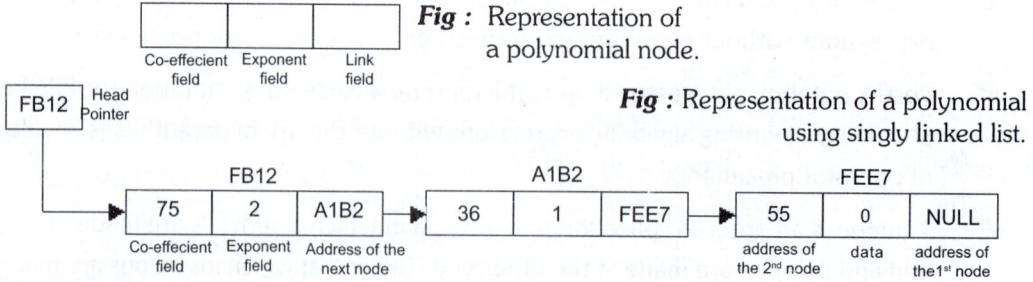

Fig : Representation of a polynomial node.

Fig : Representation of a polynomial using singly linked list.

3. *Define a stack.*

Stack is an ordered collection of elements in which insertions and deletions are restricted to one end. The end from which elements are added and/or removed is referred to as top of the stack. Stacks are also referred as "piles" and "push-down lists".

4. *List out the basic opeartions that can be performed on a stack and a queue.*

The basic operations that can be performed on a stack and queue are,

- Push operation
- Pop operation
- View stack contents.

5. *State the different ways of representing expressions.*

The different ways of representing expressions are,

- Infix notation
- Prefix notation
- Postfix notation.

6. *State the avantages of using infix notations.*

The advantages of using infix notations are,

- It is the mathematical way of representing the expression.
- It's easier to see visually which operation is done from first to LAST.

7. *State the avantages of using postfix notations.*

The advantages of using postfix notations are,

- You need not worry about the rules of precedence.
- You need not worry about the rules for right to left associativity.
- You need not need parenthesis to override the above rules.

8. *State the rules to be followed during infix to postfix conversions.*

The rules to be followed during infix to postfix conversions are,

- Fully parenthesize the expression starting from left to right (During parenthesizing, the operators having higher precedence are first parenthesized).
- Move the operators one by one to their right, such that each operator replaces their corresponding right parenthesis.
- The part of the expression, which has been converted into postfix, is to be treated as single operand.
- Once the expression is converted into postfix form, remove all parenthesis.

9. *Mention the advantages of representing stacks using linked lists than arrays.*

The advantages of representing stacks using linked lists than arrays.

- It is not necessary to specify the number of elements to be stored in a stack during its declaration (since memory is allocated dynamically at run time when an element is added to the stack).
- Insertions and deletions can be handled easily and efficiently.
- Linked list representation of stacks can grow & shrink in size without wasting the memory space, depending upon the insertion & deletion that occurs in the list.
- Multiple stacks can be represented efficiently using a chain for each stack.

10.   *State the rules to be followed during infix to prefix conversions.*

The rules to be followed during infix to prefix conversions are,

- Fully parenthesize the expression starting from left to right (During parenthesizing, the operators having higher precedence are first parenthesized).
- Move the operators one by one to their left, such that each operator replaces their corresponding left parenthesis.
- The part of the expression, which has been converted into prefix, is to be treated as single operand.
- Once the expression is converted into postfix form, remove all parenthesis.

11.   *State the difference between stacks and linked lists.*

The difference between stacks and linked lists is that insertions and deletions may occur any where in a linked list, but only at the top of the stack.

12.   *Mention the advantages of representing stacks using linked lists than arrays.*

The advantages of representing stacks using linked lists than arrays.

- It is not necessary to specify the number of elements to be stored in a stack during its declaration (since memory is allocated dynamically at run time when an element is added to the stack).
- Insertions and deletions can be handled easily and efficiently.
- Linked list representation of stacks can grow & shrink in size without wasting the memory space, depending upon the insertion & deletion that occurs in the list.
- Multiple stacks can be represented efficiently using a chain for each stack.

13.   *Define a queue.*

Queue is an ordered collection of elements in which insertions and deletions are restricted to one end. The end from which elements are added and/or removed is referred to as the rear end, and the end from which deletions are made is referred to as the front end.

14.   *Define a priority queue.*

Priority queue is a collection of elements, each containing a key referred as the priority for that element. Elements can be inserted in any order (i.e., of alternating priority), but are arranged in order of their priority value in the queue. The elements are deleted from the queue in the order of their priority (i.e., the elements with the highest priority is deleted first). The elements with the same priority are given equal importance and processed accordingly.

15.   *State the difference between queues and linked lists.*

The difference between queues and linked lists is that insertions and deletions may occur anywhere in linked list, but in queues insertions can be made only in the rear end and deletions can be made only in the front end.

16.   *Define a deque.*

Deque (Double–ended queue) is another form of a queue in which insertions and deletions are made at both the front and rear ends of the queue. There are two variations of a deque, namely, input restricted deque and output restricted deque. The input restricted deque allows insertion at one end (it can be either front or rear) only. The output restricted deque allows deletion at one end (it can be either front or rear) only.

Chapter 3
Non-Linear Data Structures
—Trees

3.1 Introduction

The data structures that we have seen in **Chapter 1** is linear data structures, as they have a linear relationship between its adjacent elements. The data structures that we are going to see in this chapter are non-linear data structures, since they don't have a linear relationship between its adjacent elements. In a linear data structure, each node has a link which points to another node, where as in a non-linear data structure, each node may point to several other nodes. Some of the non-linear data structures include, trees and graphs.

A *tree* is a non-linear, two-dimensional data structure, which represents hierarchical relationships between individual data items. *Fig. 3.1* shows a simple tree structure. Natural trees grow upwards from the ground into the air. But the tree data structure grows downwards from top to bottom. This is the universally accepted way of representing tree data structure. A *tree* is a non-empty collection of nodes and edges that satisfies the following requirements.

- It has a special data item referred as the root of the tree.
- All remaining data items are partitioned into number of subsets, each of which itself is a tree, and are referred as **subtrees**.

Each data item in a tree is referred as a *node*. It is the basic structure of a tree. It specifies the information part of each data item. There are totally 24 nodes in the tree represented in *Fig. 3.1*. An *edge* also referred as a *link* is a connection between two nodes. A *path* in a tree is a sequence of distinct nodes in which successive nodes are connected by edges in the tree. In *Fig. 3.1,* the path between A and X is given by the node pairs (A,C), (C,H), (H,Q) and (Q, X). An important property of a tree is that there should be precisely one path connecting any two nodes. If there is no path between some pair of nodes, or if there is more than one path between some pair of nodes, then we call the structure as a *graph* and not a tree.

The highest level or the first level in a tree is referred as a *root* or *root node*. In *Fig. 3.1*, A is referred as the root node. Each link to the root node refers to a *child* or *child node*. In *Fig. 3.1,* nodes B, C, D and E are referred as child nodes to the parent node A. A link between a parent node and its child node is also referred as a *branch*. All nodes in a tree, except the root node must descend from a parent node via a branch. The child nodes of a given parent node are referred as *siblings*. In *Fig. 3.1,* nodes B, C, D and E are referred as siblings to its parent node A, where as F and G are siblings of its parent node B and so on.

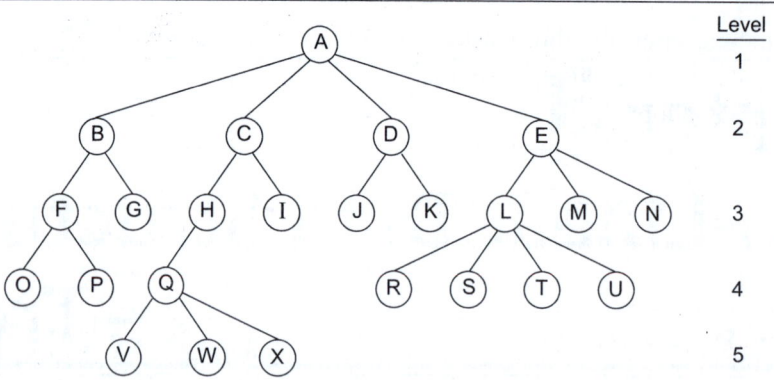

Fig. 3.1 : A tree structure.

In the hierarchy represented by a tree, the child nodes of a parent are one level lower than the parent node. The entire tree structure is leveled in such a way that the root node is always at level 1. Then, its immediate children are at level 2 and their immediate children are at level 3 and so on. In general, if a node is at level n, then its children will be at level (n+1).Thus in *Fig. 3.1,* the root node A is at level 1, its child nodes B, C, D and E are at level 2 and so on. A subset of a tree that is itself a tree is called as a **subtree**. The number of subtrees in a node isn referred as its **degree**. In *Fig. 3.1,* the degree of the root node A is 4, degree of node B is 2, where as the degree of the node L is 4.

The ancestors of a node are all the nodes along the path from the root to that node. The root node of the tree is the ancestor of all the nodes in the tree. In *Fig. 3.1,* the ancestors of node O is A, B, and F. Each node in a tree can be a parent and can have any number of child nodes to it. A node that has no children (i.e., with zero degree) is called as a *leaf* or *terminal node*. All other intermediate nodes that traversing the given tree from its root node to the terminal nodes are referred as ***non-terminal nodes***. In *Fig. 3.1,* there are totally 15 terminal nodes (i.e., G, I, K, M, N, O, P, R, S, T, U, V, W and X) and 9 non-terminal nodes (i.e., A, B, C, D, E, F, H, L, Q and X).

The *height* or *depth* of a tree is defined as the maximum level of any node in the tree. In *Fig. 3.1,* root node A has the maximum level, which descends to the bottom of the tree at V, W and X. The height of the tree shown in *Fig. 3.1* is 5. In a given tree, if you remove the root node, then it becomes a forest. In *Fig. 3.1,* if you remove the root node A, then it becomes a forest with four trees.

3.2 Binary Tree Traversal

One of the most important operations performed on a binary tree is its traversal. *Traversing a binary tree means moving through all the nodes in the binary tree, visiting each node in the tree exactly once.* For linked list, the nodes are in natural order from first to last and hence traversal follows the same order. However, for trees the nodes are not in order, hence we have to follow a different procedure for traversing all the nodes. One thing to be kept in mind while traversing a binary tree is that treat each node and its subtrees in the same fashion. The tasks performed while traversing a binary tree are,

- Visiting a node (denoted by the letter V)
- Traversing the left subtree (denoted by the letter L)
- Traversing the right subtree (denote by the letter R).

Depending upon the three tasks there are six possible combinations of traversals. They are VLR, LVR, LRV, VRL, RVL, and RLV. These six traversals can be reduced to three combinations by adopting the convention, that we always traverse the left subtree before the right subtree. Depending on the factor, the possible combinations are,

- V L R (designated as Preorder traversal)
- L V R (designated as Inorder traversal)
- L R V (designated as Postorder traversal).

3.2.1 Preorder Traversal

The steps for traversing a binary tree in preorder traversal are,

- Process the root node.
- Traverse the left subtree.
- Traverse the right subtree.

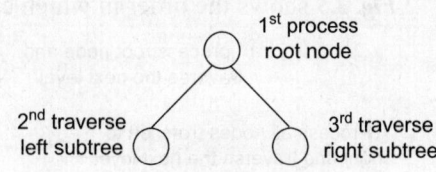

Fig. 3.2 :
Preorder traversal.

The value of in each node is processed as the node is visited. Preorder traversal leads to prefix expressions. *Fig. 3.2* shows the order in which each node is visited in preorder traversal.

3.2.2 Inorder Traversal

The steps for traversing a binary tree in preorder traversal also referred as *symmetric order traversal* are,

- Traverse the left subtree.
- Process the root node.
- Traverse the right subtree.

Fig. 3.3 :
Inorder traversal.

Inorder traversal leads to infix expressions. *Fig. 3.3* shows the order in which each node is visited in inorder traversal. The inorder traversal of a binary tree points the values always in ascending order, and hence this process is referred as the binary tree sort.

3.2.3 Postorder Traversal

The steps for traversing a binary tree in postorder traversal also referred as *end order traversal* are,

- Traverse the left subtree.
- Traverse the right subtree.
- Process the root node.

Fig. 3.4 :
Postorder traversal.

Postorder traversal leads to postfix expressions. *Fig. 3.4* shows the order in which each node is visited in postorder traversal.

3.2.4 Level order Traversal

In level order traversal, we traverse the nodes according to their levels. The steps for traversing a binary tree in level order traversal are,

- Process the root node at level 1.
- Traverse the next level (i.e, level 2), below the root node.
- Process the nodes from left to right in that level.
- Similarly traverse the next level and process the nodes from left to right and continue till the end of levels.

Fig. 3.5 shows the order in which each node is visited in level order traversal.

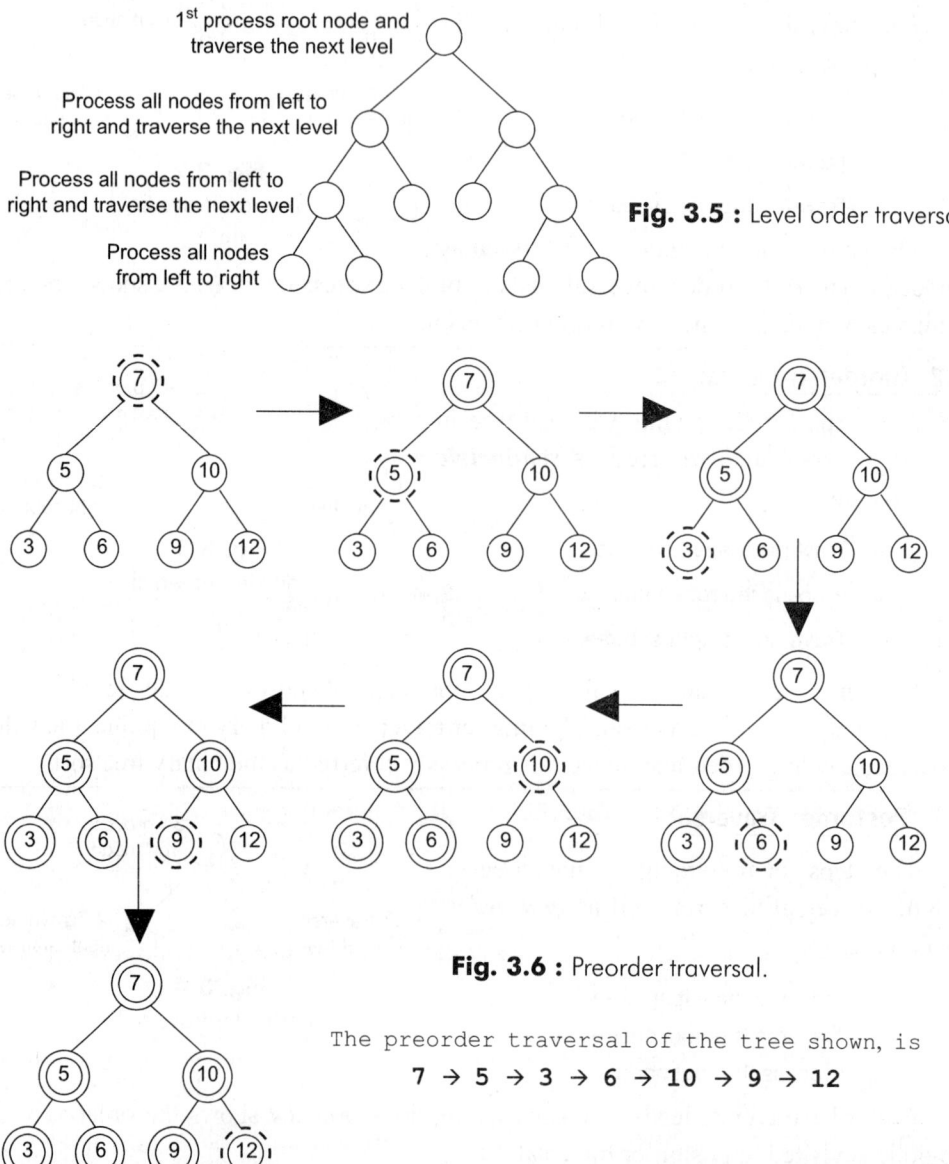

Fig. 3.5 : Level order traversal.

Fig. 3.6 : Preorder traversal.

The preorder traversal of the tree shown, is

7 → 5 → 3 → 6 → 10 → 9 → 12

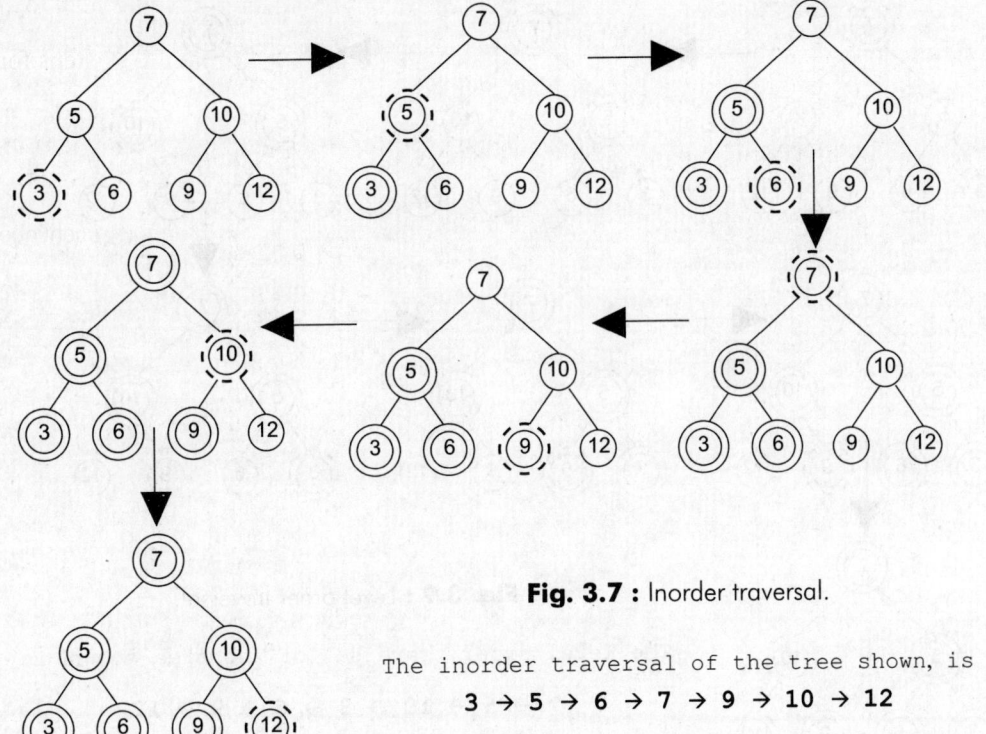

Fig. 3.7 : Inorder traversal.

The inorder traversal of the tree shown, is

3 → 5 → 6 → 7 → 9 → 10 → 12

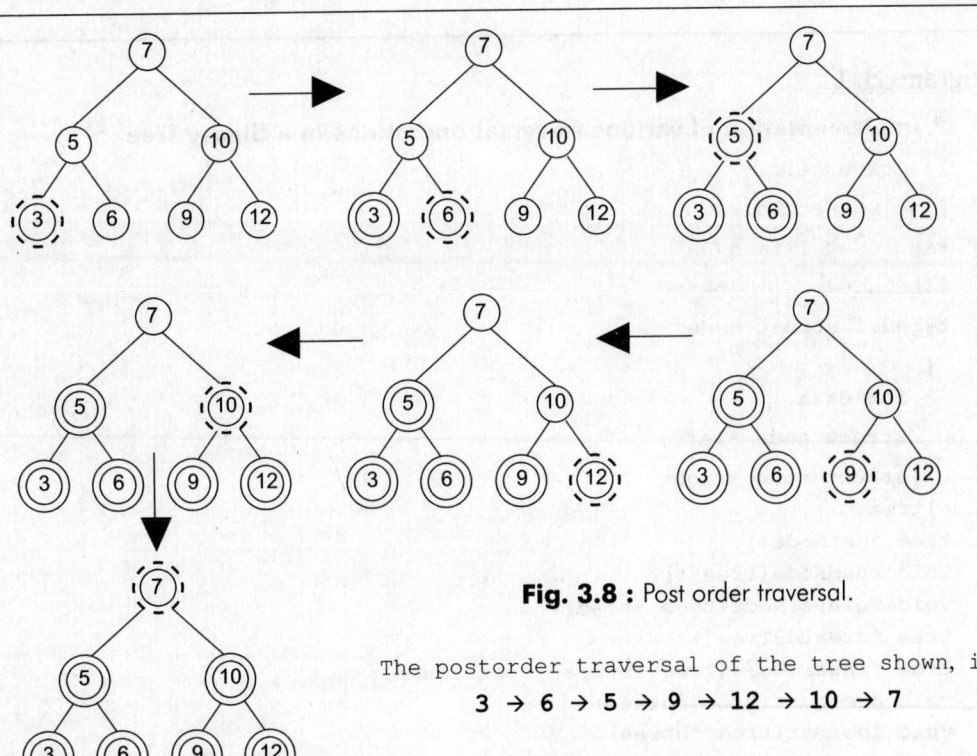

Fig. 3.8 : Post order traversal.

The postorder traversal of the tree shown, is

3 → 6 → 5 → 9 → 12 → 10 → 7

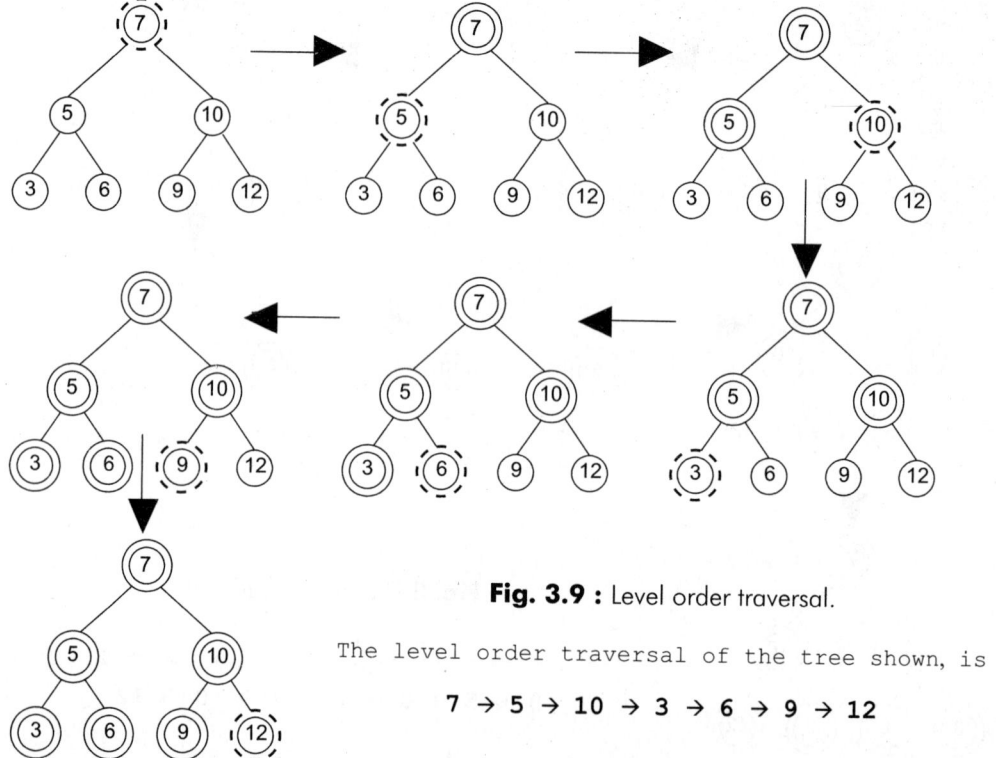

Fig. 3.9 : Level order traversal.

The level order traversal of the tree shown, is

$$7 \to 5 \to 10 \to 3 \to 6 \to 9 \to 12$$

<u>**Program 3.1 :**</u>

/* **Implementation of various traversal operations in a Binary Tree.** */

```c
/* traverse.c */
#include<stdio.h>
#include<alloc.h>
#include<stdlib.h>
typedef struct node
  {
    int data;
    struct node *left;
    struct node *right;
  }tree;
tree *getNode();
void readNode(tree *);
void releaseNode(tree *head);
tree *createBTree();
tree *insertNode(tree *btree, tree *temp);
void preorder(tree *btree);
void inorder(tree *btree);
```

```c
void postorder(tree *btree);
void levelorder(tree *btree);
tree *queue[30];
int front, rear;
int isEmpty();
void enqueue(tree* btree);
int dequeue(tree **dqdata);
void main()
 {
   int choice;
   tree *btree;
   printf("\nCreate a New Binary Tree");
   btree = createBTree();
   printf("\n TREE TRAVERSAL ");
   printf("\n\t 1. Preorder Traversal ");
   printf("\n\t 2. Inorder Traversal ");
   printf("\n\t 3. Postorder Traversal ");
   printf("\n\t 4. Levelorder Traversal ");
   printf("\n ? ");
     scanf("%d", &choice);
   if(btree == NULL)
    {
      printf("Binary Tree is Empty");
      return;
    }
   switch(choice)
    {
      case 1 :
              printf("Preorder Binary tree traversal is ... \n");
              preorder(btree);
              break;
      case 2 :
              printf("Inorder Binary tree traversal is ... \n");
              inorder(btree);
              break;
      case 3 :
              printf("Postorder Binary tree traversal is ... \n");
              postorder(btree);
              break;

      case 4 :
              printf("Levelorder Binary tree traversal is ... \n");
              levelorder(btree);
              break;
    }
```

```
      releaseNode(btree);
   }
tree* getNode()
   {
      int size;
      tree * newnode;
      size = sizeof(tree);
      newnode = (tree *)malloc(size);
      return(newnode);
   }
void readNode(tree* newnode)
   {
      printf("\nEnter the Data : ");
         scanf("%d", &newnode->data);
      newnode->left  = NULL;
      newnode->right = NULL;
   }
void releaseNode(tree* head)
   {
      free(head);
   }
tree *createBTree()
   {
      char ch;
      tree *btree = NULL, *temp;
      do
       {
          temp = getNode();
          readNode(temp);
          btree = insertNode(btree, temp);
          fflush(stdin);
          printf("Do u wish to Add Data in the Tree (y/n) ? ");
             scanf("%c", &ch);
       }while( (ch == 'y') || (ch == 'Y') );
      return btree;
   }
tree *insertNode(tree *btree, tree *temp)
   {
      if(btree == NULL)
         return temp;

      else if(temp->data < btree->data)
         btree->left = insertNode(btree->left,temp);
      else if(temp->data > btree->data)
         btree->right = insertNode(btree->right,temp);
      else if(temp->data == btree->data)
```

```
      {
         printf("\n Data is already Existing ... ");
         return btree;
      }
      return btree;
   }

   void inorder(tree *btree)
   {
      if(btree != NULL)
       {
         inorder(btree->left);
         printf(" %d ", btree->data);
         inorder(btree->right);
       }
   }

   void preorder(tree *btree)
   {
      if(btree != NULL)
       {
         printf(" %d ", btree->data);
         preorder(btree->left);
         preorder(btree->right);
       }
   }

   void postorder(tree *btree)
   {
      if(btree != NULL)
       {
         postorder(btree->left);
         postorder(btree->right);
         printf(" %d ", btree->data);
       }
   }

   void levelorder(tree *btree)
   {
      enqueue(btree);
      while(!isEmpty())
       {
         dequeue(&btree);

         if(btree != NULL)
          {
            printf(" %d ", btree->data);
            enqueue(btree->left);
            enqueue(btree->right);
          }
       }
   }
```

```
    int isEmpty()
    {
       if(front == -1 && rear == -1)
         return 1;
       else
         return 0;
    }
    void enqueue(tree* btree)
    {
       if(isEmpty())
         front = rear = 0;
       else
         rear = rear + 1;
       queue[rear] = btree;
       return 0;
    }

    int dequeue(tree **dqdata)
    {
       if(isEmpty())
         return -1;
       *dqdata = queue[front];
       if(front == rear)
         front = rear = -1;
       else
         front = front + 1;
       return 0;

    }
```

The program displays the following output

RUN 1

```
    Enter data to Create a New Binary Tree ...

    Enter the Data : 7
    Do u wish to Add Data in the Tree (y/n) ? y

    Enter the Data : 5
    Do u wish to Add Data in the Tree (y/n) ? y

    Enter the Data : 10
    Do u wish to Add Data in the Tree (y/n) ? y


    Enter the Data : 3
    Do u wish to Add Data in the Tree (y/n) ? y

    Enter the Data : 6
    Do u wish to Add Data in the Tree (y/n) ? y

    Enter the Data : 9
    Do u wish to Add Data in the Tree (y/n) ? y
```

```
Enter the Data : 12
Do u wish to Add Data in the Tree (y/n) ? n

 TREE TRAVERSAL
            1. Preorder Traversal
            2. Inorder Traversal
            3. Postorder Traversal
            4. Levelorder Traversal
 ? 1
```

Preorder Binary tree traversal is ...
7   5   3   6   10   9   12

RUN2

```
Enter data to Create a New Binary Tree ...

Enter the Data : 7
Do u wish to Add Data in the Tree (y/n) ? y

Enter the Data : 5
Do u wish to Add Data in the Tree (y/n) ? y

Enter the Data : 10
Do u wish to Add Data in the Tree (y/n) ? y

Enter the Data : 3
Do u wish to Add Data in the Tree (y/n) ? y

Enter the Data : 6
Do u wish to Add Data in the Tree (y/n) ? y

Enter the Data : 9
Do u wish to Add Data in the Tree (y/n) ? y

Enter the Data : 12
Do u wish to Add Data in the Tree (y/n) ? n

 TREE TRAVERSAL
            1. Preorder Traversal

            2. Inorder Traversal

            3. Postorder Traversal

            4. Levelorder Traversal
 ? 2
```

Inorder Binary tree traversal is ...
3   5   6   7   9   10   12

RUN3

```
Enter data to Create a New Binary Tree ...

Enter the Data : 7
Do u wish to Add Data in the Tree (y/n) ? y

Enter the Data : 5
Do u wish to Add Data in the Tree (y/n) ? y

Enter the Data : 10
```

```
Do u wish to Add Data in the Tree (y/n) ? y

Enter the Data : 3
Do u wish to Add Data in the Tree (y/n) ? y

Enter the Data : 6
Do u wish to Add Data in the Tree (y/n) ? y

Enter the Data : 9
Do u wish to Add Data in the Tree (y/n) ? y

Enter the Data : 12
Do u wish to Add Data in the Tree (y/n) ? n

  TREE TRAVERSAL
              1. Preorder Traversal

              2. Inorder Traversal

              3. Postorder Traversal

              4. Levelorder Traversal
? 3
```

Postorder Binary tree traversal is ...
3   6   5   9   12   10   7

```
Enter data to Create a New Binary Tree ...

Enter the Data : 7
Do u wish to Add Data in the Tree (y/n) ? y

Enter the Data : 5
Do u wish to Add Data in the Tree (y/n) ? y

Enter the Data : 10
Do u wish to Add Data in the Tree (y/n) ? y

Enter the Data : 3
Do u wish to Add Data in the Tree (y/n) ? y

Enter the Data : 6
Do u wish to Add Data in the Tree (y/n) ? y

Enter the Data : 9
Do u wish to Add Data in the Tree (y/n) ? y

Enter the Data : 12
Do u wish to Add Data in the Tree (y/n) ? n

  TREE TRAVERSAL
              1. Preorder Traversal

              2. Inorder Traversal

              3. Postorder Traversal

              4. Levelorder Traversal
? 4
```

Level Binary tree traversal is ...
7   5   10   3   6   9   12

3.3 Binary Trees

One of the most important tree structures is the binary tree. *A **binary tree** is a tree that has nodes either empty or not more than two child nodes, each of which may be a leaf node. Fig. 3.10* shows the structure of a binary tree. Each node in a binary tree has two subtrees, the

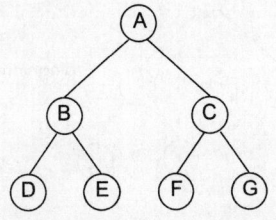

Fig. 3.10 : A binary tree structure.

left subtree and the right subtree. All the nodes to the left of a given node in a binary tree are referred as *left subtrees*. All the nodes to the right of a given node in a binary tree are referred as the *right subtrees*. In *Fig. 3.10* B, D, and F are the left subtrees and C, E and G are the right subtrees.

3.3.1 Types of Binary Trees

Left-skewed binary tree   A binary tree, which has only left child nodes.

Right-skewed binary tree   A binary tree, which has only right child nodes.

Full binary tree   A binary tree in which all the leaves are on the same level and every non-leaf node has exactly two children.

Complete binary tree   A binary tree in which every non-leaf node has exactly two children not necessarily to be on the same level.

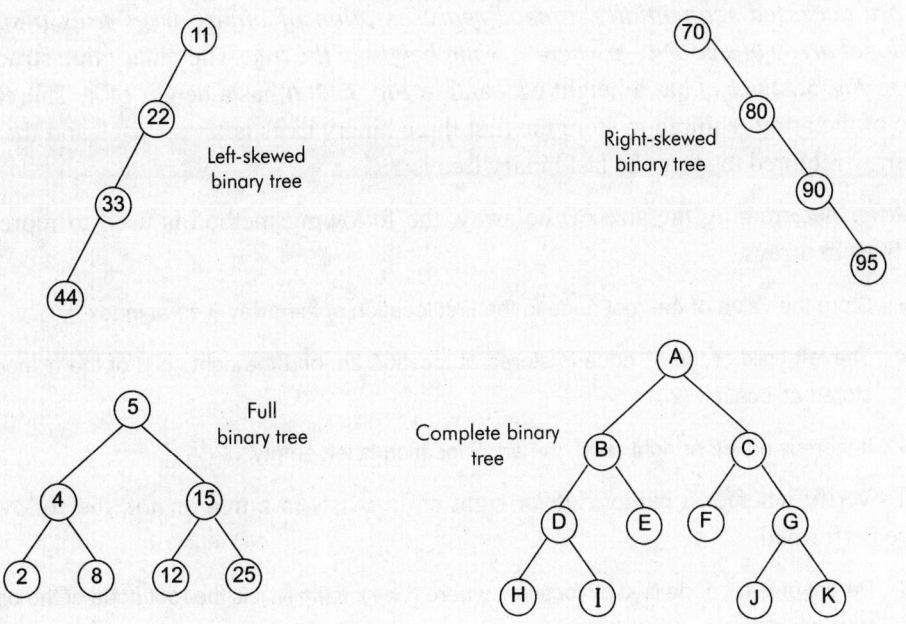

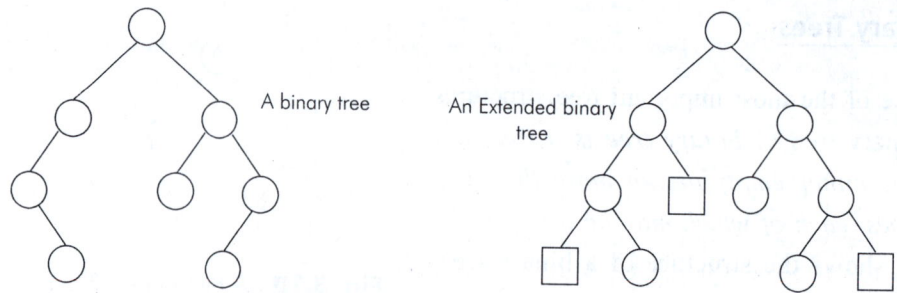

Fig. 3.11 : Examples of binary trees.

Properties of a binary tree

- The maximum number of nodes on level n of a binary tree is 2^{n-1}, where $n \geq 1$.

- The maximum number of nodes in a binary tree of height n is 2^{n-1}, where $n \geq 1$.

- For any non-empty tree, $n_l = n_d + 1$ where n_l is the number of leaf nodes and n_d is the number of nodes of degree 2.

3.4 Representation of Binary Trees

Representing a binary tree can be carried out in two ways. They are,

- Linear representation (using arrays)

- Linked representation (using pointers).

3.4.1 Linear Representation of Binary Trees

An array can be used to store the nodes of a binary tree. The nodes stored in an array are accessed sequentially. Linear representation of binary trees uses a single dimensional array of size $2^{h+1} - 1$ where h is the height of the tree. The binary tree structure shown in **Fig. 3.12 (a,b,c)** has a height of 3 and in **Fig. 3.12(d)** has a height of 4. Therefore, the size of the array required to store the first three binary trees is $2^{3+1} - 1 = 15$ and the size of the array required to store the last binary tree is $2^{4+1} - 1 = 31$.

After determining the size of the array, the following method is used to represent binary trees in arrays.

- Store the value of the root node in the first location of the array (i.e., at index = 1).

- The left child of the nth node is stored at location 2n, and the right child of the nth node is stored at location (2n+1).

- If there is no left or right child, the array location is left empty.

To verify whether a parent, left or right child exists in a tree or not, the following steps are performed.

- Parent of the ith node is at i/2 location, where (i ≠ 1). If (i =1), it is the root node of the binary tree, which has no parent node.

- Left child of the ith node is at $2i$ where $(2i \leq n)$. If $(2i > n)$, then the ith node has no left child.

- Right child of the ith node is at $(2i + 1)$, where $(2i + 1) \leq n$. If $(2i + 1) > n$, then the ith node has no right child.

Fig. 3.13 shows the linear representation using arrays for binary trees in ***Fig. 3.12***. The main advantage of representing a binary tree using arrays is simplicity and ease of implementation, but in most cases, there will be a lot of unutilized space. A full binary tree will not waste any spaces, where as complete binary trees or skewed binary trees, utilises a considerable amount of space. Insertions and deletions in a node, take an excessive amount of processing time, due to up and down data movement in an array.

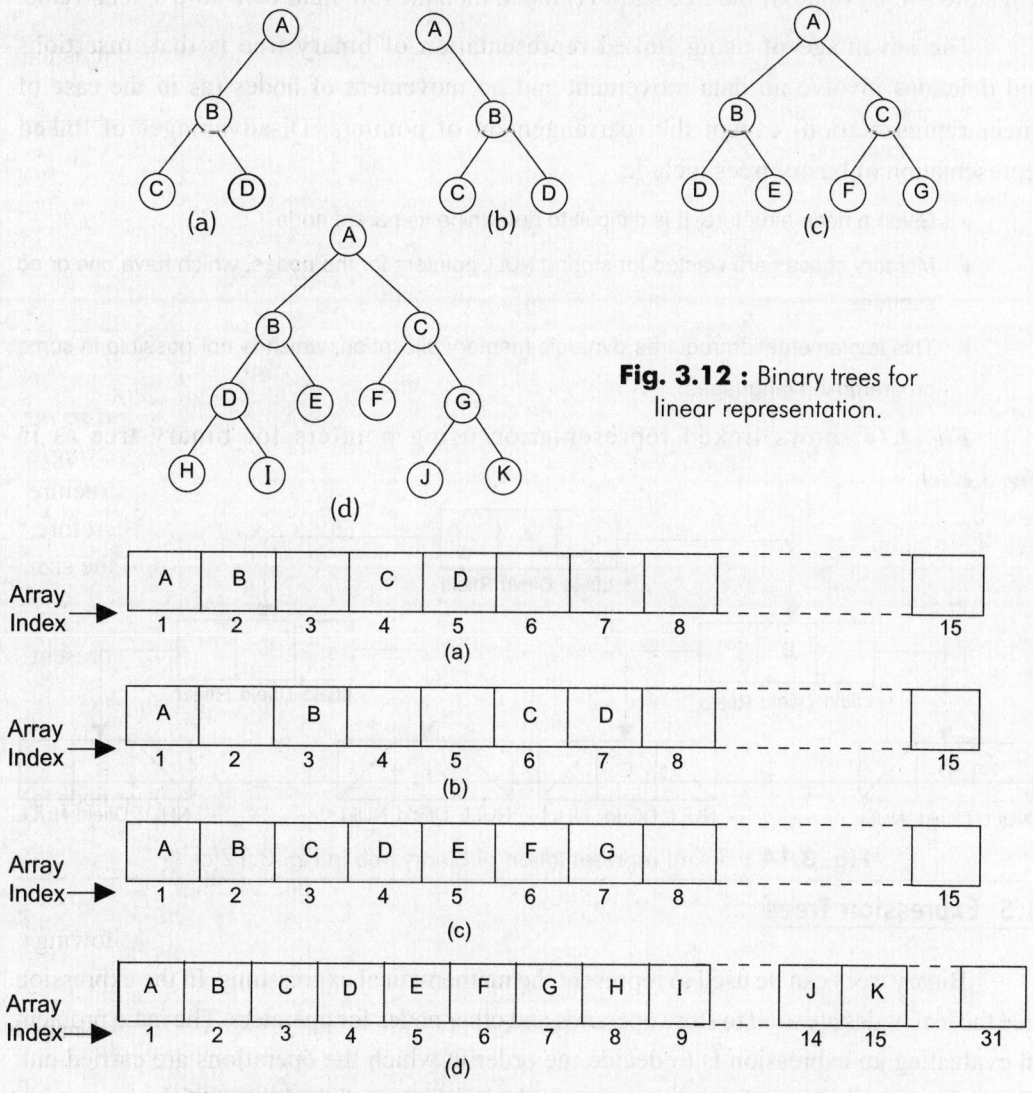

Fig. 3.12 : Binary trees for linear representation.

Fig. 3.13 : Linear representation of binary trees in Fig. 3.12.

3.4.2   Linked Representation of Binary Trees

The disadvantages of linear representation of binary trees, such as wasting memory space and difficulty in inserting and deleting a node in a tree are overcome by representing binary trees in linked representation. As we know that each node in a binary tree has two child nodes, each node in a linked representation requires 3 fields, the left child field (denoted as *Lfield*), the right child field (denoted as *Rfield*) and the data field (denoted as *Dfield*). Further, the root field contains the location of the root node. Hence, it requires 3 arrays and a variable to implement linked representation of binary trees. If any subtree is empty, then the corresponding pointers (i.e., Lfield and Rfield) will store a NULL value. If the tree itself is empty, then the root field will store a NULL value.

The advantage of using linked representation of binary tree is that, insertions and deletions involve no data movement and no movement of nodes (as in the case of linear representation) except the rearrangement of pointers. Disadvantages of linked representation of binary trees include,

- Given a node structure, it is difficult to determine its parent node.
- Memory spaces are wasted for storing NULL pointers for the nodes, which have one or no subtrees.
- This implementation requires dynamic memory allocation, which is not possible in some programming languages.

Fig. 3.14 shows linked representation using pointers for binary tree as in *Fig. 3.12(c)*.

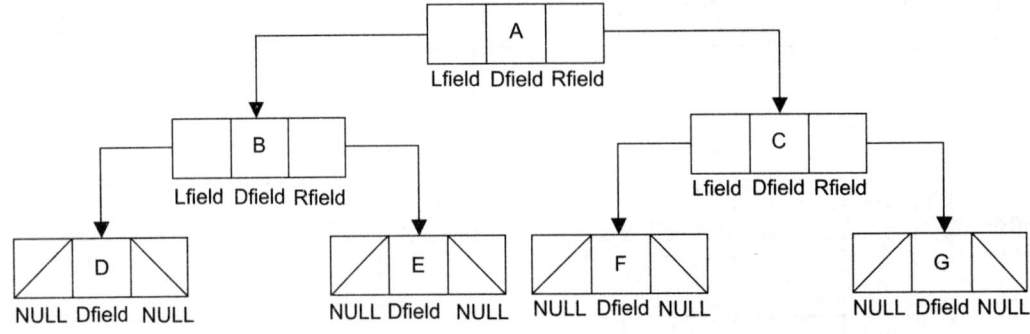

Fig. 3.14 : Linked representation of binary tree in Fig. 3.12(c).

3.5   Expression Trees

Binary trees can be used to represent the mathematical expressions. In the expression tree the leaf nodes are used to store operands and other nodes for operaters. The main problem in evaluating an expression is to decide the order in which the operations are carried out. The order of evaluation of the expression (a+b) is quite simple, where as if the expression is complex, we require knowledge of the operators, their precedence to specify the order of evaluation of the expression.

To fix the order of evaluation for an expression, we assign priority for operators. The operators with the highest priority will be evaluated first. Since we give more importance to binary operators, the most important binary operations according to their order of priority are listed in Table 3.1. Note that by using parenthesis we can override the default precedence of operators.

Priority	Operation (symbol)
1	Exponentiation (#)
2	Multiplication (*), Division (/)
3	Addition (+), Subtraction (–)

Table 3.1 :
Binary opreations in their order of priority.

All the symbols listed in Table 3.1 are as usual, except that for exponentiation we have used the symbol (#). The priority is listed in the order of highest to lowest. When unparenthesized operators of the same precedence are scanned, the order of evaluation is assumed from right to left (except for exponentiation whose precedence is left to right). For example, the representation of the expression (P + Q) / (R - S) is shown in the **Fig. 3.15.**

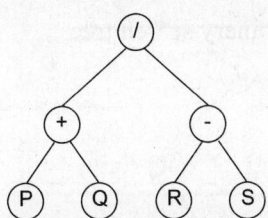

Fig. 3.15 : Expression tree.

The above expression can be evaluated by using other tree traversal methods.
In pre order traversal the expression is represented as / + P Q – R S.
In post order traversal the expression is represented as P Q + R S – /.
In the in order traversal the expression is represented as P + Q / R – S.

Here, it is clear that the post order traversal turn out to its postfix representation, in order to its infix and pre order is same as the arthimetic expression.

3.6 Applications of Trees

- Trees represent hierarchical relationships between individual data items. We can use trees to store information that naturally forms a hierarchy. For example, in

Windows, go to command line and type tree. You can see the folder structure organized and stored as a tree structure.

- Binary trees are used to represent arithmetic expressions. This feature is used in calculators and in compilers for parsing the expressions and executing them.

- Binary search tree arranges its node elements in a sorted manner, so the information can be easily inserted, deleted and searched.

- Spell check and auto correct suggestions during typing are enabled using tree structure.

- Used in router algorithms to identify where the next path/route of the packet to be sent.

3.7 Binary Search Trees

A *binary search tree* is a special binary tree, that satisfy the following characteristics.

- Every node has a value and no two nodes should have the same value (i.e., the values in the binary search tree are distinct).

- The values in any left subtree is less than the value of its parent node.

- The values in any right subtree is greater than the value of its parent node.

- The left and right subtrees of each node are again binary search trees.

Fig. 3.16 shows the structure of a binary search tree.

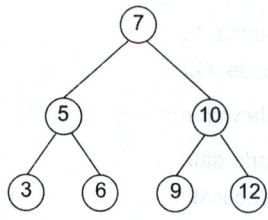

Fig. 3.16 : A binary search tree.

3.7.1 Basic Operations in a Binary Search Tree

The basic operations that can be performed on a binary search tree are,

- Creation of a binary search tree.
- Insertion of a node
- Deletion of a node
- Searching a node
- Modification of a node
- View the contents of the binary search tree.

Creation of a Binary Search Tree

Every node of a binary search tree have two parts, data part and the link part. Creation of binary search tree involves three processes. They are,

- Creating a node.
- Read details for the node from the user.
- Insert the node in the binary search tree.

In *Program 3.2,* getNode() function is used to create a node. After allocating memory for the structure of type node, the information for the node has to be read from the user. In readNode() function is used for reading details for the node from the user. In insertNode() function is used for inserting a new node in the binary search tree. The functions getNode(), readNode() and insertNode() are called repeatedly, to insert any number of nodes in the binary search trees.

Insertion of a Node

One of the most primitive operations that can be done in a binary search tree is the insertion of a node. Memory is to be allocated for the new node (in a similar way that is done while creating a tree) before reading the data. The new node will contain empty data field and empty link field. The data field of the new node is then stored with the information read from the user. The link field of the new node is assigned to NULL.

- Check whether the root node of the binary search tree is NULL.
- If the condition is true, it means, that the binary search tree is empty, hence consider the new node as the root node. Otherwise, follow the next steps.
- Compare the new node data with root node data, for the following three conditions.
- If the content of the new node data is equal to the root node data, insertion operation is terminated (because of duplication).
- If the content of the new node data is lesser than the root node data, check whether the left child of the root node is NULL. If the condition is true, insert the new data and terminate the process. Otherwise, consider the left child of the root node as the root node and check for the three conditions again.
- If the content of the new node data is greater than the root node data, check whether the right child of the root node is NULL. If the condition is true, insert the new data and terminate the process. Otherwise, consider the right child of the root node as the root node and check for the three conditions again.

In *Program 3.2,* insertNode() function is used for inserting a new node in the binary search tree. *Fig. 3.17* explains insertion operation in a binary search in detail.

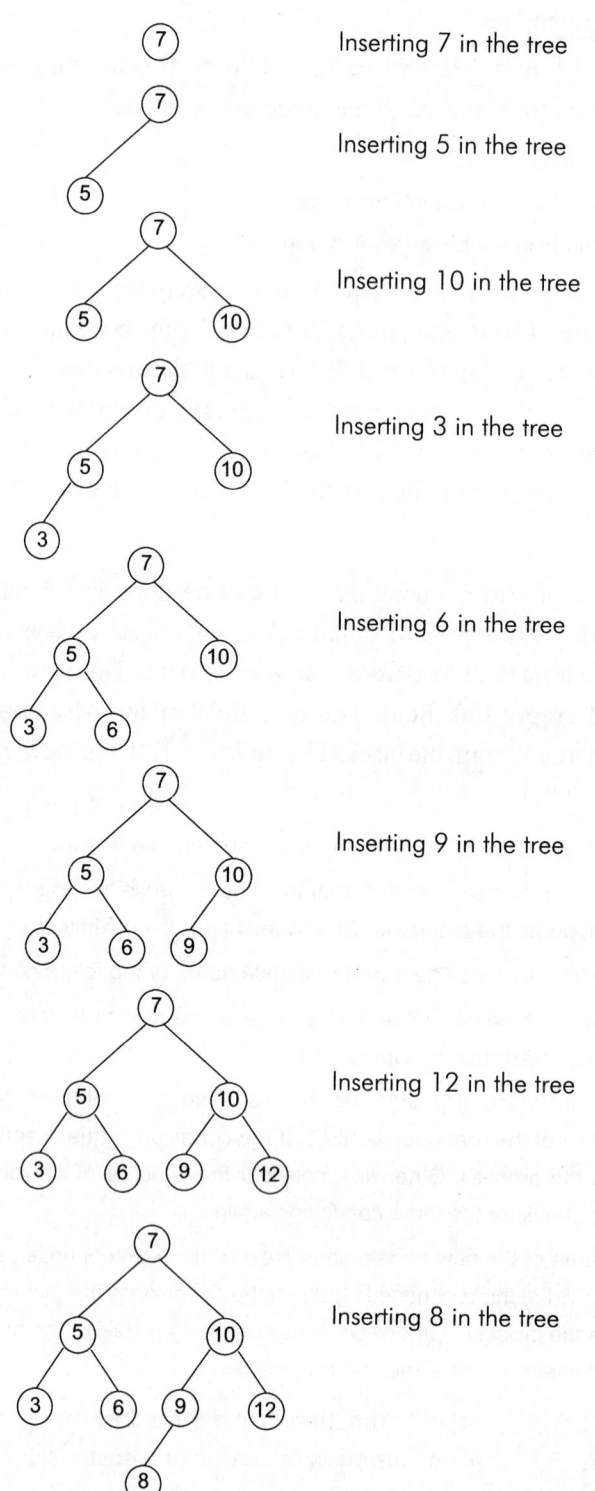

Inserting 7 in the tree

Inserting 5 in the tree

Inserting 10 in the tree

Inserting 3 in the tree

Inserting 6 in the tree

Inserting 9 in the tree

Inserting 12 in the tree

Inserting 8 in the tree

Fig. 3.17 : Steps for insertion operation in a binary search tree.

Deletion of a Node

Another primitive operation that can be done in a binary search tree is the deletion of a node. *Memory is to be released for the node to be deleted.* A node can be deleted from the tree from three different places namely,

- Deleting the leaf node
- Deleting the node with only one child
- Deleting the node with two children.

Deleting the leaf node

Steps followed to delete a leaf node from the binary search tree.

- Search the parent of the leaf node, and make the link to the leaf node as NULL.
- Release the memory for the deleted node.

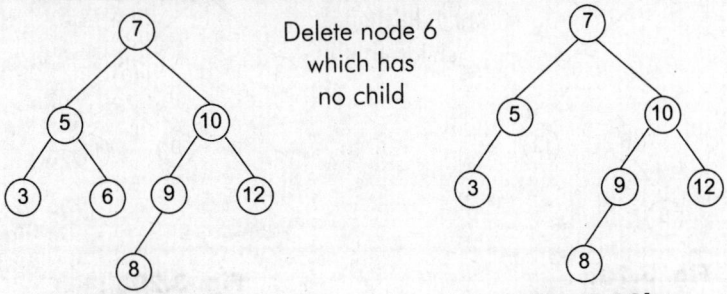

Fig. 3.18a :
Before deleting the leaf node 6.

Fig. 3.18b :
After deleting the leaf node 6.

Fig. 3.18 : Steps for deleting the leaf node.

Deleting the node with only one child

Steps followed to delete the node (with only one child) from the binary search tree.

- Search the parent of the node to be deleted (with only one child).
- Assign the link of the parent node to the child of the node to be deleted.
- Release the memory for the deleted node.

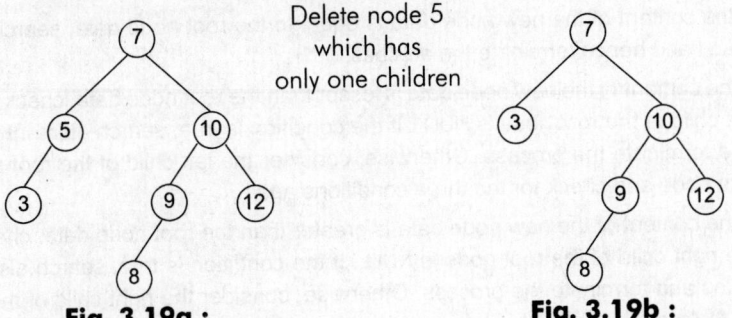

Fig. 3.19a :
Before deleting the node 5.

Fig. 3.19b :
After deleting the node 5.

Fig. 3.19 : Steps for deleting a node that has only one children.

Deleting the node with two children

Steps followed to delete the node (with two children) from the binary search tree.

- Search the parent of the node to be deleted (with two children).
- Copy the content of the inorder successor to the node to be deleted (with two children).
- Delete the inorder successor node. If the inorder successor node has no child, follow the steps given in the deleting the leaf node. If the inorder successor node has only one child, follow the steps given in the *deleting the node with one child*.
- Release the memory for the inorder successor node.
- Replace the contents of the node to be deleted with the copy of the content of the inorder successor node.

In *Program 3.2,* `deleteNode()` function is used for deleting the node from binary search tree.

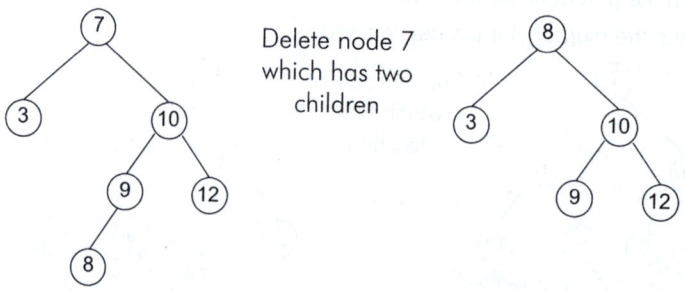

Delete node 7 which has two children

Fig. 3.20a :
Before deleting the node 7.

Fig. 3.20b :
After deleting the node 7.

Fig. 3.20 : Steps of deleting a node that has two children.

Searching a Node

One of the most important operations that can be done in a binary search tree is searching a node.

- Check whether the root node of the binary search tree is NULL. If yes, binary search tree is empty and hence terminate the search operation.
- If the binary search tree is not empty, compare the new node data with root node data, for the following three conditions.
- If the content of the new node data is equal to the root node data, search element is found and hence terminate the process.
- If the content of the new node data is lesser than the root node data, check whether the left child of the root node is NULL. If the condition is true, search element is not found and terminate the process. Otherwise, consider the left child of the root node as the root node and check for the three conditions again.
- If the content of the new node data is greater than the root node data, check whether the right child of the root node is NULL. If the condition is true, search element is not found, and terminate the process. Otherwise, consider the right child of the root node as the root node and check for the three conditions again.

In *Program 3.2* `searchNode()` function is used for searching a node in the binary search tree.

Modification of a Node

Steps followed to modify a node in a binary search tree.

- First search the node in the binary search tree using the steps given in the *searching of a node* and then modify the content of the node.

In *Program 3.2,* modifyNode() function is used for modifying a node in the binary search tree.

View the contents of the binary search tree

To display the information in a binary search tree, you have to traverse (move) a binary search tree. *The contents of binary search tree is displayed in 90° anti-clockwise position, to view the contents of the binary search tree in the fashion of a tree.*

Program 3.2 :

```c
/* Implementation of basic operations in a Binary Search Tree. */
/* bst.c */
#include<stdio.h>
#include<alloc.h>
#include<stdlib.h>
typedef struct node
  {
    int data;
    struct node *left, *right;
  }tree;
tree *getNode();
void displayMenu();
void readNode(tree *);
void releaseNode(tree* head);
tree *createBTree();
tree *insertNode(tree *btree, tree *temp);
tree *deleteNode(int digit, tree *btree);
tree *searchNode(tree *btree, int key);
void view(tree *btree, int level);
tree *findParNode(tree *btree, int item, tree **par);
tree *delNoChild(tree *btree, tree *par, tree *loc);
tree *delOneChild(tree *btree, tree *par, tree *loc);
tree *delTwoChild(tree *btree, tree *par, tree *loc);
void main()
  {
    int choice, key;
```

```
          tree *btree = NULL, *temp, *par, *loc;
      displayMenu();
      while(1)
       {
          printf("\n ? ");
            scanf("%d", &choice);
          switch(choice)
           {
            case 0 :
                        displayMenu();
                        break;
            case 1 :
                        btree = NULL;
                        printf("\nCreate a New Binary Tree");
                        btree = createBTree();
                        break;
            case 2 :
                        printf("\nInsert the Node in the Tree");
                        temp = getNode();
                        readNode(temp);
                        btree = insertNode(btree,temp);
                        break;
            case 3 :
                        if(btree == NULL)
                          printf("Binary Tree is Empty ...");
                        else
                          {
                             printf("\nDelete the Node from the Tree");
                             printf("\nEnter the Element for Deleting the Node : ");
                                  scanf("%d", &key);
                             btree = deleteNode(key, btree);
                          }
                        break;
              case 4 :
                        if(btree == NULL)
                           printf("Binary Tree is Empty ...");
                        else
                           {
                             printf("\nSearch the Node in the Tree");
                             printf("\nEnter the Searching Element : ");
```

```
                              scanf("%d", &key);
                        temp = searchNode(btree, key);
                        if(temp == NULL)
                          printf("Search Element %d is Not Found",key);
                        else
                          printf("Search Element %d is Found",temp->data);
                    }
                 break;
          case 5 :
                 if(btree == NULL)
                    printf("Binary Tree is Empty ...");
                 else
                    {
                      printf("Binary Search tree is ...\n");
                      view(btree, 1);
                    }
                 break;
          default :
                 printf("\n End of Run of your Program . . .");
                 releaseNode(btree);
                 exit(0);
         }
      }
  }
void displayMenu()
  {
    printf("\n Basic operations in a Binary Search Tree ");
    printf("\n\t 0. Show Menu ");
    printf("\n\t 1. Create a Binary Tree ");
    printf("\n\t 2. Insert a Node ");
    printf("\n\t 3. Delete a Node ");
    printf("\n\t 4. Search a Node ");
    printf("\n\t 5. View the Binary Tree ");
    printf("\n\t 6. Exit ");
  }
tree* getNode()
  {
    int size;
```

```
         tree *newnode;
         size = sizeof(tree);
         newnode = (tree *)malloc(size);
         return(newnode);
     }
void readNode(tree* newnode)
   {
      printf("\nEnter the Data : ");
        scanf("%d", &newnode->data);
      newnode->left = NULL;  newnode->right = NULL;
   }
void releaseNode(tree* head)
   {
      free(head);
   }
tree *createBTree()
   {
      char ch;
      tree *btree = NULL, *temp;
      do
       {
          temp = getNode();
          readNode(temp);
          btree = insertNode(btree, temp);
          fflush(stdin);
          printf("Do u wish to Add Data in the Tree (y/n) ? ");
            scanf("%c", &ch);
       }while( (ch == 'y') || (ch == 'Y') );
      return btree;
   }
tree *findParNode(tree *btree, int data, tree **par)
   {
      if(btree == NULL)
        return NULL;
      else if(data < btree->data)
        {
         *par = btree;
         return findParNode(btree->left,data, par);
        }
      else if(data > btree->data)
        {
```

```
        *par = btree;
        return findParNode(btree->right, data, par);
    }
  else if(data == btree->data)
      return btree;
}
tree *insertNode(tree *btree, tree *temp)
{
    tree *par = NULL, *loc = NULL;
    loc = findParNode(btree, temp->data, &par);
    if(loc != NULL)
     {
      printf("\n Data is already Existing ... ");
      return btree;
     }
    if(btree == NULL)
      return temp;
    else if(temp->data < par->data)
      par->left = temp;
    else
      par->right = temp;
    return btree;
}
tree *deleteNode(int key, tree *btree)
{
    tree *par = NULL, *loc = NULL;
    loc = findParNode(btree, key, &par);
    if(loc == NULL)
     {
       printf("\nItem Not Present ");
       return btree;
     }
    if(loc->left == NULL && loc->right == NULL)
      btree = delNoChild(btree, par, loc);
    if((loc->left != NULL && loc->right == NULL) ||
       (loc->left == NULL && loc->right != NULL))
      btree = delOneChild(btree, par, loc);
    if(loc->left != NULL && loc->right != NULL)
```

```
        btree = delTwoChild(btree, par, loc);
    releaseNode(loc);
    return btree;
 }
tree *delNoChild(tree *btree, tree *par, tree *loc)
 {
    if(par == NULL)
      return NULL;
    else if(loc == par->left)
      par->left = NULL;
    else if(loc == par->right)
      par->right = NULL;
    return btree;
 }
tree *delOneChild(tree *btree, tree *par, tree *loc)
 {
    tree *temp;
    if(loc->left != NULL)
      temp = loc->left;
    else
      temp = loc->right;
    if(par == NULL)
      btree = temp;
    else if(loc == par->left)
      par->left = temp;
    else if(loc == par->right)
      par->right = temp;
    return btree;
 }
tree *delTwoChild(tree *btree, tree *par, tree *loc)
 {
    tree *suc, *parSuc;
    parSuc = loc;
    for(suc = loc -> right; suc->left != NULL;suc = suc->left)
      parSuc = suc;
    if(suc->left==NULL&&suc->right==NULL)
      delNoChild(btree, parSuc, suc);
    else
```

```
          delOneChild(btree, parSuc, suc);
      if(par == NULL)
        btree = suc;
      else if(loc == par->left)
        par->left = suc;
      else if(loc == par->right)
        par->right = suc;
      suc->left = loc->left;
      suc->right = loc->right;
      return btree;
    }
tree *searchNode(tree *btree, int key)
    {
      if(btree == NULL)
        return NULL;
      else if(key < btree->data)
        return searchNode(btree->left,key);
      else if(key > btree->data)
        return searchNode(btree->right,key);
      else if(key == btree->data)
        return btree;
    }
void view(tree *btree, int level)
    {
      int k;
      if(btree == NULL)
        return;
      view(btree -> right, level+1);
      printf("\n");
      for(k = 0; k < level; k++)
        printf("     ");
      printf("%d", btree -> data);
      view(btree -> left, level+1);
    }
```

The program displays the following output

```
Basic operations in a Binary Search Tree
        0. Show Menu
        1. Create a Binary Tree
```

```
                2. Insert a Node
                3. Delete a Node
                4. Search a Node
                5. View the Binary Tree
                6. Exit
? 3
Binary Tree is Empty ...
? 4
Binary Tree is Empty ...
? 5
Binary Tree is Empty ...
? 1
Create a New Binary Tree
Enter the Data : 20
Do u wish to Add Data in the Tree (y/n) ? y
Enter the Data : 10
Do u wish to Add Data in the Tree (y/n) ? y
Enter the Data : 30
Do u wish to Add Data in the Tree (y/n) ? n
? 5
Binary search tree is ...
        30
    20
        10
? 2
Insert the Node in the Tree
Enter the Data : 25
? 5
Binary search tree is ...
        30
            25
    20
        10
? 2
Insert the Node in the Tree
Enter the Data : 15
```

```
? 5
Binary search tree is ...
        30
            25
    20
            15
        10
? 2
Insert the Node in the Tree
Enter the Data : 5

? 5
Binary search tree is ...
        30
            25
    20
            15
        10
            5
? 2
Insert the Node in the Tree
Enter the Data : 40
? 5
Binary search tree is ...
            40
    30
            25
    20
            15
        10
            5
? 4
Search the Node in the Tree
Enter the Searching Element : 50
Search Element 50 is Not Found
```

```
? 4

Search the Node in the Tree

Enter the Searching Element : 5

Search Element 5 is Found

? 4

Search the Node in the Tree

Enter the Searching Element : 40

Search Element 40 is Found

? 3

Delete the Node from the Tree

Enter the Element for Deleting the Node : 5

? 5

Binary search tree is ...

                40
        30
                25
    20
                15
        10


? 3

Delete the Node from the Tree

Enter the Element for Deleting the Node : 30

? 5

Inorder Binary tree traversal is ...

        40
                25
    20
                15
        10

? 3

Delete the Node from the Tree

Enter the Element for Deleting the Node : 10

? 5

Binary search tree is ...

        40
                25
    20
        15
```

```
? 3
Delete the Node from the Tree
Enter the Element for Deleting the Node : 20
? 5
Binary search tree is ...
        40
    25
        15
? 3
Delete the Node from the Tree
Enter the Element for Deleting the Node : 25
? 5
Binary search tree is ...
    40
        15
? 3
Delete the Node from the Tree
Enter the Element for Deleting the Node : 40
? 5
Binary search tree is ...
    15
? 3
Delete the Node from the Tree
Enter the Element for Deleting the Node : 15
? 5
Binary Tree is Empty ...
? 6
End of Run of your Program . . .
```

3.8 Threaded Binary Trees

In linked representation of binary trees, we can see that all leaf nodes and some non-leaf nodes have NULL values. Instead of storing NULL values in the left and right pointer fields, we can store some useful information, such as, inorder predecessor in the left pointer field and inorder successor in the right pointer field. These links are considered as *threads*. A binary tree, which implements these threads are referred to as ***threaded binary tree***.

If you use only the left pointer fields (for storing inorder predecessor) as threads, then the binary tree is referred to as ***left in-threaded binary tree***. If you use only the right pointer fields (for storing inorder successor) as threads, then the binary tree is referred to as ***right in-threaded binary tree***. If you use both left and right pointer fields as threads, then the binary tree is referred to as ***fully in-threaded binary tree***. ***Fig. 3.21*** shows the structure of a threaded binary tree. **Note that solid lines in *Fig. 3.21* show usual links, and dotted lines in *Fig. 3.21* shows threads.**

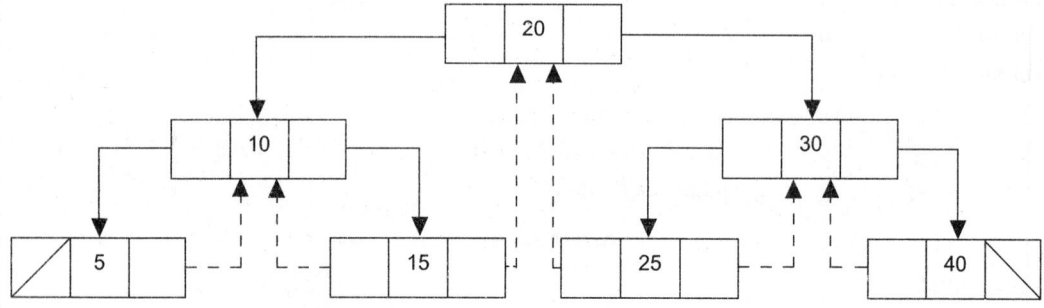

Fig. 3.21 : Fully-in threaded binary tree.

3.8.1 Basic Operations in a Threaded Binary Tree

The basic operations that can be performed on a threaded binary tree are,

- Creation of a threaded binary tree
- Insertion of a node
- Deletion of a node
- Searching a node
- Modification of a node
- Inorder traversal of threaded binary tree
- Preorder traversal of threaded binary tree
- Postorder traversal of threaded binary tree
- View the contents of the threaded binary tree.

Creation of a threaded binary tree

Every node in a threaded binary tree has three parts, data part, link part and thread flag. Creation of threaded binary tree involves three processes. They are,

- Creating a node
- Read details for the node from the user
- Insert the node in the threaded binary tree.

In ***Program 3.3*** getNode() function, is used to create a node. After allocating memory for the structure of type node, the information for the node has to be read from the user. In readNode() function is used for reading details for the node from the user. In insertNode() function is used for inserting a new node in the threaded binary tree. The functions getNode(), readNode() and insertNode() are called repeatedly, to insert any number of nodes in the threaded binary trees.

Insertion of a Node

One of the most primitive operations that can be done in a threaded binary tree is insertion of a node. Memory is to be allocated for the new node (in a similar way that is done while creating a tree) before reading the data. The new node will contain empty data field, empty link field and an empty thread flag. The data field of the new node is then stored with the information read from the user. The link field of the new node is assigned to NULL. The thread flag of the new node is set for both the left and right threads.

- To find the parent node (using `findParNode()`) of the new node to be inserted.

- If parent node is empty, it means, that the threaded binary tree is empty, hence consider the new node as the root node. Otherwise, follow the next steps.

- Compare the new node data with parent node data, for the following three conditions.

- If the content of the new node data is equal to the parent node data, insertion operation is terminated (because of duplication).

- If the content of the new node data is lesser than the parent node data (i.e., the new node is inserted as the left child of the parent node), perform the following three operations.

  - Insert the new node in the left child of the parent, and reset the left thread flag of the parent node.

  - Find the inorder predecessor for the new node, and store the reference, in the left pointer field of the new node.

  - Find the inorder successor for the new node, and store the reference, in the right pointer field of the new node.

- If the content of the new node data is greater than the parent node data (i.e., the new node is inserted as the right child of the parent node), perform the following three operations.

  - Insert the new node in the right child of the parent, and reset the right thread flag of the parent node.

  - Find the inorder predecessor for the new node, and store the reference, in the left pointer field of the new node.

  - Find the inorder successor for the new node, and store the reference, in the right pointer field of the new node.

In *Program 3.3* `insertNode()` function is used for inserting a new node in the binary search tree.

Deletion of a Node

Another primitive operation that can be done in a threaded binary tree is the deletion of a node. Memory is to be released for the node to be deleted.

A node can be deleted from the tree from three different places namely,

- Deleting the leaf node

- Deleting the node with only one child

- Deleting the node with two children.

Deleting the leaf node

Steps followed to delete a leaf node from the threaded binary tree.

- Search the location and parent of the node to be deleted (using `findParNode()`).
- Compare the parent node data, for the following three conditions.
- If parent node is empty, it means, that the threaded binary tree contains only one node (i.e., the node to be deleted), hence the tree becomes empty after deletion of the node, and returns NULL.
- If the node to be deleted is the left child of the parent node, perform the following two operations.
  - Set the left thread flag of the parent node.
  - The left child of the node to be deleted, is assigned to left child of the parent.
- If the node to be deleted is the right child of the parent node, perform the following two operations.
  - Set the right thread flag of the parent node.
  - The right child of the node to be deleted, is assigned to right child of the parent.
- Release the memory for the node to be deleted.

Deleting the node with only one child

Steps followed to delete the node (with only one child) from the threaded binary tree.

- Search the location and parent of the node to be deleted with only one child (using `findParNode()`).
- Copy the location of the child node.
- Compare the parent node data, for the following three conditions.
  - If parent node is empty, it means, that the threaded binary tree contains two nodes (i.e., the node to be deleted and its only child). Now assign the location of the child node as the root node.
  - If the node to be deleted is the left child of the parent node, assign the location of the child node as the left child of the parent node.
  - If the node to be deleted is the right child of the parent node, assign the location of the child node as the right child of the parent node.
- Find the inorder predecessor and successor for the location.
- The left child of the inorder successor of the location is inorder predecessor of the location.
- The right child of the inorder predecessor of the location is inorder successor of the location.
- Release the memory for the node to be deleted.

Deleting the node with two children

Steps followed to delete the node (with two children) from the binary search tree.

- Search the location and parent of the node to be deleted with two child (using `findParNode()`).

- Delete the inorder sucessor of the location, and replace the deleted node with inorder sucessor. If the inorder successor of the location has no child, follow the steps given in the *deleting the leaf node*. If the inorder successor node has only one child, follow the steps given in the *deleting the node with only one child*.

- Replace the contents of the node to be deleted with the contents of the inorder successor node.

- Release the memory for the inorder successor of the node to be deleted.

In *Program 3.3* deleteNode() function is used for deleting the node from a threaded binary tree.

Searching a Node

One of the most important operations that can be done in a threaded binary tree is searching a node.

- Check whether the root node of the threaded binary tree is NULL. If yes, threaded binary tree is empty and hence terminate the search operation.
- If the threaded binary search tree is not empty, compare the search node data with root node data, for the following three conditions.
- If the content of the search node data is equal to the root node data, search element is found, and hence terminate the process.
- If the content of the search node data is lesser than the root node data, check whether the left thread of the root node is set. If the condition is true, search element is not found, and terminate the process. Otherwise, consider the left child of the root node as the root node and check for the three conditions again.
- If the content of the search node data is greater than the root node data, check whether the right thread of the root node is set. If the condition is true, search element is not found,and terminate the process. Otherwise, consider the right child of the root node as the root node and check for the three conditions again.

In *Program 3.3* searchNode() function is used for searching a node in a threaded binary tree.

Modification of a Node

Steps followed to modify a node in a threaded binary tree.

- First search the node in the binary search tree using the steps given in the searching of a node and then modify the content of the node.

In *Program 3.3* modifyNode() function is used for modifying a node in a threaded binary tree.

View the contents of the threaded binary tree

To display the information in a threaded binary tree, you have to traverse (move) the threaded binary tree similar to a binary tree. *The contents of the threaded binary tree is displayed in 90° anti-clockwise position, to view the contents of threaded binary tree in the fashion of a tree.*

Inorder Traversal

The steps for traversing a threaded binary tree in inorder traversal is,

- Traverse the left subtree.
- Process the root node.
- Traverse the right subtree.

Preorder Traversal

The steps for traversing a threaded binary tree in preorder traversal is,

- Process the root node
- Traverse the left subtree
- Traverse the right subtree.

Postorder Traversal

The steps for traversing a threaded binary tree in postorder traversal is,

- Traverse the left subtree
- Traverse the right subtree
- Process the root node.

Program 3.3 :

```c
/* Implementation of Basic operations in a Threaded Binary Tree. */
/* tbt.c */
#include<stdio.h>
#include<alloc.h>
#include<stdlib.h>
#define LINK 0
#define LTHREAD 1
#define RTHREAD 2
#define LRTHREAD 3
typedef struct node
  {
    int data;
    unsigned int status;
    struct node *left, *right;
  }tree;
tree *getNode();
void displayMenu();
void readNode(tree *);
void releaseNode(tree* head);
tree *createBinTree();
tree *insertNode(tree *tbtree, tree *temp);
tree *deleteNode(int digit, tree *tbtree);
tree *searchNode(tree *tbtree, int key);
```

```
void view(tree *tbtree, int level);

tree *inSuc(tree *loc);

tree *inPre(tree *loc);

tree *findParNode(tree *tbtree, int item, tree **par);

tree *delNoChild(tree *tbtree, tree *par, tree *loc);

tree *delOneChild(tree *tbtree, tree *par, tree *loc);

tree *delTwoChild(tree *tbtree, tree *par, tree *loc);

void inorder(tree *tbtree);

void preorder(tree *tbtree);

void postorder(tree *tbtree);

void main()
  {
    int choice, key, item;
    tree *tbtree = NULL, *temp, *par, *loc;
    displayMenu();
    while(1)
      {
        fflush(stdin);
        printf("\n ? ");
          scanf("%d", &choice);
        switch(choice)
          {
            case 0 : displayMenu();
                    break;
            case 1 : tbtree = NULL;
                    printf("\nCreate a New Threaded Binary Tree");
                    tbtree = createBinTree();
                    break;
            case 2 : printf("\nInsert Node in Threaded Binary Tree");
                    temp = getNode();
                    readNode(temp);
                    tbtree = insertNode(tbtree,temp);
                    break;
            case 3 : if(tbtree == NULL)
                        printf("Threaded Binary Tree is Empty ...");
                    else
                      {
                        fflush(stdin);
                        printf("\nDelete the Node from the Tree");
                        printf("\nEnter Element for Deleting the Node : ");
```

```
                              scanf("%d", &key);
                          tbtree = deleteNode(key, tbtree);
                        }
                    break;
        case 4 : if(tbtree == NULL)
                    printf("Binary Tree is Empty ...");
                 else
                  {
                    fflush(stdin);
                    printf("\nSearch the Node in the Tree");
                    printf("\nEnter the Searching Element : ");
                      scanf("%d", &key);
                    temp = searchNode(tbtree, key);
                    if(temp == NULL)
                       printf("Search Element %d is Not Found\n",key);
                    else
                       printf("Search Element %d is Found\n",temp->data);
                  }
                    break;
        case 5 : printf("Inorder Threaded Binary tree traversal ...\n");
                    if(tbtree == NULL)
                      printf("Threaded Binary Tree is Empty ...");
                    else
                      inorder(tbtree);
                    break;
        case 6 : printf("Preorder Threaded Binary tree traversal ...\n");
                    if(tbtree == NULL)
                      printf("Threaded Binary Tree is Empty ...");
                    else
                      preorder(tbtree);
                    break;
        case 7 : printf("Postorder Threaded Binary tree traversal ...\n");
                    if(tbtree == NULL)
                      printf("Threaded Binary Tree is Empty ...");
                    else
                      postorder(tbtree);
                    break;
```

```
                    case 8 : printf("Threaded Binary tree view is ...\n");
                            if(tbtree == NULL)
        \                      printf("Threaded Binary Tree is Empty ...");
                            else
                               view(tbtree, 1);
                            break;
                  default :printf("\n End of Run of your Program . . .");
                            releaseNode(tbtree);
                            exit(0);
              }
        }
   }
void displayMenu()
   {
      printf("\n Basic operations in a Threaded Binary Tree ");
      printf("\n\t 0. Show Menu ");
      printf("\n\t 1. Create a Threaded Binary Tree ");
      printf("\n\t 2. Insert a Node ");
      printf("\n\t 3. Delete a Node ");
      printf("\n\t 4. Search a Node ");
      printf("\n\t 5. Inorder Threaded Binary Tree Traversal ");
      printf("\n\t 6. Preorder Threaded Binary Tree Traversal ");
      printf("\n\t 7. Postorder Threaded Binary Tree Traversal ");
      printf("\n\t 8. View the Threaded Binary Tree ");
      printf("\n\t 9. Exit ");
   }
tree* getNode()
   {
      int size;
      tree * newnode;
      size = sizeof(tree);
      newnode = (tree *) malloc(size);
      return (newnode);
   }
void readNode(tree* newnode)
   {
      fflush(stdin);
      printf("\nEnter the Data : ");
        scanf("%d", &newnode->data);
      newnode->left  = NULL;
```

```
    newnode->right = NULL;
    newnode->status = LRTHREAD;
}

void releaseNode(tree* head)
{
    free(head);
}

tree *inSuc(tree *loc)
{
    if((loc->status & RTHREAD) == RTHREAD)
        return loc->right;
    loc = loc->right;
    while((loc->status & LTHREAD) == LINK)
        loc = loc->left;
    return loc;
}

tree *inPre(tree *loc)
{
    if((loc->status & LTHREAD) == LTHREAD)
        return loc->left;
    loc = loc->left;
    while((loc->status & RTHREAD) == LINK)
        loc = loc->right;
    return loc;
}

tree *createBinTree()
{
    char ch;
    tree *tbtree = NULL, *temp;
    do
      {
        temp = getNode();
        readNode(temp);
        tbtree = insertNode(tbtree, temp);
        fflush(stdin);
        printf("Do u wish to Add Data in the Tree (y/n) ? ");
          scanf("%c", &ch);
      }while( (ch == 'y') || (ch == 'Y') );
```

```
          return tbtree;
      }
   tree *insertNode(tree *tbtree, tree *temp)
    {
       tree *par = NULL, *loc = NULL;
       loc = findParNode(tbtree, temp->data, &par);
       if(loc != NULL)
        {
           printf("\n Data is already Existing ... ");
           return tbtree;
        }
       if(tbtree == NULL)
         return temp;
       else if(temp->data < par->data)
        {
           temp->left = par->left;
           temp->status |= LTHREAD;
           temp->right = par;
           temp->status |= RTHREAD;
           par->left = temp;
           par->status = par->status & (~LTHREAD);
        }
       else
        {
           temp->left = par;
           temp->status |= LTHREAD;
           temp->right = par->right;
           temp->status |= RTHREAD;
           par->right = temp;
           par->status = par->status & (~RTHREAD);
        }
       return tbtree;
      }
   tree *deleteNode(int key, tree *tbtree)
    {
       tree *par = NULL, *loc = NULL;
       loc = findParNode(tbtree, key, &par);
       if(loc == NULL)
        {
           printf("\nItem Not Present ");
           return tbtree;
        }
```

```
        if(loc->status == LRTHREAD)
          tbtree = delNoChild(tbtree, par, loc);
        if((loc->status & LTHREAD)== LINK && (loc->status & RTHREAD)== RTHREAD)
            tbtree = delOneChild(tbtree, par, loc);
        if((loc->status & LTHREAD)==LTHREAD&&(loc->status & RTHREAD)== LINK)
            tbtree = delOneChild(tbtree, par, loc);
        if(loc->status == LINK)
            tbtree = delTwoChild(tbtree, par, loc);
        return tbtree;
    }
tree *delNoChild(tree *tbtree, tree *par, tree *loc)
    {
        if(par == NULL)
          return NULL;
        else if(loc == par->left)
          {
            par->status |= LTHREAD;
            par->left = loc->left;
          }
        else if(loc == par->right)
          {
            par->status |= RTHREAD;
            par->right = loc->right;
          }
        releaseNode(loc);
        return tbtree;
    }
tree *delOneChild(tree *tbtree, tree *par, tree *loc)
    {
        tree *temp, *suc, *pre;
        if((loc->status & LTHREAD)== LINK)
          temp = loc->left;
        else
          temp = loc->right;
        if(par == NULL)
          tbtree = temp;
        else if(loc == par->left)
          par->left = temp;
```

```
      else if(loc == par->right)
        par->right = temp;
    suc = inSuc(loc);
    pre = inPre(loc);
    if((loc->status & RTHREAD) == LINK)
      suc->left = pre;
    else if((loc->status & LTHREAD) == LINK)
      pre->right = suc;
    releaseNode(loc);
    return tbtree;
 }
tree *delTwoChild(tree *tbtree, tree *par, tree *loc)
 {
    tree *suc, *parSuc;
    parSuc = loc;
    for(suc = loc -> right; (suc->status & LTHREAD)==LINK;suc=suc->left)
      parSuc = suc;
    loc->data = suc->data;
    if(suc->status == LRTHREAD)
      delNoChild(tbtree, parSuc, suc);
    else
      delOneChild(tbtree, parSuc, suc);
    releaseNode(suc);
    return tbtree;
 }
tree *searchNode(tree *tbtree, int key)
 {
    if(tbtree == NULL)
      return NULL;
    else if(key < tbtree->data)
      return (((tbtree->status & LTHREAD) == LINK) ?
            searchNode(tbtree->left, key): NULL);
    else if(key > tbtree->data)
      return (((tbtree->status & RTHREAD) == LINK) ?
            searchNode(tbtree->right, key): NULL);
    else if(key == tbtree->data)
      return tbtree;
 }
```

```
tree *findParNode(tree *tbtree, int data, tree **par)
{
    if(tbtree == NULL)
      return NULL;
    else if(data < tbtree->data)
     {
        *par = tbtree;
        if((tbtree->status & LTHREAD) == LINK)
          return findParNode(tbtree->left,data, par);
        else
          return NULL;
     }
    else if(data > tbtree->data)
     {
        *par = tbtree;
        if((tbtree->status & RTHREAD) == LINK)
          return findParNode(tbtree->right,data, par);
        else
          return NULL;
     }
    else if(data == tbtree->data)
      return tbtree;
}
void inorder(tree *tbtree)
{
    if(tbtree == NULL)
      return;
    if((tbtree->status & LTHREAD) == LINK)
      inorder(tbtree->left);
    printf("Data = %-5d", tbtree->data);
    if((tbtree->status & LTHREAD) == LTHREAD && tbtree->left != NULL)
      printf(" inorder Predecessor = %-5d",tbtree->left->data);
    if((tbtree->status & RTHREAD) == RTHREAD & tbtree->right != NULL)
      printf(" inorder Successor = %-5d", tbtree->right->data);
    printf("\n");
    if((tbtree->status & RTHREAD) == LINK)
      inorder(tbtree->right);
}
```

```
void preorder(tree *tbtree)
 {
   if(tbtree == NULL)
     return;
   printf("%5d", tbtree->data);
   if((tbtree->status & LTHREAD) == LINK)
     preorder(tbtree->left);
   if((tbtree->status & RTHREAD) == LINK)
     preorder(tbtree->right);
 }
void postorder(tree *tbtree)
 {
   if(tbtree == NULL)
     return;
   if((tbtree->status & LTHREAD) == LINK)
     postorder(tbtree->left);
   if((tbtree->status & RTHREAD) == LINK)
     postorder(tbtree->right);
   printf("%5d", tbtree->data);
 }
void view(tree *tbtree, int level)
 {
   int k;
   if(tbtree == NULL)
     return;
   if((tbtree->status & RTHREAD) == LINK)
     view(tbtree -> right, level+1);
   printf("\n");
   for(k = 0; k < level; k++)
     printf("    ");
   printf("%d", tbtree -> data);
   if((tbtree->status & LTHREAD) == LINK)
     view(tbtree -> left, level+1);
 }
```

The program displays the following output

```
Basic operations in a Threaded Binary Tree
      0. Show Menu
      1. Create a Threaded Binary Tree
      2. Insert a Node
      3. Delete a Node
      4. Search a Node
```

```
            5. Inorder Threaded Binary Tree Traversal

            6. Preorder Threaded Binary Tree Traversal

            7. Postorder Threaded Binary Tree Traversal

            8. View the Threaded Binary Tree

            9. Exit

? 3

Threaded Binary Tree is Empty ...

? 4

Binary Tree is Empty ...

? 5

Inorder Threaded Binary tree traversal ...

Threaded Binary Tree is Empty ...

? 6

Preorder Threaded Binary tree traversal ...

Threaded Binary Tree is Empty ...

? 7

Postorder Threaded Binary tree traversal ...

Threaded Binary Tree is Empty ...

? 8

Threaded Binary tree view is ...

Threaded Binary Tree is Empty ...

? 1

Create a New Threaded Binary Tree

Enter the Data : 20

Do u wish to Add Data in the Tree (y/n) ? y

Enter the Data : 10

Do u wish to Add Data in the Tree (y/n) ? y

Enter the Data : 30

Do u wish to Add Data in the Tree (y/n) ? n

? 5

Inorder Threaded Binary tree traversal ...

Data = 10    inorder Successor = 20

Data = 20

Data = 30    inorder Predecessor = 20

? 6

Preorder Threaded Binary tree traversal ...

    20   10   30

? 7

Postorder Threaded Binary tree traversal ...

    10   30   20
```

```
? 8
Threaded Binary tree view is ...
        30
    20
        10
? 2
Insert the Node in the Threaded Binary Tree
Enter the Data : 25
? 2
Insert the Node in the Threaded Binary Tree
Enter the Data : 15
? 2
Insert the Node in the Threaded Binary Tree
Enter the Data : 5
? 2
Insert the Node in the Threaded Binary Tree
Enter the Data : 40
? 5
Inorder Threaded Binary tree traversal ...
Data = 5      inorder Successor = 10
Data = 10
Data = 15     inorder Predecessor = 10     inorder Successor = 20
Data = 20
Data = 25     inorder Predecessor = 20     inorder Successor = 30
Data = 30
Data = 40     inorder Predecessor = 30
? 6
.Preorder Threaded Binary tree traversal ...
    20    10    5    15    30    25    40
? 7
Postorder Threaded Binary tree traversal ...
    5    15    10    25    40    30    20
? 8
Threaded Binary tree view is ...
            40
        30
            25
    20
            15
        10
            5
```

```
? 4

Search the Node in the Tree

Enter the Searching Element : 50

Search Element 50 is Not Found
? 4
Search the Node in the Tree

Enter the Searching Element : 5

Search Element 5 is Found
? 4
Search the Node in the Tree

Enter the Searching Element : 40

Search Element 40 is Found
? 3
Delete the Node from the Tree

Enter the Element for Deleting the Node : 14

Item not present
? 3

Delete the Node from the Tree

Enter the Element for Deleting the Node : 5
? 5
Inorder Threaded Binary tree traversal ...

Data = 10

Data = 15      inorder Predecessor = 10      inorder Successor = 20

Data = 20

Data = 25      inorder Predecessor = 20      inorder Successor = 30

Data = 30

Data = 40      inorder Predecessor = 30
? 6

Preorder Threaded Binary tree traversal ...

   20    10    15    30    25    40
? 7

Postorder Threaded Binary tree traversal ...

   15    10    25    40    30    20
? 8

Threaded Binary tree view is ...

            40

           30

              25

     20

              15

      10
```

```
? 3
Delete the Node from the Tree
Enter the Element for Deleting the Node : 30
? 5
Inorder Threaded Binary tree traversal ...
Data = 10
Data = 15      inorder Predecessor = 10      inorder Successor = 20
Data = 20
Data = 25      inorder Predecessor = 20      inorder Successor = 40
Data = 40
? 6
Preorder Threaded Binary tree traversal ...
   20    10    15    40    25
? 7
Postorder Threaded Binary tree traversal ...
   15    10    25    40    20
? 8
Threaded Binary tree view is ...
        40
             25
    20
         15
         10
? 3
Delete the Node from the Tree
Enter the Element for Deleting the Node : 10
? 5
Inorder Threaded Binary tree traversal ...
Data = 15      inorder Successor = 20
Data = 20
Data = 25      inorder Predecessor = 20      inorder Successor = 40
Data = 40
? 6
Preorder Threaded Binary tree traversal ...
   20    15    40    25
? 7
Postorder Threaded Binary tree traversal ...
   15    25    40    20
```

```
? 8
Threaded Binary tree view is ...
        40
            25
    20
        15
? 3
Delete the Node from the Tree
Enter the Element for Deleting the Node : 20
? 5
Inorder Threaded Binary tree traversal ...
Data = 15     inorder Successor = 25
Data = 25
Data = 40     inorder Predecessor = 25
? 6
Preorder Threaded Binary tree traversal ...
   25    15    40
? 7
Postorder Threaded Binary tree traversal ...
   15    40    25
? 8
Threaded Binary tree view is ...
        40
    25
        15
? 3
Delete the Node from the Tree
Enter the Element for Deleting the Node : 25

? 5
Inorder Threaded Binary tree traversal ...
Data = 15     inorder Successor = 40
Data = 40
? 6
Preorder Threaded Binary tree traversal ...
   40    15
? 7
Postorder Threaded Binary tree traversal ...
   15    40
```

```
? 8

Threaded Binary tree view is ...
    40
        15
? 3

Delete the Node from the Tree

Enter the Element for Deleting the Node : 40

? 5

Inorder Threaded Binary tree traversal ...

Data = 15

? 6

Preorder Threaded Binary tree traversal ...

    15

? 7

Postorder Threaded Binary tree traversal ...

    15

? 8

Threaded Binary tree view is ...

    15

? 3

Delete the Node from the Tree

Enter the Element for Deleting the Node : 15

? 5

Inorder Threaded Binary tree traversal ...

Threaded Binary Tree is Empty ...

? 6

Preorder Threaded Binary tree traversal ...

Threaded Binary Tree is Empty ...

? 7

Postorder Threaded Binary tree traversal ...

Threaded Binary Tree is Empty ...

? 8

Threaded Binary tree view is ...

Threaded Binary Tree is Empty ...

? 9

End of Run of your Program . . . .
```

3.9 AVL Trees

We know that the height of a tree is the length of the longest path from the root to a leaf. A binary search tree is a height-balanced k-tree or HB[k]-tree, if each node in the tree has the HB[k] property. A node is said to have the HB[k] property, if the height of the left and right sub trees of the node differ in height by at most k. A HB[1] tree is referred to as *AVL trees*. That is, a binary search tree in which the heights of the left and right sub trees of the root differ by at most 1 are referred as *AVL trees*, also the left and right sub trees are themselves AVL trees. AVL trees was named after the Russian mathematicians, *Adel'son-Vel'skii* and *Landis*, who first defined HB[1] trees.

AVL trees keep an additional piece of information at each node, an associated balance factor indicating the relative heights of its left and right sub trees. In representing an AVL tree, each node N also has a balance factor BF(N) which shows the difference in height between its left and right sub trees. In an AVL tree, the BF(N) should be -1, 0, or 1 for all nodes. AVL trees are height-balanced trees, meaning that, they are built, to maintain the balance within the binary tree. Any insertion or deletion into the tree will be analyzed to see if it violates the balance condition or not. If it violates, then we need to reorganize the tree by a series of rotations to make it balanced. Thus, the insertion and deletion methods should be sensitive to maintaining this balance. The height of an AVL tree with N nodes never exceeds `1.44 log N` and is typically much closer to log N. In an n-element AVL tree can be searched in `O(log n)` time. Insertions and deletions in an AVL tree can be carried in a `O(log n)` time.

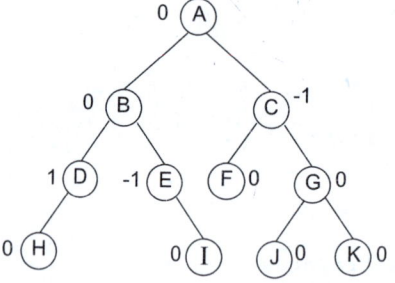

Fig. 3.22 : An AVL tree, with balancing factors.

3.10 Basic Operations in a AVL Tree

The basic operations that can be performed on a binary search tree are,

- Creation of an AVL tree
- Insertion of a node
- Deletion of a node
- Searching a node
- Modification of a node
- View the contents of the binary search tree.

The operations, creation, searching a node, modification of a node, viewing the contents of the AVL tree are similar to the binary search tree, as discussed in *Section 3.6.1*. Only the insertion and deletion process differs from the binary search tree, since the nodes are balanced, depending upon the balance factor in the AVL tree. Insertions and deletions are performed as in binary search trees, and followed by rotations to correct imbalances in the trees. In the case of insertions, one rotation is sufficient. In the case of deletions, `O(log n)` rotations at most are needed.

Inserting a Node in an AVL Tree

- Find the place to insert the new node in the tree. Traverse the node from the inserted position, until you end with a node with a balance factor +1 or -1. Denote this node, as X. AVL trees do not allow for duplicate keys, so if you find one, terminate the process.

- If node X was not found, make another pass from the root, updating the balance factors as you go and terminate the process.

- If BF(X) = 1 and new node was inserted in X's right sub tree or BF(X) = -1 and new node was inserted in X's left sub tree, BF(X) = 0. Update the balance factor on path to X and terminate the process.

- Otherwise, classify the imbalance at X and perform the any of the following 4 rotations.

Types of Rotation in an AVL Tree

- Left to Left rotation

- Right to Right rotation

- Left to Right rotation

- Right to Left rotation.

Left to Left Rotation

Insertion into the left sub tree of x's left child causes imbalance to the tree. The root of x's left sub tree (which we'll call Y) becomes the new root of this entire sub tree, and Y's right sub tree becomes x's new left sub tree.

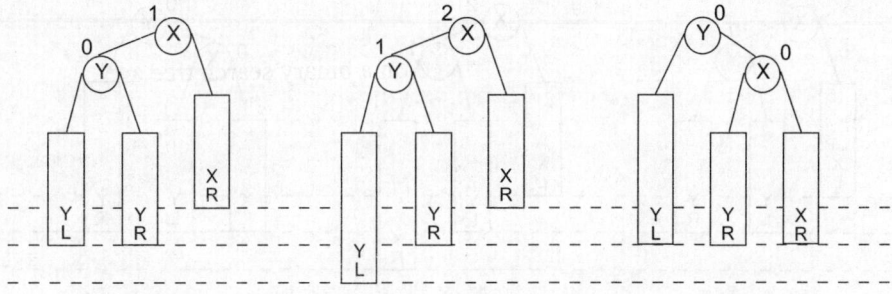

Fig. 3.23 : Left-to-left rotation of an AVL tree with balancing factors.

Left to Right Rotation

Insertion into the right sub tree of x's left child causes the imbalance. The root of Y's right sub tree (which we will call z) becomes the new root of this entire sub tree. Y is now the root of z's left sub tree, x is the root of z's right sub tree. Y's right sub tree is whatever used to be z's left sub tree, and x's left sub tree is whatever used to be z's right sub tree.

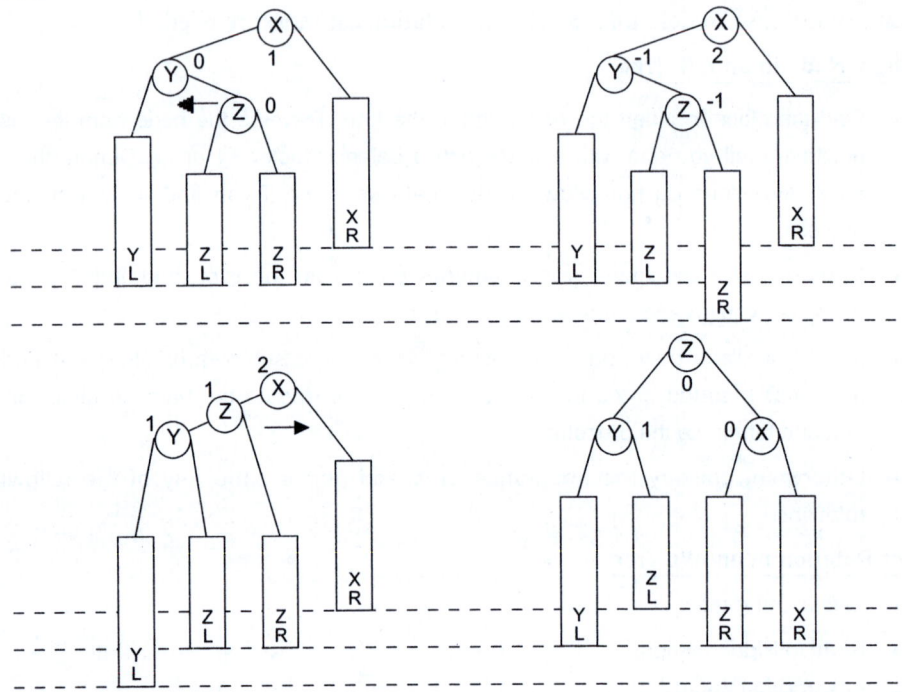

Fig. 3.24 : Left-to-right rotation of an AVL tree with balancing factors.

Right to Right Rotation

Insertion into the right sub tree of x's right child causes the imbalance. The root of x's right sub tree (Y) becomes the new root of this entire sub tree, and Y's former left sub tree becomes x's right sub tree.

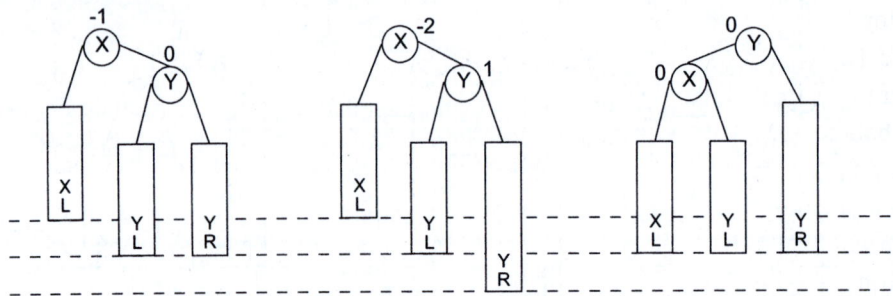

Fig. 3.25 : Right-to-right rotation of an AVL tree with balancing factors.

Right to Left Rotation

Insertion into the left sub tree of x's right child causes the imbalance. The root of Y's left sub tree (z) becomes the new root of the structure. Y is now the root of z's left sub tree, x of its right sub tree.

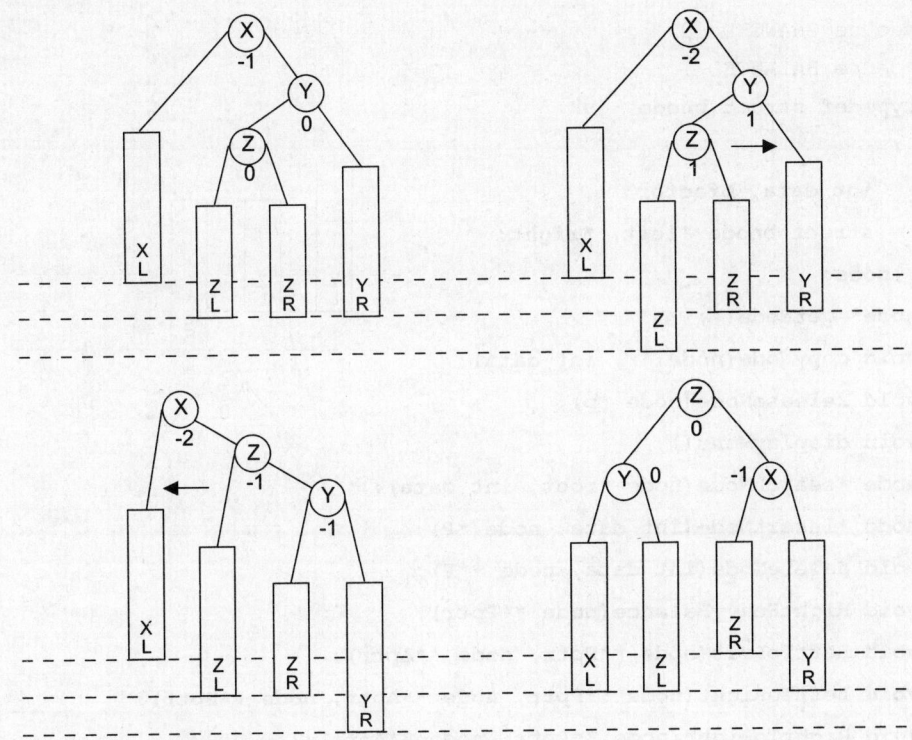

Fig. 3.26 : Right-to-left rotation of an AVL tree with balancing factors.

Deleting a Node from the AVL Tree

Like insertion, deletion initially proceeds similar to a binary search tree. The node whose key is to be removed is located using a search, and the key is replaced with its successor or predecessor. Due to removal of a node, an AVL tree may be unbalanced. So for balancing the tree as in insertion, the first unbalanced ancestor of the removed node (the leaf node that contained the successor or predecessor) is located and rearranged. Unlike in insertion, however, a single rearrangement may not restore the balance to the AVL tree. So after the rearranging operation, it is necessary to keep going upward in the tree up to the root, rearranging as necessary. Deletion as similar to a binary search tree, requires O(lg n), and then rearranging the nodes for balancing if necessary, also requires O(lg n) time. A maximum of one rearrangement per level is required, so at most O(lg n) rearranging operations need to be done. So removal also takes O(lg n) time.

Program 3.4 :

/* **Implementation of Basic operations in an AVL Tree.** */

```c
/* avltree.c */
#include<stdio.h>
#include<malloc.h>
#define CHANGED  0
#define BALANCED 1
typedef struct bnode
 {
   int data, bfactor;
   struct bnode *left, *right;
 }node;
node* getNode();
void copyNode(node *r, int data);
void releaseNode(node *p);
void displayMenu();
node *searchNode(node *root, int data);
node *insertNode(int data, node *P);
void deleteNode(int data, node **P);
void RightHeavyBalance(node **Pptr);
void LeftToLeft(node **Pptr, node **Aptr);
void LeftToRight(node **Pptr, node **Aptr, node **Bptr);
void RightToRight(node **Pptr, node **Aptr);
void RightToLeft(node **Pptr, node **Aptr, node **Bptr);
void inorder(node *root);
void view(node *root,int level);
void del(node **N, node **C);
int height;
node* getNode()
 {
   int size;
   node * newnode;
   size = sizeof(node);
   newnode = (node *)malloc(size);
   return(newnode);
 }
```

```
void main()
 {
   int data, ch, choice = 'y';
   node *root = NULL;
   displayMenu();
   while( (choice == 'y') || (choice == 'Y') )
    {
      printf("\n? ");
      fflush(stdin);
        scanf("%d", &ch);
      switch(ch)
       {
         case 0:
                   displayMenu();
                   break;
         case 1:
                   printf("\nEnter the value to be inserted : ");
                     scanf("%d", &data);
                   if(searchNode(root, data) == NULL)
                     root = insertNode(data, root);
                   else
                     printf("\n Data is already exist");
                   break;
         case 2:
                   printf("\nEnter the value to be Deleted : ");
                     scanf("%d", &data);
                   if(searchNode(root, data) != NULL)
                     deleteNode(data, &root);
                   else
                     printf("\n Element to be deleted is not Found");
                   break;
         case 3:
                   if(root == NULL)
                    {
                       printf("\n AVL Tree is Empty\n");
                       continue;
                    }
                   printf("\n Inorder Traversal of the AVL Tree : ");
                   inorder(root);
                   printf("\n AVL Tree is :\n");
                   view(root, 1);
                   break;
```

```
              default:
                          printf("\n End of Run of your Program . . .");
                          releaseNode(root);
                          return;
            }
        }
}
void displayMenu()
{
    printf("\n Basic operations in an AVL Tree ...");
    printf("\n 0. Display Menu List ");
    printf("\n 1. Insert a Node in the AVL tree");
    printf("\n 2. Delete a Node in the AVL tree");
    printf("\n 3. View the AVL Tree");
    printf("\n 4. Exit");
}
void copyNode(node *r, int data)
{
    r -> data = data;
    r -> left = NULL;
    r -> right = NULL;
    r -> bfactor = 0;
}
void releaseNode(node *p)
{
    free(p);
}
node *searchNode(node *root, int data)
{
    if(root != NULL)
      if(data < root -> data)
        root = searchNode(root -> left, data);
      else if( data > root -> data)
        root = searchNode(root -> right, data);
    return(root);
}
node *insertNode(int data, node *P)
{
    node *A, *B;
    if(P == NULL)
      {
        P = getNode();
        copyNode(P, data);
        height = CHANGED;
        return(P);
      }
```

```
    if(data < P -> data)
     {
       P -> left = insertNode(data, P -> left);

       if(height == CHANGED)
        {
          switch(P -> bfactor)
           {
             case -1:
                       P -> bfactor = 0;    /* Right Heavy Tree */

                       height = BALANCED;

                       break;
             case 0 :
                       P -> bfactor = 1;    /* Balanced Tree */

                       break;
             case 1 :
                       A = P -> left;        /* Left Heavy Tree */

                       if(A -> bfactor == 1)

                         LeftToLeft(&P, &A);

                       else

                         LeftToRight(&P, &A, &B);

                       height = BALANCED;

                       break;
           }
        }
     }
    if(data > P -> data)
     {
       P -> right = insertNode(data, P -> right);

       if(height == CHANGED)
        {
          switch(P -> bfactor)
           {
             case 1 :
                       P -> bfactor = 0;    /* Left Heavy Tree */

                       height = BALANCED;

                       break;
             case 0 :
                       P -> bfactor = -1;   /* Balanced Tree */

                       break;
```

```
                   case -1:
                            A = P -> right;        /* Right heavy Tree */
                            if(A -> bfactor == -1)
                               RightToRight(&P, &A);
                            else
                               RightToLeft(&P, &A, &B);
                            height = BALANCED;
                            break;
                   }
              }
          }
       return(P);
    }
  void deleteNode(int data, node **P)
    {
       node *A, *B, *C;
       if(*P == NULL)
        {
          printf("\n AVL Tree is Empty ...\n");
          return;
        }
       if(data < (*P) -> data)
        {
          deleteNode(data, &((*P) -> left));
          if(height == CHANGED)
            {
              switch((*P) -> bfactor)
               {
                  case 1 :
                            (*P) -> bfactor = 0;
                            break;
                  case 0 :
                            (*P) -> bfactor = -1;
                            height = BALANCED;
                            break;
                  case -1:
                            A = (*P) -> right;
                            if(A -> bfactor <= 0)
                               RightToRight(P, &A);
                            else
                               RightToLeft(P, &A, &B);
                            break;
                }
            }
        }
```

```
else if(data > (*P) -> data)
 {
   deleteNode(data, &((*P) -> right));
   if(height == CHANGED)
    {
      switch((*P) -> bfactor)
       {

         case -1:
                  (*P) -> bfactor = 0;
                  break;
         case 0 :
                  (*P) -> bfactor = 1;
                  height = BALANCED;
                  break;
         case 1:
                  A = (*P) -> left;
                  if(A -> bfactor >= 0)
                     LeftToLeft(P, &A);
                  else
                     LeftToRight(P, &A, &B);
                  break;
       }
    }
 }
else
 {
   C = *P;
   if(C -> right == NULL)
    {
      *P = C -> left;
      height = CHANGED;
      releaseNode(C);
    }
   else if(C -> left == NULL)
    {
      *P = C -> right;
```

```
                 height = CHANGED;
                 releaseNode(C);
              }
          else
           {
              del(&(C -> left), &C);
              if(height == CHANGED)
                {
                  switch((*P) -> bfactor)
                   {
                     case 1 :
                              (*P) -> bfactor = 0;
                              break;
                     case 0 :
                              (*P) -> bfactor = -1;
                              height = BALANCED;
                              break;
                     case -1:
                              A = (*P) -> right;
                              if(A -> bfactor <= 0)
                                 RightToRight(P, &A);
                              else
                                 RightToLeft(P, &A, &B);
                              break;
                   }
                }
           }
    }
void del(node **N, node **C)
  {
      node *T, *A, *B;
      node **P;
      T = (*N);
      if((*N) -> right != NULL)
        {
          del(&((*N) -> right), C);
```

```
      if(height == CHANGED)
       {
         P = N;
         switch((*P) -> bfactor)
          {
            case -1:
                      (*P) -> bfactor = 0;
                      break;
            case 0 :
                      (*P) -> bfactor = 1;
                      height = BALANCED;
                      break;
            case 1 :
                      A = (*P) -> left;
                      if(A -> bfactor >= 0)
                        LeftToLeft(P, &A);
                      else
                        LeftToRight(P, &A, &B);
                      break;
          }
       }
    else
     {
       (*C) -> data = (*N) -> data;
       (*N) = (*N) -> left;
       releaseNode(T);
       height = CHANGED;
     }
 }
void LeftToLeft(node **Pptr, node **Aptr)
 {
   node *P = *Pptr, *A = *Aptr;
   printf("\n Left to Left AVL Rotation \n");
   P -> left = A -> right;
```

```
    A -> right = P;
    if(A -> bfactor == 0)
      {
        P -> bfactor = 1;
        A -> bfactor = -1;
        height = BALANCED;
      }
    else
      {
        P -> bfactor = 0;
        A -> bfactor = 0;
      }
    P = A;
    *Pptr = P;
    *Aptr = A;
  }
void LeftToRight(node **Pptr, node **Aptr, node **Bptr)
  {
    node *P = *Pptr, *A = *Aptr, *B = *Bptr;
    printf("\n Left to Right AVL Rotation \n");
    B = A -> right;
    A -> right = B -> left;
    B -> left = A;
    P -> left = B -> right;
    B -> right = P;
    if(B -> bfactor == 1)
      P -> bfactor = -1;
    else
      P -> bfactor = 0;
    if(B -> bfactor == -1)
      A -> bfactor = 1;
    else
      A -> bfactor = 0;
    B -> bfactor = 0;
    P = B;
    *Pptr = P;
    *Aptr = A;
    *Bptr = B;
  }
```

```
    void RightToRight(node **Pptr, node **Aptr)
     {
        node *P = *Pptr, *A = *Aptr;
        printf("\n Right to Right AVL Rotation \n");
        P -> right= A -> left;
        A -> left = P;
        if(A -> bfactor == 0)
         {
           P -> bfactor = -1;
           A -> bfactor = 1;
           height = BALANCED;
         }
        else
         {
           P -> bfactor = 0;
           A -> bfactor = 0;
         }
        P = A;
        *Pptr = P;
        *Aptr = A;
     }
    void RightToLeft(node **Pptr, node **Aptr, node **Bptr)
     {
        node *P = *Pptr, *A = *Aptr, *B = *Bptr;
        printf("\n Right to Left AVL Rotation \n");
        B = A -> left;
        A -> left = B -> right;
        B -> right = A;
        P -> right = B -> left;
        B -> left = P;
        if(B -> bfactor == -1)
          P -> bfactor = 1;
        else
          P -> bfactor = 0;
        if(B -> bfactor == 1)
          A -> bfactor = -1;
        else
          A -> bfactor = 0;
```

```
        B -> bfactor = 0;
        P = B;
        *Pptr = P;
        *Aptr = A;
        *Bptr = B;
    }
void inorder(node *root)
    {
        if(root == NULL)
            return;
        inorder(root -> left);
        printf("%4d",root -> data);
        inorder(root -> right);
    }
void view(node *root, int level)
    {
        int k;
        if(root == NULL)
            return;
        view(root -> right, level+1);
        printf("\n");
        for(k = 0; k < level; k++)
            printf("      ");
        printf("%d", root -> data);
        view(root -> left, level+1);
    }
```

The program displays the following output

```
Basic operations in an AVL Tree ...
  0. Display Menu List
  1. Insert a Node in the AVL tree
  2. Delete a Node in the AVL tree
  3. View the AVL Tree
  4. Exit
? 3
AVL Tree is Empty ...
? 1
```

```
Enter the value to be inserted : 23
? 1
Enter the value to be inserted : 15
? 3
Inorder Traversal of the AVL Tree :    15   23
AVL Tree is :
     23
         15
? 1
Enter the value to be inserted : 13
Left to Left AVL Rotation
? 3
Inorder Traversal of the AVL Tree :    13   15   23
AVL Tree is :
          23
     15
          13
? 1
Enter the value to be inserted : 27
? 1
Enter the value to be inserted : 20
? 1
Enter the value to be inserted : 18
Right to Left AVL Rotation
? 3
Inorder Traversal of the AVL Tree :    13   15   18   20   23   27
AVL Tree is :
               27
          23
     20
               18
          15
               13
? 1
Enter the value to be inserted : 32
Right to Right AVL Rotation
```

```
    ? 3
    Inorder Traversal of the AVL Tree :    13  15  18  20  23  27  32
    AVL Tree is :
                    32
              27
                    23
          20
                    18
              15
                    13


    ? 1
    Enter the value to be inserted : 9
    ? 1
    Enter the value to be inserted : 12
    Left to Right AVL Rotation
    ? 3
    Inorder Traversal of the AVL Tree :     9  12  13  15  18  20  23  27  32
    AVL Tree is :
                    32
              27
                    23
          20
                    18
              15
                        13
                    12
                        9
    ? 2
    Enter the value to be Deleted : 13
    ? 2
    Enter the value to be Deleted : 27
    ? 2
    Enter the value to be Deleted : 15
    ? 2
```

```
Enter the value to be Deleted : 23

? 3

Inorder Traversal of the AVL Tree :     9  12  18  20  32

AVL Tree is :
            32

       20

                18

       12

             9

? 4

End of Run of your Program . . .
```

3.11 B-Tree

B-trees stands for ***Balanced trees***, where all the leaves are of the same distance from the root. A B-tree of order n has a root node containing from 1 to n-1 elements that should satisfy the following characteristics.

- All leaves are on the same level
- They are built upwards from the leaves
- The root has at least two children, if it is not a leaf node
- Every node has a maximum of n children
- All non-leaf nodes except the root have at least |n/2| children
- The number of keys in each non-leaf node is one less than the number of its children and these keys partition the keys in the children in the fashion of a search tree
- A leaf node contains at least |n/2|-1 children and has not more than n - 1 keys.

B-trees are specialized multiway trees designed especially for use to search an info from a large database, such as an external hard disk, RAID and so on. In a B-tree each node may contain a large number of keys and the number of subtrees of each node may also be large. A B-tree is designed to branch out in large number of directions and contains lot of keys in each node so that the height of the tree is relatively small. This means that only a small number of nodes will be read from a disk to search an item. The goal is to get fast access to the data from disk drives, which means reading a very small number of records. B-trees are generally wider than binary trees and are kept balanced automatically by the use of carefully constructed insertion and deletion algorithms so that the height of all the leaf elements is the same. B-trees with lower order are used for internal memory dictionaries and B-trees with higher order are used to represent very large dictionaries that reside on disk.

3.12 Basic Operations in a B-Tree

The basic operations that can be performed in a B-tree are,
- Creation of a B-tree

- Insertion of a node
- Deletion of a node
- Searching a node
- Finding the minimum value in the tree
- Finding the maximum value in the tree
- View the contents of the B-Tree.

3.12.1 Insertion of a Node

One of the most primitive operations that can be done in a B-tree is insertion of a node. The following steps helps you to understand things better.

- When inserting an data, first do a search for the data in the B-tree. If the data doesn't exist in the B-tree, the unsuccessful search will end at a leaf. If the data already exists, the new data will not be inserted, since B-tree will not allow duplication.

- If there is place to insert in the leaf node, then fill the new data. This may require that some existing keys be moved one to the right to give space for the new data.

- If there is no space to insert the new data, then the node must be split with about half of the keys going into a new node to the right of this one. The median or the middle key is moved up into the parent node.

- If the root node is ever split, the median key moves up into a new root node, thus causing the tree to increase its height by one. This strategy might have to be repeated all the way to the top.

3.12.2 Deletion of a Node

Another primitive operation that can be done in a B-tree is deletion of a node. There are two special cases to consider when deleting an element. They are,

- Deleting an element may put it under the minimum number of elements and children
- Deleting an element from an internal node may be a separator for its child nodes.

Search for the data to be deleted

- If the data is in present in the leaf node, simply delete the data from the node, leaving the node with too few keys, so some additional changes to the tree will be required

- If the data is not present in the leaf node, then it is guaranteed that its predecessor (largest element in the left subtree) or successor (smallest element in the right subtree) will be in a leaf node and we can delete the key and promote the predecessor or successor key to the non-leaf deleted key's position

- If both the above steps leads to a leaf node containing less than the minimum number of keys then we have to look at the siblings immediately adjacent to the leaf node.

Rebalancing the tree after deletion

- If the right sibling has more than the minimum number of keys borrow one, adjust the separator.

- Otherwise, if the left sibling has more than the minimum number of keys borrow one, adjust the separator.

- If both immediate siblings have only the minimum number of elements

  ▪ Create a new node with all the elements from the deficient node, all the elements from one of its siblings and the separator in the parent between the two combined sibling nodes.

  ▪ Remove the separator from the parent and replace the two children, if separated with the combined node.

  ▪ If it brings the number of elements in the parent node under minimum, repeat the steps with that deficient node, unless it is the root.

Program 3.5 :

```
/* Program to demonstrate the Basic Operations in a B-Tree */
/* btree.c */
#include<stdio.h>
#define MAX 3
#define MIN 1
typedef enum {FALSE, TRUE} Boolean;
typedef int KeyType;
int levels = 3;
typedef struct Node
 {
     int count;
     KeyType key[MAX+1];
     struct Node *branch[MAX+1];
 }BNode;
typedef BNode *BTree;
BTree Insert(KeyType newkey, BTree root);
Boolean PushDown(KeyType newkey,BTree p,KeyType *x, BTree *xr);
Boolean SeqSearch(KeyType target,BTree p, int *k);
void PushIn(KeyType x,BTree xr,BTree p, int k);
void Split(KeyType x, BTree xr, BTree p, int k, KeyType *y, BTree *yr);
BTree Delete(KeyType target, BTree root);
Boolean RecDelete(KeyType target,BTree p);
void Successor(BTree p, int k);
void Remove(BTree p,int k);
void Restore(BTree p, int k);
void MoveLeft(BTree p,int k);
```

```
void MoveRight(BTree p,int k);

void Combine(BTree p,int k);

void DFS(BTree p, int depth);

void viewTree(BTree p, int depth);

void viewTreeAsc(BTree p);

void viewTreeDes(BTree p);

void releaseNode(BTree Node);

void displayMenu();

void Search(KeyType key, BTree p, int depth, int *pos);


void main()
 {
     BTree   T = NULL;
     int i, j, ch, Key, pos;
     char choice;
     displayMenu();
     while(1)
      {
        fflush(stdin);
        printf("\n\n ? ");
          scanf("%d", &ch);
        switch(ch)
         {
             case 0 : /* Show Menu Operation */
                     displayMenu();
                     break;
             case 1 : /* Create New B-Tree Operation */
                     printf("\n Create a New B-Tree");
                     do
                       {
                             fflush(stdin);
                             printf("\n Enter The Key : ");
                               scanf("%d", &Key);
                             T = Insert(Key, T);
                     fflush(stdin);
                     printf("Do u wish to add Data in the Tree (y/n) ? ");
                        scanf("%c", &choice);
                   }while((choice == 'y') || (choice == 'Y'));
                break;
```

```
        case 2 : /* Insert Node Operation */
          printf("\nInsert the Node in the Tree");
          fflush(stdin);
          printf("\n Enter The Key : ");
          scanf("%d", &Key);
          T = Insert(Key, T);
          break;
        case 3 : /* Delete Node Operation */
          if(T == NULL)
            printf("\nB-Tree is Empty.");
          else
              {
                  printf("\nDelete the Node from the Tree");
                  printf("\n Enter the Key for Deleting the Node : ");
                  fflush(stdin);
                    scanf("%d", &Key);
                  T = Delete(Key, T);
              }
          break;
        case 4 : /* Search Node Operation */
          if(T == NULL)
            printf("\nB-Tree is Empty.");
          else
            {
                  printf("\nSearch the Node in the Tree");
                  printf("\n Enter the Searching Key : ");
                    scanf("%d", &Key);
                  pos = -1;
                  Search(Key, T, 0, &pos);
                  if(pos >= 0)
                    printf("Search Element %d is Found at Level %d",
                                                        Key, pos);
                  else
                    printf("Search Element %d is Not Found", Key);
              }
            break;
        case 5 : /* View the B-Tree in Ascending Order Operation */
          if(T == NULL)

            printf("\nB-Tree is Empty.");
```

```
            else
             {
                    printf("\nB-Tree in Ascending Order is...\n");
                    viewTreeAsc(T);
             }
            break;
        case 6 : /* View the B-Tree in Descending Order Operation */
            if(T == NULL)
              printf("\nB-Tree is Empty.");

            else
             {
                    printf("\nB-Tree in Descending Order is...\n");
                    viewTreeDes(T);
             }
            break;
        case 7 : /* View the B-Tree in Level Order Operation */
            if(T == NULL)
              printf("\nB-Tree is Empty.");
            else
                {
                    printf("\nB-Tree in Level Order is...\n");
                    viewTree(T, 0);
                }
            break;
        default : /* Deallocate Memory & Exit Operation */
            printf("\n End of Run of your Program ...");
            releaseNode(T);
            exit(0);
     }
   }
 }
void viewTreeAsc(BTree p)
 {
     int i;
     if(p != NULL)
       {
         for(i = 0; i <= p->count; i++)
            {
                if(i > 0)
                   printf("--> %d ", p->key[i]);
                viewTreeAsc(p->branch[i]);
            }
       }
 }
```

```
void viewTreeDes(BTree p)
{
    int i;
    if (p != NULL)
    {
        for(i=p->count; i>=0; i--)
        {
            viewTreeDes(p->branch[i]);
            if(i > 0)
                printf("--> %d ", p->key[i]);
        }
    }
}

BTree Insert(KeyType newkey, BTree root)
{
    KeyType x; BTree xr, p; Boolean pushup;
    pushup = PushDown(newkey,root,&x,&xr);
    if(pushup)
    {
        p = (BTree)malloc(sizeof(BNode));
        p->count = 1;
        p->key[1] = x;
        p->branch[0] = root;
        p->branch[1] = xr;
        return p;
    }
    return root;
}

Boolean PushDown(KeyType newkey,BTree p,KeyType *x, BTree *xr)
{
    int k;
    if(p == NULL)
    {
        *x = newkey;
        *xr = NULL;
        return TRUE;
    }
    else
    {
        if(SeqSearch(newkey, p, &k))
            printf("inserting duplicate key");
```

```
         if(PushDown(newkey,p->branch[k], x, xr))
           if(p->count < MAX)
            {
                 PushIn(*x, *xr, p, k);
                 return FALSE;
            }
           else
            {
                 Split(*x,*xr,p,k,x,xr);
                 return TRUE;
            }
           return FALSE;
        }
    }
Boolean SeqSearch(KeyType target, BTree p, int *k)
    {
        if(target < p->key[1])
         {
             *k = 0;
             return FALSE;
         }
        else
         {
             *k = p->count;
             while((target < p->key[*k]) && *k > 1)
              {
                   (*k)--;
              }
             return (target == p->key[*k]);
         }
    }
void PushIn(KeyType x, BTree xr, BTree p, int k)
    {
        int i;
        for(i = p->count; i > k; i--)
         {
             p->key[i+1] = p->key[i];
             p->branch[i+1] = p->branch[i];
         }
```

```
            p->key[k+1] = x;
            p->branch[k+1] = xr;
            p->count++;
    }
    void Split(KeyType x, BTree xr, BTree p, int k, KeyType *y, BTree *yr)
    {
            int i, median;
            if(k <= MIN)
              median = MIN;
            else
              median = MIN + 1;
            *yr = (BTree)malloc(sizeof(BNode));
            for (i = median+1; i <= MAX; i++)
             {
                  (*yr)->key[i-median] = p->key[i];
                  (*yr)->branch[i-median] = p->branch[i];
             }
            (*yr)->count = MAX - median;
            p->count = median;
            if (k <= MIN)
              PushIn(x, xr, p, k);
            else
              PushIn(x, xr, *yr, k - median);
            *y = p->key[p->count];
            (*yr)->branch[0] = p->branch[p->count];
            p->count--;
    }
    BTree Delete(KeyType target, BTree root)
    {
            BTree p, t;
            t = root;
            if(!RecDelete(target, t))
              printf("Target was not in the B-tree.");
            else if(root->count == 0)
             {
                  p = root;
                  root = root->branch[0];
                  free(p);
             }
```

```
        return root;
    }
Boolean RecDelete(KeyType target,BTree p)
    {
        int k;
        Boolean found;
        if(p == NULL)
          {
              return FALSE;
          }
        else
          {
            found = SeqSearch(target, p, &k);
            if(found)
              {
                    if(p->branch[k-1])
                      {
                            Successor(p,k);
                            if(!(found = RecDelete(p->key[k],p->branch[k])))
                                printf("Key not found.");
                      }
                    else
                      {
                            Remove(p,k);
                      }
              }
            else
              {
                    found = RecDelete(target, p->branch[k]);
              }
            if(p->branch[k] != NULL)
              {
                    if(p->branch[k]->count < MIN)
                        Restore(p,k);
              }
            return found;
          }
    }
```

```
    void Successor(BTree p, int k)
    {
        BTree q;
        for(q = p->branch[k]; q->branch[0]; q = q->branch[0]);
        p->key[k] = q->key[1];
    }

    void Remove(BTree p,int k)
    {
        int i;
        for(i = k+1; i <= p->count; i++)
        {
            p->key[i-1] = p->key[i];
            p->branch[i-1] = p->branch[i];
        }
        p->count--;
    }

    void Restore(BTree p, int k)
    {
        if(k == 0)
          if(p->branch[1]->count > MIN)
            MoveLeft(p,1);
          else
            Combine(p,1);
        else if(k == p->count)
          if(p->branch[k-1]->count > MIN)
            MoveRight(p,k);
          else
            Combine(p,k);
        else if (p->branch[k-1]->count > MIN)
          MoveRight(p, k);
        else if (p->branch[k+1]->count > MIN)
          MoveLeft(p, k+1);
        else
          Combine(p,k);
    }

    void MoveLeft(BTree p,int k)
    {
        int c;
        BTree t;
```

```
        t = p->branch[k-1];

        t->count++;

        t->key[t->count] = p->key[k];

        t->branch[t->count] = p->branch[k]->branch[0];

        t = p->branch[k];

        p->key[k] = t->key[1];

        t->branch[0] = t->branch[1];

        t->count--;

        for (c=1; c<=t->count; c++)

          {

                t->key[c] = t->key[c+1];

                t->branch[c] = t->branch[c+1];

          }

    }

void MoveRight(BTree p,int k)

  {

        int c;

        BTree t;

        t = p->branch[k];

        for(c = t->count; c > 0; c--)

          {

                t->key[c+1] = t->key[c];

                t->branch[c+1] = t->branch[c];

          }

        t->branch[1] = t->branch[0];

        t->count++;

        t->key[1] = p->key[k];

        t = p->branch [k-1];

        p->key[k] = t->key[t->count];

        p->branch[k]->branch[0] = t->branch[t->count];

        t->count--;

    }

void Combine(BTree p,int k)

  {

        int c;

        BTree l, q;

        q = p->branch[k];

        l = p->branch[k-1];
```

```
        l->count++;
        l->key[l->count] = p->key[k];
        l->branch[l->count] = q->branch[0];
        for (c=1; c<=q->count; c++)
         {
             l->count++;
             l->key[l->count] = q->key[c];
             l->branch[l->count] = q->branch[c];
         }
        for(c = k; c < p->count; c++)
         {
             p->key[c] = p->key[c+1];
             p->branch[c] = p->branch[c+1];
         }
        p->count--;
        free(q);
  }
void viewTree(BTree p, int depth)
  {
      int i;
      if(p != NULL)
       {
         if(depth > levels)
           levels = depth;
         for (i = 0; i <= p->count; i++)
          {
              if(i == 0)
                printf("\nLevel %d : ==> ",depth);
              if(i > 0 && i < p->count)
                printf(" %d --> ", p->key[i]);
              if(i == p->count)
                printf(" %d\n", p->key[i]);
          }
         printf("\n");
         for (i = 0; i <= p->count; i++)
           viewTree(p->branch[i],depth+1);
       }
  }
```

```
void Search(KeyType key, BTree p, int depth, int *pos)
{
    int i;
    if(p != NULL)

    {
        if(depth > levels)
            levels = depth;
        for(i = 0; i <= p->count; i++)
            if(i > 0 && p->key[i] == key)
                *pos = depth;
        for (i = 0; i <= p->count; i++)
            Search(key, p->branch[i], depth+1, pos);
    }
}
void displayMenu()
{
    printf("\n Basic Operations in a B-Tree . . .");
    printf("\n\t 0. Show Menu ");
    printf("\n\t 1. Create a New B-Tree ");
    printf("\n\t 2. Insert a Node ");
    printf("\n\t 3. Delete a Node ");
    printf("\n\t 4. Search a Node ");
    printf("\n\t 5. View the B-Tree in Ascending Order ");
    printf("\n\t 6. View the B-Tree in Descending Order ");
    printf("\n\t 7. View the B-Tree in Level order");
    printf("\n\t 8. Exit ");
}
void releaseNode(BTree Node)
{
    free(Node);
}
```

The program displays the following output

```
Basic Operations in a B-Tree . . .
        0. Show Menu
        1. Create a New B-Tree
        2. Insert a Node
        3. Delete a Node
```

```
            4. Search a Node
            5. View the B-Tree in Ascending Order
            6. View the B-Tree in Descending Order
            7. View the B-Tree in Level order
            8. Exit
? 3
B-Tree is Empty.
? 4
B-Tree is Empty.
? 5
B-Tree is Empty.
? 6
B-Tree is Empty.
? 7
B-Tree is Empty.
? 1
Create a New B-Tree
Enter The Key : 55
Do u wish to add Data in the Tree (y/n) ? y
Enter The Key : 44
Do u wish to add Data in the Tree (y/n) ? y
Enter The Key : 33
Do u wish to add Data in the Tree (y/n) ? n
? 5
B-Tree in Ascending Order is...
--> 33 --> 44 --> 55
? 6
B-Tree in Descending Order is...
--> 55 --> 44 --> 33
? 7
B-Tree in Level Order is...
Level 0 : ==>   33 -->   44 -->   55
? 2
Insert the Node in the Tree
Enter The Key : 22
```

```
? 7

B-Tree in Level Order is...

Level 0 : ==>  33

Level 1 : ==>  22

Level 1 : ==>  44 -->  55

? 2

Insert the Node in the Tree

Enter The Key : 25

? 7

B-Tree in Level Order is...

Level 0 : ==>  33

Level 1 : ==>  22 -->  25

Level 1 : ==>  44 -->  55

? 2

Insert the Node in the Tree

Enter The Key : 66

? 7

B-Tree in Level Order is...

Level 0 : ==>  33

Level 1 : ==>  22 -->  25

Level 1 : ==>  44 -->  55 -->  66

? 2

Insert the Node in the Tree

Enter The Key : 30

? 7

B-Tree in Level Order is...

Level 0 : ==>  33

Level 1 : ==>  22 -->  25 -->  30

Level 1 : ==>  44 -->  55 -->  66

? 2

Insert the Node in the Tree

Enter The Key : 32

? 7

B-Tree in Level Order is...

Level 0 : ==>  25 -->  33

Level 1 : ==>  22
```

```
Level 1 : ==>  30 -->  32

Level 1 : ==>  44 -->  55 -->  66

? 2

Insert the Node in the Tree

Enter The Key : 40

? 7

B-Tree in Level Order is...

Level 0 : ==>  25 -->  33 -->  44

Level 1 : ==>  22

Level 1 : ==>  30 -->  32

Level 1 : ==>  40

Level 1 : ==>  55 -->  66

? 5

D Tree in Ascending Order is...

--> 22 --> 25 --> 30 --> 32 --> 33 --> 40 --> 44 --> 55 --> 66

? 6

B-Tree in Descending Order is...

--> 66 --> 55 --> 44 --> 40 --> 33 --> 32 --> 30 --> 25 --> 22

? 2

Insert the Node in the Tree

Enter The Key : 11

? 7

B-Tree in Level Order is...

Level 0 : ==>  25 -->  33 -->  44

Level 1 : ==>  11 -->  22

Level 1 : ==>  30 -->  32

Level 1 : ==>  40

Level 1 : ==>  55 -->  66

? 2

Insert the Node in the Tree

Enter The Key : 26

? 7

B-Tree in Level Order is...

Level 0 : ==>  25 -->  33 -->  44

Level 1 : ==>  11 -->  22

Level 1 : ==>  26 -->  30 -->  32
```

```
Level 1 : ==>  40

Level 1 : ==>  55 -->  66

? 2

Insert the Node in the Tree

Enter The Key:35

? 7

B-Tree in Level Order is...

Level 0 : ==>  25 -->  33 -->  44

Level 1 : ==>  11 -->  22

Level 1 : ==>  26 -->  30 -->  32

Level 1 : ==>  35 -->  40

Level 1 : ==>  55 -->  66

? 2

Insert the Node in the Tree

Enter The Key : 50

? 7

B-Tree in Level Order is...

Level 0 : ==>  25 -->  33 -->  44

Level 1 : ==>  11 -->  22

Level 1 : ==>  26 -->  30 -->  32

Level 1 : ==>  35 -->  40

Level 1 : ==>  50 -->  55 -->  66

? 2

Insert the Node in the Tree

Enter The Key : 31

? 7

B-Tree in Level Order is...

Level 0 : ==>  30

Level 1 : ==>  25

Level 2 : ==>  11 -->  22

Level 2 : ==>  26

Level 1 : ==>  33 -->  44

Level 2 : ==>  31 -->  32

Level 2 : ==>  35 -->  40

Level 2 : ==>  50 -->  55 -->  66

? 3

Delete the Node from the Tree

Enter the Key for Deleting the Node : 30
```

```
? 0

Basic Operations in a B-Tree . . .

         0. Show Menu

         1. Create a New B-Tree

         2. Insert a Node

         3. Delete a Node

         4. Search a Node

         5. View the B-Tree in Ascending Order

         6. View the B-Tree in Descending Order

         7. View the B-Tree in Level order

         8. Exit

? 5

B-Tree in Ascending Order is...

--> 11 --> 22 --> 25 --> 26 --> 31 --> 32 --> 33 --> 35 --> 40 --> 44
--> 50 --> 55 --> 66

? 6

B-Tree in Descending Order is...

--> 66 --> 55 --> 50 --> 44 --> 40 --> 35 --> 33 --> 32 --> 31 --> 26
--> 25 --> 22 --> 11

? 7

B-Tree in Level Order is...

Level 0 : ==>   31

Level 1 : ==>   25

Level 2 : ==>   11 -->  22

Level 2 : ==>   26

Level 1 : ==>   33 -->  44

Level 2 : ==>   32

Level 2 : ==>   35 -->  40

Level 2 : ==>   50 -->  55 -->  66

? 4

Search the Node in the Tree

Enter the Searching Key : 30

Search Element 30 is Not Found

? 3

Delete the Node from the Tree

Enter the Key for Deleting the Node : 30
```

```
        Target was not in the B-tree.

        ? 4

        Search the Node in the Tree

        Enter the Searching Key : 32

        Search Element 32 is Found at Level 2

        ? 4

        Search the Node in the Tree

        Enter the Searching Key : 33

        Search Element 33 is Found at Level 1

        ? 4

        Search the Node in the Tree

        Enter the Searching Key : 31

        Search Element 31 is Found at Level 0

        ? 8

        End of Run of your Program . . .
```

3.13 B+ Tree

B+ (spelled as B plus) tree is a close sibling of B tree, with a slight variation. B+ tree combines the features of B tree and ISAM (Index Sequential Access Method). Like B trees, all the leaves are of the same distance from the root.The main difference between them is the nodes are divided into two types they are: index node and the data node. *Index node* is a node, which stores the key value and pointer, also holds the details of the internal nodes whereas the *data node* stores all the elements and holds the details of external nodes. The leaf nodes of the B+ tree are linked together to provide ordered access on the search field to therecords. Internal nodes of a B+ tree is used to guide the search.For faster access all the data nodes are linked together to form a doubly linked list. In B+ trees, all the data are stored only in data nodes.B+ tree of order n has a root node from 1 to n-1 elements. Usually, these trees will occupy more spaces compared to B trees since it holds large number of children per node.

Characteristics of B+ trees

- All the leaves node are on the same level

- They are build upwards from the leaves

- All the elements are stored only in leaves

- Key values are stored in the internal nodes

- FIND (search) operation is more easy since all the data nodes are interconnected

- Keys act as the indices for directing to the search node

- All the non leaf nodes except the root have at least |n/2| children

- A leaf node contains at least |n/2|-1 children and has not more than n-1 keys

- It require O(n) work to store the tree

- Insert and delete operation require O (log n) work to fix up all the information at the node.

B+ trees have very high distribution, which helps to reduce the number of input and output operations in order to search an element in the tree. B+ trees are specialized multi way trees designed especially for retrieving the data, which is stored in file systems. Many file systems like JFS, XFS, NSS, BFS, ReiserFS, etc., uses B+ tree for metadata indexing used for storing the directories, for file extent indexing and also provides security related metadata indexing. The main goal of B+ tree is to get fast access to the data from disk drives, which means reading a very small number of records. These trees are generally wider than binary trees and are kept balanced automatically by the use of carefully constructed insertion and deletion algorithms so that, the height of all the leaf elements remain the same.

Fig. 3.27 shows the example structure of B+ trees of order 3. The leave nodes (level 3) are data node and the above layer (i.e.,) level 2 are index nodes. The top layer is the root of B+ tree.

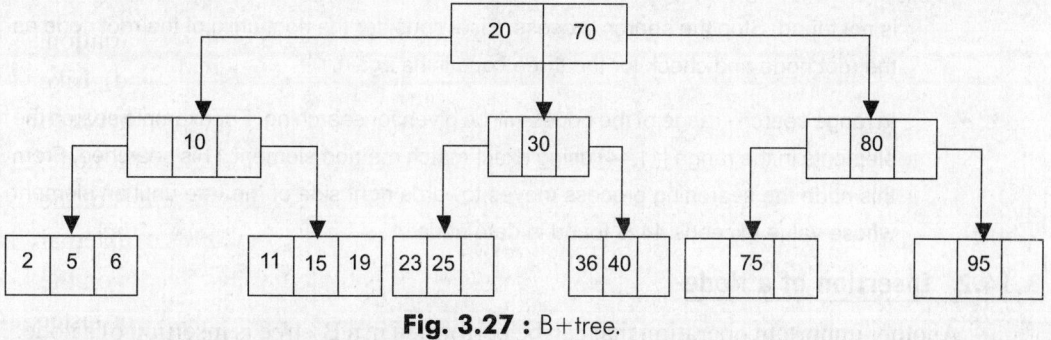

Fig. 3.27 : B+tree.

3.14 Basic operations in a B+ tree

The basic operations that can be performed in a B+ tree are,

- Creation of B+ tree

- Insertion of node

- Deletion of node

- Searching a node

- Finding the minimum value in the tree

- Finding the maximum value in the tree

- View the contents of the B+ tree.

3.14.1 Searching of a node

One of the most important operations performed in a B+ tree is searching a node.

- Check whether the root node of the B+ tree is NULL. If yes, B+ tree is empty and hence stop the search operation. If the tree is not empty, then the start the search operation

- Search process is of two types, exact match search and range search.

- In exact match search, we compare the new node data with root node data, for the following three conditions.

- If the content of the new node is equal to the content of the root node, search element is found, and hence stop the search process.

- If the content of the new node data is lesser than the content of the root node, check whether the left child of the root node is NULL. If the condition is true, search element is not found. Stop the search process. Else, consider the left child of the root node as the root node and check for the three conditions again.

- If the content of the new node data is greater than the content of the root node, check whether the right child of the root node is NULL. If the condition is true, search element is not found. Stop the search process. Else, consider the right child of the root node as the root node and check for the three conditions again.

- In range search - range of the nodes will be given for searching. For example search the elements in the range [11,44] using exact match method element 11 is searched. From this node the searching process moves towards right side of the tree until an element whose value exceeds 44 is found in data node.

3.14.2 Insertion of a Node

Another important operation that can be performed in a B+ tree is insertion of a node. The following steps helps you to understand things better.

- When inserting an data, first do a search for the data in the B-tree. If the data doesn't exist in the B-tree, the unsuccessful search will end at a leaf. If the data already exists, the new data will not be inserted, since B-tree will not allow duplication.

- If there is place to insert in the leaf node, then fill the new data. This may require that some existing keys be moved one to the right to give space for the new data.

- If there is no space to insert the new data, then the node must be split with about half of the keys going into a new node to the right of this one. The median or the middle key is moved up into the parent node.

- If the root node is ever split, the median key moves up into a new root node, thus causing the tree to increase its height by one. This strategy might have to be repeated all the way to the top.

3.14.3 Deletion of a Node

Another important operation that can be performed in a B+ tree is deletion of a node. There are two specific cases to be considered before deleting an element. They are,

- Deleting an element may put it under the minimum number of elements and children
- Deleting an element from an internal node may be a separator for its child nodes.

Search for the data to be deleted

- If the data is present in the leaf node, simply delete the data from the node, leaving the node with few keys, so some additional changes to the tree will be required
- If the data is not present in the leaf node, then it is guaranteed that its predecessor (largest element in the left subtree) or successor (smallest element in the right subtree) will be in a leaf node and we can delete the key and promote the predecessor or successor key to the non-leaf deleted key's position
- If both the above steps leads to a leaf node containing less than the minimum number of keys then we have to look at the siblings immediately adjacent to the leaf node.

Rebalancing the tree after deletion

- If the right sibling has, more than the minimum number of keys borrow one and adjust the separator.
- If the left sibling has more than the minimum number of keys borrow one and adjust the separator.
- If both immediate siblings have only the minimum number of elements
  - Create a new node with all the elements from the deficient node, all the elements from one of its siblings and the separator in the parent between the two combined sibling nodes.
  - Remove the separator from the parent and replace the two children, if separated with the combined node.
  - If it brings the number of elements in the parent node under minimum, repeat the steps with that deficient node, unless it is the root.

3.15 Binary Heaps

A *binary heap* is an array that is viewed as a complete binary tree. A complete binary tree is completely filled on all levels except possibly the lowest, and the lowest level is filled from the left. The root of the tree is stored in array element 0. The parent of the node n is stored at node (n/2). The right child of node is stored at node 2n, and the left child at node is stored at 2n+1.

Properties of binary Heap

- A heap satisfies the **max-heap property** if for every node n except the root, has a value lesser than its parent.
- A heap satisfies the **min-heap property** if for every node n except the root, has a value greater than its parent.

A heap is a *max-heap* or a *min-heap* if it satisfies the corresponding heap property. The *height* of a node in a heap is the number of edges on the longest simple downward path from the node to a leaf, and the height of the heap is the height of the root. Conceptually, a heap is a kind of binary tree. That is, it is a collection of nodes with a root node and in which each node can potentially have a left child node and a right child node. Every node in the binary tree, except for the root node, has exactly one parent node.

When a heap is used to implement a priority queue, each node contains one of the items in the queue along with the number that specifies the priority of that item. As far as the structure of the heap goes, it is only the priority, not the item itself. A heap must satisfy the heap property, which says that the priority of every node is greater than or equal to the priority of any child nodes of that node. Another way of saying this is that the priority of each non-root node must be less than or equal to the priority of its parent node. Note that the heap property implies that the priority of any node is greater than or equal to the priorities of all its descendant nodes, not just the nodes immediately below it. In particular, the priority of the root node is greater than or equal to the priority of every other node in the heap.

In terms of priority queues, the root node contains the item that is at the head of the queue. A heap has one more important property: It is a full binary tree. In a full binary tree, there are no missing nodes in the interior of the tree. If you think of the tree being built up by adding nodes one at a time, then the nodes are added level-by-level from top to bottom, and within a level they are added from left to right. A heap (or any full binary tree) can be represented as an array. All you have to do is line up the nodes in the array, starting with the root node, then the children of the root, then the grandchildren, and so on. The important thing about this array is that the structure of the binary tree can be described completely in terms of the array. In order to use a heap to implement a priority queue, we need to implement the heap's insert and remove operations in terms of operations on the heap. Note that after we insert or remove an item, the resulting data structure must still be a full binary tree, and it must still have the heap property.

We can implement the heap as an array of objects, where each object contains an item of type, along with its associated priority. For generality, we should make it a dynamic array, but to keep things simple, let's make it a static array with a maximum capacity given by a constant MAX SIZE. We also need an integer variable to keep track of the actual number of items currently in the queue. When we add a new item to the heap, a new node must be added in the next available position, at the end of the array. However, simply placing the new item in that node is likely to violate the heap property. That is, the new item might have a priority that is greater than the priority of its parent. The solution is simple, place the new item in the next available spot, but then have a contest between the new item and its parent in the tree. If the new item has higher priority, swap it with its parent. Now, the new item might still be out of place in its new position, so have another contest between it and its new parent. Repeat this process until the new item is in correct position in the heap or reaches the root node. Using these ideas implement a priority queue using a heap.

3.16 Applications of Heaps

- Heaps are used to implement priority queues. Each node contains the data to be stored in the queue along with the number that specifies the priority of the data being stored

- Another important application of the heap is sorting (Heap Sort). Heap sort is nothing but the binary tree in which the elements to be sorted are stored. Heap Sort is discussedin Chapter 5.

3.17 Summary

- A tree is a non-linear, two-dimensional data structure, which represents hierarchical relationship between individual data items.

- A path in a tree is a sequence of distinct nodes in which successive nodes are connected by edges in the tree.

- A node that has no children is called as a terminal node. It is also referred as a leaf node. These nodes have zero degree.

- All intermediate nodes that traverse the given tree from its root node to the terminal nodes are referred as non-terminal nodes.

- A binary tree is a tree, which has nodes either empty or not more than two child nodes, each of which may be a leaf node.

- A full binary tree is a tree in which all the leaves are on the same level and every non-leaf node has exactly two children.

- A complete binary tree is a tree in which every non-leaf node has exactly two children not necessarily to be on the same level.

- Postorder traversal leads to postfix expressions. Preorder traversal leads to prefix expressions. Inorder traversal leads to infix expressions.

- **Left-skewed binary tree is a** binary tree, which has only left child nodes.

- **Right-skewed binary tree is a** binary tree, which has only right child nodes.

- An extended binary tree is a transformation of any binary tree in to a complete binary tree, which replaces every null subtree of original binary tree with special nodes. The nodes from the original tree are referred as internal nodes, while the special nodes are referred as external nodes.

- A **general tree** (i.e., a tree with nodes having any number of children) can be converted into an equivalent binary tree using the leftmost child right siblings representation.

- Traversing a binary tree, means moving through all the nodes in the binary tree, visiting each node in the tree only once.

- The different binary tree traversal techniques are preorder traversal, inorder traversal, and postorder traversal.

- ✍ A binary search tree in which the heights of the left and right sub trees of the root differ by at most 1 are referred as **AVL trees**, also the left and right sub trees are themselves AVL trees.

- ✍ In representing an AVL tree, each node N also has a balance factor BF(N) which shows the difference in height between its left and right sub trees. In an AVL tree, the BF(N) should be -1, 0, or 1 for all nodes.

- ✍ AVL trees are height-balanced trees, meaning that, they are built, to maintain the balance within the binary tree.

- ✍ In linked representation of binary trees, we can see that all leaf nodes and some non-leaf nodes have NULL values. Instead of storing NULL values in the left and right pointer fields, we can store some useful information, in left and right pointer fields. These links are considered as threads. A binary tree, which implements these threads are referred to as threaded binary tree.

- ✍ If you use only the left pointer fields (for storing inorder predecessor) as threads, then the binary tree is referred to as left in-threaded binary tree.

- ✍ If you use only the right pointer fields (for storing inorder successor) as threads, then the binary tree is referred to as right in-threaded binary tree.

- ✍ If you use both left and right pointer fields as threads, then the binary tree is referred to as fully in-threaded binary tree.

- ✍ An appropriate data structure that supports the operations for inserting a new element and deleting the largest element is referred to as a **priority queue**.

- ✍ Btrees stands for Balanced trees, where all the leaves are of the same distance from the root. A B-tree of order n has a root node containing from 1to n-1 elements that should satisfy the following characteristics as mentioned in section 3.11.

- ✍ The basic operations that can be performed in a Btree are, creation of a B-tree, insertion of a node, deletion of a node, searching a node, finding the minimum value in the tree, finding the maximum value in the tree, and view the contents of the B-Tree.

- ✍ B+ tree is a close sibling of B tree, with a slight variation. B+ tree combines the features of B tree and ISAM (Index Sequential Access Method).

- ✍ A binary tree, which implements a thread is referred to as threaded binary tree. Instead of storing NULL values in the left and right pointer fields, we can store some useful information, such as, inorder predecessor in the left pointer field and inorder successor in the right pointer field. These links are considered as threads.

- ✍ A **binary heap** is an array that is viewed as a complete binary tree. A complete binary tree is completely filled on all levels except possibly the lowest, and the lowest level is filled from the left.

3.18 Short-answer Questions

1.   *Define a tree.*

A tree is a non-linear, two-dimensional data structure, which represents hierarchical relationship between individual data items.

2.   *Define a path in a tree.*

A path in a tree is a sequence of distinct nodes in which successive nodes are connected by edges in the tree.

3.   *Define terminal nodes in a tree.*

A node that has no children is called as a terminal node. It is also referred as a leaf node. These nodes have degree has zero.

4.   *Define a binary tree.*

A binary tree is a tree, which has nodes either empty or not more than two child nodes, each of which may be a leaf node.

5.   *Define a full binary tree.*

A full binary tree is a tree in which all the leaves are on the same level and every non-leaf node has exactly two children.

6.   *Define a complete binary tree.*

A complete binary tree is a tree in which every non-leaf node has exactly two children not necessarily to be on the same level.

7.   *State the properties of a binary tree.*

The properties of a binary tree includes,
- The maximum number of nodes on level n of a binary tree is 2^{n-1}, where $n \geq 1$.
- The maximum number of nodes in a binary tree of height n is 2^{n-1}, where $n \geq 1$.
- For any non-empty tree, $n_l = n_d + 1$ where n_l is the number of leaf nodes and n_d is the number of nodes of degree 2.

8.   *What are the different binary tree traversal techniques ?*

The different binary tree traversal techniques are
- Preorder traversal.
- Inorder traversal.
- Postorder traversal.
- Levelorder traversal.

9.   *What are the tasks performed while traversing a binary tree ?*

The tasks performed while traversing a binary tree are,
- Visiting a node.
- Traverse the left subtree.
- Traverse the right subtree.

10. **What are the tasks performed during preorder traversal.**

The tasks performed during preorder traversal,
- Process the root node.
- Traverse the left subtree.
- Traverse the right subtree.

11. **What are the tasks performed during inorder traversal.**

The tasks performed during inorder traversal,
- Traverse the left subtree.
- Process the root node.
- Traverse the right subtree.

12. **What are the tasks performed during postorder traversal.**

The tasks performed during postorder traversal,
- Traverse the left subtree.
- Traverse the right subtree.
- Process the root node.

13. **What are the tasks performed during levelorder traversal.**

The tasks performed during levelorder traversal,
- Process the root node at level 1.
- Traverse the next level (i.e, level 2), below the root node.
- Process the nodes from left to right in that level.
- Similarly traverse the next level and process the nodes from left to right and continue till the end of levels.

14. **State the merits and demerits of linked representation of a binary tree.**

The merits of linked representation of binary trees include
- Insertions and deletions in a node, involves no data movement except the re-arrangement of pointers, hence less processing time.

The demerits of linked representation of binary trees include
- Given a node structure, it is difficult to determine its parent node.
- Memory spaces are wasted for storing null pointers for the nodes, which have one or no subtrees.
- It requires dynamic memory allocation, which is not possible in some programming languages.

15. **Define a binary search tree.**

A binary search tree is a special binary tree, which is either empty or if it is empty it should satisfy the following characteristics.
- Every node has a value and no two nodes should have the same value (i.e., the values in the binary search tree are distinct.
- The values in any left subtree is less than the value of its parent node.
- The values in any right subtree is greater than the value of its parent node.
- The left and right subtrees of each node are again binary search trees.

Chapter 4
Non-Linear Data Structures
— Graphs

4.1 Graphs

*A **graph** is a non-linear data structure that represents less relationship between its adjacent elements. There is no hierarchical relationship between the adjacent elements in case of graphs. A **graph** consists of a set of non-empty vertices (referred as **nodes** in case of trees), together with a set of edges, and each edge joins two different vertices. A **path** is a sequence of distinct vertices each adjacent to the next, except possibly the first vertex and last vertex is different. In **Fig. 4.1** 1, 2, 3 is path and 3, 4, 1 is also a path. A **cycle** is a path containing atleast three vertices such that the starting and the ending vertices are the same. In **Fig. 4.1,** the path formed by vertices 1, 2, 3, 4 is a cycle.*

4.1.1 Definitions in Graphs

Graphs are generally classified as,

- Undirected graph
- Directed graph.

*If an edge between any two nodes is not directionally oriented, a graph is referred as an **undirected graph** or **unqualified graph**. **Fig. 4.1** shows an undirected graph* in which 12 or 21, 23 or 32, 34 or 43 and 14 or 41 are edges that are not oriented directionally. *If an edge between any two nodes is directionally oriented, a graph is referred as a **directed graph** or **digraph**. **Fig. 4.2** shows a digraph which consists of* directed edges from 1 to 2, 2 to 3, 3 to 4, 4 to 5, 5 to 6 and 6 to 7. The reverse is not an edge (i.e., 2 to 1, 3 to 2 and so on). In a digraph, all edges are in same direction, which follows a path always moving in the same direction indicated by arrows. Such a path is referred as a **directed path**. In a digraph, the cycle is referred as a **directed cycle**.

A graph is called as a **null graph**, if it has no vertices. A graph is called as a **sub graph** of another graph, if all the vertices and edges, are also available in the another graph. A graph is called as a **connected graph**, if there exists a path from any one vertex to all other vertex. In a pair of distinct vertices if there is a directed path from every vertex to all other vertex then the directed graph is said to be **strongly connected graph**. It is also referred as a **complete graph**. A complete digraph with n vertices will have n(n-1) edges. A complete undirected graph with n vertices will have n(n-1)/2 edges.

Fig. 4.3 shows a strongly connected digraph. A directed graph is said to be *weakly connected graph*,if any vertex does not have a directed path to any other vertices. *Fig. 4.4* shows the weakly connected digraph.

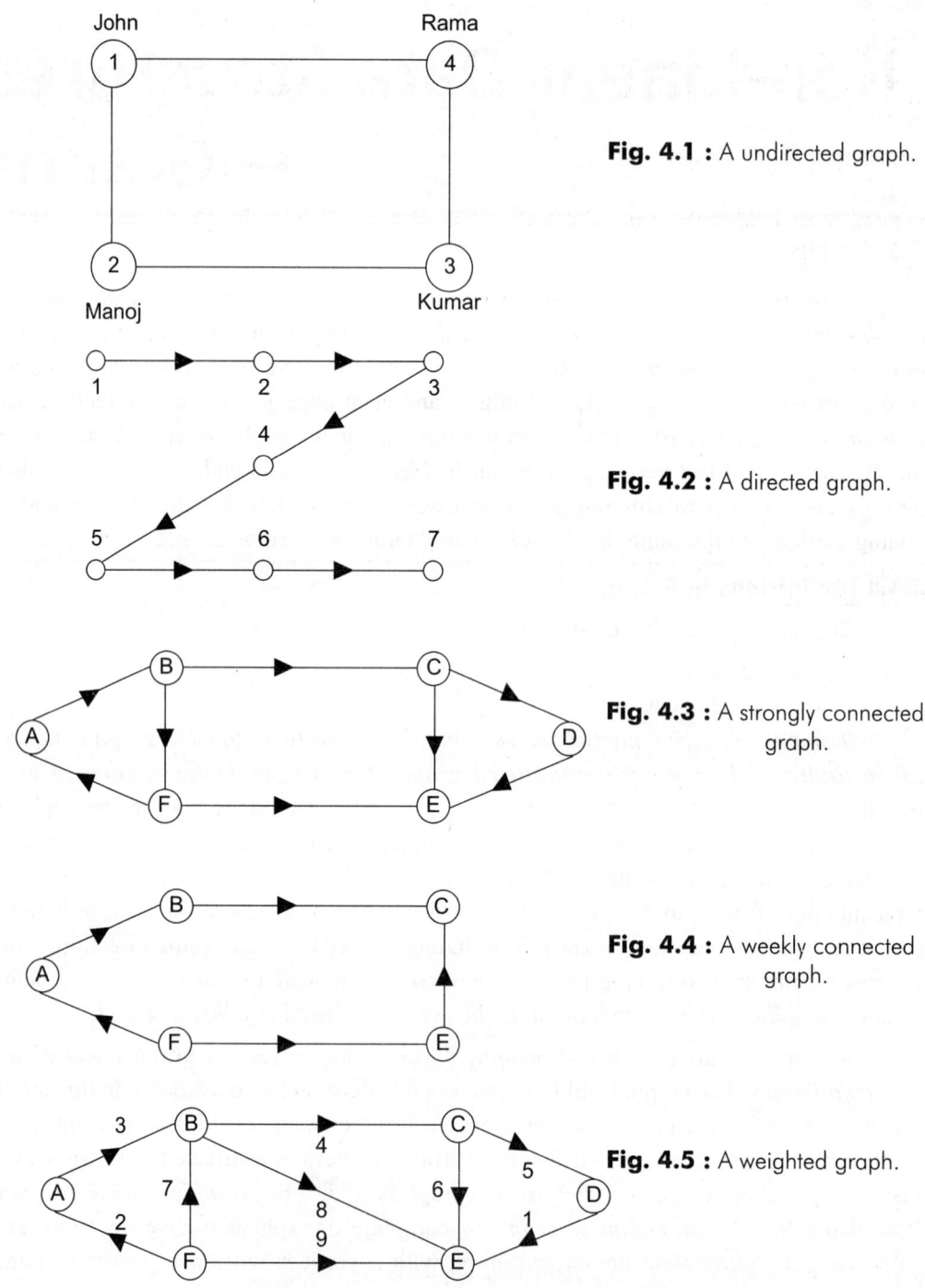

Fig. 4.1 : A undirected graph.

Fig. 4.2 : A directed graph.

Fig. 4.3 : A strongly connected graph.

Fig. 4.4 : A weekly connected graph.

Fig. 4.5 : A weighted graph.

The *indegree* of a vertex in a digraph is the number of edges entering into the vertex. The *outdegree* of a vertex in a digraph is the number of edges exiting from the vertex. The *degree* of a vertex is calculated by the sum of indgree and outdegree in a digraph. In *Fig. 4.4,* the indegree of the vertex c is 2, whereas the outdegree of the vertex c is 0. A vertex whose indegree is 0 is referred as *source vertex* and the vertex whose outdegree is 0 is referred as a *sink vertex*. A vertex, which has no edge is referred to as an *isolated vertex*. A vertex whose indegree is 1 and outdegree is 0 is referred to as *pendant vertex*. A graph is said to be a *weighted graph* if every edge in the graph is assigned some weight or value. The weight of an edge is a positive value that may be representing the distance between the vertices or the weights of the edges along the path. *Fig. 4.5* shows the weighted graph.

4.2 Graph Representation and its Operations

Graphs are generally represented in the following scheme as,

- Incidence Matrix
- Adjacency Matrix
- Adjacency List.

4.2.1 Incidence Matrix

A graph containing m vertices and n edges can be represented by a matrix with m rows and n columns. The matrix is formed by storing 1 in its ith row and j^{th} column if there exists a ith vertex, connected to one end of the jth edge, and a 0, if there is no i^{th} vertex, connected to any end of the jth edge of the graph, such a matrix is referred as an *incidence matrix*.

IncMat[i][j] = 1, if there is an edge E_j from vertex V_i.
        = 0, Otherwise.

Fig. 4.6 shows three undirected graphs and *Fig. 4.7* shows the incidence matrices for the undirected graphs shown in *Fig. 4.6*.

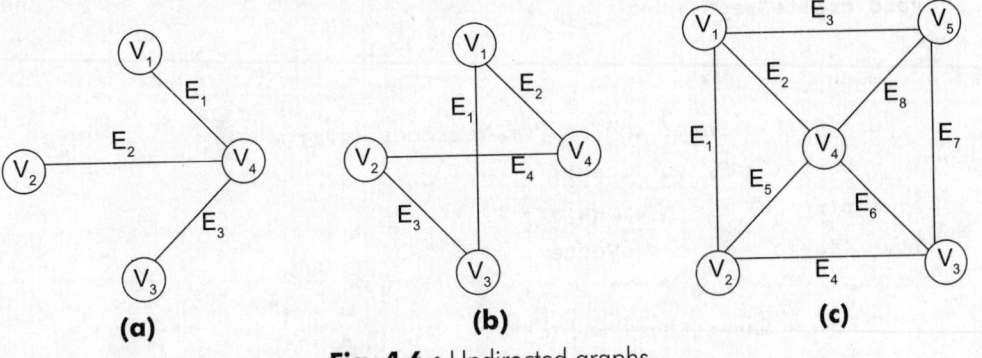

(a)   **(b)**   **(c)**

Fig. 4.6 : Undirected graphs.

	E₁	E₂	E₃	
V₁	1	0	0	
V₂	0	1	0	**(a)**
V₃	0	0	1	
V₄	1	1	1	

	E₁	E₂	E₃	E₄
V₁	1	1	0	0
V₂	0	0	1	1
V₃	1	0	1	0
V₄	0	1	0	1

(b)

(c)

	E₁	E₂	E₃	E₄	E₅	E₆	E₇	E₈
V₁	1	1	1	0	0	0	0	0
V₂	1	0	0	1	1	0	0	0
V₃	0	0	0	1	0	1	1	0
V₄	0	1	0	0	1	1	0	1
V₅	0	0	1	0	0	0	1	1

Fig. 4.7 : Incidence matrices for the undirected graphs shown in Fig. 4.6.

Program 4.1 :

```
/* Program to create and view the incidence Matrix. */
#include <stdio.h>
#define VSIZE 20
int nVertex, nEdges, incMat[VSIZE][VSIZE];
void insertEdge(int vStart, int vEnd);
void createGraph();
void viewGraph();
void main()
{
    createGraph();
    printf("\n Incidence Matrix is . . . \n");
    viewGraph();
}
void createGraph()
{
    int r, c;
    printf("\n Enter the no. of Vertices : ");
        scanf("%d", &nVertex);
    for(r = 0; r < nVertex; r++)
        for(c = 0; c < nVertex; c++)
            if(r != c)
                insertEdge(r+1, c+1);
}
```

```
    void insertEdge(int vStart, int vEnd)
    {
        int i, ie;
        if(vStart > nVertex || vStart < 1 || vEnd > nVertex || vEnd < 1)
            return;
        printf("Enter the Weight of the Edge from V%d to V%d : ",
                    vStart, vEnd);
            scanf("%d", &ie);
        if(ie <= 0)
            return;
        for(i = 0;  i < nEdges; i++)
            if(incMat[vEnd-1][i] == 1 && incMat[vStart-1][i] == 1)
                return;
        incMat[vEnd-1][nEdges] = incMat[vStart-1][nEdges] = 1;
        nEdges++;
    }
    void viewGraph()
    {
        int e, v, c;
        for(e = 0; e < nEdges; e++)
            printf("     E%d",e+1);
        for(v = 0; v < nVertex; v++)


        {
            printf("\nV%-2d   ",v+1);
            for(c = 0; c < nEdges; c++)
                printf("%-2d    ", incMat[v][c]);
        }
        printf("\n Total No. of Vertices : %d", nVertex);
        printf("\n Total No. of Edges : %d", nEdges);
    }
```

The program displays the following output

RUN 1   Enter the no. of Vertices : 4
           Enter the Weight of the Edge from V1 to V2 :0
           Enter the Weight of the Edge from V1 to V3 :0
           Enter the Weight of the Edge from V1 to V4 :1

```
          Enter the Weight of the Edge from V2 to V1 :0
          Enter the Weight of the Edge from V2 to V3 :0
          Enter the Weight of the Edge from V2 to V4 :1
          Enter the Weight of the Edge from V3 to V1 :0
          Enter the Weight of the Edge from V3 to V2 :0
          Enter the Weight of the Edge from V3 to V4 :1
          Enter the Weight of the Edge from V4 to V1 :1
          Enter the Weight of the Edge from V4 to V2 :1
          Enter the Weight of the Edge from V4 to V3 :1

     Incidence Matrix is

          E1      E2      E3

     V1    1       0       0
     V2    0       1       0
     V3    0       0       1
     V4    1       1       1

     Total No. of Vertices : 4

     Total No. of Edges : 3

Run2     Enter the no. of Vertices : 5
          Enter the Weight of the Edge from V1 to V2 : 1
          Enter the Weight of the Edge from V1 to V3 : 0
          Enter the Weight of the Edge from V1 to V4 : 1
          Enter the Weight of the Edge from V1 to V5 : 1
          Enter the Weight of the Edge from V2 to V1 : 1
          Enter the Weight of the Edge from V2 to V3 : 1
          Enter the Weight of the Edge from V2 to V4 : 1
          Enter the Weight of the Edge from V2 to V5 : 0
          Enter the Weight of the Edge from V3 to V1 : 0
          Enter the Weight of the Edge from V3 to V2 : 1
          Enter the Weight of the Edge from V3 to V4 : 1
          Enter the Weight of the Edge from V3 to V5 : 1
          Enter the Weight of the Edge from V4 to V1 : 1
          Enter the Weight of the Edge from V4 to V2 : 1
          Enter the Weight of the Edge from V4 to V3 : 1
          Enter the Weight of the Edge from V4 to V5 : 1
          Enter the Weight of the Edge from V5 to V1 : 1
          Enter the Weight of the Edge from V5 to V2 : 0
          Enter the Weight of the Edge from V5 to V3 : 1
          Enter the Weight of the Edge from V5 to V4 : 1
```

```
Incidence Matrix is . . .
        E1      E2      E3      E4      E5      E6      E7      E8
V1      1       1       1       0       0       0       0       0
V2      1       0       0       1       1       0       0       0
V3      0       0       0       1       0       1       1       0
V4      0       1       0       0       1       1       0       1
V5      0       0       1       0       0       0       1       1
Total No. of Vertices : 5
Total No. of Edges : 8
```

4.2.2 Adjacency Matrix

A graph containing n vertices can be represented by a matrix with n rows and n columns. The matrix is formed by storing the edge weight in its ith row and j^{th} column of the matrix, if there exists an edge between i^{th} and j^{th} vertex of the graph, and a 0, if there is no edge between i^{th} and j^{th} vertex of the graph. Such matrix is referred as an *adjacency matrix*. *Note that for an unweighted graph, the edge weight is 1.*

AdjMat[i][j] = Weight of the edge, if there is a path from vertex Vi to Vj.

= 0, Otherwise.

Fig. 4.8 shows the adjacency matrices for the undirected graphs shown in *Fig. 4.6*. Even though adjacency matrix is an easy way of representing graphs, a graph with considerable number of nodes could use a large amount of memory. Most of the adjacency matrices will be sparse matrices (a matrix with lot of zeros in it) only.

(a)

	V_1	V_2	V_3	V_4
V_1	0	0	0	1
V_2	0	0	0	1
V_3	0	0	0	1
V_4	1	1	1	0

(b)

	V_1	V_2	V_3	V_4
V_1	0	0	1	1
V_2	0	0	1	1
V_3	1	1	0	0
V_4	1	1	0	0

(c)

	V_1	V_2	V_3	V_4	V_5
V_1	0	1	0	1	1
V_2	1	0	1	1	0
V_3	0	1	0	1	1
V_4	1	1	1	0	1
V_5	1	0	1	1	0

Fig. 4.8 :
Adjacency matrices for the undirected graphs shown in Fig. 4.7.

Program 4.2 :

```c
/* Program to create, insert, delete and view the adjacency matrix. */
/* adjmat.c */
#include <stdio.h>
#define VSIZE 20
int checkWt();
int checkDir();
void insertVertex();
void deleteVertex(int vDel);
void insertEdge(int vStart, int vEnd);
void deleteEdge(int vStart, int vEnd);
void createGraph();
void viewGraph();
void display_menu();
int nVertex, adjMat[VSIZE][VSIZE];
void main()
 {
    char choice = 'y';
    int ch, vs, ve, vd;
    display_menu();
    while( (choice == 'y') || (choice == 'Y') )
     {
        printf("\n? ");
        fflush(stdin);
         scanf("%d", &ch);
        switch(ch)
         {
            case 0 :
                    display_menu();
                    break;
            case 1 :
                    createGraph();
                    break;
            case 2 :
                    insertVertex();
                    break;
            case 3 :
                    printf("\n Enter the Starting & Ending Vertex to
                    insert an edge : ");
```

```
                        scanf("%d %d", &vs, &ve);
                        insertEdge(vs, ve);
                        break;
            case 4 :
                        printf("\n Enter the Vertex to delete : ");
                        scanf("%d", &vd);
                        deleteVertex(vd);
                        break;
            case 5 :
                        printf("\n Enter the Starting & Ending Vertex to
                        delete an edge : ");
                        scanf("%d %d", &vs, &ve);
                        deleteEdge(vs, ve);
                        break;
            case 6 :
                        viewGraph();
                        break;
            default:
                        printf("End of run of your program . . .");
                        exit(0);
        }
    }
}
void insertEdge(int vStart, int vEnd)
{
    int ie;
    if(vStart > nVertex || vStart < 1 || vEnd > nVertex || vEnd < 1)
        return;
    printf("Enter Weight of the Edge from V%d to V%d : ", vStart, vEnd);
        scanf("%d",&adjMat[vStart-1][vEnd-1]);
}


void deleteEdge(int vStart, int vEnd)
{
    if(vStart > nVertex || vStart < 1 || vEnd > nVertex || vEnd < 1)
        return;
    if(!checkDir()) adjMat[vEnd-1][vStart-1] = 0;
        adjMat[vStart-1][vEnd-1] = 0;
}
```

```
void insertVertex()
{
    int rc;
    nVertex++;
    for(rc = 0; rc < nVertex; rc++)
        adjMat[rc][nVertex-1] = adjMat[nVertex-1][rc] = 0;
}
void deleteVertex(int vDel)
{
    int r, c;
    if(vDel > nVertex || vDel < 1)
        return;
    for(r = vDel-1; r < nVertex; r++)
        for(c = 0; c < nVertex; c++)
            adjMat[r][c] = adjMat[r+1][c];
    for(c = vDel-1; c < nVertex; c++)
        for(r = 0; r < nVertex; r++)
            adjMat[r][c] = adjMat[r][c+1];
    nVertex--;
}
int checkDir()
{
    int r, c;
    for(r = 0; r < nVertex; r++)
        for(c = 0; c < nVertex; c++)
            if(adjMat[r][c] != adjMat[c][r])
                return 1;
    return 0;
}
int checkWt()
{
    int r, c;
    for(r = 0; r < nVertex; r++)
        for(c = 0; c < nVertex; c++)
            if(adjMat[r][c] > 1)
                return 1;
    return 0;
}
```

```
void createGraph()
{
   int r, c;
   printf("\n Enter the no. of Vertices : ");
     scanf("%d", &nVertex);
   for(r = 0; r < nVertex; r++)
     for(c = 0; c < nVertex; c++)
      {
         adjMat[r][c] = 0;
         if(r != c)
            insertEdge(r+1, c+1);
      }
}
void viewGraph()
{
   int v, r, c, edges, inDeg[VSIZE], outDeg[VSIZE];
   for(v = 0; v < nVertex; v++)
     printf("     V%d",v+1);
   for(r = 0; r < nVertex; r++)
     {
        printf("\nV%-2d   ", r+1);
        for(c = 0; c < nVertex; c++)
           printf("%-2d     ", adjMat[r][c]);
     }
   for(v = 0; v < nVertex; v++)
      inDeg[v] = outDeg[v] = 0;
   edges = 0;
   for(r = 0; r < nVertex; r++)
     for(c = 0; c < nVertex; c++)
        if(adjMat[r][c] != 0)
          {
            edges++;
            outDeg[r]++;
            inDeg[c]++;
          }
   if(!checkDir())
     edges = edges / 2;
   printf("\n %s Graph",(checkDir())? "Directed" : "Undirected");
   printf("\n %s Graph",(checkWt())? "Weighted" : "Unweighted");
```

```
            printf("\nTotal No. of Vertices : %d", nVertex);
            printf("\nTotal No. of Edges : %d", edges);
            printf("\nVertex Indegree Outdegree");
            for(r = 0; r < nVertex; r++)
              {
                  printf("\n V%-2d     %-9d %-9d", r+1, inDeg[r], outDeg[r]);
                  if(inDeg[r] == 0 && outDeg[r] != 0)
                     printf(": %s", "SOURCE");
                  if(inDeg[r] != 0 && outDeg[r] == 0)
                     printf(": %s", "SINK");
                  if(inDeg[r] == 1 && outDeg[r] == 0)
                     printf(": %s", "PENDANT");
                  if(inDeg[r] == 0 && outDeg[r] == 0)
                     printf(": %s", "ISOLATED");
              }
      }
  void display_menu()
    {
      printf("\n\nBasic Operations in an Adjacency Matrix . . . ");
      printf("\n\t 0. Display Menu");
      printf("\n\t 1. Creation of Graph");
      printf("\n\t 2. Insert a Vertex ");
      printf("\n\t 3. Insert an Edge");
      printf("\n\t 4. Delete a Vertex");
      printf("\n\t 5. Delete an Edge");
      printf("\n\t 6. View the Graph");
      printf("\n\t 7. Exit");
    }
```

The program displays the following output

```
Basic Operations in an Adjacency Matrix . . .
            0. Display Menu
            1. Creation of Graph
            2. Insert a Vertex
            3. Insert an Edge
            4. Delete a Vertex
            5. Delete an Edge
            6. View the Graph
            7. Exit
```

```
? 1

Enter the no. of Vertices : 5
Enter the Weight of the Edge from V1 to V2 :1
Enter the Weight of the Edge from V1 to V3 :0
Enter the Weight of the Edge from V1 to V4 :1
Enter the Weight of the Edge from V1 to V5 :1
Enter the Weight of the Edge from V2 to V1 :1
Enter the Weight of the Edge from V2 to V3 :1
Enter the Weight of the Edge from V2 to V4 :1
Enter the Weight of the Edge from V2 to V5 :0
Enter the Weight of the Edge from V3 to V1 :0
Enter the Weight of the Edge from V3 to V2 :1
Enter the Weight of the Edge from V3 to V4 :1
Enter the Weight of the Edge from V3 to V5 :1
Enter the Weight of the Edge from V4 to V1 :1
Enter the Weight of the Edge from V4 to V2 :1
Enter the Weight of the Edge from V4 to V3 :1
Enter the Weight of the Edge from V4 to V5 :1
Enter the Weight of the Edge from V5 to V1 :1
Enter the Weight of the Edge from V5 to V2 :0
Enter the Weight of the Edge from V5 to V3 :1
Enter the Weight of the Edge from V5 to V4 :1

? 6

        V1      V2      V3      V4      V5
V1      0       1       0       1       1
V2      1       0       1       1       0
V3      0       1       0       1       1
V4      1       1       1       0       1
V5      1       0       1       1       0

Undirected Graph
Unweighted Graph
Total No. of Vertices : 5
Total No. of Edges : 8
Vertex Indegree Outdegree
  V1          3               3
  V2          3               3
  V3          3               3
  V4          4               4
  V5          3               3
```

```
? 2
? 6
        V1      V2      V3      V4      V5      V6
V1       0       1       0       1       1       0
V2       1       0       1       1       0       0
V3       0       1   .   0       1       1       0
V4       1       1       1       0       1       0
V5       1       0       1       1       0       0
V6       0       0       0       0       0       0
Undirected Graph
Unweighted Graph
Total No. of Vertices : 6
Total No. of Edges : 8
Vertex Indegree Outdegree
  V1      3               3
  V2      3               3
  V3      3               3
  V4      4               4
  V5      3               3
  V6      0               0           : ISOLATED
? 3
Enter the Starting & Ending Vertex to insert edge : 1 6
Enter the Weight of the Edge from V1 to V6 : 1
? 6
        V1      V2      V3      V4      V5      V6
V1       0       1       0       1       1       1
V2       1       0       1       1       0       0
V3       0       1       0       1       1       0
V4       1       1       1       0       1       0
V5       1       0       1       1       0       0
V6       0       0       0       0       0       0
Directed Graph
Unweighted Graph
Total No. of Vertices : 6
Total No. of Edges : 17
```

```
Vertex Indegree Outdegree
  V1       3         4
  V2       3         3
  V3       3         3
  V4       4         4
  V5       3         3
  V6       1         0          : SINK: PENDANT
? 4
Enter the Vertex to delete : 5
? 6
        V1      V2      V3      V4      V5
  V1    0       1       0       1       1
  V2    1       0       1       1       0
  V3    0       1       0       1       0
  V4    1       1       1       0       0
  V5    0       0       0       0       0
Directed Graph
Unweighted Graph
Total No. of Vertices : 5
Total No. of Edges : 11
Vertex Indegree Outdegree
  V1       2         3
  V2       3         3
  V3       2         2
  V4       3         3
  V5       1         0          : SINK: PENDANT
? 5
Enter the Starting & Ending Vertex to delete edge : 4  3
? 6
        V1      V2      V3      V4      V5
  V1    0       1       0       1       1
  V2    1       0       1       1       0
  V3    0       1       0       1       0
  V4    1       1       0       0       0
  V5    0       0       0       0       0
Directed Graph
Unweighted Graph
Total No. of Vertices : 5
```

```
Total No. of Edges : 10
Vertex Indegree Outdegree
  V1       2         3
  V2       3         3
  V3       1         2
  V4       3         2
  V5       1         0          : SINK: PENDANT
? 7
End of run of your program . . .
```

4.2.3 Adjacency List

A graph containing m vertices and n edges can be represented using a linked list, referred to as **adjacency list**. The number of vertices in a graph forms a singly linked list. Each vertex has a seperate linked list, with nodes equal to the number of edges connected from the corresponding vertex. *Fig. 4.9* and *Fig. 4.10* show the undirected and directed graph. *Fig. 4.11* shows the adjacency lists for the graph shown in *Fig. 4.9* and *Fig. 4.10*. Even though adjacency list is a difficult way of representing graphs, a graph with large number of nodes will use small amount of memory.

Fig. 4.9 :
An undirected graph.

Fig. 4.10 :
A directed graph.

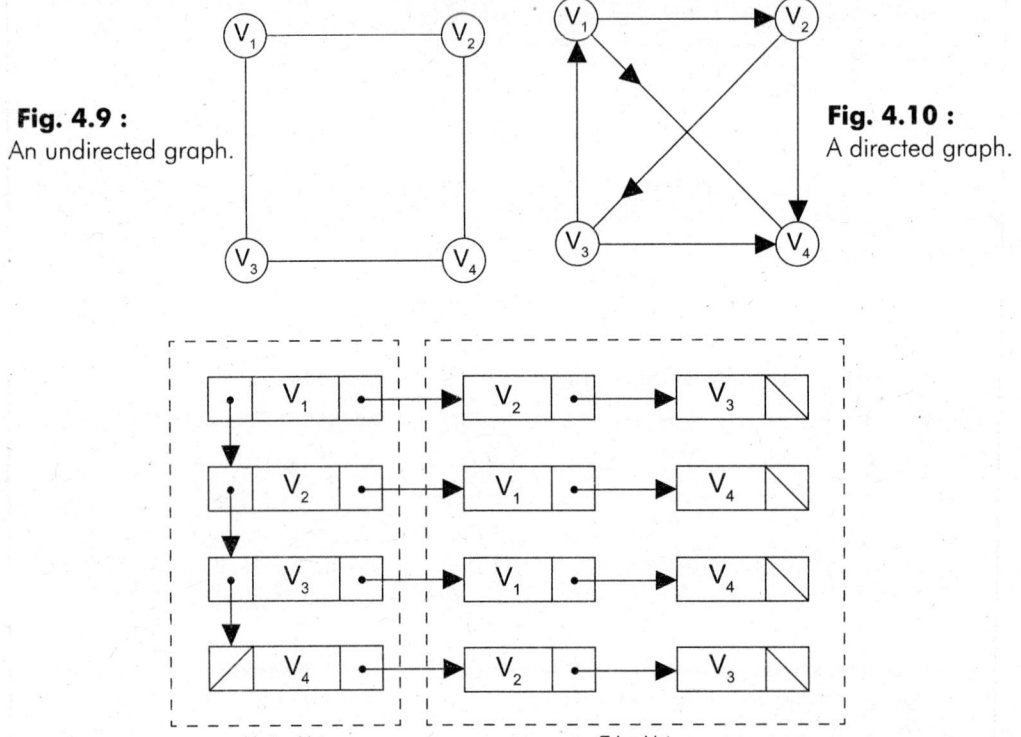

Vertex List   Edge List

Fig. 4.11 : Adjacency list for the undirected graph shown in Fig. 4.9.

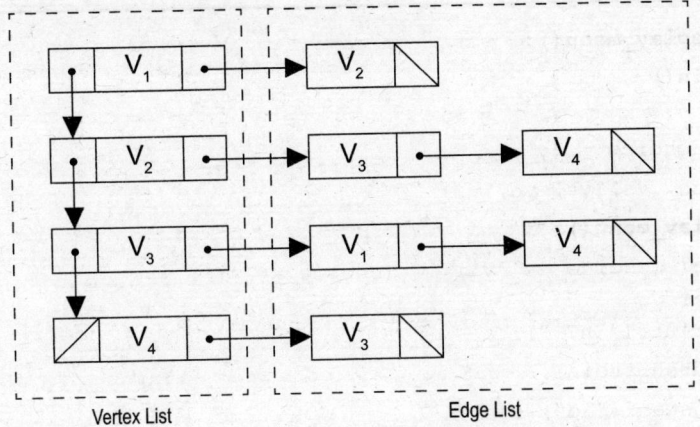

Fig. 4.12 : Adjacency list for the directed graph shown in Fig. 4.10.

Program 4.3 :

/* Program to create, insert, delete and view the adjacency list. */

```c
/* adjlist.c */
#include <stdio.h>
typedef struct vnode
  {
    int vName;
    struct vnode *vlink;
    struct enode *elink;
  }vnode;
typedef struct enode
  {
    int vName;
    int eWeight;
    struct enode *elink;
  }enode;
vnode *adjList = NULL;
vnode* getvNode();
enode* geteNode();
void insertVertex();
void insertEdge(int vStart, int vEnd);
void deleteVertex(int vDel);
void deleteEdge(int vStart, int vEnd);
void createGraph();
void viewGraph();
```

```c
void display_menu();
void main()
{
    char choice = 'y';
    int ch, vs, ve, vd, vi;
    display_menu();
    while( (choice == 'y') || (choice == 'Y') )
    {
        printf("\n? ");
        fflush(stdin);
        scanf("%d", &ch);
        switch(ch)
        {
            case 0 :
                    display_menu();
                    break;
            case 1 :
                    createGraph();
                    break;
            case 2 :
                    insertVertex();
                    break;
            case 3 :
                    printf("\n Enter the Starting & Ending Vertex to
                            insert Edge : ");
                      scanf("%d %d", &vs, &ve);
                    insertEdge(vs, ve);
                    break;
            case 4 :
                    printf("\n Enter the Vertex to delete : ");
                      scanf("%d", &vd);
                    deleteVertex(vd);
                    break;
            case 5 :
                    printf("\n Enter the Starting & Ending Vertex to
                            delete Edge : ");
                      scanf("%d %d", &vs, &ve);
                    deleteEdge(vs, ve);
                    break;
```

```
                   case 6 :
                           viewGraph();
                           break;
               default :
                           printf("End of run of your program . . .");
                           exit(0);
           }
      }
}
vnode* getvNode()
{
    int size;
    vnode *newvnode;
    size = sizeof(vnode);
    newvnode = (vnode *)malloc(size);
    newvnode->vlink = NULL;
    newvnode->elink = NULL;
    return(newvnode);
}

enode* geteNode()
{
    int size;
    enode *newenode;
    size = sizeof(enode);
    newenode = (enode *) malloc(size);
    newenode->elink = NULL;
    return (newenode);
}
void insertVertex()
{
    vnode *tv, *nv;
    nv = getvNode();
    nv->vName = 1;
    if(adjList == NULL)
      {
        adjList = nv;
        return;
      }
```

```
      for(tv = adjList; tv->vlink != NULL; tv=tv->vlink);
      tv->vlink = nv;
      nv->vName = tv->vName + 1;
   }
 void insertEdge(int vStart, int vEnd)
   {
      vnode *pv;
      enode *te, *pe;
      for(pv = adjList; pv != NULL && pv->vName != vStart; pv = pv->vlink);
      if(pv == NULL)
         return;

      te = geteNode();
      printf("Enter Edge Weight from V%d to V%d : ", vStart, vEnd);
         scanf("%d",&te->eWeight);
      te->vName = vEnd;
      if(pv->elink == NULL)
       {
          pv->elink = te;
          return;
       }
      for(pe = pv->elink; pe->elink != NULL; pe = pe->elink);
      pe->elink = te;
   }
 void deleteVertex(int vDel)
   {
      vnode *pv, *tv;
      enode *pe, *te;
      if(adjList == NULL)
         return;
      if(adjList->vName == vDel)
        {
          tv = adjList;
          adjList = adjList->vlink;
          free(tv);
          return;
        }
      for(pv = adjList; pv->vlink != NULL && pv -> vlink -> vName != vDel;
          pv = pv->vlink);
      if(pv ->vlink == NULL)
         return;
```

```
        else
         {
           tv = pv -> vlink;
           pv->vlink = pv->vlink->vlink;
           free(tv);
         }
       for(pv = adjList; pv != NULL; pv = pv->vlink)
        {
          if(pv->elink == NULL)
             continue;
          if(pv->elink->vName == vDel)
           {
              te = pv->elink;
              pv->elink = pv->elink->elink;
              free(te);
              continue;
           }
        for(pe = pv->elink; pe->elink != NULL && pe -> elink -> vName != vDel;
           pe = pe -> elink);
        if( pe->elink!= NULL)
         {
           te = pe->elink;
           pe->elink = pe->elink->elink;
           free(te);
         }
        }
     }

void deleteEdge(int vStart, int vEnd)
 {
    vnode *pv, *tv;
    enode *pe, *te;
    if(adjList == NULL)
       return;
    for(pv = adjList; pv != NULL && pv->vName!=vStart;pv=pv->vlink);
    if(pv == NULL)
       return;
    if(pv->elink == NULL)
       return;
```

```
      if(pv->elink->vName == vEnd)

       {

         te = pv->elink;

         pv->elink = pv->elink->elink;

         free(te);

         return;

       }

      for(pe = pv->elink; pe->elink != NULL && pe -> elink -> vName != vEnd;
          pe = pe->elink);

      if(pe->elink!= NULL)

       {

         te = pe->elink;

         pe->elink = pe->elink->elink;

         free(te);

       }

    }

void createGraph()

  {

    int r, c, v, nVertex;

    printf("\n Enter the no. of Vertices : ");

      scanf("%d", &nVertex);

    adjList = NULL;

    for(v = 0; v < nVertex; v++)

        insertVertex();

    for(r = 0; r < nVertex; r++)

      for(c = 0; c < nVertex; c++)

        if(r != c)

            insertEdge(r+1, c+1);

  }

void viewGraph()

  {

    int edges = 0, wStatus = 0, nVertex = 0;

    vnode *pv;   enode *pe;

    for(pv = adjList; pv!= NULL; pv = pv->vlink)

      {

        printf("\nV%-2d to ", pv->vName);

        nVertex++;

        for(pe = pv->elink; pe != NULL; pe = pe->elink)
```

```
            {
                edges++;
                printf("V%-2d(%d) -> ", pe->vName, pe->eWeight);
                if(pe->eWeight > 1)
                    wStatus = 1;
            }
            printf("NULL");
        }
    if(adjList != NULL)
    {
        printf("\n %s Graph", (wStatus) ? "Weighted" : "Unweighted");
        printf("\n Number of Vertices : %5d", nVertex);
        printf("\n Number of Edges    : %5d", edges);
    }
}

void display_menu()
{
    printf("\n\n Basic Operations in a Adjacency List . . .");
    printf("\n\t 0. Display Menu");
    printf("\n\t 1. Creation of Graph");
    printf("\n\t 2. Insert a Vertex ");
    printf("\n\t 3. Insert an Edge");
    printf("\n\t 4. Delete a Vertex");
    printf("\n\t 5. Delete an Edge");
    printf("\n\t 6. View the Graph");
    printf("\n\t 7. Exit");
}
```

The program displays the following output

```
Basic Operations in an Adjacency List . . .
        0. Display Menu
        1. Creation of Graph
        2. Insert a Vertex
        3. Insert an Edge
        4. Delete a Vertex
        5. Delete an Edge
        6. View the Graph
        7. Exit
? 1
Enter the no. of Vertices : 4
```

```
Enter Edge Weight from V1 to V2 : 1

Enter Edge Weight from V1 to V3 : 1

Enter Edge Weight from V1 to V4 : 0

Enter Edge Weight from V2 to V1 : 1

Enter Edge Weight from V2 to V3 : 0

Enter Edge Weight from V2 to V4 : 1

Enter Edge Weight from V3 to V1 : 1

Enter Edge Weight from V3 to V2 : 0

Enter Edge Weight from V3 to V4 : 1

Enter Edge Weight from V4 to V1 : 0

Enter Edge Weight from V4 to V2 : 1

Enter Edge Weight from V4 to V3 : 1

? 6

V1  to  V2 (1) -> V3 (1) -> V4 (0) -> NULL

V2  to  V1 (1) -> V3 (0) -> V4 (1) -> NULL

V3  to  V1 (1) -> V2 (0) -> V4 (1) -> NULL

V4  to  V1 (0) -> V2 (1) -> V3 (1) -> NULL

Unweighted Graph

Number of Vertices :    4

Number of Edges    :    12

? 2

? 6

V1  to  V2 (1) -> V3 (1) -> V4 (0) -> NULL

V2  to  V1 (1) -> V3 (0) -> V4 (1) -> NULL

V3  to  V1 (1) -> V2 (0) -> V4 (1) -> NULL

V4  to  V1 (0) -> V2 (1) -> V3 (1) -> NULL

V5  to  NULL

Unweighted Graph

Number of Vertices :    5

Number of Edges    :    12

? 3

Enter the Starting & Ending Vertex to insert Edge : 5 2

Enter Edge Weight from V5 to V2 : 1
```

```
? 6

V1  to  V2 (1) -> V3 (1) -> V4 (0) -> NULL

V2  to  V1 (1) -> V3 (0) -> V4 (1) -> NULL

V3  to  V1 (1) -> V2 (0) -> V4 (1) -> NULL

V4  to  V1 (0) -> V2 (1) -> V3 (1) -> NULL

V5  to  V2 (1) -> NULL

Unweighted Graph

Number of Vertices :      5

Number of Edges    :      13

? 4

Enter the Vertex to delete : 3

? 6

V1  to  V2 (1) -> V4 (0) -> NULL

V2  to  V1 (1) -> V4 (1) -> NULL

V4  to  V1 (0) -> V2 (1) -> NULL

V5  to  V2 (1) -> NULL

Unweighted Graph

Number of Vertices :      4

Number of Edges    :      7

? 5

Enter the Starting & Ending Vertex to delete Edge : 4 2

? 6

V1  to  V2 (1) -> V4 (0) -> NULL

V2  to  V1 (1) -> V4 (1) -> NULL

V4  to  V1 (0) -> NULL

V5  to  V2 (1) -> NULL

Unweighted Graph

Number of Vertices :      4

Number of Edges    :      6

? 7

End of run of your program . . .
```

4.3 Graph Traversals

Traversing a graph means visiting all the nodes in the graph. In many practical applications, traversing a graph is important, such that each vertex is visited once systematically by traversing through minimum number of paths. The two important graph traversal methods are

- Depth-first traversal (or) Depth-first search (DFS)
- Breadth-first traversal (or) Breadth-first search (BFS).

4.3.1 Depth–First Traversal

The logic of DFS is similar to the preorder traversal of a tree. Visit the first node initially and then find the unvisited node which is adjacent to the first node. Then the unvisited node is visited and a depth first search is initiated from the adjacent node (considering it as the first node). If all the adjacent nodes have been visited, backtrack to the last node visited, and find another adjacent node and again initiate the depth-first search from the adjacent node. This traversal continues until allnodes have been visited once. The following algorithm describes DFS in a graph.

Algorithm for Depth First Traversal

Step 1 : Consider that the DFS is beginning from the starting vertex A. Process the vertex A and mark it as visited.

Step 2 : Using the adjacency matrix of the graph find the vertex along the path which begins vertex A, that has not been visited yet. Process the vertex and consider this as the new vertex and mark the vertex as visited.

Step 3 : Repeat **Step 2** using the new search vertex. If no vertices (i.e., if a dead end if reached) back track to the previous node and continue the search from there.

Step 4 : When backtracking to the previous search node in **Step 3** is impossible, the search from the originally chosen search node is complete.

Step 5 : If the graph still contains unvisited nodes, choose any vertex that has not been visited and repeat **Step 1** to **Step 4**.

The above algorithm executes in a recursive manner, which can also be implemented non-recursively using stacks. To understand the traversal clearly, consider the graph shown in *Fig. 4.6(c)* and its adjacency matrix shown in *Fig. 4.8(c)*. *Program 4.4* helps you to understand things better.

Program 4.4 :

/* Program to demonstrate Depth First Search. */

```
/* dfs.c */
#include<stdio.h>
int a[10][10], visited[10], n;
void searchFrom(int k);
```

```
    void main()
    {
        int i, j;
        printf("Enter the no. of Nodes : ");
            scanf("%d", &n);
        printf("Enter the adjacency matrix . . . \n");
        for(i = 1; i <= n; i++)
            for(j = 1; j <= n; j++)
                if(i != j)
                {
                    printf("Enter the value of %d, %d element : ", i, j);
                        scanf("%d", &a[i][j]);
                }
        printf("Nodes are visited in this order ");
        for(i = 1; i <= n; i++)
            if(visited[i] == 0)
                searchFrom(i);
    }
    void searchFrom(int k)
    {
        int i;
        printf("-> %d ", k);
        visited[k] = 1;
        for(i = 1; i <= n; i++)
            if(visited[i] == 0)
                if(a[k][i] != 0)
                    searchFrom(i);
    }
```

The program displays the following output

```
Enter the no. of Nodes : 5
Enter the adjacency matrix . . .
Enter the value of 1, 2 element : 1
Enter the value of 1, 3 element : 0
Enter the value of 1, 4 element : 1
Enter the value of 1, 5 element : 0
Enter the value of 2, 1 element : 0
```

```
Enter the value of 2, 3 element : 1
Enter the value of 2, 4 element : 1
Enter the value of 2, 5 element : 0
Enter the value of 3, 1 element : 0
Enter the value of 3, 2 element : 0
Enter the value of 3, 4 element : 0
Enter the value of 3, 5 element : 1
Enter the value of 4, 1 element : 0
Enter the value of 4, 2 element : 0
Enter the value of 4, 3 element : 1
Enter the value of 4, 5 element : 1
Enter the value of 5, 1 element : 1
Enter the value of 5, 2 element : 0
Enter the value of 5, 3 element : 0
Enter the value of 5, 4 element : 0
Nodes are visited in this order –> 1 –> 2 –> 3 –> 5 –> 4
```

4.3.2 Breadth–First Traversal

Another widely used traversal technique in graphs is the breadth-first traversal. *The traversal technique begins at a given vertex and then proceeds to all the vertices connected to that vertex.* Visit the first node initially, and then find all the unvisited nodes which is adjacent to the first node. Then unvisited nodes are visited and a breadth first search is initiated from the adjacent node (considering it as the first node). This traversal continues until all nodes have been visited once. The following algorithm describes BFS in a graph.

Algorithm for Breadth First Traversal
Step 1 : Consider any vertex in the graph. Process the vertex and mark it as visited.
Step 2 : Using the adjacency matrix of the graph proceed to the next vertex which has an edge connection wise the vertex considered in **Step 1** .
Step 3 : Backtrack to the vertex considered in **Step 1** descend along an edge towards an unvisited vertex and mark the new vertex as visited.
Step 4 : Repeat **Step 3** until all vertices adjacent to the node in **Step 1** have been marked as visited.
Step 5 : Repeat **Step 1** to **Step 4** starting from vertex visited in **Step 2**, then start again from vertices visited in **Step 3** in the order visited.

The above algorithm executes in a recursive manner, which can also be implemented non-recursively using queues. To understand the traversal clearly, consider the graph shown in in *Fig. 4.7(c)* and its adjacency matrix shown in *Fig. 4.9(c)*. *Program 4.5* helps you to understand things better.

Program 4.5 :

```c
/* Program to demonstrate Breadth-First Search. */
/* bfs.c */
#include<stdio.h>
int visited[10], a[10][10], n;
void searchFrom(int k);
void main()
 {
   int i,j;
   printf("Enter the No. of Nodes : ");
     scanf("%d", &n);
   printf("Enter the adjacency matrix ... \n");
   for(i = 1; i <= n; i++)
     for(j = 1; j <= n; j++)
       if(i != j)
         {
             printf("Enter the value of %d, %d element : ", i, j);
               scanf("%d", &a[i][j]);
         }
   printf("Nodes are visited in this order ");
   for(i = 1; i <= n; i++)
     if(visited[i] == 0)
        searchFrom(i);
 }

 void searchFrom(int k)
  {
    int i;
    printf("--> %d ", k);
    visited[k] = 1;
    for(i = 1; i <= n; i++)
      {
        if(visited[i] == 0)
          {
```

```
        if(a[k][i] != 0)

        {

            searchFrom(i);

        }

    }

    break;

    }

}
```

The program displays the following output

```
Enter the No. of Nodes : 5

Enter the adjacency matrix ...

Enter the value of 1, 2 element : 1

Enter the value of 1, 3 element : 0

Enter the value of 1, 4 element : 1

Enter the value of 1, 5 element : 0

Enter the value of 2, 1 element : 0

Enter the value of 2, 3 element : 1

Enter the value of 2, 4 element : 1

Enter the value of 2, 5 element : 0

Enter the value of 3, 1 element : 0

Enter the value of 3, 2 element : 0

Enter the value of 3, 4 element : 0

Enter the value of 3, 5 element : 1

Enter the value of 4, 1 element : 0

Enter the value of 4, 2 element : 0

Enter the value of 4, 3 element : 1

Enter the value of 4, 5 element : 1

Enter the value of 5, 1 element : 1

Enter the value of 5, 2 element : 0

Enter the value of 5, 3 element : 0

Enter the value of 5, 4 element : 0
```

Nodes are visited in this order --> 1 --> 2 --> 3 --> 4 --> 5

4.4 Application of DFS – Topological Sorting

Topological sorting is a natural subproblem used on directed acyclic graphs. Topological sorting, orders the vertices and edges of a directed acyclic graph in a simple way and can be used to schedule tasks under precedence constraints. Let us assume, that we have to do a set of jobs. But certain jobs have to be performed after completion of other jobs. These precedence constraints form a directed acyclic graph, and any topological sort defines an order to do these jobs such that each job is performed only after all of its constraints are satisfied. *Note that every directed acyclic graph can be topologically sorted, so there must be always at least one schedule for any reasonable precedence constraints among the given jobs.*

Topological sorting is an ordering of the vertices in a directed acyclic graph, such that, if there is a path from **x** to **y**, then **y** appears after **x** in the ordering. As each vertices is visited, push the vertex in to the stack. Finally print the stack elements in order. The following algorithm describes the topological sorting in a graph.

Algorithm for Topological Sorting

    Step 1 :   Find the indegree for each vertex.

    Step 2 :   Remove the vertices, whose indegree is zero.

    Step 3 :   Decrement the indegree of the vertices, at the end of the outgoing edges.

    Step 4 :   Repeat **Step 2**, until all the vertices are removed.

The basic algorithm of topological sorting performs a depth-first search of the directed acyclic graph to identify the complete set of source vertices, where source vertices are vertices without incoming edges (i.e., with indegree zero). At least one such source must exist in any directed acyclic graph. Note that source vertices can appear at the start of any schedule without violating any constraints. After deleting all the outgoing edges of the source vertices, we will create new source vertices, by reducing the indegree by the number of incoming edges, from removed vertices. Repeat until all vertices has been removed. Consider the directed acyclic graphs shown in *Fig. 4.13* and their corresponding topological orders for each graph.

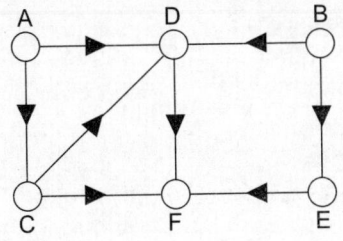

A, B, C, E, D, F

A, C, B, E, D, F

B, A, E, C, D, F

B, E, A, C, D, F

(a)

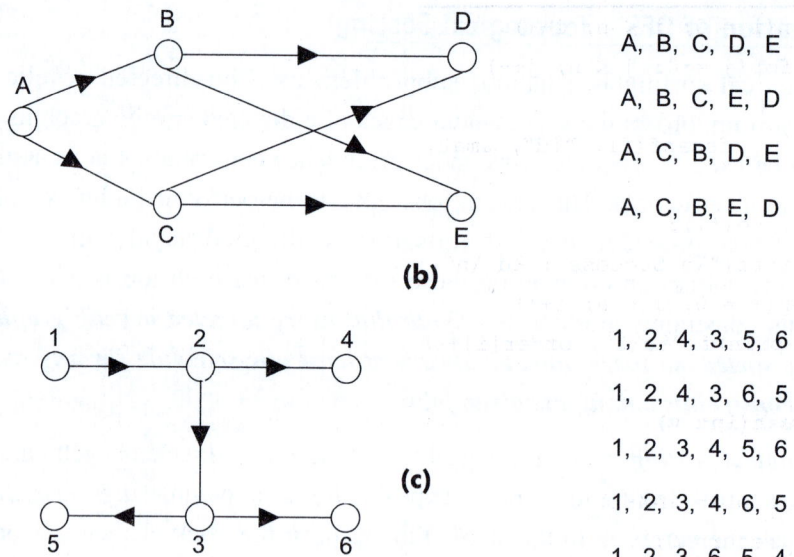

	A, B, C, D, E
	A, B, C, E, D
	A, C, B, D, E
	A, C, B, E, D

(b)

	1, 2, 4, 3, 5, 6
	1, 2, 4, 3, 6, 5
	1, 2, 3, 4, 5, 6
(c)	1, 2, 3, 4, 6, 5
	1, 2, 3, 6, 5, 4

Fig. 4.13 : Directed acyclic graphs with its topological orders.

Program 4.6 :

```
/* Program to demonstrate Topological Sorting. */
/* tpl_sort.c */
#include<stdio.h>
#define MAX 30
int stack[MAX], top = -1;
int push(int v);
int pop(int *v);
int topologicalOrder(int mat[MAX][MAX], int n, int order[MAX]);
void main()
{
    int i, j, n, mat[MAX][MAX], order[MAX];
    FILE *f1;
    printf("Enter the No. of Vertices : ");
      scanf("%d", &n);
    if((f1 = fopen("C:\\Graph.txt", "rt")) == NULL)
    {
        fprintf(stderr, "Cannot open input file. \n");
        return ;
    }
```

```
        for(i = 0; i < n; i++)
          for(j = 0; j < n; j++)
            {
                fscanf(f1, "%d", &mat[i][j]);
            }
        fclose(f1);
        printf("\n Success : %d \n", topologicalOrder(mat, n, order));
        for(i = 0; i < n; i++)
          printf("%c\t", order[i]+65);
}
int push(int v)
{
    if(top == MAX-1)
        return 0;
    else
        stack[++top] = v;
    return -1;
}
int pop(int *v)
{
    if(top == -1)
        return 0;
    else
      *v = stack[top--];
    return -1;
}
int topologicalOrder(int mat[MAX][MAX], int n, int order[MAX])
{
    int indegree[MAX], v, i, k, m;
    for(i = 0; i < n; i++)
     {
       indegree[i] = 0;
       for(k = 0; k < n; k++)
         if(mat[k][i] == 1)
           indegree[i]++;
         if(indegree[i] == 0)
           push(i);
     }
    m = 0;
```

```
        while(pop(&v))
        {
          order[m++] = v;
          for(k = 0;  k < n;  k++)
            if(mat[v][k] == 1 && indegree[k] > 0)
            {
                indegree[k]--;
                if(indegree[k] == 0)
                    push(k);
            }
        }
      return (i == n);
   }
```

The text in the file graph.txt is

```
0 0 1 1 0 0
0 0 0 1 1 0
0 0 0 1 0 1
0 0 0 0 0 1
0 0 0 0 0 1
0 0 0 0 0 0
```

The program displays the following output

```
Enter the No. of Vertices : 6
Success : 1
B       E       A       C       D       F
```

4.5 Application of Graphs

Some important applications of graphs include,

- Bi-connectivity in Graphs
- Euler circuits
- Hamilton circuits.

4.5.1 Bi-connectivity and Cut Vertex in Graphs

An undirected graph is said to be a *connected graph* if for any pair of nodes of the graph, there exists a path between them (i.e., two nodes are reachable from one another). If it is able to visit all other vertices starting from any vertex of a graph, then we can say that the graph is connected. *Fig. 4.14* below shows the connected graph.

If a vertex whose removal from the graph makes a disconnected graph then the vertex is referred to as *cut-vertex* or an *articulation point*. In *Fig. 4.14*, "R" is an articulation point. If we remove the articulation point "R", then the connected graph becomes two disconnected graphs. If the removal of an edge disconnects the graph, then the edge is referred to as a *bridge*. A bridge will have at least one articulation point at its end, but an articulation point doesn't necessarily need to be linked to a bridge. In *Fig. 4.15*, (R,S) and (S,T) are bridges.

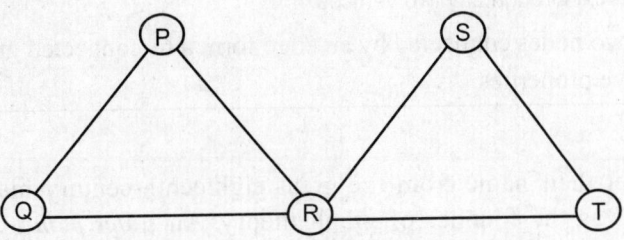

Fig. 4.14 : A connected graph.

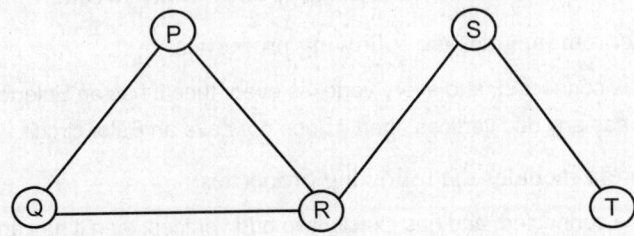

Fig. 4.15 : A connected graph.

A graph with no articulation points and no bridges is referred to as *bi-connected graph*. In other words, a connected, undirected graph is said to bi-connected, if the graph is still connected after removing any one vertex. Any graph containing a node of degree 1 cannot be bi-connected. *Fig. 4.16* below shows the different bi-connected graphs. Removing any one vertex, doesn't make the graph as non bi-connected. Biconnected graphs have at least two vertex-disjoint paths between any pair of vertices, hence to disconnect a biconnected graph, we must remove at least two vertices. A depth frist search algorithm can be used to find the articulation poinxts of a graph, and hence find the biconnected components in a graph.

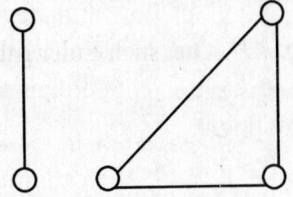 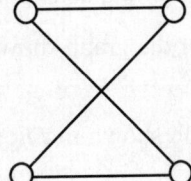 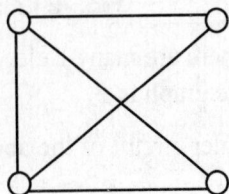

Fig. 4.16 : Bi-connected graphs.

Properties of bi-connected components includes,

- An edge belongs to exactly one bi-connected component
- A non-separation vertex belongs to exactly one bi-connected component
- A separation vertex belongs to two or more bi-connected components
- There are two disjoint paths between any two vertices
- There is a cycle through any two vertices.

By convention, two nodes connected by an edge form a bi-connected graph, but this does not verify the above properties.

4.5.2 Euler Circuits

Euler circuits get their name from the great eighteenth-century mathematician *Leonhard Euler*, who was the founder of graph theory. An *Euler path* is a path that passes through each edge of a graph exactly only once. If the start and end point are the same, the Euler path is referred to as an *Euler circuit*. A circuit that covers each edge of a graph once but not more than once, is referred to as an *Euler circuit*.

Euler'circuit theorem includes the following properties.

- If a graph is connected, and every vertex is even, then it has an Euler circuit.
- If a graph has any odd vertices, then it does not have an Euler circuit.

Euler'path theorem includes the following properties.

- If a graph is connected, and has exactly two odd vertices, then it has an Euler path (at least one, usually more). Any such path must start at one of the odd vertices and end at the other one.

- If a graph has more than two odd vertices, then it cannot have an Euler path.

Fig. 4.17 below shows graphs with Euler paths and Euler circuits.

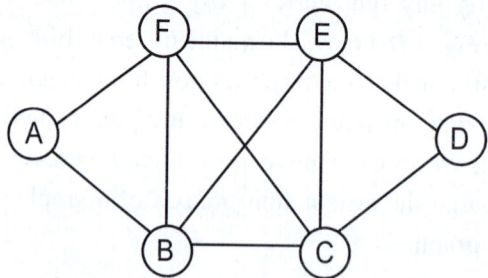

Fig. 4.17 : Graph showing euler path and euler circuits..

There are many Euler paths for the graph shown in *Fig. 4.17*. One such Euler path of the above graph is D -> E -> B -> C -> A -> B -> D -> C -> E.

Euler circuit of the above graph shown in *Fig. 4.17* is D -> E -> B -> C -> A -> B -> D -> C -> E -> F -> D.

A depth first search algorithm can be used to find whether an Euler circuit exists for a graph or not.

4.5.3 Hamilton Circuits

A *hamilton circuit* is a closed path in a graph, in which each node appears exactly once. The hamilton circuit problem asks whether such a path exists for the given graph. The hamilton circuit problem is an NP-hard problem, and so no polynomial time algorithm is available for it. Properties of Hamilton circuits includes,

- A simple circuit that includes all the vertex of a graph.
- A sequence of adjacent vertices and distinct edges in which every vertex of graph appears exactly once, except for the first and last, which are the same.

4.6 Summary

✍ A graph is a non-linear data structure that represents less relationship between its adjacent elements. There is no hierarchical relationship between the adjacent elements in case of graphs.

✍ If an edge between any two nodes in a graph is not directionally oriented, a graph is called as undirected graph. It is also referred as unqualified graph.

✍ If an edge between any two nodes in a graph is directionally oriented, a graph is called as directed graph. It is also referred as a digraph.

✍ A path in a graph is defined as a sequence of distinct vertices each adjacent to the next, except possibly the first vertex and last vertex is different.

✍ A cycle is a path containing atleast three vertices such that the starting and the ending vertices are the same.

✍ A directed graph is said to be a strongly connected graph if, for every pair of distinct vertices there is a directed path from every vertex to every other vertex. It is also referred as a complete graph.

✍ A directed graph is said to be weakly connected graph, if any vertex doesn't have a directed path to any other vertices.

✍ A graph is said to be a weighted graph if every edge in the graph is assigned some weight or value. The weight of an edge is a positive value that may be representing the distance between the vertices or the weights of the edges along the path.

✍ Adjacency matrix is a representation used to represent a graph with zeros and ones. A graph containing n vertices can be represented by a matrix with n rows and n columns.

✍ Traversing a graph means visiting all the nodes in the graph. The two important graph traversal methods are depth-first traversal and breadth-first traversal.

✍ **Topological sorting** is an ordering of the vertices in a directed acyclic graph, such that, if there is a path from **x** to **y**, then **y** appears after **x** in the ordering.

✍ An undirected graph is said to be a connected graph if for any pair of nodes of the graph, there exists a path between them (i.e., two nodes are reachable from one another).

✍ If a vertex whose removal from the graph makes a disconnected graph then the vertex is referred to as cut-vertex or an articulation point.

✍ A graph with no articulation points and no bridges is referred to as bi-connected graph.

✍ If the removal of an edge also referred to as seperation vertex, disconnects the graph, then the edge is referred to as a bridge.

✍ An Euler path is a path that passes through each edge of a graph exactly only once. If the start and end point are the same, the Euler path is referred to as an Euler circuit.

✍ A hamilton circuit is a closed path in a graph, in which each node appears exactly once.

4.7 Short-answer Questions

1. *Define a graph.*

   A graph is a non-linear data structure that represents less relationship between its adjacent elements. There is no hierarchical relationship between the adjacent elements in case of graphs.

2. *Define undirected graph.*

   If an edge between any two nodes in a graph is not directionally oriented, a graph is called as undirected graph. It is also referred as unqualified graph.

3. *Define directed graph.*

   If an edge between any two nodes in a graph is directionally oriented, a graph is called as directed graph. It is also referred as a digraph.

4. *Define a path in a graph.*

   A path in a graph is defined as a sequence of distinct vertices each adjacent to the next, except possibly the first vertex and last vertex is different.

5. *Define a cycle in a graph.*

   A cycle is a path containing atleast three vertices such that the starting and the ending vertices are the same.

6. *Define a strongly connected graph.*

   A directed graph is said to be a strongly connected if, for every pair of distinct vertices their is a directed path from every vertex to every other vertex. It is also referred as a complete graph.

7.   Define a weakly connected graph.

A directed graph is said to be weakly connected graph, if any vertex doesn't have a directed path to any other vertices.

8.   Define a weighted graph.

A graph is said to be a weighted graph if every edge in the graph is assigned some weight or value. The weight of an edge is a positive value that may be representing the distance between the vertices or the weights of the edges along the path.

9.   Define incidence matrix.

incidence matrix is a representation used to represent a graph with zeros and ones. A graph containing m vertices and n edges can be represented by a matrix with m rows and n columns. The matrix is formed by storing 1 in its ith row and j^{th} column corresponding to the matrix, if there exists a ith vertex, connected to one end of the jth edge, and a 0, if there is no i^{th} vertex, connected to any end of the jth edge of the graph.

10.   Define adjacency matrix.

Adjacency matrix is a representation used to represent a graph with zeros and ones. A graph containing n vertices can be represented by a matrix with n rows and n columns. The matrix is formed by storing 1 in its ith row and j^{th} column of the matrix, if there exists an edge between i^{th} and j^{th} vertex of the graph, and a 0, if there is no edge between i^{th} and j^{th} vertex of the graph.

11.   Define adjacency list.

A graph containing m vertices and n edges can be represented using a linked list, referred to as adjacency list.

12.   What is meant by traversing a graph ? State the different ways of traversing a graph.

Traversing a graph means visiting all the nodes in the graph. In many practical applications, traversing a graph is important, such that each vertex is visited once systematically by traversing through minimum number of paths. The two important graph traversal methods are

- Depth-first traversal (or) Depth-first search (DFS)
- Breadth-first traversal (or) Breadth-first search (BFS).

13.   Determine the incidence matrix for the undirected graph shown below.

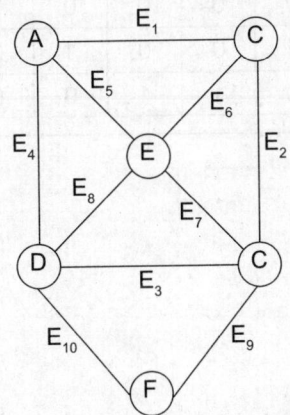

The incidence matrix for the undirected graph shown above is as follows,

	E_1	E_2	E_3	E_4	E_5	E_6	E_7	E_8	E_9	E_{10}
A	1	0	0	1	1	0	0	0	0	0
B	1	1	0	0	0	1	0	0	0	0
C	0	1	1	0	0	0	1	0	1	0
D	0	0	1	1	0	0	0	1	0	1
E	0	0	0	0	1	1	1	1	0	0
F	0	0	0	0	0	0	0	0	1	1

14.   Determine the incidence matrix for the directed graph shown below.

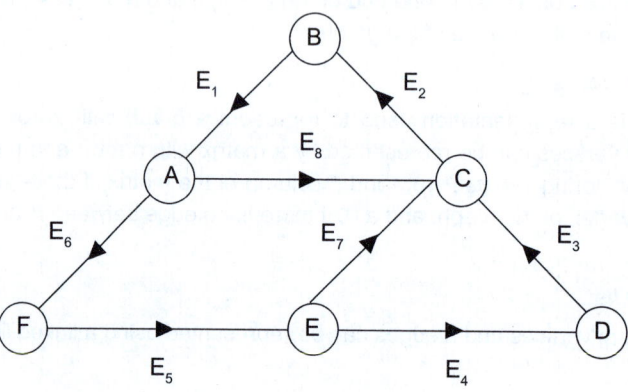

The incidence matrix for the directed graph shown above is as follows,

	E_1	E_2	E_3	E_4	E_5	E_6	E_7	E_8
A	0	0	0	0	0	0	0	1
B	1	0	0	0	0	0	0	0
C	0	1	0	0	0	0	0	0
D	0	0	1	0	0	0	0	0
E	0	0	0	1	0	0	1	0
F	0	0	0	0	1	1	0	0

Chapter 5

Searching, Sorting and Hashing Techniques

5.1 Introduction

In this chapter, we are going to see two most important techniques used in programming, sorting and searching. ***Sorting** a group or sequence of elements or data items means rearranging them in either ascending or descending order depending upon the relationship among the data items present in the group.* ***Searching** is a programming technique that determines whether an element or a data item is present in a group of elements or not.*

Sorting is, without doubt, the most fundamental algorithmic problem. Many different approaches lead to useful sorting algorithms and these ideas can be used to solve many other problems. Finding better algorithms to sort a given set of data is an ongoing problem in the field of computer science. Simple sorting techniques sort data in ascending and descending order. The same algorithm can be used for sorting in increasing or decreasing order but all we need is to change $\leq$ to $\geq$ in the comparison algorithm as we desire. In this chapter some important sorting techniques are being discussed. For easier approach and understanding the data is sorted only in ascending order. The factors to be considered while choosing a sorting technique are

- Programming time of the sorting technique.
- Execution time of the sorting technique.
- Number of comparisons required for sorting the group of elements.
- Main or auxiliary memory space needed for sorting technique.

One reason why sorting is so important is that once a set of items are sorted, many other problems become easy. Speeding up searching is perhaps the most important application of sorting. Once the elements are placed in sorted order in an array, the kth largest element can be found in constant time by simply looking in the kth position of the array.

All data processing requires accessing records efficiently and quickly. Search techniques are most efficient only when the data items are already sorted according to some specified keys. If the number of elements is large and not sorted, searching an element takes more time. Therefore sorting becomes a necessary technique. A sorting method is said to be stable when it has minimum number of swaps i.e., if the two data items of matching value are guaranteed not to be rearranged with respect to each other when the algorithm progresses.

Some of the important sorting techniques are

- Bubble sort
- Quick sort
- Insertion sort
- Merge sort
- Heap sort
- Selection sort
- Shell sort
- Radix sort

Some of the important searching techniques are

- Linear search
- Binary search

5.2 Linear Search

Linear search also referred as *sequential search*, is the simplest searching technique. *The search begins at one end of the list and searches for the required element one by one until the element is found or till the end of the list is reached.* The search is said to be successful if the search element is found and unsuccessful if the search element is not found in the list. The data items in the list need not be in a sorted order for linear search technique.

Algorithm for Linear Search

LINEAR_SEARCH (ARR, N, FIND)

where ARR is an array of N elements in which the element FIND is to be searched.

Step 1 : Repeat For I = 0, 1, 2, . . . , N–1

Step 2 : If (ARR[I] = FIND) Then

RETURN I

[End of If structure]

Step 3 : [End of **Step 1** For loop]

Step 4 : RETURN –1

END LINEAR_SEARCH()

Program 5.1 :

/* **Program to search an element using linear search.** */

```
/* linear.c */
#include<stdio.h>
int linear_search(int [], int, int);
void main()
{
    int i, n, pos, find, list[100];
    printf("Enter the limit : ");
        scanf("%d", &n);
    printf("Enter the elements : ");
    for(i = 0 ; i < n ; i++)
        scanf("%d", &list[i]);
```

```
            printf("Enter the element to be searched : ");

        scanf("%d", &find);

    if((pos = linear_search(list, n, find)) == -1)

        printf("The element is not present");

    else

        printf("The element is in the %d position", pos+1);

}

int linear_search(int list[], int n, int find)

{

    int i;

    for(i = 0 ; i < n ; i++)

        if(list[i] == find)

            return i;

    return -1;

}
```

The program displays the following output

RUN 1   Enter the limit : 5

Enter the elements : 78   88   89   98   65

Enter the element to be searched : 65

The element is in the 5 position

RUN 2   Enter the limit : 5

Enter the elements : 90   8   3   2   1

Enter the element to be searched : 5

The element is not present

The given list may be in any particular order and it is just as likely that the element to be found may be present in the first position or in the last position. The best case is 1, which occurs when the element to be searched occurs in the first position of the list. The worst case is n, which occurs when the element to be searched occurs in the last position of the list. The still worst case is n+1, which occurs when the element to be searched is not present in the list. On an average, the number of comparisons carried by the linear search algorithm, is half the elements present in the list and is given by (n+1)/2. The linear searching method searches well for small-unsorted arrays, but becomes inefficient when the size of the list is large.

5.3 Binary Search

The binary search algorithm is one of the most efficient searching techniques, which requires the list to be sorted in ascending order. *To search for an element in the list, the binary search algorithm splits the list and locates the middle element of the list. It is then compared with the search element.* If the search element is less than the middle element, the first part of the list is searched else the second part of the list is searched. The algorithm again reduces the list into two halves, locates the middle element, and compares with the search element. If the search element is less than the middle element, the first part of the list is searched. This process continues until the search element is equal to the middle element or the list consists of only one element that is not equal to the search element.

Algorithm for Binary Search

BINARY_SEARCH (ARR, FIND, BEG, END)

where ARR is an array in which the element FIND is to be searched, BEG refers to the initial index position of the list, END refers to the final position of the list.

Step 1 :   If (BEG > END) Then

RETURN –1

[End of If structure]

Step 2 :   Assign MID = (BEG + END) / 2

Step 3 :   If (FIND = ARR[MID]) Then

RETURN MID

Else If (FIND < ARR[MID]) Then

RETURN BINARY_SEARCH (ARR, FIND, BEG, MID–1)

Else

RETURN BINARY_SEARCH (ARR, FIND, MID+1, END)

[End of If structure]

END BINARY_SEARCH()

Program 5.2 :

```c
/* Program to search an element using binary search. */
/* binarys.c */
#include<stdio.h>
int binary_search(int [], int, int, int);
void main()
 {
    int i, n, find, pos = 0, list[100];
    printf("Enter the limit : ");
     scanf("%d", &n);
```

```
    printf("Enter the elements : ");
    for(i = 0 ; i < n ; i++)
       scanf("%d", &list[i]);
    printf("Enter the element to be searched : ");
       scanf("%d", &find);
    pos = binary_search(list, find, 0, n);
    if(pos != -1)
       printf("The element is in the %d position", pos+1);
    else
       printf("The element is not present");
 }

 binary_search(int list[], int find, int beg, int end)
 {
    int mid;
    if(beg > end)
       return(-1);
    mid = (beg + end)/2;
    if(find == list[mid]);
       return(mid);
    else if(find < list[mid])
       return binary_search(list, find, beg, mid-1);
    else
       return binary_search(list, find, mid+1, end);
 }
```

The program displays the following output

RUN1 Enter the limit : 5

Enter the elements : 3   12   56   98   987

Enter the element to be searched : 12
The element is in the 2 position

RUN2 Enter the limit : 4

Enter the elements : 23   34   45   108

Enter the element to be searched : 78
The element is not present

The binary_search() function used in *Program 5.2* takes 4 arguments, an integer array a, the element to be searched, beginning array subscript beg and the end array subscript end. If the search element is less than the middle element the 4th argument i.e., end subscript is set to mid-1 and the search continues from the beginning of the array subscript to `mid-1`. If the search element is greater than the middle element, the beginning subscript is set to `mid+1` and the search continues from `mid+1` to the end of the array. This process continues until the search element is equal to the middle element or the list consists of only one element that is not equal to the element to be searched. Since we eliminate elements by half in each pass, the binary search algorithm works faster when compared with the linear search algorithm. Therefore, the running time for average case as well as worst case are almost the same.

5.4 Bubble Sort

The easiest and the most widely used sorting technique among students and engineers is the bubble sort. This sort is also referred as *sinking sort*. *The idea of bubble sort is to repeatedly move the smallest element to the lowest index position in the list.* To find the smallest element, the bubble sort algorithm begins by comparing the first element of the list with its next element and upto the end of the list and interchanges the two elements if they are not in proper order. In either case, after such a pass, the smaller element will be in the lowest index position of the list. The focus then moves to the next smaller element and the process is repeated. Swapping occurs only among successive elements in the list and hence only one element will be placed in its sorted order after each pass. Also, note that once the elements are placed in its sorted order they are not considered for comparison in successive passes. When the focus reaches the end of the list, the smallest element will be "`bubbled`" from whatever has been its original position to the first index position in the list and the larger values "`sink`" to the last index position in the list. The sort terminates after a pass in which no elements are interchanged.

Algorithm for Bubble Sort

BUBBLE (ARR, N)

where ARR is an array of N elements.

Step 1 :   Repeat For I = 0, 1, 2, . . . , N–1•

Step 2 :   Repeat For J = I+1 to N–1

Step 3 :   If (ARR[I] > ARR[J]) Then

        Interchange ARR[I] and ARR[J]

        [End of If structure]

Step 4 :   Increment J by 1

Step 5 :   [End of **Step 2** For loop]

Step 6 :   [End of **Step 1** For loop]

Step 7 :   Print the sorted array ARR.

END BUBBLE()

Program 5.3 :

/* Program to sort the numbers using bubble sort. */

```c
/* bubble.c */
#include<stdio.h>
void bubble(int a[], int n);
int i, j, n, temp, a[25];
void main()
  {
    printf("Enter the limit : ");
      scanf("%d", &n);
    printf("Enter the elements : ");
    for(i = 0 ; i < n ; i++)
      scanf("%d", &a[i]);
    bubble(a, n);                    /* Calling the function bubble() */
    printf("The sorted list is : ");
    for(i = 0 ; i < n ; i++)
      printf("%d   ", a[i]);
  }
void bubble(int a[], int n)
  {
    for(i = 0 ; i <= n-1 ; i++)
      for(j = i+1 ; j <= n-1 ; j++)
        if(a[i] > a[j])
          {
              temp = a[i];
              a[i] = a[j];
              a[j] = temp;
          }
  }
```

The program displays the following output

```
Enter the limit : 6
Enter the elements : 56   91   35   72   48   68
The sorted list is : 35   48   56   68   72   91
```

Unsorted List	56	91	35	72	48	68
	56	91	35	72	48	68
	35	56	91	72	48	68
	35	48	91	72	56	68
	35	48	56	91	72	68
	35	48	56	68	91	72
Sorted List	35	48	56	68	72	91

Fig. 5.1 : Trace of a bubble sort.

The bubble sort algorithm makes (n-1) comparisons, in the first pass to place the smallest element in the first position of the list. The second pass makes (n-2) comparisons, to place the next smallest element in the second position of the list and so on. Thus, the number of comparisons required by the bubble sort is given by

$$[n-1] + [n-2] + \ldots\ldots + 2 + 1 = \frac{n[n-1]}{2} = \frac{[n^2-n]}{2} = o[n^2]$$

Therefore, the time required to execute the binary sort algorithm is proportional to n^2 where n is the number of elements in the list. This sorting method works well only for simple lists. The best case occurs when the input data elements are almost in sorted order. The worst case occurs when the input data elements are in descending order.

5.5 Selection Sort

Another easiest method for sorting elements in the list is the selection sort. The main idea of selection sort is to search for the smallest element in the list. When the element is found, it is swapped with the first element in the list. The second smallest element in the list is then searched. When the element is found, it is swapped with the second element in the list. The process of searching the next smallest element is repeated, until all the elements in the list have been sorted in ascending order.

Algorithm for Selection Sort

SELECT (ARR, N)

where ARR is an array of N elements.

Step 1 :   Repeat For I = 1, 2, 3, . . ., N–1

Step 2 :   Assign K = I, MIN = ARR[I]

Step 3 :   Repeat For J = I+1 to N–1

Step 4 :   If (ARR[J] < MIN) Then

　　　　　　MIN = ARR[J]

　　　　　　K = J

[End of If structure]

Step 5 :   [End of **Step 3** For loop]

Step 6 :   Assign ARR[K] = ARR[I], ARR[I] = MIN

Step 7 :   [End of **Step 1** For loop]

Step 8 :   Print the sorted array ARR

END SELECT()

Program 5.4 :

/* **Program to sort the numbers using selection sort.** */

```c
/* select.c */
#include<stdio.h>
void select(int a[], int n);
int i, j, k, n, min, array[25];
void main()
 {
    printf("Enter the limit : ");
      scanf("%d", &n);
    printf("Enter the elements : ");
    for(i = 0 ; i < n ; i++)
       scanf("%d", &array[i]);
    select(array, n);              /* calling the function select() */
    printf("The sorted list is : ");
    for(i = 0 ; i < n ; i++)
       printf("%d  ", array[i]);
 }
 void select(int a[], int n)
  {
     for(i = 0 ; i <= n-1 ; i++)
      {
         k = i;
         min = a[i];
         for(j = i+1 ; j <= n-1 ; j++)
           if(a[j] < min)
            {
               min = a[j];
               k = j;
            }
```

```
        a[k] = a[i];
        a[i] = min;
    }

}
```

The program displays the following output

```
Enter the limit : 6
Enter the elements : 56   91   35   72   48   68
The sorted list is : 35   48   56   68   72   91
```

Unsorted List	56	91	35	72	48	68
	56	91	35	72	48	68
	35	91	56	72	48	68
	35	48	56	72	91	68
	35	48	56	72	91	68
	35	48	56	68	91	72
Sorted List	35	48	56	68	72	91

Fig. 5.2 : Trace of a selection sort.

The selection sort requires only (n-1) passes to search for the location of the smallest element in the list and to place the element in its proper location. The first pass makes (n-1) comparisons, the second pass makes (n-2) comparisons and so on. The number of comparisons is given by,

$$[n - 1] + [n - 2] + [n - 3] + \ldots + 1 = n[n - 1] = o[n^2]$$

Note that the algorithm always performs the same steps, independent of the state of the list, i.e., the best case and worst case of a selection sort are identical. The major advantage of selection sort is that, if an element is placed in its correct position it will never be moved, since during each pass no more than one interchange is required for each element present in the list. In each pass, a pair of elements is swapped, and in each pass, an element moves into its final position. The selection sort minimizes data movement and overcomes the disadvantage of insertion sort. However, selection sort becomes inefficient when size of n becomes large.

5.6 Insertion Sort

The main idea of insertion sort is to consider each element at a time, into the appropriate position relative to the sequence of previously ordered elements, such that the resulting sequence is also ordered. The insertion sort can be easily understood if you know to play cards. Imagine that you are arranging cards after it has been distributed before you in front of the table. As each new card is taken, it is compared with the cards in hand. The card is inserted in proper place within the cards in hand, by pushing one position to the left or right. This procedure proceeds until all the cards are placed in the hand are in order.

Algorithm for Insertion Sort

INSERT (ARR, N)

where ARR is an array of N elements.

Step 1 :   Repeat For I = 1, 2, 3, . . . , N–1

Step 2 :   Assign TEMP = ARR[I]

Step 3 :   Repeat For J = I to 1

Step 4 :   If (TEMP < ARR[J–1]) Then

   ARR[J] = ARR[J–1]

   Else

      Goto **Step 7**

   [End of If structure]

Step 5 :   Decrement J by 1

Step 6 :   [End of **Step 3** For loop]

Step 7 :   Assign ARR[J] = TEMP

Step 8 :   [End of **Step 1** For loop]

Step 9 :   Print the sorted array ARR.

END INSERT()

Program 5.4 :

```
/* Program to sort the numbers using insertion sort. */
/* insert.c */
#include<stdio.h>
void insert(int a[], int n);
int i, j, n, temp, a[25];
void main()
{
   printf("Enter the limit : ");
      scanf("%d", &n);
   printf("Enter the elements : ");
      for(i = 0 ; i < n ; i++)
         scanf("%d", &a[i]);
   insert(a, n);                    /* Calling the function insert() */
   printf("The sorted list is : ");
   for(i = 0 ; i < n ; i++)
      printf("%d  ", a[i]);
}
void insert(int a[], int n)
{
   for(i = 1 ; i <= n-1 ; i++)
   {
      temp = a[i];
```

```
for(j = i ; j >= 1 ; j--)
    {
        if(temp < a[j-1])
            a[j] = a[j-1];
        else
            break;
    }
    a[j] = temp;
}
```

The program displays the following output

```
Enter the limit : 6
Enter the elements : 56   91   35   72   48   68
The sorted list is : 35   48   56   68   72   91
```

Unsorted List	56	91	35	72	48	68
	56	91	35	72	48	68
	35	56	91	72	48	68
	35	48	56	91	72	68
	35	48	56	91	72	68
	35	48	56	68	91	72
	35	48	56	68	72	91
Sorted List	35	48	56	68	72	91

Fig. 5.2 : Trace of an insertion sort.

The number of comparisons, when the list is initially sorted is $O(n^2)$, since only one comparison is made in each pass. In the worst case, (i.e., if the list is arranged in descending order) the number of comparisons required by the insertion sort is given by

$$1 + 2 + 3 + \ldots + [n-2] + [n-1] = \frac{n[n-1]}{2} = \frac{[n^2-n]}{2}$$

Therefore, the number of comparisons is $O(n^2)$. On an average case the number of comparisons is given by

$$\frac{1}{2} + \frac{2}{2} + \frac{3}{2} + \ldots + \frac{[n-2]}{2} + \frac{[n-1]}{2} = \frac{n[n-1]}{4} = \frac{[n^2-n]}{4} = O[n^2]$$

Even though the insertion sort is better than the bubble sort, the number of comparisons are almost the same. Insertion sort is more efficient and takes less time if the list is almost in sorted order. The timing of the insertion sort can be improved by using binary search, rather than a linear search to find the proper position to insert the element in the list. This reduces the total number of comparisons to O(log n) from O(n²). Even, if the correct position is found, the sorting time of O(log n) steps it has to move (n-1)/2 elements forward. Thus, the use of binary search in insertion does not significantly improve time requirements in the sort. Since insertion sort is efficient when 'n' is small, linear search is almost efficient as binary search when n is small.

5.7 Shell Sort

Shell sort, named after its developer ***Donald.L.shell*** in 1959 is an extension of the insertion sort, which has the limitation, that it compares only the consecutive elements and interchanges the elements by only one space. The smaller elements that are far away require many passes through the sort, to properly insert them in its correct position.

Shell sort overcomes this limitation, gains speed than insertion sort, by comparing elements that are at a specific distance from each other, and interchanges them if necessary. Shell sort divides the list into smaller sub lists, and then sorts the sub lists seperately using insertion sort. This is done by considering the input list being n-sorted. This method splits input list into h-independent sorted files. The procedure of h-sort is insertion sort considering only the hth element (starting anywhere). The value of h will be initially high and is repeatedly decremented until it reaches 1. When h is equal to 1, a regular insertion sort is performed on the list, but by then the list of elements is guaranteed to be almost sorted. Using the above procedure for any sequence values of h, always endingin 1 will produce a sorted list.

Algorithm for Shell Sort

SHELL (ARR, N)
where ARR is an array of N elements.

Step 1 :   Repeat For I = (N+1) / 2 to 1

Step 2 :   Repeat For J = I to N–1

Step 3 :   Assign TEMP = ARR[J], K = J–I

Step 4 :   Repeat While (K >= 0 AND TEMP < ARR[K])

Step 5 :   Assign ARR[K+I] = ARR[K], K = K–I

Step 6 :   [End of **Step 4** While loop]

Step 7 :   Assign ARR[K+I] = TEMP

Step 8 :   Increment J by 1

Step 9 :   [End of **Step 2** For loop]

Step 10 :   Assign I = I / 2

Step 11 :   [End of **Step 1** For loop]

Step 12 :   Print the sorted array ARR.

END SHELL()

Program 5.6 :

```
/* Program to sort the numbers using shell sort. */
/* shell.c */
#include<stdio.h>
void shell(int a[],int n);
int i, j, k, n, temp, array[25];
void main()
  {
    printf("Enter the limit : ");
      scanf("%d",&n);
    printf("Enter the elements : ");
    for(i = 0 ; i < n ; i++)
      scanf("%d", &array[i]);
    shell(array, n);                    /* Calling the function shell() */
    printf("The sorted list is : ");
    for(i = 0 ; i < n ; i++)
      printf("%d  ", array[i]);
  }
void shell(int a[], int n)
  {
    for(i = (n+1)/2 ; i >= 1 ; i /= 2)
      {
        for(j = i ; j <= n-1 ; j++)
          {
            temp = a[j];
            k = j-i;
            while(k >= 0 && temp < a[k])
              {
                a[k+i] = a[k];
                k = k-i;
              }
            a[k+i] = temp;
          }
      }
  }
```

The program displays the following output

```
Enter the limit : 5
Enter the elements : 4857  36  6794  35  535
The sorted list is : 35  36  535  4857  6794
```

In the first pass, for a list of 6 elements, shell sort takes 3 groups of 2 elements and sorts the elements within each by straight insertion. In the second pass the shell sort takes 2 groups of 3 elements and sorts the elements within each, and in the next pass it takes all the elements and sorts the entire list.

Shell sort is the method of choice for many sorting applications because it has acceptable running time for moderately large arrays (containing more than 5000 elements) and requires only a very small amount of code for its operation. The shell sort is also referred as *diminishing increment sort*, because the number of elements compared in a group continuously decreases in each pass.

Unsorted List	56	91	35	72	48	68
Pass 1 Span 3	56	91	35	72	48	68
Pass 2 Span 2	56	48	35	72	91	68
Pass 3 Span 1	35	48	56	68	91	72
Sorted List	35	48	56	68	72	91

Fig 5.4 : Trace of a shell sort.

An important thing to consider when implementing shell sort is the increment sequence (spacing between the numbers). The value chosen for this sequence affects the running time of shell sort drastically. Relatively prime values (numbers that are not multiples of each other) of the increments are better because they ensure distinct increments that will not divide evenly into each other so that data that have been compared to each other are less likely to be compared again. The best case for the shell sort algorithm is a data set with the data already in order. The worst case is a data set arranged in descending order, because every data element in the array is out of order and there will be maximum number of swaps.

The running time of shell sort is not yet known. **Knuth** has mathematically estimated that the running time of the shell sort can be approximated by $O(n(\log n)^2)$ if appropriate sequence of increments is used. If the increment sequence is not chosen correctly the running time of the shell sort will be $O(nb)$ where b ranges from 1 to 2. For large values of n, the number of comparisons required to sort the list is in the range of $n^{1.25}$ to $1.6n^{1.25}$, which seems to be faster than the insertion sort.

5.8 Radix Sort

The sorting techniques that we have seen so far sorts the list of elements by comparing the sequence of elements and swaps them if necessary. Radix sort also referred, as **bucket sort** is little bit different. It manages to sort values without actually performing any comparisons on the input data. Values are successively ordered on digit positions from right to left (i.e., lower order byte to higher order byte). This is accomplished by copying the values into buckets, where the index is given by the position of the digit being sorted. Once all digit positions have been examined, the list must be sorted.

Radix is just a position in a number. In hexadecimal representation of a decimal number, a radix indicates a digit. Radix sort gets its name from the radices, because the method first sorts the input values according to their first radix, then according to the second and so on. The number of passes in the radix sort equals the number of radices in the input values. For example you will need 2 passes to sort 16-bit integers and 4 passes to sort 32-bit integers. In a hexadecimal number system, radix is referred as a byte, and hence the radix sort is often referred as a **byte sort**. Radix sort uses 255 buckets for placing 1 byte data from 00 to FF.

Algorithm for Radix Sort

    RADIX (ARR, N)

    where ARR is an array of N elements

Step 1 :	Repeat For I = 1, 2, 3, . . ., 255
Step 2 :	Initialize bucket_size[I] = 0
Step 3 :	[End of **Step 1** For loop]
Step 4 :	Repeat For M = 1 to 4 where M refers to the byte position
	(from lower order to higher order)
Step 5 :	Assign DATA1 = Mth lower order byte of ARR[J],
	bucket_size[DATA1] = bucket_size[DATA1]+1, TEMP[J] = ARR[J]
Step 6 :	[End of **Step 4** For loop]
Step 7 :	Assign bucket_size[0] = 0
Step 8 :	Repeat For K = 1, 2, 3, . . ., 255
Step 9 :	Assign FIRST_IN_BUCKET[K] = FIRST_IN_BUCKET[K–1] + BUCKET_SIZE[K–1]
Step 10 :	[End of **Step 1** For loop]
Step 11 :	Repeat For R = 1, 2, . . ., N–1
Step 12 :	Assign DATA2 = Mth lower order byte of TEMP[R]
	ARR[FIRST_IN_BUCKET[DATA2]] = TEMP[R]
	FIRST_IN_BUCKET[DATA2] = FIRST_IN_BUCKET[DATA2]+1
Step 13 :	[End of **Step 11** For loop]
Step 14 :	Print the sorted array ARR

    END RADIX()

Program 5.7 :

```c
/* Program to sort the numbers using radix sort. */
/* radix.c */
#include<stdio.h>
void radix(int arr[], int n);
int i, j, k, n, r, data, array[25], temp[25];
int shift, bucket_size[256], first_in_bucket[256];
void main()
 {
    printf("Enter the limit : ");
      scanf("%d", &n);
    printf("Enter the elements : ");
    for(i = 0 ; i < n ; i++)
      scanf("%d", &array[i]);

    radix(array, n);                    /* Calling the function radix() */
    printf("The sorted list is : ");
    for(i = 0 ; i < n ; i++)
      printf("%d  ", array[i]);
 }
void radix(int arr[], int n)
 {
    for(shift = 0 ; shift < 32 ; shift += 8)
     {
       for(i = 0 ; i <= 255 ; i++)
       bucket_size[i] = 0;
       for(j = 0 ; j <= n-1 ; j++)
        {
          data = (arr[j] >> shift) & 255;
          bucket_size[data]++;
          temp[j] = arr[j];
        }
       first_in_bucket[0] = 0;
       for(k = 1 ; k <= 255 ; k++)
         first_in_bucket[k] = first_in_bucket[k-1] + bucket_size[k-1];
       for(r = 0 ; r < n ; r++)
        {
          data = (temp[r] >> shift) & 255;
```

```
                    arr[first_in_bucket[data] = temp[r];

                    first_in_bucket[data]++;

            }

        }

    }
```

The program displays the following output

```
Enter the limit : 6

Enter the elements : 4563   789   31539   15632   489   56

The sorted list is :  56   489   789   4563   15632   31539
```

Unsorted List	4563	789	31539	15632	489	56
Hexadecimal equivalent	4563 11D3	789 0315	31539 7B33	15632 3D10	489 01E9	56 0038
Hexadecimal equivalent	15632 3D10	789 0315	31539 7B33	56 0038	4563 11D3	489 01E9
Hexadecimal equivalent	56 0038	489 01E9	789 0315	4563 11D3	15632 3D10	31539 7B33
Sorted List	56	489	789	4563	15632	31539

Fig 5.5 : Trace of a radix sort.

The radix sort is the most efficient sort that we have seen so far, since it requires only $O(kn)$ time for its sort. The running time of the radix sort clearly depends upon the number of digits k, which is equal to the number of passes and the number of elements n to be sorted in the list. Radix sort is relatively efficient only if the number of digits k is not too large. If the number of digits is less, even a simple bubble sort works faster than the radix sort, since the bubble sort reads the input data and swaps them if they are not in correct order, where as the radix sort has to read the data and sorts them digit by digit. Another drawback of radix sort is that, you may need k*n memory locations for storing each byte of the numbers to be sorted. The memory requirement can be minimized to 2n by using linked lists instead of using arrays.

5.9 Heap Sort

A heap is defined to be a complete binary tree with the property that the value of each node is at least as large as the value of its child nodes, if they exist. The root node of the heap has the largest value in the tree. There are three types of heaps. They are,

- Max heap

- Min heap

- Ternary heap.

A max heap also referred as descending heap of size n is defined as a complete binary tree of n nodes such that the content of each node is less than or equal to the contents of its parent node. A min heap also referred as ascending heap of size n is defined as a complete binary tree of n nodes such that the content of each node is greater than or equal to the contents of its parent node. A ternary heap of size n is defined as a complete binary tree of n nodes in which the contents of each node is greater than or equal to the contents of all its descendants. A heap in a heap sort is nothing but the binary tree in which the elements to be sorted are stored. Then, a loop is used to remove each element of the heap. When an element is removed, it is still part of the list, and is swapped with the last item of the heap. This process continues and each time the largest item is pushed to the end of the heap, which is directly before the item to be discarded in the previous iteration, since the heap becomes smaller.

Algorithm for heap sort

CREATE_HEAP (ARR, N)

where ARR is an array of N elements.

Step 1 :   Repeat For Q = 0, 1, 2, . . . , N

Step 2 :   Assign I = Q

Step 3 :   Assign KEY = ARR[Q]

Step 4 :   Assign J = I / 2

Step 5 :   Repeat While (I > 0 AND KEY > ARR[J])

Step 6 :   Assign ARR[I] = ARR[J]

Step 7 :   Assign I = J

Step 8 :   Assign J = I / 2

Step 9 :   If (J < 0) Then

　　　　　　　　J = 0

　　　　　　　　[End of If structure]

Step 10 :   [End of Step 5 While loop]

Step 11 :   Assign ARR[I] = KEY

Step 12 :   [End of Step 1 For loop]

END CREATE_HEAP()

HEAP (ARR, N)

where ARR is an array of N elements.

Step 1 :   CREATE_HEAP (ARR, N)

Step 2 :   Repeat For Q = N–1, . . . , 1

Step 3 :   Assign TEMP = ARR[0]

Step 4 :   Assign ARR[0] = ARR[Q]

Step 5 :   Assign ARR[Q] = TEMP

Step 6 :   Assign I = 0

Step 7 :   Assign KEY = ARR[0]

Step 8 :   Assign J = 1

Step 9 :   If (J+1 < Q) Then

        If (ARR[J+1] > ARR[J]) Then

            J = J + 1

        [End of If structure]

        [End of If structure]

Step 10 :   Repeat While (J <= Q–1 AND ARR[J] > KEY)

Step 11 :   Assign ARR[I] = ARR[J]

Step 12 :   Assign I = J

Step 13 :   Assign J = 2 * I

Step 14 :   If (J+1 < Q) Then

        If (ARR[J+1] > ARR[J]) Then

            J = J + 1

        Else If (J > N–1) Then

            J = N – 1

        [End of If structure]

        [End of If structure]

Step 15 :   Assign ARR[I] = KEY

Step 16 :   [End of Step 10 While loop]

Step 17 :   Decrement Q by 1

Step 18 :   [End of Step 2 For loop]

Step 19 :   Print the sorted array ARR.

END HEAP()

Program 5.8 :

/* Program to sort the numbers using heap sort. */

```c
#include<stdio.h>
void heap(int a[], int n);
void create_heap(int a[], int n);
void main()
{
    int a[50], i, n;
    printf("Enter the limit : ");
```

```
       scanf("%d", &n);
     printf("Enter the elements : ");
     for(i = 0; i < n; i++)
       scanf("%d", &a[i]);
     heap(a, n);          /* calling the function heap() */
     printf("The sorted list is : ");
     for(i = 0; i < n; i++)
       printf("%d  ", a[i]);
  }
  void create_heap(int a[], int n)
  {
     int i, j, q, key;
     for(q = 1 ; q < n ; q++)
      {
        i = q;
        key = a[q];
        j = (int) (i/2);
        while((i > 0) && (key > a[j]))
         {
           a[i] = a[j];
           i = j;
           j = (int) (i/2);
           if(j < 0)
              j = 0;
         }
        a[i] = key;
      }
  }
  void heap(int a[],int n)
  {
     int i, j, q, key, temp;
     create_heap(a, n);
     for(q = n-1 ; q >= 1 ; q--)
      {
        temp = a[0];
        a[0] = a[q];
        a[q] = temp;
        i = 0;
        key = a[0];
```

```
        j = 1;
        if((j+1) < q)
           if(a[j+1] > a[j])
              j = j + 1;
        while((j <= (q-1)) && (a[j] > key))
         {
            a[i] = a[j];
            i = j;
            j = 2 * i;
            if((j + 1) < q)
               if(a[j+1] > a[j])
                  j = j + 1;
               else if(j > n-1)
                  j = n-1;
            a[i] = key;
         }
        }
    }
```

The program displays the following output

```
Enter the limit : 6
Enter the elements : 56   91   35   72   48   68
The sorted list is : 35   48   56   68   72   91
```

The create_heap() function is used to make an array into a heap. The create_heap() function begins at the first non-leaf node and works up the array, sorting each sub tree with the heap()function. Since leafs can't travel down any further, they do not need to be processed. Instead, they will fall into their proper place by being exchanged with a node on a higher level if necessary, when that node comes down. Suppose that the root of the tree is in array element A[0]. The left child of the root is found at A[1]and the root's right child is at A[2]. The left and right children of the node at A[1]are found at A[3]and A[4], respectively and so on. In general, the left child of the node is stored in array element A[i] is found in A[2*i+1], and the right child is stored in array element A[2*i+2].

By working up, the sub trees of a node are made into heaps first, which allows the heap()function to be used. After all elements have been added to the heap, we can sort the array relatively easily. The heap()function relies on the fact that the node's sub trees are heaps. This is because it compares the node to its children, and swaps if necessary. The idea is that the largest element in the heap is at the root. Suppose we swap the element at the root with the one in the last position of the array. Now the largest element is where it belongs, and all that has to occur is to restore the heap property on the remaining elements. If the elements did not follow the heap property, larger items on lower levels would never be brought to the top, since a comparison is made with the node's children and not the node's parent.

The time complex y of heap() is O(log n) because, in worst case, the function moves a value from the root to a leaf of a complete binary tree. The time to carry out that operation is proportional to the height of the tree, which is O(log n). So the time complexity of the sort is also O(n log n). The time to build the tree is also O(n log n), so the entire heap sorting algorithm is also O(n log n).

Heap sort is interesting because its time complexity in worst and best case is also O(n log n). By comparison, the worst-case time complexity for quick sort is O(n²), with an expected time complexity of O(n log n). For well-chosen pivots, quick sort is much faster than heap sort. But heap sort is better than quick sort, when the list is nearly sorted, since it begins the heap sort algorithm.

5.10 Hashing

Hashing is a data structure that allows insertion, deletion and search operations to be carried out in O(1) time. However, hashing is not efficient in operation that requires any ordering information among the elements, such as sorting, finding minimum and maximum element.

Let us assume we need to keep information about 500 students. Hence, we can assign an identification number to each student between 0 and 499 and then use a multidimensional array of 500 elements. Accessing elements in an array is extremely efficient. Array elements are usually accessed by index (also referred as its subscript). To search for a particular record, we have to search the whole array sequentially till we find the required record. Hence, the search time to find a particular data item in the array is proportional to the number of data items in the list, since the item to be searched may be at the first position, any intermediate position or at the last position. Similarly, if we want to store Reg_No (which is supposed to be a 11-digit number) of each student in an array, if we want to directly use the Reg_No as an index, the table should have much more elements than the number of the students, which is a great waste of space. The modern approach is that to make the entries in the table in sorted order of the primary key. Then we apply any of the sorting and searching techniques to get the desired record, which reduces the search time considerably. But the movement of existing records of the table in sorted order is unnecessary and it is a difficult task. To overcome this problem, we generate a table for the records in the file. Then we take the primary key of each record, and apply a function to manipulate it and generate an address value and store the record, at the generated address. Hence, if we map the 500 Reg_Nos of the students and the numbers between 0-499, then we can use the Reg_Nos as search keys and still use an array of 500 elements to store the records. If we can find a mapping between the search keys and indices, we can store each record in the element with the corresponding index. Thus each element would be found with one operation only, such a technique is referred to as *hash addressing* or *hashing*.

This hashing technique is used in searching for a particular record in a file. So we will use the concept of files to analyze this technique. Let us assume a file F having

N records. This file has a set of fields SF that forms the primary key PK of the file (i.e., Roll_No field in the students record is unique for every student in the college). This primary key PK is used to uniquely identify a particular record in a file. We assume that this file is maintained by a table kept in memory, which stores the primary key PK and the address part of the record with the primary key PK., which directly refers records in a table by doing arithmetic operations on keys to map them onto the respective table addresses. Such a table which maintains the key (of the item that is mapped to an index value) is referred to as the *hash table*. The hash table is sometimes referred to as *scatter table*, because we are trying to scatter the data throughout the table. Each slot in the array (which is considered as an hash table) is sometimes referred to as a *bucket*.

A hash table is a data structure that works just like an array, except instead of forcing you to use integers as your index you can use any arbitrary data type as your index. Basically a function is needed to map a key K to an integer index i of the hash table (which has indices 0 to n), such a function is referred as the *hashing function*. Ideally, the hash function is used to determine the location (table index) of any record, given its key value.

Hash functions transform the keys into numbers within a predetermined interval (0 to N). These numbers are then used as indices in an array in the hash table to store the records. If the indices are numbers and if N is the size of the array, then h(key) = key % N. This will map all the keys into numbers within the interval (0 to N-1). If the indices are strings of characters, treat the binary representation of a key as a number and then apply them as before. If each character is represented with m bits, then the string can be treated as base-m number.

We should choose a hash function such that it gives us distinct values for different values of primary key. Unfortunately, sometimes, two different values may hash to the same address. This situation, where two different key values hash to the same hash address, is referred to as *collision*.

In this collision condition for inserting the new pair, another possible location has to be found. And if all the buckets are filled then this condition is called *overflow*. so, we should have some resolution methods to avoid such overflow.

The methods for handling overflow are

- Open addressing.
- Chaining.

The integer, generated by a hash function between 0 and N-1 is used as an index in a hash table of N elements. Initially all slots in the hash table are blank. To insert values into the hash table, use the hash function to generate an address for each value to be inserted. To search for a key in the table the same hash function is reused. An important consideration in hashing performance is value of the *load factor*, which is denoted by (L) and is defined as the ratio between the number of records to be stored and the size of the table. As the load factor increases, the hashing performance will degrade because of the time required to search collision chains.

The value that the hash function returns for a given key is its hash address. A perfect hash function maps every key into a different table location. It has been proved that if P is a prime number, we obtain better (more even) distribution of the keys over the table. The key obtained by transforming the string into a number using the modulus operation utilizes most of the information in the string. We can use different methods to generate an address from the key value in hash function. Some methods of importance are,

- Truncation method.
- Folding method.
- Mid square method.
- Division method.

5.10.1 Truncation Method

Truncation method is the simplest and easiest method for computing keys using the hash function. Let us consider that you want to generate hash table address for the following keys,

987456   125978   963294   852137

The truncation method truncates a part of the given keys, depending upon the size of the hash table. If we assume that the size of the hash table is 1000, then the right most (or left most) 3 digits are truncated and used as hash table addresses. The hash table addresses for the given keys are,

456   978   294   137

Since, we are using only the last three digits for computing the hash table address, chances of collisions are more in this method.

5.10.2 Folding Method

In this method, the given keys are broken into groups of digits, and these groups are added to get the hash table address. For example, if the key to be mapped is 143765980, break it into 3 groups of 3 digit numbers (143), (765), (980) and add them up resulting in 1888. You can use the result as it is, as the hash table address. But if the size of the hash table is small, you can truncate the result to last 2 or 3 digits, depending upon the size of the hash table. ***Note that it is not necessary that you have to add the digits in this method, you can also multiply the digits, or multiply each group by a base number, to get the hash address to be stored in the hash table.***

5.10.3 Mid-Square Method

In mid-square method of generating the hash table addresses, after reading the keys, square them and choose the middle digits which are the random address to be stored in the hash table. Let us consider, that you want to generate hash table address for the following keys,

    456   978   294   137

Now squaring these keys, will result in the following values,

    207936   956484   86436   18769

Now take the two middle digits from each squared value and use that as hash addresses for these keys. The hash table addresses for the given numbers will be,

    79   64   43   76

5.10.4 Division Method

This is the one of the best method to get the address, for the key to be mapped. *Take the key, depending upon the size of the hash table choose a prime member and do the modulus operation and store the result of modulus operation as the address of the hash table.* Let us consider, that you want to generate hash table address for the key 987456782. Use any prime number for the modulus operation. Let us consider, the table size is 61 and hence the hash address will be 46 (i.e., 987456883 % 61).

Note that you can also combine all or any combinations of the above methods, to generate the hash address for the corresponding key.

Properties of a good hash function

- The function should compute quickly.
- The function should be easy to compute (with few simple instructions) and understand.
- The function should rely on all or most bits of key.
- The function should distribute the key apparently and randomly.
- It should distribute values uniformly over the address range and avoid collisions as far as possible. To uniformly distribute the values over the address range we have to know the address bound before and define the hash function.

5.11 Overflow Resolution Technique --- Open Addressing

When a data item cannot be placed at the index calculated by the hash function (because of collision), we look for availability of another empty location in the hash table. This process is referred to as *open addressing*. Open addressing is generally used where storage space is large and hence it uses only the space in the hash table and does not use any space outside the hash table for storing the key values. In open addressing, arrays are used as storage for hash tables.

5.11.1 Linear Probing

Linear probing method arises when there is no space for new value insertion. In order to solve this, the size of the table is increased and this change in the table size leads to change in the hash function.

For example, Let us use division function method, to find the hash address for the keys specified. Let the keys to be mapped in the hash table be 18, 72, 65, 34 and 13. Using the prime number 7, for the modulus operation, the hash address mapped for the keys are as follows,

```
H(18) = 18 % 7 = 4
H(72) = 72 % 7 = 2
H(65) = 65 % 7 = 2
H(34) = 34 % 7 = 6
H(13) = 13 % 7 = 6
```

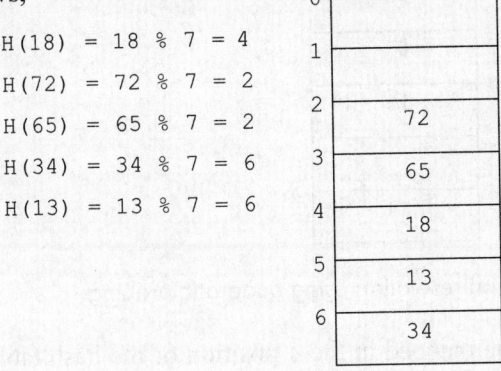

Fig. 5.6 : Collision resolution using linear probing.

The first key (i.e., 18) will be mapped in the 4 position of the hash table. The next key (i.e., 72) will be mapped in the 2nd position of the hash table. The third key (i.e., 65) will try to map the key in the 2nd position of the hash table, since it is already mapped, it will search for the next free place, which is the 3rd position in the hash table. The fourth key (i.e., 34) will be mapped in the 6th position of the hash table. The fifth key (i.e., 13) will try to map the key in the 6th position of the hash table, since it is already mapped, it will search for the next free place, which is the 0th position (since the size of the hash table is 7) in the hash table.

To search an element in the hash table, we check hash address position, corresponding to the key, if the key is not found at that position, then we linearly search the element, following the hash address position. *The main disadvantage* of this resolution technique is the primary clustering problem. That is, if half of hash table is filled or an overflow occurs, it is difficult to find an empty location in the hash table and hence the insertion process takes a longer time.

5.11.2 Quadratic Probing

Quadratic probing is similar to linear probing, except that, instead of looking just one more index ahead each time until we find an empty index, we do the following. On the method we look ahead 1 position, and place the key in the hash table. On the second collision we look 4 (2^2) positions ahead, and on the third we look 9 (3^3) positions ahead and so on. If i is the position in the array in quadratic probing, the step sizes are i+1, i+4, i+9, i+16, and so on. Let us assume, that we want to map the keys considered in the previous example,

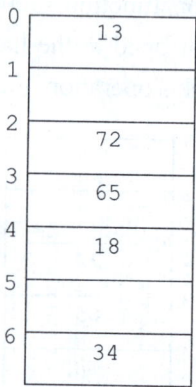

Fig. 5.7 : Collision resolution using quadratic probing.

The first key (i.e., 18) will be mapped in the 4 position of the hash table. The next key (i.e., 72) will be mapped in the 2nd position of the hash table. The third key (i.e., 65) will try to map the key in the 2nd position of the hash table, since it is already mapped, it will search for the next free place, by shifting 1 position ahead, which is the 3rd position in the hash table, and since it is empty, maps the key in that location. The fourth key (i.e., 34) will be mapped in the 6th position of the hash table. The fifth key (i.e., 13) will try to map the key in the 6th position of the hash table, since it is already mapped, it searches for the next free place, by shifting 4 positions ahead, which is the 3rd position in the hash table (since the size of the hash table is 7), since it is already occupied, it searches for the next free place, by shifting 9 positions ahead, which is the 5th position in the hash table and since it is empty, it maps the key in that location.

Quadratic probing is just as easy to implement as linear probing, and has less of a clustering effect than linear probing. The problem with quadratic probing is that it gives rise to secondary clustering. This method will not search all locations in the hash table to find an empty slot. Due to this insertion takes a longer time when compared to linear probing.

5.11.3 Rehashing

Rehashing is similar to Quadratic Probing, except that the size of the table is doubled [i.e., resized]. When the table is almost filled and when the overflow occurs, the new table is created which is double the size of the old one. Let us assume that, we want to insert 23,87 in the table of the Fig. 5.7. The table is almost full and if we try to insert more elements collission will occur. Inorder to overcome the failure the size of the table is doubled. The size of the table in the Fig. 5.7 is 7 on doubling it will be 14. But 14 is not the prime number . So, the immediate prime number 17 is used as the table size, for the modulus opeartion. The hash address mapped for the keys are as follows,

$$H(18) = 18 \ \% \ 17 = 1$$
$$H(72) = 72 \ \% \ 17 = 4$$
$$H(65) = 65 \ \% \ 17 = 14$$
$$H(34) = 34 \ \% \ 17 = 0$$
$$H(13) = 13 \ \% \ 17 = 13$$
$$H(23) = 23 \ \% \ 17 = 6$$
$$H(87) = 87 \ \% \ 17 = 2$$

Index	Value
0	34
1	18
2	87
3	
4	72
5	
6	23
7	
8	
9	
10	
11	
12	
13	13
14	65
15	
16	

Fig. 5.8 : Rehashing Technique.

The first key (i.e., 18) will be mapped in the 1st position of the hash table. The next key (i.e., 72) will be mapped in the 4 th position. The 3rd key (i.e., 65) will be mapped in the 14 th position of the hash table. The 4th, 5th, 6th, and 7th (i.e., 34, 13, 23 and 87) key will map to the 0th, 13th, 6th and 2nd position of the hash table.

The main advantage of rehashing is the perfect collision resolution. Since, the table size is double, there is more wastage of memory.

5.11.4 Extendible Hashing

Extensible Hashing is the dynamic hashing which is used to handle very large amount of data. The table size can be altered according to the insertion and deletion of the data. Like B⁺ tree, it also used to find the exact match query with better cost of the query. The extensible hashing is implemented by using directory which is usually available in the main memory. All the datas are stored in buckets, which holds the enquire address in disk. In this hashing technique, the overflow is handled by doubling the size of the directory. (i.e.,) the overfloing bucket is splitted and doubled.

The size of the directory is always 2^d where d is the global depth and d' is the local depth. Here, the hash values are converted to its equivalent binary representation.

In the extensible hashing method, we use division function method, to find the hash address for the keys specified. Let the key to be mapped in the hash table are 18, 72, 65, 34, 13, 14, 23, 42, and 54 and their binary representations are 10010, 1001000, 1000001, 100010, 1101,1110, 10111, 101010 and 111010.

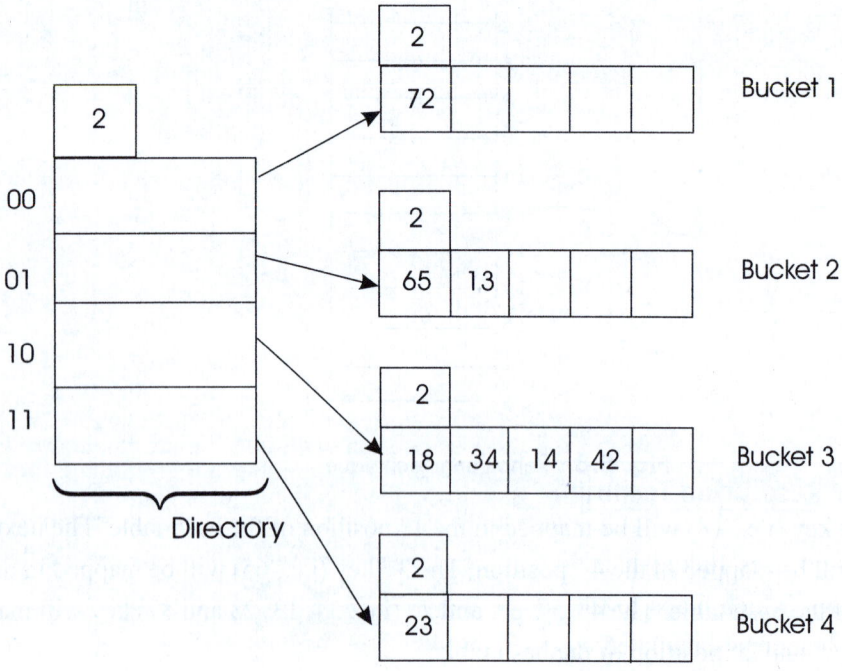

The bucket 2 is almost full and collision occurs. So, to solve the directory is expanded and the bucket 2 is splitted and doubled. Here, the last 3 digits are considered,like 10010, 1001000,1000001, 100010, 1101, 1110, 10111, 101010, 111010.

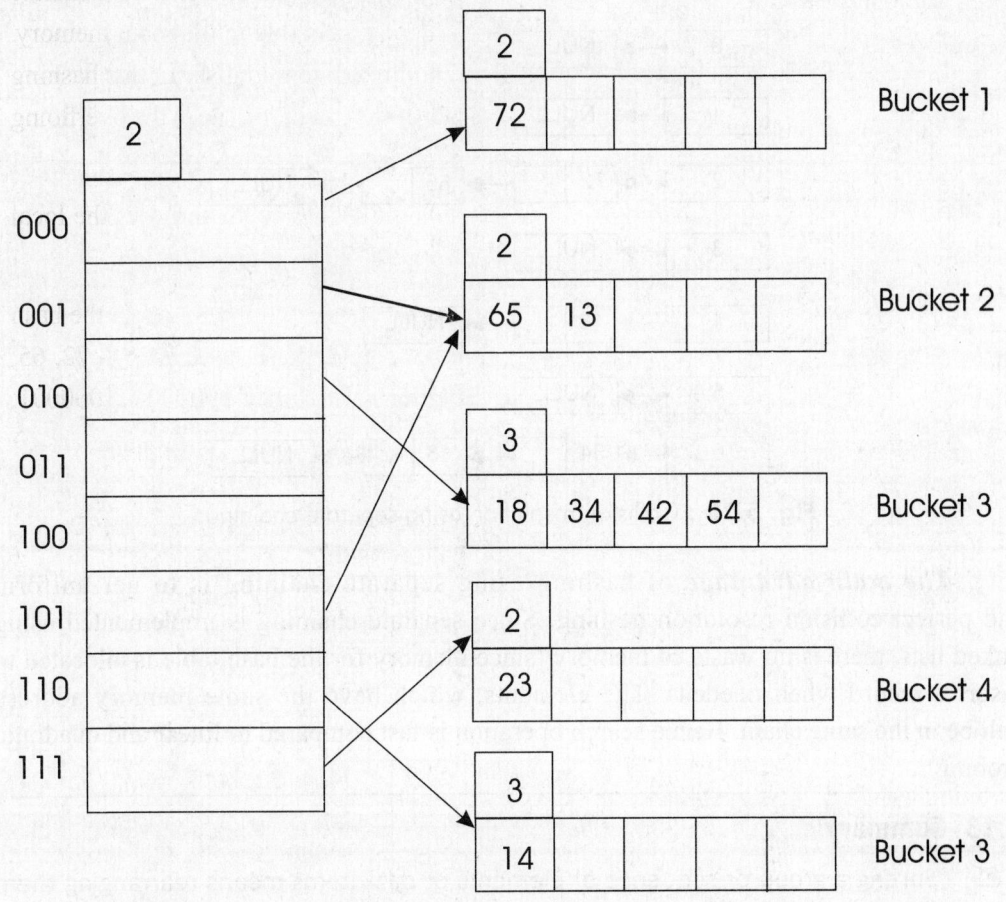

Fig. 5.9 : Extensible Hashing.

5.12 Overflow Resolution Technique --- Separate Chaining

This method uses linked lists for storage as hash tables. It maintains separate chains of elements, which maps to the same hash address. When a data item cannot be placed at the hash address calculated by the hash function, a chain or link is allocated and stores the key element in that chain. This allows an unlimited number of elements to the same hash address and does not require a prior knowledge on number of elements stored in the hash table. This method is referred to as *separate chaining*, because you have a bunch of separate chains in your hash table. In this method, there is no problem of limited storage hence insertions and searching elements are carried out in no time. When we want to map the keys (18, 72, 65, 34 and 13) in the previous example, the hash address mapped for the keys using division function method is 4, 2, 2, 6 and 6. The keys are mapped as shown in *Fig. 5.10.*

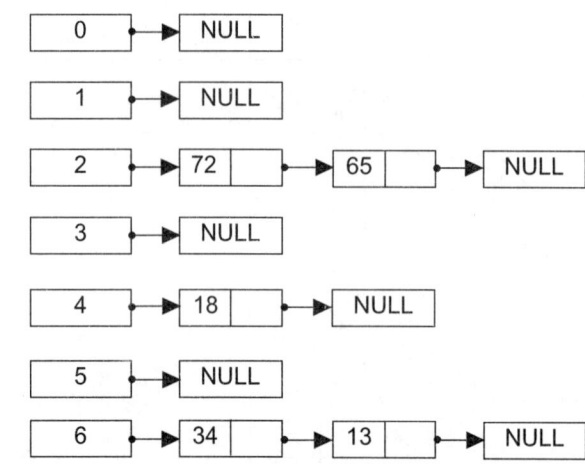

Fig. 5.10 : Collision resolution using seperate chaining.

The main advantage of hashing using separate chaining is to get uniform and perfect collision resolution hashing. Since separate chaining is implemented using linked lists, there is no waste of memory (since memory for the hash table is allocated to insert a record when needed). The elements, which have the same memory address will be in the same chain. Hence search operation is fast compared to linear and quadratic probing.

5.13 Summary

- Sorting a group or sequence of elements or data items means rearranging them in either ascending or descending order depending upon the relationship among the data items present in the group.

- Searching is a programming technique that determines whether an element or a data item is present in the given list or not.

- Bubble sort derives its name from the fact that while sorting the data, the smallest data item bubbles to the initial position of the partially sorted list.

- Insertion sort derives its name from the fact that while sorting the data, each data item is inserted in its correct position among the initially placed data items.

- Selection sort derives its name from the fact that while sorting the data, it selects the smallest element in the list and swaps with the first element in the list. Then the next smallest element is selected and swapped with the second element in the list and so on until all the elements have been sorted in ascending order.

✍ Shell sort divides the list into smaller sub lists, and then sorts the sub lists seperately using the insertion sort by comparing elements that are at a specific distance from each other and swaps them if necessary.

✍ Radix sort derives its name from the fact that while sorting the data, it considers the radix (digit position) of elements from lower order byte to higher order byte and sorts the data items in the list.

✍ In sequential search, the value to be found is searched, from left to right one by one until the element is found or until the end of the list is reached. This search doesn't require that the data items in the list to be in sorted order.

✍ Binary search algorithm splits the list into two and locates the middle element in the list. If the search element is less than the middle element, the first part of the list is searched else the second part of the list is searched. This process continues until the search element is equal to the middle element or the list consists of only one element that is not equal to the search element.

✍ A possible improvement in binary search is not to use the middle element at each step, but to guess more precisely where the key being sought falls within the current interval of interest. This improved version is called Fibonacci search.

✍ A table which maintains key (of the item that is mapped to an index value) is referred to as the **hash table**.

✍ Hash table is also referred as **scatter table**, since we are trying to scatter the data throughout the table.

✍ We basically need a function to map a key K to an integer index i of the hash table (which has indices 0 to n), such a function is referred as the **hashing function**.

✍ An important consideration in hashing performance is value of the **load factor**, which is denoted by (L), and is defined as the ratio between the number of records to be stored and the size of the table.

✍ **When a data item cannot be placed at the index calculated by the hash function (because of collision), we look for availability of another empty location in the hash table has to be found, this process is referred to as** open addressing.

5.14 Short-answer Questions

1.   Define sorting.

Sorting a group or sequence of elements or data items means rearranging them in either ascending or descending order depending upon the relationship among the data items present in the group.

2.   What are the factors to be considered while choosing a sorting technique ?

The factors to be considered while choosing a sorting technique are

- Programming time
- Running time of the sorting technique
- Number of comparisons required for sorting the list
- Main or auxiliary memory space needed for the sorting technique.

3.   What is the necessity for sorting techniques ?

All data processing requires accessing records efficiently and quickly. Search techniques are most efficient only when the data items are sorted according to some specified keys. If the list/file is not sorted, searching a record takes more time when the list/file is large.

4.   Mention some of the sorting techniques.

Sorting techniques includes

- Bubble sort   • Shell sort
- Insertion sort   • Radix sort
- Selection sort

5.   When is sorting method is said to be stable ?

A sorting method is said to be stable when it has minimum number of swaps i.e., if the two data items of matching value are guaranteed not to be rearranged with respect to each other when the algorithm progresses.

6.   List out some of the stable and unstable sorting techniques.

Stable sorting techniques includes

- Bubble sort
- Selection sort
- Insertion sort
- Merge sort.

Unstable sorting techniques includes

- Shell sort
- Radix sort
- Quick sort.

7.   Why is the bubble sort called by that name ?

The bubble sort derives its name from the fact that while sorting the data, the smallest data item bubbles to the initial position of the partially sorted list.

8.   Why is the bubble sort is also called as sinking sort ?

Bubble sort also referred as sinking sort derives its name from the fact that while sorting the data, the largest data item sinks to the final position of the list.

9.   Why is the insertion sort called by that name ?

The insertion sort derives its name from the fact that while sorting the data, each data item is inserted in its correct position among the initially placed data items.

10.   Why is the insertion sort most efficient when the original data are almost in sorted order?

Data exchange in insertion sort is minimal when list to be sorted is in almost sorted order.

11.   Mention the limitation of insertion sort.

Insertion sort has the limitation, that it compares only the consecutive elements and interchanges the elements by only one space. The smaller elements that are far away require many passes through the sort to properly place them in its correct position.

12.   Why is the selection sort called by that name ?

The selection sort derives its name from the fact that while sorting the data, it selects the smallest element in the list and swaps with the first element in the list. Then the next smallest element is selected and swapped with the second element in the list and so on until all the elements have been sorted in ascending order.

13.   How sorting is performed in shell sort ?

The shell sort divides the list into smaller sub lists, and then sorts the sub lists seperately using the insertion sort by comparing elements that are at a specific distance from each other and swaps them if necessary.

14. *Why is the shell sort is also called as diminishing increment sort ?*

Shell sort is also called as diminishing increment sort because the number of elements compared in a list continuously decreases.

15. *State the advantage of shell sort over insertion sort.*

The shell sort overcomes the limitation of insertion sort and gains speed, by comparing elements that are at a specific distance from each other, and interchanges them if necessary hence, the sorting time is reduced in case of shell sort.

16. *Why is the radix sort called by that name ?*

The radix sort derives its name from the fact that while sorting the data, it considers the radix (digit position) of elements from lower order byte to higher order byte and sorts the data items in the list.

17. *Why is the radix sort is also called as bucket sort ?*

Radix sort is also referred as the bucket sort because the elements to be sorted are compared digit by digit and the values are stored into buckets, where the index is given by the position of the digit being sorted. Once all digit positions have been examined, the l

18. *Define searching.*

Searching is a programming technique that determines whether an element or a data item is present in the given list or not.

19. *Mention some of the searching techniques.*

Searching techniques includes

- Linear search
- Indexed sequential search
- Binary search
- Fibonacci search.

20. *What is meant by sequential search ?*

In sequential search, the value to be found is searched, from left to right one by one until the element is found or until the end of the list is reached. This search is also referred as linear search and it doesn't require that the data items in the list to be in sorted order.

21. *Stat the advantages of sequential search ?*

In sequential search, the value to be found is searched normally on unsorted data. The logic of this search is simply straight forward, hence the coding is simple and easily understandable.

22. *What is meant by binary search ?*

The binary search algorithm is one of the most efficient sorting techniques, which requires the list to be sorted in ascending order. To search for an element in the list, the binary search algorithm splits the list into two and locates the middle element in the list. If the search element is less than the middle element, the first part of the list is searched else the second part of the list is searched. This process continues until the search element is equal to the middle element or the list consists of only one element that is not equal to the search element.

23. *Which is the fastest internal sorting technique & why ?*

As the name indicates, the quick sort technique is the fastest sorting technique. The purpose of quick sort is to move a data item in the correct position just enough to reach its final position in the list. This method therefore reduces unnecessary swaps. The quick sort technique has an advantage of moving a data item to a great distance in one move to place it in its exact position.

24. *Sort the following numbers using bubble sort 30, 5, 95, 6, 3, 15.*

The steps for sorting the numbers using bubble sort includes,

```
30,   5, 95,   6,   3, 15
 3,   5, 95,   6, 30, 15
 3,   5, 95,   6, 30, 15
 3,   5,  6,  95, 30, 15
 3,   5,  6,  15, 30, 95
 3,   5,  6,  15, 30, 95
```

25. *Sort the following numbers using insertion sort 30, 5, 95, 6, 3, 15.*

The steps for sorting the numbers using insertion sort includes,

```
30,   5, 95,   6,   3, 15
 5,  30, 95,   6,   3, 15
 5,  30, 95,   6,   3, 15
 5,   6, 30,  95,   3, 15
 3,   5,  6,  30,  95, 15
 3,   5,  6,  15,  30, 95
```

26. ***Sort the following numbers using selection sort 30, 5, 95, 6, 3, 15.***

The steps for sorting the numbers using selection sort includes,

```
30,   5,  95,   6,   3,  15
 3,   5,  95,   6,  30,  15
 3,   5,  95,   6,  30,  15
 3,   5,   6,  95,  30,  15
 3,   5,   6,  15,  30,  95
 3,   5,   6,  15,  30,  95
```

27. ***Sort the following numbers using shell sort 30, 5, 95, 6, 3, 15.***

The steps for sorting the numbers using shell sort includes,

```
30,   5,  95,   6,   3,  15
 6,   5,  95,  30,   3,  15
 6,   3,  95,  30,   5,  15
 6,   3,  15,  30,   5,  95
 3,   6,  15,  30,   5,  95
 3,   6,  15,  30,   5,  95
 3,   6,  15,  30,   5,  95
 3,   5,   6,  15,  30,  95
 3,   5,   6,  15,  30,  95
```

28. ***Sort the following numbers using radix sort 30, 5, 95, 6, 3, 15.***

The steps for sorting the numbers using radix sort includes,

```
  30,     5,    95,     6,     3,    15
0014, 0005, 005F, 0006, 0003, 000F
0003, 0014, 0005, 0006, 005F, 0008
0003, 0005, 0006, 000F, 0014, 005F
0003, 0005, 0006, 000F, 0014, 005F
0003, 0005, 0006, 000F, 0014, 005F
   3,     5,     6,    15,    30,    95
```

TECHNICAL Q & A IN C

I – CHOOSE THE CORRECT ANSWER(S) FROM THE CHOICES GIVEN

1. Which rules determine the meaning of instructions?
   (a) semantic rules   (b) syntax rules
   (c) programming rules   (d) language rules

2. An expression that evaluates to true or false is called as _____ expression.
   (a) logical (boolean)   (b) int
   (c) char   (d) data

3. An expression that has operands of different data types is called a _____ expression.
   (a) unary   (b) binary
   (c) dual   (d) mixed

4. Which of the following is not a legal identifier?
   (a) first   (b) conversion
   (c) payRate   (d) 'primary

5. Every character in a string has a relative _____ in the string.
   (a) position   (b) hierarchy
   (c) importance   (d) area

6. The maximum number of significant digits is called the _____.
   (a) significance   (b) position
   (c) location   (d) precision

7. Preprocessor directives are processed by a program called a(n) _____.
   (a) compiler   (b) linker
   (c) preprocessor   (d) postprocessor

8. A set of rules, symbols, and special words that enable you to write code is known as _____.
   (a) syntax rules   (b) semantic rules
   (c) programming language   (d) syntax

9. When a value of one data type is automatically changed to another data type a(n) _____ type coercion is said to have occurred.
   (a) intrinsic   (b) explicit
   (c) implicit   (d) singular

10. Every C program has a function called _____.
    (a) master   (b) index
    (c) main   (d) default

11. Which is a data type that deals with integers, or numbers without a decimal part?
    (a) integral   (b) enumeration type
    (c) floating-point   (d) numeric

12. Which of the following is an arithmetic operator?
    (a) * multiplication   (b) / division
    (c) % remainder   (d) all of the above

13. The letters that make up a reserved word are always _____.
    (a) lowercase   (b) uppercase
    (c) camel case   (d) capcase

14. A sequence of zero or more characters is known as a(n) _____.
    (a) character   (b) string
    (c) enumeration   (d) set

15. The EBCDIC character set has _____ values.
    (a) 64   (b) 128
    (c) 256   (d) 512

16. A sequence of characters from the computer to an output device is known as a(n) _____.
    (a) output stream   (b) input stream
    (c) common output   (d) common input

17. Characters that consist of blanks and certain nonprintable characters, such as tabs, newline characters, are known as _____.
    (a) openspace   (b) emptyspace
    (c) blankspace   (d) whitespace

18. One printable character except the blank is valid input for which simple data type?
    (a) char   (b) int
    (c) double   (d) both b and c

19. Which logical operator represents not?
    (a) !   (b) &
    (c) || (d) *

20. The syntax of one-way selection is _____.
    (a) if expression statement
    (b) if(expression) statement
    (c) expression(if) statement
    (d) if(statement) expression

21. Which of the following is a binary operator?
    (a) !   (b) &&
    (c) || (d) both b and c

22. A two-way selection in C is the _____.
    (a) if..else   (b) if..then
    (c) if..only   (d) if

23. Since relational and logical operators are evaluated from left to right, the _____ of these operators is said to be from left to right.

(a) associativity   (b) relativity
(c) evaluation   (d) calculation

24. An informal mixture of C and ordinary language is known as _____.

(a) coder   (b) pseudocode
(c) langcode   (d) program code

25. Which operator represents equal to?

(a) =   (b) ==
(c) EQUAL   (d) EQUAL TO

26. The expression used in a switch statement to determine which case to process is called the _____.

(a) action   (b) selector
(c) purpose   (d) declaration

27. Which logical operator represents OR operation?

(a) OR   (b) or
(c) | (d) ||

28. The statement following the expression in an if statement is sometimes called the _____ statement.

(a) decision   (b) declarative
(c) purpose   (d) action

29. Control structures provide alternatives to _____ program execution.

(a) controlled   (b) sequential
(c) repetitive   (d) iterative

30. Which of the following operators has the highest order of precedence?

(a) increment (++)   (b) Unary minus (-)
(c) decrement (--)   (d) Unary Plus (+)

31. A compound statement consists of a sequence of statements enclosed in _____.

(a) square braces   (b) parentheses
(c) curly braces   (d) angle braces

32. Which operator allows you to make comparisons in a program?

(a) comparison   (b) conditional
(c) relational   (d) logical

33. A process in which the computer evaluates a logical expression from left to right and stops as soon as the value of the expression is known is called _____.

(a) circuit evaluation   (b) short-circuit evaluation
(c) short evaluation   (d) logical evaluation

34. Which operators enable you to combine logical expressions?

(a) formatted   (b) conditional
(c) valued   (d) logical (boolean)

35. The primary purpose of a(n) _____ is to simplify the writing of count-controlled loops.

(a) for loop   (b) if loop
(c) while loop   (d) if..else loop

36. The do..while loop is useful when it does not make sense to check a condition until after the _____ occurs.

(a) trigger   (b) action
(c) condition   (d) opening

37. A flag-controlled while loop uses a _____ variable to control the loop.

(a) control   (b) loop-control
(c) boolean   (d) flag

38. In C, do is a(n) _____ word.

(a) unique   (b) reserved
(c) action   (d) special

39. What kind of while loop is used when you know how many items of data there are to be read?

(a) iterative while loop
(b) counter-controlled while loop
(c) limited while loop
(d) specific while loop

40. A(n) _____ statement, when executed in a switch structure, provides an immediate exit from the switch structure.

(a) continue   (b) break
(c) halt   (d) end

41. In a while loop, the expression acts as a(n) _____ maker.

(a) primary key   (b) condition
(c) expression   (d) decision

42. A break and continue statement alters the flow of _____.

(a) information   (b) location
(c) action   (d) control

43. What kind of while loop is used when the sentinel value is not known?

(a) Counter-controlled while loop
(b) EOF-(End Of File) controlled while loop
(c) Flag-controlled while loop
(d) Unknown sentinel-controlled while loop

44. If the expression in a do..while loop evaluates to _____, the statement executes again.

(a) true   (b) false
(c) open   (d) closed

45. In a counter-controlled while loop, the counter is sometimes _____ 0.

(a) defined as   (b) decremented as
(c) initialized as   (d) incremented as

46. In a for statement, if the loop condition is omitted, it is assumed to be _____.

(a) true   (b) false
(c) open   (d) closed

47. A loop that continues to execute endlessly is called a(n) _____.

(a) unending loop   (b) endless loop
(c) infinite loop   (d) elongated loop

48. In a for loop, if the loop condition is initially _____, the loop body does not execute.

(a) true   (b) false
(c) open   (d) closed

49. Which of the following is not a looping structure in C?

(a) if   (b) do..while
(c) while   (d) for

50. A while loop that uses a sentinel value to end the loop is known as a _____ controlled while loop.

(a) numerically   (b) counter
(c) variable   (d) sentinel

51. Using one control structure statement inside another is referred as _____.

(a) organizing   (b) grouping
(c) stacking   (d) nesting

52. To call a function, use its name together with the actual _____ list.

(a) function   (b) module
(c) parameter   (d) group

53. The header file _____ contains mathematical functions.

(a) math   (b) cmath
(c) fmath   (d) stdio

54. Which of the following is not a predefined function?

(a) pow   (b) islower
(c) abs   (d) sum

55. The syntax of the actual parameter list is _____.

(a) expression, variable, ..
(b) expression variable, variable, ...
(c) expression, expression or variable, ...
(d) expression or variable, expression or variable

56. Functions enable you to divide a program into manageable _____.

(a) tasks   (b) groups
(c) modules   (d) nodes

57. In C, predefined functions are organized into separate _____.

(a) divisions   (b) areas
(c) groups   (d) libraries

58. Functions that have a data type are known as _____ functions.

(a) user-defined   (b) predefined
(c) void   (d) value-returning

59. The syntax of the formal parameter list is _____.

(a) identifier, dataType identifier, dataType, ...
(b) dataType identifier, identifier, ...
(c) dataType identifier, dataType identifier, ...
(d) identifier, dataType identifier, ...

60. An integer that reads forward and backward in the same way is known as a _____.

(a) unique integer
(b) bidirectional number
(c) forward/backward number
(d) palindrome

61. What lets you divide complicated programs into manageable pieces?

(a) nodes   (b) subnodes
(c) functions   (d) packets

62. Which function returns the lowercase value of x if x is uppercase; otherwise, it returns x?

(a) toupper(x)   (b) tolower(x)
(c) upper(x)   (d) lower(x)

63. The variable declared in the heading of the function is known as the _____.

(a) formal parameter   (b) heading parameter
(c) actual parameter   (d) primary parameter

64. The function heading without the body of the function is known as the _____.

(a) function header   (b) function prototype
(c) header prototype   (d) function head prototype

65. The function heading and the body of the function are called the _____ of the function.

(a) main module   (b) definition
(c) main group   (d) description

66. The function type is the data type of the _____ value returned by the function.

(a) final

(b) first

(c) unique

(d) only

67. When a function exits, the control goes back to the _____.

(a) controller

(b) caller

(c) master

(d) organizer

68. If the function's formal parameter list is empty, it takes the form of _____.

(a) functionType functionName()

(b) functionType Name()

(c) functionType functionParam()

(d) functionType functionList()

69. In a function call, the number of actual parameters and their types must match with the _____ parameters in the order given.

(a) unique

(b) function

(c) specific

(d) formal

70. Functions that do not have a data type are known as _____ functions.

(a) user-defined

(b) predefined

(c) void

(d) value-returning

71. What is the syntax for the formal parameter list of void functions with parameters that are passed by reference?

(a) dataType variable, dataType variable, ...

(b) dataType variable, dataType variable, ...

(c) dataType& variable, dataType& variable, ...

(d) dataType& variable, dataType& variable, ...

72. During data manipulation, the content of the formal parameter directs the computer to manipulate the data of the memory cell indicated by its _____.

(a) location

(b) variable

(c) arguments

(d) content

73. To declare an external variable inside a function use the _____ reserved word.

(a) external

(b) extern

(c) outside

(d) global

74. What is the syntax for the function call of void functions with parameters?

(a) functionName(formal parameter);

(b) functionName(actual parameter list);

(c) functionName(global variables);

(d) functionName(void);

75. A value-returning function returns _____.

(a) a single value

(b) multiple values

(c) void values

(d) control variables

76. Any function that uses global variables is not _____ and typically cannot be used in more than one program.

(a) independent

(b) stand-alone

(c) unique

(d) globally accessible

77. As with value-returning functions, in a function call the number of actual parameters together with their data types must _____ the formal parameters.

(a) match

(b) duplicate

(c) replace

(d) be different from

78. A variable for which memory is allocated at block entry and deallocated at block exit is called a(n) _____ variable.

(a) static

(b) short term

(c) permanent

(d) automatic

79. A formal parameter that receives a copy of the content of the corresponding actual parameter is known as a(n) _____.

(a) reference parameter

(b) open parameter

(c) value parameter

(d) specified parameter

80. Which exactly refer to the accessibility(visibility) of an identifier in a program?

(a) the location of an identifier

(b) the scope of an identifier

(c) the memory address of an identifier

(d) the accessibility of an identifier

81. A variable for which memory remains allocated as long as the program executes is called a(n) _____ variable.

(a) static

(b) short term

(c) permanent

(d) automatic

82. A formal parameter that receives the location (memory address) of the corresponding actual parameter is known as a(n) _____.

(a) reference parameter

(b) open parameter

(c) value parameter

(d) specified parameter

83. Identifiers declared within a function (or block) are known as _____ identifiers.

(a) local

(b) global

(c) functional

(d) unique

84. You can declare a reference (formal) parameter as a constant by using the keyword _____.

(a) con

(b) const

(c) constant

(d) none of the above

85. Identifiers declared outside every function definition are known as _____ identifiers.

(a) local

(b) global

(c) functional

(d) unique

86. You cannot assign a constant value as a default

value to a(n) _____ parameter.

(a) reference
(b) automatic
(c) default
(d) formal

87. Which identifiers are not accessible outside the function (block)?

(a) local
(b) global
(c) functional
(d) unique

88. Because an enumeration is an ordered set of values, the _____ operators can be used with the enumeration type.

(a) relational
(b) arithmetic
(c) numeric
(d) order

89. The general syntax of the typedef statement is _____.

(a) typedef existing Name newTypeName;
(b) typedef existingTypeName newTypeName;
(c) typedef newTypeName existingTypeName;
(d) typedef existingTypeName newTypeName

90. In C, a sequence of zero or more characters enclosed in double quotation marks is known as a(n) _____.

(a) variable
(b) char
(c) string
(d) word

91. A user-defined simple data type is known as a(n) _____ type.

(a) user-defined
(b) enumeration
(c) unique
(d) specified

92. The enumeration type is a(n) _____ type.

(a) relational
(b) integral
(c) arithmetic
(d) unique

93. Which of the following statements creates an alias, integer, for the data type int?

(a) type def integer;
(b) typedef int integer;
(c) typedef int real;
(d) typedef int integer;

94. The values that you specify for the data type must be _____.

(a) numbers
(b) variables
(c) characters
(d) identifiers

95. Which function returns the number of characters currently in the string?

(a) strlen()
(b) strlength()
(c) stringlen()
(d) stringlength()

96. What is the syntax for an enumeration type?

(a) enum typeName{value1, value2, ...};
(b) enum typeValue{value1, value2, ...};
(c) enum typeValue{name1, name2, ...};
(d) enum typeName{object1, object2, ...};

97. You can pass the enumeration type as a(n) _____ to functions just like any other simple data type.

(a) identifier
(b) parameter
(c) enumerated value
(d) character value

98. If a global identifier in a program has the same name as one of the global identifiers in the header file, the compiler generates a(n) _____ error.

(a) undefined
(b) identifier
(c) syntax
(d) duplex

99. A collection of a fixed number of components wherein all of the components are of the same data type is known as a(n) _____.

(a) database
(b) array
(c) organization
(d) area

100. Which statement declares an array list of 10 components?

(a) int list[9];
(b) int list[10];
(c) int list[11];
(d) int list[12];

101. If either (index < 0) or (index > arraySize - 1), we say that the array is _____ bounds.

(a) between
(b) maximized
(c) in
(d) out of

102. To copy one array into another array, you must copy it _____.

(a) all at once
(b) manually
(c) in sub groups
(d) component-wise

103. The address of the first array component is known as the _____ address of an array.

(a) primary
(b) memory
(c) first
(d) base

104. A sequence of zero or more characters is known as a(n) _____.

(a) string
(b) char unit
(c) alphanumeric
(d) data group

105. An array in which the components are arranged in a list form is known as a(n) _____ array.

(a) one-dimensional
(b) two-dimensional
(c) multi-dimensional
(d) list

106. Which of the following is not a basic operation performed on an array?

(a) initialize
(b) input data
(c) output data
(d) change array bounds

107. C does not check whether the index value is within _____.
   (a) scope
   (b) range
   (c) indices
   (d) formula

108. Other than integers, C allows any _____ type to be used as an array index.
   (a) float
   (b) char
   (c) string
   (d) value

109. Which function copies string s2 into string variable s1?
   (a) strcopy(s1, s2)
   (b) strcopy(s1, s2)
   (c) strcpy(s1, s2)
   (d) strcpy(s2, s1)

110. The general form of declaring a one-dimensional array is _____.
   (a) Type arrayName[intExp];
   (b) dataType Name[intExp];
   (c) dataType array[intExp];
   (d) dataType arrayName[intExp];

111. If the data in an array is numeric, you can find the sum and _____ of the elements of the array.
   (a) average
   (b) product
   (c) quantity
   (d) value

112. Like any other simple variable, an array can also be _____ while it is being declared.
   (a) initialized
   (b) manipulated
   (c) resized
   (d) deleted

113. Because arrays are passed by reference only, you do not use the symbol _____ when declaring an array as a formal parameter.
   (a) *
   (b) %
   (c) $
   (d) &

114. An array whose components are of the type char is known as a(n) _____ array.
   (a) char
   (b) character
   (c) alpha
   (d) alphanumeric

115. Which data type has variables of that type which can store only one value at a time?
   (a) structured
   (b) single
   (c) simple
   (d) unary

116. To compare struct variables, you compare them _____.
   (a) in sorted order
   (b) aggregately
   (c) group-wise
   (d) member-wise

117. The members of a struct are enclosed in _____.

   (a) square brackets
   (b) angle brackets
   (c) curly braces
   (d) parentheses

118. The syntax for accessing a struct member is _____.
   (a) structMemberName.VariableName;
   (b) structVariableName.memberName;
   (c) structVariableName.[memberName];
   (d) struct[VariableName].memberName;

119. A struct variable can be passed as a(n) _____ either by value or by reference.
   (a) variable
   (b) control
   (c) parameter
   (d) object

120. The component employees[50] is the _____ component of the array employees.
   (a) 49th
   (b) 50th
   (c) 51st
   (d) 52nd

121. A collection of a fixed number of components in which the components are accessed by name is known as a(n) _____.
   (a) object
   (b) group
   (c) array
   (d) struct

122. In arrays, you access a component by using the _____ together with the relative position (index) of the component.
   (a) array index
   (b) component name
   (c) array name
   (d) function name

123. As with an array, no aggregate _____ operations are performed on a struct.
   (a) binary
   (b) relational
   (c) Boolean
   (d) arithmetic

124. The struct statement must end with a(n) _____.
   (a) ampersand
   (b) period
   (c) colon
   (d) semicolon

125. In C, the dot, (.), is an operator, called the _____.
   (a) access operator
   (b) member access operator
   (c) function access operator
   (d) member operator

126. An array is a(n) _____ data structure.
   (a) open
   (b) closed
   (c) heterogeneous
   (d) homogeneous

127. To convert a number from base 2 to base 10, we first find the _____ of each bit in the binary number.

(a) weight   (b) position

(c) location   (d) amount

128. The body of the recursive function contains a statement that causes the same function to execute before completing the _____ call.

(a) current   (b) last

(c) final   (d) single

129. We can also write an algorithm to find the factorial of a non-negative integer by using a(n) _____ control structure.

(a) iterative   (b) direct

(c) integer   (d) factorial

130. Every recursive call requires the system to allocate _____ space for its formal parameters and (automatic) local variables.

(a) variable   (b) memory

(c) storage   (d) result

131. Every call to a recursive function has its own copy of the _____ of the function.

(a) header   (b) variables

(c) body   (d) footer

132. Every recursive definition must have one or more _____ cases.

(a) open   (b) base

(c) general   (d) specific

133. A very powerful way to solve certain problems for which the solution would otherwise be very complicated is known as _____.

(a) iteration   (b) lineation

(c) circular programming   (d) recursion

134. Solutions that use a looping structure, such as while, for, or do...while, to repeat a set of statements are known as having _____ control structures.

(a) iterative

(b) duplicating

(c) repeating

(d) circular

135. What are the two ways usually used to solve a particular problem?

(a) logically and recursively

(b) logically and iteratively

(c) iteratively and recursively

(d) linearly and recursively

136. When a function terminates, the memory space that is allocated for its formal parameters is then _____.

(a) cleared   (b) deallocated

(c) reallocated   (d) deleted

137. The process of solving a problem by reducing it to smaller versions of itself is called _____.

(a) circular programming   (b) recursion

(c) rounding   (d) fractalization

138. The base case _____ the recursion.

(a) stops   (b) starts

(c) closes   (d) opens

139. When we are inserting an item in a doubly linked list, the insertion of a node in the list requires the adjustment of _____ pointers in certain nodes.

(a) one   (b) two

(c) three   (d) no

140. A list of items, called nodes, in which the order of the nodes is determined by the address stored in each node is known as a(n) _____ list.

(a) linked   (b) object

(c) node   (d) item

141. Building a list in the backward manner, a new node is always inserted at the _____ of the list.

(a) beginning   (b) middle

(c) end   (d) lowest position

142. When building a list backward, the list is empty so the pointer first must be initialized to _____.

(a) open   (b) NULL

(c) closed   (d) the first data record

143. A linked list is a collection of components, called _____.

(a) objects   (b) items

(c) classes   (d) nodes

144. When building a list backward, the new node becomes the _____ node in the list.

(a) end   (b) middle

(c) first   (d) last

145. The function _____ deallocates the memory occupied by each node.

(a) dealloc()   (b) free()

(c) realloc()   (d) freealloc()

146. The function retrieveFirst returns the _____ contained in the first node.

(a) address   (b) link

(c) info   (d) pointer

147. **To delete a given item from an ordered linked list, _____.**

   (a) first we search the list to see whether the item to be deleted is in the list

   (b) delete the info component of the node

   (c) first sort the nodes

   (d) first organize the info sections of the nodes

148. **Suppose that current is a pointer of the same type as the pointer head; then the statement _____ copies the value of head into current.**

   (a) head = current   (b) head = current;

   (c) current = head;   (d) current = head

149. **We need _____ pointers to build the list forward.**

   (a) two   (b) three

   (c) four   (d) no

150. **If a list is _____, then we can insert a new item at either the end or the beginning.**

   (a) flexible   (b) closed

   (c) open   (d) arbitrary

151. **To print the data contained in each node, we must _____ the list starting at the first node.**

   (a) initialize   (b) organize

   (c) preprocess   (d) traverse

152. **When searching an ordered list, we compare the search item with the _____ node in the list.**

   (a) first   (b) middle

   (c) last   (d) current

153. **The length of a list is the number of _____ in the list.**

   (a) objects   (b) nodes

   (c) items   (d) functions

154. **Every node (except the last node) contains the address of the _____ node.**

   (a) first   (b) next

   (c) last   (d) end

155. **When implementing a stack as an array, to keep track of the top position of the array, we can simply declare another _____, called top.**

   (a) class   (b) array

   (c) stack   (d) variable

156. **The queue is empty if front is _____.**

   (a) equal to rear   (b) NULL

   (c) destroyed   (d) set to 9

157. **Because the value of top indicates whether the stack is empty, we can simply set top to _____ to initialize the stack.**

   (a) 0   (b) 1

   (c) 2   (d) 3

158. **The addQueue operation adds a new element at the _____ of the queue.**

   (a) front   (b) middle

   (c) rear   (d) head

159. **Many compilers now first translate arithmetic expressions into some form of _____ notation.**

   (a) postfix   (b) infix

   (c) prefix   (d) refix

160. **If we set the value of top to 0, even though there are elements are in the stack, they are treated as _____.**

   (a) updated information (b) valuable data

   (c) unlinked data   (d) garbage

161. **A list of homogenous elements, wherein the addition and deletion of elements occurs only at one end, is known as a _____.**

   (a) list   (b) stack

   (c) queue   (d) top

162. **A queue is also called a _____ data structure.**

   (a) Last In Last Out (LILO)

   (b) First In Last Out (FILO)

   (c) Last In First Out (LIFO)

   (d) First In First Out (FIFO)

163. **The end of the stack where additions and deletions occur is known as the _____ of the stack.**

   (a) top   (b) middle

   (c) bottom   (d) initial element

164. **A data structure in which the elements are added at one end, called the rear, and deleted from the other end, called the front, is known as a(n) _____.**

   (a) stack   (b) queue

   (c) tree   (d) list

165. **A stack is also called a _____ data structure.**

   (a) Last In Last Out (LILO)

   (b) First In Last Out (FILO)

   (c) Last In First Out (LIFO)

   (d) First In First Out (FIFO)

166. **A queue is a set of elements of the same type in which the elements are added at one end, called the _____.**

   (a) rear   (b) top

   (c) back   (d) front

167. Adding, or pushing, an element onto the stack is a _____ step process.

(a) one   (b) two
(c) three   (d) four

168. Since new items can be added to the stack, we can perform the add operation, called _____.

(a) push   (b) pop
(c) add   (d) pull

169. We call the add operation on a queue _____.

(a) incQueue   (b) enQueue
(c) deQueue   (d) addQueue

170. If we try to add a new item to a full stack, the resulting condition is called _____.

(a) overflow   (b) underflow
(c) flow error   (d) flow control

171. The remove operation for a stack is called _____.

(a) push   (b) pop
(c) add   (d) pull

172. A sequential search is also called a(n) _____ search.

(a) linear   (b) directed
(c) arrow   (d) binary

173. The algorithms for sequential and binary searches search the list by comparing the target with the list elements and these are called _____ search algorithms.

(a) direction-based   (b) target-based
(c) comparison-based   (d) object-based

174. A sequence of branches from a node x to another node y is called a _____ from x to y.

(a) leaf   (b) branch
(c) path   (d) root

175. If the search item is found in a sequential search, its _____ is returned.

(a) data content   (b) search variable
(c) function   (d) index

176. The most important operation on a list is the _____.

(a) initialization   (b) search
(c) insert   (d) delete

177. The selection sort algorithm sorts a list by selecting the smallest element in the unsorted portion of the list, and then moving this element to the _____ of the list.

(a) bottom   (b) top

(c) middle   (d) next open position

178. Like the quick sort, the merge sort uses the _____ technique to sort a list.

(a) divide-and-conquer
(b) float-to-top
(c) sink-to-bottom
(d) bubble

179. The unique member of an item that uniquely identifies the item in the data set is called the _____ of the item.

(a) index   (b) identifier
(c) object   (d) key

180. The _____ sort algorithm sorts the list by moving each element to its proper place.

(a) insertion   (b) selection
(c) location   (d) place

181. The merge sort and the quick sort differ in how they _____ the list.

(a) link   (b) partition
(c) categorize   (d) update

182. The sequential search always starts at the _____ element in the list.

(a) first   (b) middle
(c) last   (d) index

183. If the list is stored in an array, we can traverse the list in either direction using a(n) _____ variable.

(a) linking   (b) list
(c) traversal   (d) index

184. Once the sublists are sorted, the next step in the merge sort is to _____ the sorted sublists.

(a) further divide   (b) contrast
(c) compare   (d) merge

185. The sequential search continues until either the item is found in the list or _____.

(a) a sentinel value is reached
(b) the search restarts
(c) the entire list is searched
(d) the search list becomes too large

186. If the list is stored in a linked list, we can traverse the list in only one direction starting at the _____ node.

(a) key   (b) controlling
(c) first   (d) last

187. The sequential search is good for _____ lists.

(a) medium sized   (b) very short
(c) single element   (d) very long

188. *If the search item is the first element in the list, _____ is/are required.*

(a) one comparison

(b) two comparisons

(c) no comparison

(d) multiple comparisons

189. *A binary search requires the list _____ to be in order.*

(a) elements   (b) variables

(c) functions   (d) operations

190. *A list is ordered if its _____ are ordered according to some criteria.*

(a) end points   (b) starting point

(c) elements   (d) variables

191. *If the binary tree is empty, then the height is _____.*

(a) 0   (b) 1

(c) undetermined   (d) pruned

192. *The performance of the search algorithm depends on the _____ the binary search tree.*

(a) data contained in

(b) shape of

(c) type of variables in

(d) type of search used with

193. *A node in the binary tree is called a(n) _____ if it has no left and right children.*

(a) parent   (b) only child

(c) root   (d) leaf

194. *If the item is found in the binary search tree, it returns _____.*

(a) found   (b) identified

(c) true   (d) false

195. *An arrow is usually called a directed edge or a(n) _____.*

(a) directed branch   (b) specific branch

(c) important branch   (d) straight branch

196. *In a(n) _____ traversal, the binary tree is traversed as follows: 1. Visit the node. 2. Traverse the left subtree. 3. Traverse the right subtree.*

(a) inorder   (b) preorder

(c) postorder   (d) levelorder

197. *In the diagram of a binary tree, each node of the binary tree is represented as a _____.*

(a) rectangle   (b) triangle

(c) circle   (d) square

198. *A binary tree is a _____ data structure.*

(a) large   (b) variable

(c) static   (d) dynamic

199. *The number of comparisons required to determine whether x is in the binary search tree T is _____ the number of comparisons required to insert x in T.*

(a) one more than   (b) one less than

(c) the same as   (d) two more than

200. *If U and V are two nodes in a binary tree, U is called a(n) _____ of V if there is a branch from U to V.*

(a) child   (b) parent

(c) sister   (d) brother

201. *If the binary search tree is _____, we first compare the search item with the info in the root node.*

(a) empty   (b) nonempty

(c) open   (d) closed

202. *Three lines at the end of an arrow indicate that the subtree is _____.*

(a) open   (b) closed

(c) empty   (d) full

203. *The root node of the binary tree is drawn at the _____ of the drawing.*

(a) top   (b) bottom

(c) middle   (d) side

204. *To make an identical copy of a binary tree, we need to create as many _____ as there are in the binary tree to be copied.*

(a) decision points   (b) nodes

(c) functions   (d) variables

205. *In the inorder traversal of a binary tree, for each node, the _____ subtree is visited first, then the node, and then the _____ subtree.*

(a) primary, secondary   (b) secondary, primary

(c) right, left   (d) left, right

206. *After inserting an item in a binary search tree, the resulting binary tree must be _____.*

(a) binary search tree   (b) resorted

(c) updated   (d) relinked

207. *Every node in a binary tree has at most _____ children.*

(a) one

(b) two

(c) three

(d) four

208. The path with the smallest weight is known as the _____ path.

(a) largest   (b) smallest

(c) longest   (d) shortest

209. Let G be a graph. A graph H is called a _____ of G if V(H) is a subset of V(G) and E(H) is a subset of E(G).

(a) directed graph   (b) undirected graph

(c) subgraph   (d) pair graph

210. A graph is empty if the number of _____ is zero.

(a) parameters   (b) functions

(c) vertices   (d) variables

211. The set of all elements that are in A or in B are known as the _____.

(a) vertices   (b) graph

(c) union   (d) intersection

212. G Is called _____ connected If any two vertices in G are connected.

(a) directly

(b) indirectly

(c) strongly

(d) weakly

213. The weight of the path P is the _____ of the weights of all edges on the path P, which is also called the weight of v from u via P.

(a) product   (b) sum

(c) inverse   (d) smallest

214. Vertices u and v are called _____ if there is a path from u to v.

(a) directed   (b) bonded

(c) connected   (d) disconnected

215. A tree in which a particular vertex is designated as a root is called a _____ tree.

(a) minimal   (b) rooted

(c) weighted   (d) spanning

216. When a graph is shown pictorially, the vertices are drawn as _____.

(a) arrows   (b) lines

(c) squares   (d) circles

217. The depth first traversal is similar to the _____ traversal of a binary tree.

(a) preorder   (b) postorder

(c) inorder   (d) levelorder

218. A graph G is a pair where G=(V,E) where V is a finite nonempty set also called a set of _____.

(a) vertices   (b) graph

(c) union   (d) intersection

219. To write programs that process and manipulate graphs, the graphs must be stored or represented in _____.

(a) a variable   (b) computer memory

(c) a function   (d) an array

220. A tree T is a simple graph such that if u and v are _____ vertices in T, there is a unique path from u to v.

(a) no   (b) two

(c) three   (d) four

221. A path in which all vertices, except possibly the first and last vertices, are distinct is known as a(n) _____ path.

(a) component   (b) cycle

(c) complex   (d) simple

222. If a weight is assigned to the edges in T, thenT is called a _____ tree.

(a) minimal   (b) rooted

(c) weighted   (d) spanning

223. When a graph is shown pictorially, the label inside the symbol for the vertices represents the _____.

(a) vertex   (b) tangents

(c) union   (d) intersection

224. The breadth first traversal of a graph is similar to traversing a _____ level by level.

(a) function   (b) binary tree

(c) variable   (d) class

❖ ❖ ❖ ❖ ❖ ❖ ❖

BASICS OF C PROGRAM

1.
```c
void main()
{
    int const * ptr = 5;
    printf("%d",++(*ptr));
}
```

2.
```c
void main()
{
    extern int i;
    i = 20;
    printf("%d",i);
}
```

3.
```c
void main()
{
    int i= -1, j= -1, k=0, l=2, m;
    m = i++ && j++ && k++ || l++;
    printf("%d %d %d %d %d",
                    i,j,k,l,m);
}
```

4.
```c
void main()
{
    printf("%x", -1 << 4);
}
```

5.
```c
void main()
{
    int a =- -2;
    printf("c = %d", a);
}
```

6.
```c
#define int char
void main()
{
    int i = 65;
    printf("sizeof(i) = %d",
                    sizeof(i));
}
```

7.
```c
void main()
{
    int i = 10;
    i = !i > 5;
    printf("i = %d",i);
}
```

8.
```c
void main()
{
    printf("\nab");
    printf("\bsi");
    printf("\rha");
}
```

9.
```c
void main()
{
    int i = 5;
    printf("%d %d %d %d %d",
            i++,--i,i--,++i,i);
}
```

10.
```c
#define square(x) x*x
void main()
{
    int i = 64 / square(4);
    printf("%d",i);
}
```

11.
```c
#define a 10
void main()
{
    #define a 50
    printf("%d", a);
}
```

12.
```c
#define clrscr() 100
void main()
{
    clrscr();
    printf("%d",clrscr());
}
```

13.
```c
void main()
{
    printf("%p",main);
}
```

14.
```c
void main()
{
    clrscr();
}
clrscr();
```

15.
```c
enum colors{BLACK,BLUE,GREEN};
void main()
{
    printf("%d - %d - %d",
            BLACK,BLUE,GREEN);
    return(1);
}
```

16.
```c
void main()
{
    char far *farther,*farthest,farless;
    printf("%d-%d-%d",sizeof(farther),
    sizeof(farthest),sizeof(farless));
}
```

17.
```c
void main()
{
    char far *a, near *b, huge *c;
    printf("%d - %d - %d",sizeof(a),
            sizeof(b),sizeof(c));
}
```

18.
```c
void main()
{
    int a = 100, b = 200;
    printf("%d - %d");
}
```

19.
```
void main()
{
    char *ptr;
    ptr = "John";
    printf("%c",*&*ptr);
}
```

20.
```
void main()
{
    int i = 5;
    printf("%d",i++ + ++i);
}
```

21.
```
void main()
{
    int i = 5;
    printf("%d",i+++++i);
}
```

22.
```
void main()
{
    int i;
    /* Input value is 234 */
    printf("%d",scanf("%d",&i));
}
```

23.
```
#define f(a,b) a##b
void main()
{
    int cd = 100;
    printf("%d",f(c,d));
}
```

24.
```
void main()
{
    extern int i;
    i = 20;
    printf("%d",sizeof(i));
}
```

25.
```
void main()
{
    printf("%d",out);
}
int out = 100;
```

26.
```
void main()
{
    extern out;
    printf("%d",out);
}
int out = 100;
```

27.
```
void main()
{
    int i = -(-1);
    printf("i = %d, i = %d\n",i,+i);
}
```

28.
```
void main()
{
    char name[10],str[12];
    scanf(" \"%[^\"]\"",str);
}
```
How will the scanf function execute?

29.
```
void main()
{
    main();
}
```

30.
```
void main()
{
    char not;
    not = !2;
    printf("%d",not);
}
```

31.
```
void main()
{
    int i = 1;
    printf("%d==1 is ""%s",
            i,i==1?"TRUE":"FALSE");
}
```

32.
```
#define MAX 3
void main()
{
    typedef char data[MAX];
    data list = {0, 1, 2};
    data name = "John";
    printf("%d %s",list[0],name);
}
```

33.
```
#define MAX 3
#define int data[MAX]
void main()
{
    data list = {0, 1, 2};
    printf("%d",list[0]);
}
```

34.
```
int i = 10;
void main()
{
    extern int i;
    {
        int i = 20;
        {
            const volatile unsigned i=30;
            printf(" %d",i);
        }
        printf(" %d",i);
    }
    printf(" %d",i);
}
```

35.
```
void main()
{
    int i = -1;
    +i;
    printf("i = %d, +i = %d",i,+i);
}
```

36.
```
void main()
{
    int i = -1;
    -i;
    printf("i = %d, -i = %d",i,-i);
}
```

```
37.#include<stdio.h>
   void main()
   {
      const int i = 4;
      float j;
      j = ++i;
      printf("%d  %f",i,++j);
   }

38.#include<stdio.h>
   void main()
   {
      register i = 4;
      char j[] = "John";
      printf("%s  %d",j,i);
   }

39.void main()
   {
      int i = 5, j = 6, z;
      printf("%d",i+++j);
   }

40.void main()
   {
      char a[] = "12345\0";
      int i = strlen(a);
      printf("The length of the
            variable a is %d\n",++i);
   }

41.void main()
   {
      int a;
      unsigned b=-1;
      printf("%u ",++b);
      printf("%u ",a=--b);
   }

42.void main()
   {
      int i=i++, j=j++, k=k++;
      printf("%d %d %d",i,j,k);
   }

43.void main()
   {
      static int i=i++, j=j++, k=k++;
      printf("i = %d j = %d k = %d",i,j,k);
   }

44.#define prod(a,b) a*b
   void main()
   {
      int x = 3, y = 4;
      printf("%d",prod(x+2,y-1));
   }

45.void main()
   {
      float a = 2;
      printf("%f\n", a >> 2);
   }
```

```
46.void main()
   {
      enum { i = 10, j = 20, k = 50 };
      printf("%d\n", ++k);
   }

47.void main()
   {
      float a = 2;
      printf("%f\n", a << 2);
   }

48.void main()
   {
      float a = 2, b = 4;
      printf("%lf\n", a % b);
   }

49.void main()
   {
      float a = 5, b = 2;
      printf("%lf\n",fmod(a,b));
   }

50.typedef enum errorType
   {
      warning, error, exception
   }error;
   void main()
   {
      error e;
      e = 1;
      printf("%d",e);
   }

51.typedef struct error
   {
      int warning, error, exception;
   }error;
   void main()
   {
      error e;
      e.error=1;
      printf("%d",e.error);
   }

52.#define something 100
   #ifdef something
   int some = 0;
   #endif
   void main()
   {
      int thing = 0;
      printf("%d %d",some,thing);
   }

53.#ifdef something
   int some = 0;
   #endif
   void main()
   {
      int thing = 0;
      printf("%d %d",some,thing);
   }
```

```
54.#ifdef something
   #if something == 0
   int some = 0;
   #endif
   void main()
     {
       int thing = 0;
       printf("%d %d",some,thing);
     }
```

```
55.void main()
     {
       int arr[2][2];
       printf("%d\n", ((arr==*arr)
              && (*arr==arr[0])));
     }
```

```
56.void main()
     {
       int i = 5;
       printf("%d",++i++);
     }
```

```
57.void main()
     {
       int i = 5;
       printf("%d",i=++i==6);
     }
```

```
58.void main()
     {
       char text[] = "%d\n";
       text[1] = 'c';
       printf(text, 65);
     }
```

```
59.void main()
     {
       int i=5, j=10;
       i = i &= j && 10;
       printf("%d %d",i,j);
     }
```

```
60.void main()
     {
       int i=5, j=10;
       i = i |= j || 10;
       printf("%d %d",i,j);
     }
```

```
61.void main()
     {
       int i=5, j=10;
       j = i = j + 10;
       printf("%d %d",i,j);
     }
```

```
62.void main()
     {
       int i=5, j=10;
       j = i = j > 1;
       printf("%d %d",i,j);
     }
```

```
63.void main()
     {
       int i = 4, j = 7;
       j=j||i++&&printf("YOU CAN WIN");
       printf("%d %d",i,j);
     }
```

```
64.void main()
     {
       register int a = 2;
       printf("Address of a = %d",&a);
       printf("Value of a = %d",a);
     }
```

```
65.void main()
     {
       extern i;
       printf("%d\n",i);
         {
           int i = 20;
           printf("%d\n",i);
         }
     }
```

```
66.#define DIM(array,type)
           sizeof(array)/sizeof(type)
   void main()
     {
       int arr[10];
       printf("The dimension of the
           array is %d",DIM(arr,int));
     }
```

```
67.void main()
     {
       printf("sizeof(void *) = %d\n",
           sizeof(void*));
       printf("sizeof(int *) = %d\n",
           sizeof(int*));
       printf("sizeof(double *) = %d\n",
           sizeof(double *));
       printf("sizeof(struct unknown*)
       =%d",sizeof(struct unknown*));
     }
```

```
68.void main()
     {
       char a[4] = "HELLO";
       printf("%s",a);
     }
```

```
69.void main()
     {
       char a[4] = "HELL";
       printf("%s",a);
     }
```

```
70.void main()
     {
       extern int i;
         {
           int i = 20;
             {
               const volatile unsigned i=30;
               printf("\t%d", i);
             }
           printf("\t%d", i);
         }
       printf("\t%d", i);
     }
```

❖ ❖ ❖ ❖ ❖ ❖

IF STATEMENTS

1.
```c
void main()
{
   float a=123.4;
   double b=123.4.;
   if(a == b)
      printf("INDIA will win match");
   else
      printf("INDIA may win match");
}
```

2.
```c
void main()
{
   static int a=5;
   printf("%d ",a--);
   if(a)
      main();
}
```

3.
```c
void main()
{
   static int i = 5;
   if(--i)
      {
      main();
      printf("%d ",i);
      }
}
```

4.
```c
void main()
{
   int i=3;
   switch(i)
      {
      default: printf("Zero");
               break;
      case 1: printf("One");
               break;
      case 2: printf("Two");
               break;
      case 3: printf("Three");
               break;
      }
}
```

5.
```c
void main()
{
   int a=1,b=2;
   switch(b)
      {
      case 1: printf("Good Morning");
              break;
      case b: printf("Bad Morning");
              break;
      }
}
```

6.
```c
#define FALSE -1
#define TRUE 1
#define NULL 0
void main()
{
   if(NULL)
      puts("NULL");
   else if(FALSE)
      puts("TRUE");
   else
      puts("FALSE");
}
```

7.
```c
void main()
{
   int year;
   /* Input value is 10 */
   scanf("%d",&year);
   if((year%4==0&&year%100!=0)
                    ||year%100==0)
    printf("%d is a leap year");
   else
    printf("%d is not a leap year");
}
```

8.
```c
void main()
{
   int i=0, j=0;
   if(i&&j++)
      printf("%d - %d",i++,j);
   printf("%d - %d",i,j);
}
```

9.
```c
void main()
{
   int a = 0;
   int b = 20;
   char c = 1;
   char d = 10;
   if(a, b, c, d)
      printf("Programming");
}
```

10.
```c
void main()
{
   char str[]="\0";
   if(printf("%s\n",str))
      printf("Good Morning");
   else
      printf("Good Night");
}
```

11.
```c
void main()
{
   int a, b = 100,c;
   if(a = b % 2)
      {
       c=100;
      }
   printf("%d - %d - %d",a,b,c);
}
```

12.
```c
void main()
{
   float a=1.5;
   switch(a)
      {
      case 1: printf("1");
              break;
      case 2: printf("2");
              break;
      default: printf("0");
               break;
      }
}
```

❖ ❖ ❖ ❖ ❖ ❖ ❖

LOOPING STATEMENTS

1. void main()
```
    {
        char str[] = "man";
        int i;
        for(i = 0; str[i]; i++)
        printf("\n%c%c%c%c",
        str[i],i[str],*(str+i),*(i+str));
    }
```

2. void main()
```
    {
        int arr[] = {2.2,3,4.4,5,6.6};
        int i, *ptr1=arr, *ptr2=arr;
        puts("");
        for(i = 0; i < 5; i++)
        {
            printf("%d ",*arr);
            ++ptr2;
        }
        for(i = 0; i < 5; i++)
        {
            printf("%d ",*ptr1);
            ++ptr1;
        }
    }
```

3. void main()
```
    {
        char *str="I Love You",*ptr;
        ptr = str;
        while(*str != '\0')
        ++*str++;
        printf("%s   %s",str,ptr);
    }
```

4. void main()
```
    {
        int a = 1;
        while(a <= 5)
        {
            printf("%d",a);
            if(a > 3)
            goto INDIA;
            a++;
        }
    }
    int func()
    {
        here:
        printf("I LOVE INDIA");
    }
```

5. void main()
```
    {
        int i;
        char *ptr;
        static char Lang[4][20]
        ={"Pascal","C","C++","Java"};
        ptr = Lang[2];
        Lang[2] = Lang[3];
        Lang[3] = ptr;
        for(i = 0; i <= 3; i++)
        puts(Lang[i]);
    }
```

6. void main()
```
    {
        int a = 0;
        for(; a++; printf("%d",a));
        printf("%d",a);
    }
```

7. int i;
```
    void main()
    {
        unsigned int i;
        for(i = 1; i > -3; i--)
        printf("c aptitude");
    }
```

8. void main()
```
    {
        while(1)
        {
            if(printf("%d",printf("%d")))
            break;
            else
            continue;
        }
    }
```

9. void main()
```
    {
        unsigned int i = 5;
        while(i-- >= 0)
        printf("%u",1);
    }
```

10. void main()
```
    {
        unsigned int i = 65000;
        while(i++ != 0);
        printf("%d",i);
    }
```

11. void main()
```
    {
        int i = 0;
        while(+(+i--) != 0)
        i-=i++;
        printf("%d",i);
    }
```

12. void main()
```
    {
        signed char i = 0;
        for(; i >= 0; i++);
        printf("%d",i);
    }
```

13. void main()
```
    {
        unsigned char i = 0;
        for(; i >= 0 ; i++);
        printf("%d",i);
    }
```

14. void main()
```
    {
        char i = 0;
        for(; i >= 0; i++);
        printf("%d",i);
    }
```

```
15. void main()
    {
        while(strcmp("John", "John\0"))
         printf("Strings Are Not Equal");
    }

16. void main()
    {
        char str1[]={'J','o','h','n'};
        char str2[]={'J','o','h','n','\0'};
        while(strcmp(str1,str2))
         printf("Strings Are Not Equal");
    }

17. void main()
    {
        int i = 3;
        for(; i++=0 ;)
            printf("%d",i);
    }

18. void main()
    {
        static int i;
        while(i <= 10)
            (i > 2) ? i++ : i--;
        printf("%d",i);
    }

19. void main()
    {
        char ch;
        for(ch=0;ch<=127;ch++);
            printf("%c  %d",ch,ch);
    }

20. void main()
    {
        int l1 = 1;
        l1:
        printf("Testing in C");
        while(l1)
            break;
        goto l1;
    }
```

❖ ❖ ❖ ❖ ❖ ❖ ❖

FUNCTIONS

```
1. void main()
   {
       char str[] = "Hello World";
       display(str);
   }
   void display(char *str)
   {
       printf("%s",str);
   }

2. void main()
   {
       show();
   }
   void show()
   {
       printf("Fashion Show");
   }

3. void main()
   {
       int i = _func(10);
       printf("%d",--i);
   }
   int _func(int i)
   {
       return(i++);
   }

4. void main()
   {
       char c = ' ', x, Convert(z);
       x = Convert(c);
       printf("%c",x);
   }
   Convert(z)
   {
       return z;
   }

5. int sum(int m, int n);
   void main(int argc, char **argv)
   {
       printf("Enter a Character : ");
       getchar();
       sum(argv[1], argv[2]);
   }
   int sum(int m, int n)
   {
       return(m+n);
   }

6. a()
   {
       printf("Hai");
   }
   b()
   {
       printf("Hello");
   }
   c()
   {
       printf("Bye");
   }
   void main()
   {
       int (*ptr[3])();
       ptr[0] = a;
       ptr[1] = b;
       ptr[2] = c;
       ptr[2]();
   }
```

7.
```
void main()
{
    int i;
    i = abc();
    printf("%d",i);
}
abc()
{
    _AX = 1000;
}
```

8. The following notations of defining functions are known as?
```
i. int abc(int a,float b)
   {
      // some code
   }
ii. int abc(a,b)
    int a; float b;
    {
       // some code
    }
```

9.
```
void main()
{
    char a[100];
    a[0] = 'a';
    a[1] = 'b';
    a[2] = 'c';
    a[3] = 'd';
    func(a);
}
func(char a[])
{
    a++;
    printf("%c",*a);
    a++;
    printf("%c",*a);
}
```

10.
```
func(int a, int b)
{
    return(a =(a == b));
}
void main()
{
    int process(), func();
    printf("The value of process
    is %d",process(func,3,6));
}
process(int(*pf)(),int val1,int val2)
int(*pf)();
{
    return((*pf) (val1,val2));
}
```

11.
```
int func(int);
void main()
{
    int a = func(sizeof(float));
    printf("Value is %d",++a);
}
int func(int func)
{
    func += 2.5;
    return(func);
}
```

12.
```
void pascal func(int, int, int);
void main()
{
    int i = 10;
    func(i++, i++, i++);
    printf(" %d",i);
}
void pascal func(integer:i,
            integer:j, integer:k)
{
    write(i, j, k);
}
```

13.
```
void pascal fun1(int i,int j,int k)
{
    printf("%d %d %d",i,j,k);
}
void cdecl fun2(int i,int j,int k)
{
    printf("%d %d %d",i,j,k);
}
void main()
{
    int i = 5;
    fun1(i++, i++, i++);
    printf(" %d\n",i);
    i = 5;
    fun2(i++, i++, i++);
    printf(" %d",i);
}
```

14. Describe the C statement.
```
void(* abc(int,void(*def)()))();
```

15.
```
int DIM(int array[])
{
    return sizeof(array)/sizeof(int);
}
void main()
{
    int arr[10];
    printf("The array dimension is
            %d",DIM(arr));
}
```

❖ ❖ ❖ ❖ ❖ ❖ ❖

POINTERS

1.
```
void main()
{
    char *ptr;
    printf("%d %d",sizeof(*ptr),
                 sizeof(ptr));
}
```

2.
```
void main()
{
    char s[] = {'a','b','c','\n',
                         'c','\0'};
    char *ptr,*str;
    ptr = &s[3];
    str = s;
    printf("%c",++*ptr + ++*str-9);
}
```

3.
```
void main()
{
    int arr[2][2][2] = {{10,2,3,4},
                         {5,6,7,8}};
    int *ptr,*qtr;
    ptr = &arr[2][2][2];
    *qtr = ***arr;
    printf("%d--%d",*ptr,*qtr);
}
```

4.
```
void main()
{
    int a[2][3][2] =
            {
             {{1,2},{3,4},{5,6}},
             {{9,8},{7,6},{5,4}}
            };
    printf("%u - %u - %u - %d \n",
                 a,*a,**a,***a);
    printf("%u - %u - %u - %d",
             a+1,*a+1,**a+1,***a+1);
}
```

5.
```
void main()
{
    int a[] = {10,20,30,40,50};
    int i, *ptr;
    for(i = 0; i < 5; i++)
      {
        printf("%d",*a);
        a++;
      }
    ptr = a;
    for(i = 0; i < 5; i++)
      {
        printf("%d",*ptr);
        ptr++;
      }
}
```

6.
```
void main()
{
static int a[]={0,1,2,3,4};
int *p[] = {a,a+1,a+2,a+3,a+4};
int **ptr = p;
ptr++;
printf("\n %d %d %d",
             ptr-p,*ptr-a, **ptr);
*ptr++;
printf("\n %d %d %d",
             ptr-p,*ptr-a,**ptr);
*++ptr;
printf("\n %d %d %d",
             ptr-p,*ptr-a,**ptr);
}
```

7.
```
void main()
{
    int arr[3][3] =   {
                        {1, 2, 3},
                        {4, 5, 6},
                        {7, 8, 9},
                      };
    printf("%d", *(*(arr)));
}
```

8.
```
void main()
{
    void *vp;
    char ch = 'A', *cp = "Hello";
    int j = 20;
    vp = &ch;
    printf("%c",*(char*)vp);
    vp = &j;
    printf("%d",*(int*)vp);
    vp = cp;
    printf("%s",(char*)vp+3);
}
```

9.
```
void main()
{
    static char *s[]  =
    {"Black","White","Green","Red"};
    char **ptr[]={s+3,s+2,s+1,s};
char ***p;
    p = ptr;
    **++p;
    printf("%s",*--*++p+3);
}
```

10.
```
void main()
{
    int  i, n;
    char *x = "John";
    n = strlen(x);
    *x = x[n];
    for(i = 0; i < n; ++i)
      {
        printf("%s\n",x);
        x++;
      }
}
```

11.
```
void main()
{
    char *cptr, c = 10;
    void *vptr, v = 0;
    cptr = &c;
    vptr = &v;
    printf("%c %v", c, v);
}
```

12.
```
void main()
{
    char *str1 = "abcd";
    char str2[] = "abcd";
    printf("%d %d %d",sizeof(str1),
       sizeof(str2),sizeof("abcd"));
}
```

```
13.void main()
   {
       int *j;
       {
         int i = 10;
         j = &i;
       }
       printf("%d",*j);
   }

14.void main()
   {
       char *p;
       int *q;
       long *r;
       p = q = r = 0;
       p++;
       q++;
       r++;
       printf("%p - %p - %p",p,q,r);
   }

15.int arr[] = {1, 2, 3};
   void main()
   {
       int *ptr;
       ptr = arr;
       ptr += 3;
       printf("%d", *ptr);
   }

16.void main()
   {
       char *ptr;
       ptr = "%d\n";
       ptr++;
       ptr++;
       printf(ptr-2,300);
   }

17.void main()
   {
       void *v;
       int integer = 2;
       int *i = &integer;
       v = i;
       printf("%d",(int*)*v);
   }

18.void main()
   {
       int a[10];
       printf("%d",*a+1-*a+3);
   }

19.void main()
   {
       char *ptr = "abcde";
       printf("%c",++*(ptr++));
   }

20.void main()
   {
       char *p = "abcde";
       printf("%c", ++*p++);
   }
```

```
21.void main()
   {
       int *mptr =(int*)malloc(sizeof(int));
       int *cptr=(int*)
       calloc(sizeof(int),1);
       printf("%d\n",*mptr);
       printf("%d",*cptr);
   }

22.void main()
   {
       int a = 2, *ptr1, *ptr2;
       ptr1 = ptr2 = &a;
       *ptr2 += *ptr2 += a += 2.5;
       printf("%d %d %d",a,*ptr1,*ptr2);
   }

23.void main()
   {
       char *ptr = "GOOD";
       char arr[ ] = "GOOD";
       printf("%d %d %d %d %d",
              sizeof(ptr),sizeof(*ptr),
              strlen(ptr),sizeof(arr),
                strlen(arr));
   }

24.int swap(int *a,int *b)
   {
       *a = *a + *b; *b = *a - *b;
       *a = *a - *b;
   }
   void main()
   {
       int x = 10, y = 20;
       swap(&x, &y);
       printf("x= %d y = %d\n", x, y);
   }

25.void main()
   {
       void swap();
       int x = 10, y = 20;
       swap(&x, &y);
       printf("x = %d y = %d",x,y);
   }
   void swap(int *a, int *b)
   {
       *a ^= *b; *b ^= *a;
       *a ^= *b;
   }

26.void main()
   {
       int i = 257; int *ptr = &i;
       printf("%d %d",*((char*)ptr),
                    *((char*)ptr+1));
   }

27.void main()
   {
       int i = 258; int *ptr = &i;
       printf("%d %d",*((char*)ptr),
                    *((char*)ptr+1));
   }

28.void main()
   {
       int i = 300;
       char *ptr = &i;
       *++ptr = 2;
       printf("%d",i);
   }
```

```
29.void main()
   {
     char *str = "hello";
     char *ptr = str, ch = 127;
     while(*ptr++)
       ch = (*ptr < ch) ? *ptr:ch;
     printf("%d", ch);
   }
```

30. What is the subtle error in the following code segment?

```
void fun(int n, int arr[])
   {
     int *ptr = 0, i = 0;
     while(i++ < n)
       ptr = &arr[i];
     *ptr = 0;
   }
```

```
31.void main()
   {
     int *i = 0x400;
     /* i points to the address 400 */
     *i = 0;
     /*sets value of memory location pointed by i*/
   }
```

```
32.void main()
   {
     int i = 10, j = 2;
     int *ip = &i, *jp = &j;
     int k = *ip / *jp;
     printf("\n\n\n%d",k);
   }
```

33. Is this code legal?
```
int *ptr;
ptr = (int *) 0x400;
```

```
34.char *someFun()
   {
     char *temp = "String constant";
     return temp;
   }
   int main()
   {
     puts(someFun());
   }
```

```
35.char *someFun1()
   {
     char temp[] = "string";
     return temp;
   }
   char *someFun2()
   {
     char temp[]={'s','t','r','i','n',
'g'};
     return temp;
   }
   int main()
   {
     puts(someFun1());
     puts(someFun2());
   }
```

❖ ❖ ❖ ❖ ❖ ❖ ❖

STRUCTURES & UNIONS

```
1. void main()
   {
     struct X
     {
       int x = 2;
       char name[] = "John";
     };
     struct X *s;
     printf("%d",s->x);
     printf("%s",s->name);
   }
```

```
2. void main()
   {
     struct X
     {
       int x;
       struct Y
       {
         char s;
         struct X *p;
       };
       struct Y *q;
     };
   }
```

```
3. void main()
   {
     struct X
     {
       int x;
       char name[5];
     };
     struct X *s=malloc(sizeof(struct X));
     printf("%d",s->x);
     printf("%s",s->name);
   }
```

```
4. void main()
   {
     struct X
     {
       int x;
       struct Y
       {
         char s;
         struct X *p;
       };
       struct Y *q;
     };
   }
```

```
5. struct A_A
   {
     struct A_A *prev;
     int i;
     struct A_A *next;
   };
   void main()
   {
     struct A_A abc,def,ghi,jkl;
     int x = 100;
     abc.i = 0;
     abc.prev = &jkl;
     abc.next = &def;
     def.i = 1;
     def.prev = &abc;
     def.next = &ghi;
     ghi.i = 2;
```

```
    ghi.prev = &def;
    ghi.next = &jkl;
    jkl.i = 3;
    jkl.prev = &ghi;
    jkl.next = &abc;
    x=abc.next->next->prev->next->i;
    printf("%d",x);
}
```

6.
```
struct A_A
{
    int x, y;
};
struct A_A origin, *ptr;
void main()
{
    ptr = &origin;
    printf("Value of ptr is %d - %d
          \n",(*ptr).x,(*ptr).y);
    printf("Value of ptr is %d - %d
          \n",ptr->x,ptr->y);
}
```

7.
```
void main()
{
    struct student
    {
        char name[30];
        struct date dob;
    }stud;
    struct date
    {
        int dd, mm, yy;
    };
    scanf("%s %d %d %d", stud.name,
    &student.dob.dd,&student.dob.mm,
                &student.dob.yy);
}
```

8.
```
void main()
{
    struct date;
    struct student
    {
        int rollno;
        char name[30];
        struct date dob;
    }stud;
    struct date
    {
        int dd, mm, yy;
    };
    scanf("%s %d %d %d", stud.name,
    &student.dob.dd,&student.dob.mm,
                &student.dob.yy);
}
```

9. There were 10 records stored in "somefile.dat" but the following program printed 11 names. What went wrong?
```
void main()
{
    struct student
    {
        char name[30];
        int rollno;
    }stud;
    FILE *fp =
        fopen("C;\somefile.dat","r");
    while(!feof(fp))
    {
```

```
        fread(&stud,sizeof(stud),1,fp);
        puts(stud.name);
        printf("%s -- %d",
                stud.name,stud.rollno);
    }
}
```

10. Is the following code legal?
```
struct a
{
    int x;
    struct a b;
};
```

11. Is the following code legal?
```
struct a
{
    int x;
    struct a *b;
};
```

12. Is the following code legal?
```
typedef struct a
{
    int x;
    Type *b;
}Type;
```

13. Is the following code legal?
```
typedef struct a Type;
struct a
{
    int x;
    Type *b;
};
```

14. Is the following code legal?
```
void main()
{
    typedef struct a Type;
    Type someVariable;
    struct a
    {
        int x;
        Type *b;
    };
}
```

15.
```
void main()
{
    struct X
    {
        int x;
        float y;
    };
    struct X v1, v2;
    v1. x = 10;
    v1.y = 20.5;
    v2 = v1;
    printf("\t%d\t%f\t%d\t%f",
            v1.x,v1.y,v2.x,v2.y);
}
```

❖ ❖ ❖ ❖ ❖ ❖ ❖

III – PREDICT THE OUTPUT FOR THE FOLLOWING QUESTIONS

1. **Which of the following are valid identifiers?**

   (a) circle area   (b) char

   (c) INT   (d) book's

   (e) no_of_side   (f) no-constraint

2. **Which of the following are valid expression?**

   (a) b*b - 4.0*a*c = d;   (b) 5.54 = e;

   (c) f = +g--h;   (d) f = +g- -h;

   (e) i = 'j' + 2;   (f) k += 8;

3. **What is the type of each of the following integer constants?**

   (a) 1234   (b) 1234u

   (c) 1234s   (d) 1234L

   (e) 1234us   (f) 1234uL

4. **What is the type of each of the following constants?**

   (a) 12   (b) -34.56

   (c) "34.56"   (d) '3'

   (e) '\n'   (f) "Son\'s"

5. **Which of the following are valid character constants?**

   (a) 'a'   (b) 'abc'

   (c) "Z_1234"   (d) '\t'

6. **Which of the following are valid string constants?**

   (a) 3 + "Program"   (b) 'book'

   (c) "1234.56789"   (d) "\n\t"

7. **What are the results of the following statements if, a = 2, b = 3 and c = 4?**

   (a) ++a + a++;   (b) c *= c + 1;

   (c) a + b * c / a;   (d) c -= a += 5;

   (e) 'a' + a;   (f) sizeof(a) + a;

8. **What is the equivalent C statement for the expression?**

   (a) b*b - 4*a*c / 2*a

   (b) b*b - 4*a*c / (2*a)

   (c) ((b*b) - (4*a*c)) / 2*a

   (d) ((b*b) - (4*a*c)) / (2*a)

9. **What are the results of the following expressions if, a = 2, b = 3 and c = 4?**

   (a) a & b | c   (b) ~a ^ b & c

   (c) a | b & c   (d) ~~b

   (e) a << b >> c   (f) a ^ b ^ c

10. **What are the results of following conditional expressions if, a = 2, b = 0 and c = 4?**

    (a) a && b || c   (b) !!b

    (c) a || b && c   (d) a && b || !c

11. **Simplify the expressions by removing the parenthesis and the logical not operator.**

    (a) !(a)   (b) !(a > b)

    (c) !(!a >= b)   (d) !(a != !b)

12. **What are the results of following conditional expressions if a = 1, b = 0, c = 3 and d = 4?**

    (a) !(a)

    (b) (a || b && c || d)

    (c) (!a && b || c && !d)

    (d) !(a && (!b || !c))

13. **What is the result of the following C statements?**

    (a) 5 / 2   (b) 5.0 / 2

    (c) 5 % 2   (d) 5 % 2.0

14. **What is the value of the following C statements.**

    (a) 38 * 1000   (b) 38.0 * 1000

    (c) 'A' * 1000   (d) 'A' * 1000.0

15. **What is the value of a in the following C statements?**

    (a) char a = '\123';   (b) char a = 0x53;

    (c) char a = 0123;   (d) char a = 83;

16. **Which of the following is not a data type in C?**

    (a) integer   (b) character

    (c) void   (d) boolean

17. **Specify the precedence order of the operators.**

    (a) arithmetic, relational, logical, assignment

    (b) arithmetic, logical, relational, assignment

    (c) relational, arithmetic, logical, assignment

    (d) logical, arithmetic, relational, assignment

18. **What are the operators which have left to right associativity?**

    (a) unary   (b) binary

    (c) ternary   (d) comma

19. **Specify the type of operators used.**

    (a) sizeof(double)   (b) abc + x_y_z

    (c) return((a>b) ? a:b) (d) a += b;

20. **Which of the following is a valid binary expression?**

    (a) -3   (b) a + b

    (c) c += 25   (d) 4 - e

21. **Which of the following is a valid assignment statement?**

    (a) i = (j++, k++);   (b) i = j = k;

    (c) i += k;   (d) 5000 = k;

22. **What is the value of x after the execution of the statements, when x = 5 initially?**

    (a) x %= 10;   (b) x = x+++3;

    (c) x >>= 1;   (d) x <<= 1;

    (e) x >>= -1;   (f) x <<= -1;

23. **What is the value of z after the execution of the statements, when x = 5 and y = 7 initially?**

    (a) z = (x++, y++);   (b) z = x += ++y;

    (c) z = x++ - --y;   (d) z = x + y-- -x + x++;

24. **Which of the following statements are true about mixed mode operation?**

    (a) Implicit cast generated by the compiler

    (b) Compiler automatically carries constant casting

    (c) Explicit cast used to change expression type

    (d) Explicit cast changes variable type in memory

25. **What is the purpose of the header files in C?**

    (a) Function decalration (b) Function definition

    (c) Both (a) and (b)   (d) None of the above

26. **What does the following scanf() format specifiers indicate?**

    (a) %d   (b) %x

    (c) %u   (d) %o

    (e) %lu   (f) %ld

27. **What does the following scanf() format specifier indicate?**

    (a) %e   (b) %f

    (c) %g   (d) %lf

28. **What does the following printf() format specifiers indicat?**

    (a) %n   (b) %X

    (c) %p   (d) %o

    (e) %i   (f) %hx

29. **What is the justification, decimal fraction and width of the format specifier %-9.2f?**

    (a) Right justify, 2, 9 (b) Left justify, 2, 9

    (c) Right justify, 9, 2 (d) Left justify, 9, 2

30. **What is the output of the C statement?**

    printf("%d", printf("ProgramminG"));

    (a) 11ProgramminG   (b) ProgramminG11

    (c) Compile time error (d) Warning

31. **Which of the following file accessing modes are used in C?**

    (a) Text   (b) Binary

    (c) Text & Binary   (d) None of the above.

32. **Which of the following specifies an infinite loop?**

    (a) for(;;);   (b) while(1);

    (c) for(;i=4;);   (d) while(true);

    (e) for(;!0;);(f)   while(a = 0);

33. **How many times the following loop executes, when the value of i = 0 initially?**

    (a) for(;i < 5; i--);   (b) while(i);

    (c) for(;i=4;i++);   (d) while(! i);

    (e) do{ }while(i = 0); (f) do{ }while(!i);

34. **What is the following C statement used to read the one line input from the keyboard?**

    (a) scanf("%s",str)

    (b) scanf("%[^\n]",str)

    (c) gets(str)

    (d) getchar()

35. **Which is the simplest file structure?**

    (a) Sequential   (b) Indexed

    (c) Random   (d) All of the above

36. What are the sizes of character, integer and float pointers.

(a) 1, 1, 1   (b) 2, 2, 2

(c) 4, 4, 4   (d) 1, 2, 4

37. Which one is not a preprocessor directive?

(a) #define   (b) #zigma

(c) #line   (d) #pragma

38. Which operator is used to concatenate (combine) two separate strings into one single string in a macro definition?

(a) #   (b) ##

(c) +   (d) strcat

39. Argument list in the scanf() is the example of

(a) Call by value   (b) Call by reference

(c) Call by pointer (d) Both (b) and (c)

40. Argument list in the printf() is the example of

(a) Call by value   (b) Call by reference

(c) Call by address (d) Both (b) and (c)

41. How many argument(s) are available in the main() function?

(a) 0   (b) 1

(c) 2   (d) 3

42. Which of the following is a valid main() function?

(a) main(int)   (b) main(int,char*)

(c) main(int,char*,char*) (d) main()

43. In switch-case statement, which accept the following as its input.

(a) Integer variable   (b) Float variable

(c) Character variable (d) String variable

(e) Character constant (f) Integer constant

44. What is the use of break statement in a switch-case control statement?

(a) Control pass to after switch block

(b) Control pass to next switch case statement

(c) Control pass to first switch case statement

(d) Control pass to default switch case statement

45. Which of the following character is not a terminating character in the string?

(a) NULL   (b) '\0'

(c) 0   (d) ';'

46. Evaluate the value of the following expressions.

(a) fabs(5)   (b) fabs(-5)

(c) fabs(5.5)   (d) fabs(-5.44)

(e) fabsl(5.5)   (f) fabsl(-5.44)

47. Evaluate the value of the following expressions.

(a) floor(5.4)   (b) ceil(5.4)

(c) floor(5.5)   (d) ceil(5.5)

(e) floor(5.6)   (f) ceil(5.6)

48. Evaluate the value of the following expressions, when x = 1.234, y = 5.678

(a) floor(x*10 + y*5)

(b) ceil(x*10 + y*5)

(c) floor(x+0.05) / 10

(d) ceil(x+0.05) / 10

(e) floor(x+y*0.5)*50

(f) ceil(x + y * 0.5) * 50

49. In the following tree structures, which is efficient interms of space and time complexities?

(a) Full Binary Tree

(b) Incomplete binary tree

(c) Complete binary tree

(d) Right skewed binary tree

50. Which of the following statements about switch-case statements is true?

(a) Two case labels can have the same value

(b) Condition in switch control expression must evaluate to an integer type

(c) It can have two default statements

(d) Break statement after every case is compulsary

51. Which of the following situations creates dangling problem in if-else statements?

(a) Any nested if statement

(b) Nested if statement without a true statement

(c) Nested if statement without a false statement

(d) Nested if statement without true or false statement

52. What is the value of the following expressions?

(a) tolower('A')   (b) toupper('A')

(c) tolower('g')   (d) toupper('g')

(e) tolower('5')   (f) toupper('5')

53. Which of the following statements about for loop is true?

(a) Initialization part is executed first

(b) Condition part is executed first

(c) If the condition is false, the loop is exited in the first check itself

(d) Multiple statements are allowed in a for loop

(e) Initialization part and increment / decrement part are compulsary in a for loop

54. Which of the following statements about while loop is true?

(a) Multiple statements are allowed in the loop

(b) It is a pre test loop

(c) If the condition is false, the loop is not exited in the first check itself

(d) While statement is terminated with a semicolon

(e) Initialization is not required in the loop

55. Which of the following is not a jump statement?

(a) break (b) continue

(c) goto (d) move

(e) jump (f) return

56. Which of the following header file contains the function prototypes for functions used in file operations?

(a) stdio.h (b) stdlib.h

(c) stdarg.h (d) stddef.h

(e) file.h (f) stdfile.h

57. Which of the following statement is correct, when a file is opened in r mode?

(a) Opens the file for reading, and sets the file pointer at the beginning of the file

(b) Opens the file for reading, and sets the file pointer at the end of the file

(c) Opens the file for reading, and clears all the text from the file

(d) Returns an error if the file doesn't exist

58. Which of the following statement is correct, when a file is opened in w mode?

(a) Opens the file for writing, and sets the file pointer at the beginning of the file

(b) Opens the file for writing, and sets the file pointer at the end of the file

(c) Opens the file for writing, and clears all the text from the file

(d) Returns an error if the file doesn't exist

59. If the file is not opened sucessfully, what happens in C?

(a) Returns an error if file doesn't exist

(b) Terminates the program

(c) Continues execution of next statement in the program

(d) Displays an error message

60. Find the odd man out in the following options.

(a) malloc() (b) calloc()

(c) realloc() (d) free()

61. Find the odd man out in the following options.

(a) getch() (b) getche()

(c) getchar() (d) kbhit()

62. Which function is used to convert string to double?

(a) atoi() (b) atof()

(c) atol() (d) strtod()

(e) fcvt() (b) gcvt()

63. What is the purpose of functions exec..(), spawn..() and system() in C?

(a) Enable the program into run the other file

(b) Enable program into run the other child process

(c) Enable the program into include other files

(d) All of the above

64. When an array is passed as an argument to a function, C uses _____.

(a) Call by value (b) Call by reference

(c) Call by pointer (d) Call by address

65. What is the equivalent of the statement a[r]?

(a) r[a] (b) *(a+r)

(c) *(&a[r]) (d) a+r

66. Which of the following statements are true regarding pointers?

(a) String constants can be assigned to character pointer

(b) String constatnts can be assigned to character array

(c) Possible to cast a pointer to int as a pointer to float

(d) Implicit cast is done, when pointers of different types are assigned

67. What is the equivalent of the statement a[r][c]?

(a) *(*(a+r)+c) (b) (*(a+r)+c)

(c) *(&a[r][0]+c) (d) *(a[r]+c)

68. Which of the following statements are true regarding array?

(a) Assign one array variable to another

(b) Array contains different type of elements

(c) Array index starts from -1

(d) Array index may be a character constant

69. Which of the following statement defines a pointer variable to a float or one dimensional float array?

(a) float *ptr   (b) float &ptr

(c) float **ptr   (d) float &&ptr

70. What is the incremented value for the following options when char *p, int *q, float *r, double *s?

(a) p++   (b) q++

(c) r++   (d) s++

71. What is the size of the following pointer variables?

(a) char *ptr   (b) char near *ptr

(c) char far *ptr   (d) char huge *ptr

72. The declaration float **p defines p is,

(a) pointer of pointer to float variable

(b) pointer of float variable

(c) pointer to address of float variable

(d) two dimesional pointer

73. Sorting is not possible by using which of the following methods?

(a) insertion   (b) selection

(c) exchange   (d) deletion

74. How many different trees are possible with 10 nodes ?

(a) 1004   (b) 1014

(c) 1024   (d) 1034

75. In construction of a tree which is the suitable and efficient data structure?

(a) array   (b) linked list

(c) stack   (d) queue

ANSWERS --- I

(1) (c)	(2) (a)	(3) (d)	(4) (d)	(5) (a)	(6) (d)	(7) (c)
(8) (c)	(9) (c)	(10) (c)	(11) (b)	(12) (d)	(13) (a)	(14) (b)
(15) (c)	(16) (a)	(17) (d)	(18) (d)	(19) (a)	(20) (b)	(21) (d)
(22) (a)	(23) (a)	(24) (b)	(25) (b)	(26) (b)	(27) (d)	(28) (a)
(29) (a)	(30) (b)	(31) (c)	(32) (c)	(33) (b)	(34) (d)	(35) (a)
(36) (c)	(37) (c)	(38) (b)	(39) (b)	(40) (b)	(41) (d)	(42) (d)
(43) (a)	(44) (a)	(45) (c)	(46) (a)	(47) (c)	(48) (b)	(49) (a)
(50) (d)	(51) (d)	(52) (c)	(53) (a)	(54) (d)	(55) (d)	(56) (a)
(57) (d)	(58) (d)	(59) (c)	(60) (d)	(61) (c)	(62) (b)	(63) (a)
(64) (b)	(65) (b)	(66) (c)	(67) (b)	(68) (a)	(69) (c)	(70) (c)
(71) (c)	(72) (b)	(73) (b)	(74) (b)	(75) (a)	(76) (b)	(77) (a)
(78) (c)	(79) (c)	(80) (b)	(81) (a)	(82) (a)	(83) (a)	(84) (b)
(85) (b)	(86) (d)	(87) (a)	(88) (c)	(89) (b)	(90) (c)	(91) (b)
(92) (b)	(93) (b)	(94) (d)	(95) (a)	(96) (a)	(97) (b)	(98) (c)
(99) (b)	(100) (b)	(101) (d)	(102) (b)	(103) (d)	(104) (a)	(105) (d)
(106) (d)	(107) (b)	(108) (b)	(109) (c)	(110) (d)	(111) (a)	(112) (a)
(113) (a)	(114) (a)	(115) (c)	(116) (d)	(117) (c)	(118) (b)	(119) (c)
(120) (c)	(121) (c)	(122) (a)	(123) (d)	(124) (d)	(125) (b)	(126) (c)
(127) (a)	(128) (a)	(129) (a)	(130) (b)	(131) (b)	(132) (b)	(133) (d)
(134) (a)	(135) (b)	(136) (b)	(137) (b)	(138) (a)	(139) (b)	(140) (a)
(141) (a)	(142) (d)	(143) (d)	(144) (c)	(145) (b)	(146) (a)	(147) (a)
(148) (c)	(149) (a)	(150) (a)	(151) (d)	(152) (a)	(153) (b)	(154) (b)
(155) (d)	(156) (b)	(157) (a)	(158) (c)	(159) (a)	(160) (d)	(161) (b)
(162) (d)	(163) (a)	(164) (b)	(165) (c)	(166) (a)	(167) (b)	(168) (a)
(169) (b)	(170) (a)	(171) (b)	(172) (a)	(173) (b)	(174) (c)	(175) (d)
(176) (b)	(177) (a)	(178) (a)	(179) (d)	(180) (a)	(181) (b)	(182) (a)
(183) (d)	(184) (d)	(185) (a)	(186) (c)	(187) (b)	(188) (a)	(189) (a)
(190) (c)	(191) (c)	(192) (a)	(193) (d)	(194) (d)	(195) (c)	(196) (a)
(197) (b)	(198) (c)	(199) (d)	(200) (c)	(201) (b)	(202) (b)	(203) (c)
(204) (a)	(205) (b)	(206) (d)	(207) (a)	(208) (b)	(209) (d)	(210) (c)
(211) (c)	(212) (c)	(213) (c)	(214) (b)	(215) (c)	(216) (d)	(217) (d)
(218) (c)	(219) (a)	(220) (d)	(221) (b)	(222) (b)	(223) (c)	(224) (a)
(225) (b)						

ANSWERS --- II

BASICS OF C PROGRAM

1. ANSWER :

Compiler error : Cannot modify a constant value.

EXPLANATION :

The variable ptr is a pointer to a "constant integer". But we tried to change the value of the "constant integer", which is impossible, hence the error.

2. ANSWER :

Linker Error : Undefined symbol i

EXPLANATION :

The extern storage class declaration (extern int i) specifies to the compiler that the memory for i is allocated in some other program and that address will be used in the current function at the time of linking. But since linker doesn't finds anyother variable of name i in the program with memory space allocated for it. Hence a linker error has occurred .

3. ANSWER :

0 0 1 3 1

EXPLANATION :

Always keep in mind, that logical operations always gives a result of 1 or 0. Logical AND (&&) operator has higher priority over the logical OR (||) operator. So the expression ("i++ && j++ && k++") is executed first. The result of this expression is 0 (since, -1 && -1 && 0). Now the next expression (i.e., 0 || 2) is evaluated, whose result evaluates to 1 (because OR operator always gives 1 except for '0 || 0' combination). So the value of m is 1. The values of other variables are also incremented by 1, hence you get the above output.

4. ANSWER :

fff0

EXPLANATION :

The constant -1 is internally represented as all 1's. When left shifted four times (since << 4) the least significant 4 bits are filled with 0's. The %x format specifier specifies that the integer value be printed as a hexadecimal value.

5. ANSWER :

a = 2;

EXPLANATION :

During initialization of a, unary minus (or negation) operator is used twice. As per maths, minus * minus= plus, same rule applies in programming also hence you get the above output.. Also note that you cannot give --2, since -- operator can only be applied to variables for decrement operation as --a).

6. ANSWER :

sizeof(i) = 1

EXPLANATION :

Since #define replaces the string int by the macro definition char.

7. ANSWER :

i = 0

EXPLANATION :

In the expression !i>5 , NOT (!) operator has more precedence than ' >' symbol. ! is a unary logical operator. !i (!10) is 0 (not of true is false). 0 > 5 is false (zero).

8. **ANSWER :**

   hai

EXPLANATION :

   \n - newline character
   \b - backspace character
   \r - linefeed character.

The first printf() function prints the string, "ab" in a new line. The second printf() function initially moves backspace by one character (i.e., \b) and removes the character b, and then prints the string, "si" in the same line. After the execution of the second line, the output is "asi". The third printf() function initially moves to the first position of the same line (i.e., \r),and then prints the string, "ha" in the same line. After the execution of the third line, the output is "hai".

9. **ANSWER :**

   4 4 6 6 5

EXPLANATION :

The arguments in a printf() function call are pushed into the stack from left to right. The evaluation is by popping out from the stack and the evaluation takes place from right to left, hence you get the above output..

10. **ANSWER :**

   64

EXPLANATION :

The macro definition called square(4) will substituted by 4 * 4 so the expression becomes i = 64 / 4 * 4. Since / and * has equal priority the expression will be evaluated as (64/4)*4 (i.e., 16 * 4 = 64).

11. **ANSWER :**

   50

EXPLANATION :

The preprocessor directives can be redefined anywhere in the program and hence the most recently assigned value will be taken.

12. **ANSWER :**

   100

EXPLANATION :

Preprocessor executes as a seperate pass before the execution of the compiler. So textual replacement of clrscr() to 100 occurs.The input program to compiler looks like this,

```
void main()
{
   100;
   printf("%d\n", 100);
}
```

Note that 100; is a perfectly executable statement but with no action, hence it doesn't rise any error.

13. **ANSWER :**

   Some address will be printed.

EXPLANATION :

Function names are just addresses (similar as array names are addresses). We know that main() is also a function. So the address of main() function will be printed. The format specifier %p in printf() function specifies that the argument is an address, which is printed as hexadecimal numbers.

14. **ANSWER :**

No output / error.

EXPLANATION :

The first declaration of clrscr() occurs inside the main() function, so it becomes a function call. In the second usage, clrscr(); is a function declaration (because it is not inside any function).

15. **ANSWER :**

0 - 1 - 2

EXPLANATION :

The enum data type assigns numbers to its enumeration list starting from 0, if not explicitly defined, hence you get the above output.

16. **ANSWER :**

4 - 2 - 1

EXPLANATION :

The first output (i.e., 4) represents the size of the character far pointer. The second output (i.e., 2) represents the size of the character pointer. The third output (i.e., 1) represents the size of the character.

17. **ANSWER :**

4 - 2 - 4

EXPLANATION :

The first output (i.e., 4) represents the size of the character far pointer. The second output (i.e., 2) represents the size of the character near pointer. The third output (i.e., 4) represents the size of the character huge pointer.

18. **ANSWER :**

200 - 100

EXPLANATION :

The printf() function takes the values of the first two assignments of the program in reverse order. Any number of printf's may be given. All of them uses only the first two assignment values. If more number of assignments are given in the program, then the printf() function will take garbage values.

19. **ANSWER :**

J

EXPLANATION :

* is a dereferencing operator and & is a reference operator. They can be used any number of times with a variable provided it is meaningful. Here ptr points to the first character in the string "John". *ptr dereferences it and so its value is 'J'. Again & references it to an address and * dereferences it to the value 'J'.

20. **ANSWER :**

12

EXPLANATION :

The input statement to the compiler looks like this (5 + 7), and hence you get the above output.

21. **ANSWER :**

Compiler Error.

EXPLANATION :

The expression i+++++i is parsed as i ++ ++ + i, which is an illegal combination of operators.

22. ANSWER :

1

EXPLANATION :

The scanf() function returns number of input items successfully read. Here 10 is given as input which should have been scanned successfully. So number of items read is 1, hence you get the above output.

23. ANSWER :

100

EXPLANATION :

The ## used in the macro definition, is a concatenation operator, used to concatenate two seperate strings into one string. In the program, we concatenate the variable name 'c' and 'd, as 'cd'. The value for the variable cd is 100, hence you get the above output.

24. ANSWER :

Linker error: undefined symbol 'i'.

EXPLANATION :

The variable i declared using the keyword extern specifies global declaration that the variable i is defined somewhere else. The compiler passes the external variable to be resolved by the linker, so compiler doesn't find an error. During linking, the linker searches for the definition of i. Since it is not found the linker raises an error.

25. ANSWER :

Compiler error: undefined symbol out in function main.

EXPLANATION :

The rule is that a variable is available for use, only from the point of declaration, hence you get an error. Even when out is a global variable, it is not available in the main() function. Hence an error.

26. ANSWER :

100

EXPLANATION :

This is the correct way of writing the previous program.

27. ANSWER :

i = 1, i = -1

EXPLANATION :

The expression -(-1) evaluates to 1, and hence you get the above output.

28. ANSWER :

First it checks for the leading white space and discards it.Then it matches with a quotation mark and then it reads all character upto another quotation mark.

29. ANSWER :

Runtime error : Stack overflow.

EXPLANATION :

The main() function calls itself again and again recursively. Each time the function is called its return address is stored in the call stack. Since there is no condition to terminate the function call, the call stack overflows at runtime and it terminates the program resulting in an run time error.

30. **ANSWER :**

   0

EXPLANATION :

   The character ! is used to denote a logical NOT operator. In C, the value 0 is considered to be the boolean value for FALSE, and any non-zero value is considered to be the boolean value for TRUE. Here 2 is a non-zero value so TRUE. !TRUE is FALSE so it prints 0.

31. **ANSWER :**

   1==1 is TRUE

EXPLANATION :

   When two strings are placed together or separated by whitespace they are concatenated (this is called as "stringization" operation). So the string is as if it is given as "%d==1 is %s". Thus conditional operator(?:) evaluates to "TRUE".

32. **ANSWER :**

   0 John

EXPLANATION :

   The typedef is used for declaring new types, hence typedef assigns 'data' as character array of size [MAX], and hence you get the above output.

33. **ANSWER :**

   Compiler Error.

EXPLANATION :

   The #define preprocessor is used for textual replacement, hence the variable data is declared in the preprocessor directive and not in the function, hence you get errors.

34. **ANSWER :**

   30 20 10

EXPLANATION :

   Each open and closed flower braces in the program introduces new block and hence a new scope. In the innermost block i is declared as, const volatile unsigned which is a valid declaration. i is assumed to be of type int and hence the printf() function prints the value of the variable 30. In the next block, i has value 20 and hence the printf() function prints the value of the variable 20. In the outermost block, i is declared as extern, so no storage space is allocated for it. After compilation is over the linker resolves it as global variable i (since it is the only variable visible there)and hence the printf() function prints the value of the variable 10.

35. **ANSWER :**

   i = -1, +i = -1

EXPLANATION :

   Unary + is the only dummy operator in C, whenever it comes you can just ignore it just because it has no effect in the unary expressions.

36. **ANSWER :**

   i = -1, -i = 1

EXPLANATION :

   -i is executed and this execution doesn't affect the value of i. In printf first you just print the value of i. After that the value of the expression -i = -(-1) is printed.

37. **ANSWER :**

   Compiler Error.

EXPLANATION :

   The variable i is declared as a constant ane hence you cannot change the value of constant variable i.

38. **ANSWER :**

   John 4

EXPLANATION :

   If you declare i as a register variable, the compiler will treat it as ordinary integer and it will take as integer value. The variable i may be stored either in register or in memory.

39. **ANSWER :**

   11

EXPLANATION :

   The expression i+++j is evaluated as (i++ + j), and hence you get the above output.

40. **ANSWER :**

   The length of the variable a is 6

EXPLANATION :

   The char array 'a' will hold the initialized string, whose length will be counted from 0 till the null character. Hence the variable 'i' will hold the value equal to 5, after the pre-increment operation, the value of i is incremented to 6, which is printed as output.

41. **ANSWER :**

   0 65535

EXPLANATION :

   The value -1 initialized to the unsigned variable 'b' is represented in 2's complement as all 1's in 16 bit format, which evaluates to 65535. The variable 'b' when incremented by 1, results in all 0's in 16 bit format, which evaluates to 0. The variable 'b' when decremented by 1, results in all 1's again in 16 bit format, which evaluates to 65535, hence you get the above output.

42. **ANSWER :**

   Garbage values.

EXPLANATION :

   An identifier is available to use in program code from the point of its declaration,,hence expressions such as i = i++ are valid statements. The variables i, j and k are automatic or local variables and hence they contain some garbage value, which will be displayed as output.

43. **ANSWER :**

   i = 1 j = 1 k = 1

EXPLANATION :

   Since static variables are initialized to zero by default, you get the above output.

44. **ANSWER :**

   10

EXPLANATION :

   The macro expands and evaluates as (x + 2 * y - 1) = (x + (2 * y)) - 1) = 10

45. **ANSWER :**

   Compiler Error : Cannot apply right shift to float.

EXPLANATION :

   Bitwise operators cannot be applied on float values, hence you get the above error.

46. **ANSWER :**

Compiler Error: Lvalue required.

EXPLANATION :

Enumeration constants cannot be modified, hence you cannot apply ++ operation with it.

47. **ANSWER :**

Compiler Error : Cannot apply left shift to float.

EXPLANATION :

Bitwise operators cannot be applied on float values, hence you get the above error.

48. **ANSWER :**

Compiler Error : Cannot apply mod to float.

EXPLANATION :

Modulus operators cannot be applied on float values, hence you get the above error.

49. **ANSWER :**

1.000000

EXPLANATION :

The fmod() function is to find the modulus values for floats similar to modulus (%) operator used for integers.

50. **ANSWER :**

Compiler error: Multiple declaration for error.

EXPLANATION :

The name error is used in the two meanings. One means that it is a enumerator constant with value 1. The another use is that it is a type name (due to typedef) for enum errorType. Given a situation the compiler cannot distinguish the meaning of error to know in what sense the error is used, hence you get the above error.

51. **ANSWER :**

1

EXPLANATION :

The three usages of the identifier error can be distinguishable by the compiler at any instance, hence it is perfectly valid since they are in different namespaces. Note that this code is given here to just explain the concept behind. In real programming don't use such overloading of names. It reduces the readability of the code.

52. **ANSWER :**

0 0

EXPLANATION :

This is a simple example for conditional compilation. The macro named 'something' is defined, hence the conditonal compilation of ifdef evaluates to true and declares the global variable 'some' and initialize the variable with a value of zero, which gets printed in the output.

53. **ANSWER :**

Compiler error : undefined symbol some

EXPLANATION :

The macro named 'something' is not defined, hence the conditonal compilation of ifdef evaluates to false, hence the declaration, int some = 0; is effectively removed from the source code and hence you get the following output.

54. ANSWER :

0 0

EXPLANATION :

This code is to show that preprocessor expressions are not the same as the ordinary expressions. If a name is not known the preprocessor treats it to be equal to zero, hence you get the above output.

55. ANSWER :

1

EXPLANATION :

The variable arr is made up of a 2 single arrays that contains 2 integers each. The variable 'arr' refers to the beginning of all the 2 arrays. *arr refers to the start of the first 1D array (of 2 integers) that is the same address as 'arr'. So the expression (arr == *arr) evaluates to true. Similarly, *arr is nothing but *(arr + 0), adding a zero doesn't change the value/meaning and again arr[0] is the another way of telling *(arr + 0). So the expression (*(arr + 0) == arr[0]) is true (1) evaluates to true. Since both parts of the expression evaluates to true the result is true and you get the above output.

56. ANSWER :

Compiler Error: Lvalue required in function main

EXPLANATION :

++i yields an rvalue. For evaluating the postfix expression ++, an lvalue is required.

57. ANSWER :

1

EXPLANATION :

The expression can be treated as i = (++i==6), because == is of higher precedence than = operator. In the inner expression, ++i is equal to 6 yielding true(1), hence you get the above output.

58. ANSWER :

A

EXPLANATION :

Initially the string text is initialized to "%d\n". Due to the assignment text[1] = 'c' the string becomes, "%c\n". Since this string becomes the format string for the printf() function and ASCII value of 65 is 'A' you get the above output.

59. ANSWER :

1 10

EXPLANATION :

The expression is evaluated as i = (i &= (j && 10)); The inner expression (j && 10) evaluates to 1 because j==10. i is 5. i = 5 & 1 is 1, hence you get the above output.

60. ANSWER :

5 10

EXPLANATION :

The expression is evaluated as i = (i |= (j || 10)); The inner expression (j || 10) evaluates to 1 because j==10. i is 5. i = 5 | 1 is 5, hence you get the above output.

61. ANSWER :

20 20

EXPLANATION :

The expression (j = i = j + 10;) is an example of a simple assignement statement, which evaluates as j = i = 20, hence you get the following output.

62. ANSWER :

1 1

EXPLANATION :

The expression (j = i = j > 10;) evaluates as j > i is 1, hence you get the following output.

63. ANSWER :

4 1

EXPLANATION :

The boolean expression needs to be evaluated only till the truth value of the expression is not known. j is not equal to zero, means that the expression's truth value is 1. Because it is followed by || and true || (anything) evaluates to true, hence the remaining expression is not evaluated and so the value of i remains the same. Similarly when && operator is involved in an expression, when any of the operands become false, the whole expression's truth value becomes false and hence the remaining expression will not be evaluated, since false && (anything) evaluates to false.

64. ANSWER :

Compier Error: '&' on register variable

EXPLANATION :

The address of (&) operator cannot be applied on register variables.

65. ANSWER :

Linker Error : Unresolved external symbol i

EXPLANATION :

The identifier i is available in the inner block and so using extern has no use in resolving it.

66. ANSWER :

10

EXPLANATION :

The size of integer array of 10 elements is 10 * sizeof(int). The macro expands to sizeof(arr)/sizeof(int) = 10 * sizeof(int) / sizeof(int) = 10.

67. ANSWER :

sizeof (void *) = 2
sizeof (int *) = 2
sizeof (double *) = 2
sizeof(struct unknown *) = 2

EXPLANATION :

The pointer to any data type are of same size.

68. ANSWER :

Compiler Error : Too many initializers.

EXPLANATION :

The array a is of size 4 but the string constant requires 6 bytes (including the terminating NULL character) to get stored.

69. ANSWER :

HELL%@!~@!@???@~~!

EXPLANATION :

The character array has the memory just enough to hold the string "HELL" and doesnt have enough space to store the terminating null character. So it prints the HELL correctly and continues to print garbage values till it accidentally comes across a NULL character. Note that you may get any combination of characters, after the string "HELL" each time you evaluate.

70. ANSWER :

30   20   0

EXPLANATION :

The first printf() function represents the value of const volatile unsigned variable 'i'. Second printf() function represents the value of local variable 'i'. Third printf() function represents the value of extern variable 'i' which is declared outside the main function.

IF STATEMENTS

1. ANSWER :

INDIA may win match

EXPLANATION :

Floating point variables declared using float, double and long double values cannot be predicted exactly. Depending on the number of bytes, the precision with of the value represented varies from compiler to complier. Float takes 4 bytes and long double takes 10 bytes. So float stores the value 123.4 with less precision than the long double value. ***Note that never compare using floating point numbers with relational operators.***

2. ANSWER :

5 4 3 2 1

EXPLANATION :

The static variable 'a' is initialized only once, and any change in the value of the static variable 'a' is retained between function calls. The main() function is treated as an ordinary function, which can be called recursively, hence you get the above output.

3. ANSWER :

0 0 0 0

EXPLANATION :

The static variable 'I' Is Initialized only once, and any change in the value of the static variable 'a' is retained between function calls. The main() function is treated as an ordinary function, which is called recursively, unless I becomes equal to 0 and hence you get the above output.

4. ANSWER :

Three

EXPLANATION :

A simple C program using switch case statement. The default case can be placed anywhere inside the loop. It is executed only when all other cases doesn't match, hence you get the above output.

5. ANSWER :

Compiler Error: Constant expression required.

EXPLANATION :

The case statement can have only constants or constant expressions (this implies that we cannot use variable names directly hence the above error).

6. ANSWER :

TRUE

EXPLANATION :

The input program to the compiler after processing by the preprocessor is,

```
void main()
  {
    if(0)
      puts("NULL");
    else if(-1)
      puts("TRUE");
    else
      puts("FALSE");
  }
```

The preprocessor replaces the values given only in the conditional statements and doesn't replace the values given inside the double quotes in the puts() function. The if condition (NULL) evaluates to a boolean value zero, which is indicated as false, hence the condition will never become true, so it goes to else if condition. In else if condition evaluates to a boolean value one, hence the condition will always be true, and exits without executing the else conditon, hence you get the above output.

7. ANSWER :

1000 is a leap year

EXPLANATION :

A simple C program to check the given year is leap year or not.

8. ANSWER :

0 - 0

EXPLANATION :

Logical operators employ a technique referred as lazy evaluation, for their operators. These operators evaluate their operand first, and then evaluate the right hand operator only if it is required. Clearly false && any operand is always false, and true || is always true. In such cases, the second and subsequent operand are not evaluated. Hence in the above case, the value of i is 0, and hence the printf statement following the if statement is not executed. The values of i and j remain unchanged and gets printed.

9. ANSWER :

Programming

EXPLANATION :

The comma operator has the associativity from left to right. Only the rightmost value is returned and the other values are ignored. Thus the value of last variable y is returned to check in the if statement. Since it is a non zero value, the if condition becomes true and hence the printf statement following the if statement is executed and, hence you get the above output.

10. ANSWER :

Good Morning

EXPLANATION :

The printf() function returns the number of characters it prints. Hence printing a null character returns 1 (note that null character is considered as a single character) which makes the if statement evaluated to true, hence you get the above output.

11. ANSWER :

0 - 100 - 9874

EXPLANATION :

The value of (b % 2) is 0, is assigned to a. The if condition reduces to if(a) or in other words if(0) and the statement(s) inside the flower braces will not be executed, hence the value of c will not be initialized. The value of c which is printed, is a garbage value. You will get different values for the same program, if you execute it in different systems and different times.

12. ANSWER :

Compiler Error: switch expression not integral

EXPLANATION :

Switch statements can be applied only to integral types.

LOOPING STATEMENTS

1. ANSWER :

mmmm

aaaa

nnnn

EXPLANATION :

str[i], i[str], *(i+str), *(str+i) are all different ways of expressing the same location in an array. Generally array name is the base address for that array. Here str is the base address for the array and i is the index number from the base address. So, indirecting it with * is same as str[i]. i[str] may be surprising. But in the case of C it is same as str[i].

2. ANSWER :

2 2 2 2 2 2 3 4 5 6

EXPLANATION :

Initially pointer arr is assigned to both ptr1 and ptr2. In the first loop, since only ptr2 is incremented and not arr, the value 2 will be printed 5 times. In second loop ptr itself is incremented, hence you get the above output.

3. ANSWER :

J!Mpwf!Zpv

EXPLANATION :

++*str++ will be parse in the following order.

- *str is the value at each location currently pointed by str will be considered.
- ++*str the retrieved value will be incremented.
- When ; is encountered the location will be incremented that is str++ will be executed.

Hence you get the above output.

4. ANSWER :

Compiler error: Undefined label 'INDIA'

EXPLANATION :

The scope of the labels is limited to functions. The label 'INDIA' is available only in function func() Hence it is not visible in main() function.

5. ANSWER :

Compiler error: Lvalue required

EXPLANATION :

Array names are pointer constants. So it cannot be modified.

6. ANSWER :

1

EXPLANATION :

Before entering into the for loop the condition is evaluated, which evaluates to 0 (i.e., false) and exits from the loop (Note the semicolon at the end of for loop), and a is incremented by 1, hence you get the above output.

7. ANSWER :

No Output.

EXPLANATION :

Inside the main() function i is an unsigned integer. It is compared with a signed value (i.e., -3). Since both data types doesn't match, the condition becomes false and control exits from loop, hence the printf() function will not be executed and you will not get any output from the program.

8. **ANSWER :**

01

EXPLANATION :

The inner printf executes first to print some garbage value. The printf returns no of characters printed and this value also cannot be predicted. Still the outer printf prints something and so returns a non-zero value. So it encounters the break statement and comes out of the while statement.

9. **ANSWER :**

5 4 3 2 1 0 65535 65534 65533 65534 . . .

EXPLANATION :

Since i is an unsigned integer it can never become negative. So the expression (i-- >= 0) will always be true, hence an infinite loop is executed and hence you get the above output.

10. **ANSWER :**

1

EXPLANATION :

Note the semicolon after the while statement. When the value of i becomes 0 it exits from the while loop. The value 1 is printed due to the post-increment operation on i, hence the value of i, increments by 1, and hence you get the above output.

11. **ANSWER :**

-1

EXPLANATION :

Unary + is the only a dummy operator in C. So it has no effect on the expression and now the while loop is, while(i-- != 0) which is false and so exits from the while loop. The value −1 is printed due to the post-decrement operation on i, hence the value of i, decrements by 1, and hence you get the above output.

12. **ANSWER :**

-128

EXPLANATION :

Note the semicolon after the for statement. The initial value of i is set to 0. The inner loop executes to increment the value from 0 to 127 (the positive maximum positive range of char) and then it rotates to the negative minimum value of -128. The condition in the for loop fails and so exits from the for loop. It prints the current value of i that is -128.

13. **ANSWER :**

Infinite loop.

EXPLANATION :

The difference between the previous question and this one is that the char is declared to be unsigned. So the i++ can never yield negative value and hence the condition (i >= 0) never becomes false so it forms an infinite for loop.

14. **ANSWER :**

Behavior is implementation dependent.

EXPLANATION :

The char is signed/unsigned by default is implementation dependent. If the implementation treats the char to be signed by default the program will print −128 and terminate. On the other hand if it considers char to be unsigned by default, it goes to infinite loop.

15. ANSWER :

No output.

EXPLANATION :

Ending the string constant with \0 explicitly makes no difference. So "John" and "John\0" are equivalent. So, the strcmp() function returns 0 (false) and hence the printf() function will not be executed and you will not get any output from the program.

16. ANSWER :

No output.

EXPLANATION :

Initializing the string constant with \0 explicitly makes no difference. So "John" and "John\0" are equivalent. So, the strcmp() function returns 0 (false) and hence the printf() function will not be executed and you will not get any output from the program.

17. ANSWER :

Compiler Error: Lvalue required.

EXPLANATION :

As we know that increment operators return rvalues and hence it cannot appear on the left hand side of an assignment operation.

18. ANSWER :

32767

EXPLANATION :

Since i is a static variable it is initialized to 0 by default, hence the condition in the while loop evaluates to true. Inside the while loop, the conditional operator evaluates to false, executing i--. This continues till the integer value rotates to positive value (32767). The while condition becomes false and hence, comes out of the while loop, printing the current value of i.

19. ANSWER :

Implementaion dependent

EXPLANATION :

The char data type may be signed or unsigned by default. If it is signed then ch++ is executed. When ch reaches 127 it rotates back to -128. Thus char is always smaller than 127.

20. ANSWER :

Infintely prints the string "Testing in C".

EXPLANATION :

Here the declaration int I1 = 1 represents I1 is a integer variable. But I1: represents label value which is used by the goto statement later. Both the things are different in C. The statement goto I1 tranfer the control flow again into label statement without any condition. So the program is infinitely prints the string "testing in C".

FUNCTIONS

1. Answer :

Compiler Error : Type mismatch in redeclaration of function display.

Explanation :

When the function call statement (i.e., display(str)) is encountered, the compiler doesn't know anything about the display() function. It assumes the arguments and return type of the display() function to be of type integers, (which is the default type). When it sees the actual function display(), the arguments and type contradicts with what it has assumed previously, hence you get the above error.

The solutions to avoid such errors are as follows,

- Use function declaration statements for all functions used in the program, above the main() function.
- Use function declaration statement atleast before its use in the function.

2. Answer :

Compiler Error: Type mismatch in redeclaration of function show.

Explanation :

When the function call statement (i.e., show(str)) is encountered, the compiler doesn't know anything about the show() function. It assumes the arguments and return type of the show() function to be of type integers, (which is the default type). When it sees the actual function show(), the arguments and type contradicts with what it has assumed previously, hence you get the above error.

The solutions to avoid such errors are as follows,

- Declare void show() in main() function.
- Define void show() before main() function.

3. Answer :

9

Explanation :

The return statement (i++) will first return i and then increments it. The returned value (i.e., 10) is first decremented and then printed in the printf() function.

4. Answer :

Compiler Error.

Explanation :

Declaration of the function convert() in the variable declaration statement is wrong.

5. Answer :

Compiler Error. Type Mismatch in call to fucntion sum().

Explanation :

The arguments argv[1] & argv[2] are strings. They are passed to the function sum without converting it to integer values.

6. Answer :

Bye

Explanation :

The varaible ptr is an array of pointers to functions of return type int. ptr[0] is assigned to address of the function a(). Similarly ptr[1] and ptr[2] for the functions b() and c() respectively. ptr[2]() is in effect of writing c(), since ptr[2] points to the function c().

7. ANSWER :

1000

EXPLANATION :

Normally the return value from the function is through the information from the accumulator. Here _AX is the pseudo global variable denoting the accumulator. Hence, the value of the accumulator is set 1000 so the function returns value 1000.

8. ANSWER :

i. ANSI C notation

ii. Kernighan & Ritche notation

9. ANSWER :

bc

EXPLANATION :

The base address is modified only in function and as a result the variable 'a' points to 'b' then after incrementing points to 'c', hence you get the above output.

10. ANSWER :

The value if process is 0 !

EXPLANATION :

The function 'process' has 3 parameters - 1, a pointer to another function 2 and 3, integers. When this function is invoked from main(), the following substitutions for formal parameters take place: func for pf, 3 for val1 and 6 for val2. This function returns the result of the operation performed by the function 'func'. The function func has two integer parameters. The formal parameters are substituted as 3 for a and 6 for b. since 3 is not equal to 6, a==b returns 0. therefore the function returns 0 which in turn is returned by the function 'process'.

11. ANSWER :

Value is 7

EXPLANATION :

In the function definition int func(int func), the function name and the argument name can be the same. The function func() is called in which the sizeof(float) (i.e., 4 is passed), after the first expression the value in func will be 6, as 'func' is an integer variable hence the value stored in 'func' will have implicit type conversion from float to int. The value of the variable 'func' is returned to main() is printed after preincrement operation, hence you get the above output.

12. ANSWER :

Compiler Error : Unknown type integer or integer cannot start a parameter declaration.
Compiler Error : Undeclared function write().

EXPLANATION :

The use of pascal keyword doesn't mean that pascal code can be used. It means that the function follows pascal argument passing mechanism in calling functions.

13. ANSWER :

5 6 7 8
5 6 7 8

EXPLANATION :

Pascal argument passing mechanism forces the arguments to be called from left to right, where as cdecl is the normal C argument passing mechanism where the arguments are passed from right to left.

14. ANSWER :

abc is a ptr to a function which takes 2 argument, an integer variable and a pointer to a funtion which returns void. The return type of the function abc() is of type void.

EXPLANATION :

Use clock-wise rule to find the result.

15. ANSWER :

The array dimension is 1

EXPLANATION :

Arrays cannot be passed to functions as arguments and only pointers can be passed, hence the argument which is equivalent to int *array (this is one of the very few places where [] and * usage are equivalent). The return statement evluates as, sizeof(int *)/ sizeof(int), which happens to be equal in this case.

POINTERS

1. ANSWER :

1 2

EXPLANATION :

The sizeof() operator gives the number of bytes of its operand. The ptr variable is a character pointer, which needs one byte for storing its value (a character), hence sizeof(*ptr) returns a value of 1. Since it needs two bytes to store the address of the character pointer sizeof(ptr) returns 2.

2. ANSWER :

d

EXPLANATION :

The statement (ptr = &s[3]), indicates that the variable ptr is pointing to character '\n'. The statement (str = s), indicates that the variable str is pointing to character 'a'. The expression ++*ptr, indicates that, ptr (pointing to '\n') is incremented by one. The ASCII value of '\n' is 10, which is then incremented to 11. The value of ++*ptr is 11. The expression ++*str, indicates that, str (pointing to 'a') is incremented by one. The ASCII value of '\a' is 97, which is then incremented to 98. The value of ++*str is 98. Now performing (11 + 98 - 9), we get 100, which is the ascii value of "d", hence we get the above output.

3. ANSWER :

SomeGarbageValue--1

EXPLANATION :

The variable declaration arr[2][2][2], in the first line declares only 2 two-dimensional arrays. But in the statement ptr = &arr[2][2][2], you are trying to access the 3rd two-dimensional array (which you are not declared) so it will take some garbage values. If you print *ptr, it will print some garbage value. The statement *qtr = ***a, assigns the starting address of the array 'arr' to an integer pointer 'qtr'. Now the variable 'qtr' is pointing to starting address of the array 'arr'. If you print *qtr, it will print first element of array 'arr'.

4. ANSWER :

100 - 100 - 100 - 1
114 - 106 - 104 - 2

EXPLANATION :

The given array is a 3-dimesional array. Let us assume the initial address of the array is 100, which means the subsequent array values are stored in contiguous memory locations. Thus, the first printf() function a, *a, **a prints the address of first element of the array, and the indirection pointer ***a gives the value of the first location of the array. The second printf() function a+1 increases in the third dimension and thus points to value at the address 114, *a+1 increments in second dimension and thus points to 106, **a+1 increments the first dimension and thus points to 104 and ***a+1 gets the value at the second location (since first location is incremented by 1) and points to the value in the second location (i.e., 2), hence you get the above output.

5. **ANSWER :**

   Compiler Error: lvalue required.

EXPLANATION :

   Error is in statement a++. The operand must be an lvalue and may be of any of scalar type for any operator, but array name only when subscripted becomes an lvalue. Simply using an array name is unalterable lvalue.

6. **ANSWER :**

   1 1 1
   2 2 2
   3 3 3

EXPLANATION :

   The given array is a 3-dimensional array. Let us assume the initial address of the array is 1000, which means the subsequent array values are stored in contiguous memory locations. The statement **ptr = p assigns the starting address of the array 'p' to the pointer variable 'ptr'. After execution of the instruction ptr++, the value in ptr becomes 1002, if scaling factor for integer is 2 bytes. The expression (ptr-p) indicates (value in ptr - the value in the starting location of array 'p'), (i.e., (1002 - 1000) / (scaling factor)) = 1. The expression (*ptr-a) indicates (value at address pointed by ptr - starting value of array 'a'), (i.e., (1002 - 1000) / (scaling factor)) = 1. The expression **ptr indicates the value stored in the location pointed by the pointer of ptr, (i.e., the value pointed by 1002) = 1. Hence the output of the first printf() function is 1 1 1. Similarly for all other printf() functions.

7. **ANSWER :**

   1

EXPLANATION :

   The given array is a 2-dimesional array, which points to its first element and hence the output.

8. **ANSWER :**

   A20lo

EXPLANATION :

   Since a void pointer (i.e., *vp) is used it can be type casted to any other type pointer. The statement (vp = &ch) stores the address of char 'ch' and the next statement prints the value stored in the pointer vp after type casting it to the proper data type pointer, whose output is 'A'. The statement (vp = &j) stores the address of integer 'j' and the next statement prints the value stored in the pointer vp after type casting it to the proper data type pointer, whose output is 20. The statement (vp = cp) stores the address of string 'cp' and the next statement prints the value stored in the pointer vp after type casting it to the proper data type pointer, whose output is "lo".

9. **ANSWER :**

   ck

EXPLANATION :

   In this problem we have an array of character pointers 's' pointing to the start of 4 strings. Then we have 'ptr' which is a pointer to a pointer of type char and a variable 'p' which is a pointer to a pointer to a pointer of type char. The vaiable 'p' holds the initial value of ptr, (i.e., p = s+3). The next statement increments value in p by 1, hence it becomes s+2. In the printf() function the expression *++p is first evaluated, thus incrementing the value of p to s+1, then the predecrement operation is evaluated, and we get s+1 - 1 = s. The indirection operator now gets the value from the array of s and adds 3 to the starting address. Thus the string is printed from the third position, hence we get the output as 'ck'.

10. **ANSWER :**

   (blank line)
   ohn
   hn
   n

EXPLANATION :

   Here a string (a pointer to char) is initialized with the value "John". The strlen() function returns the length of the string, thus n has a value 4. The next statement assigns value at the nth location (i.e., '\0') to the first location. Now the string becomes "\0ohn". Now the printf statement prints the string after each iteration it increments it starting position. Loop starts from 0 to 4. The first time x[0] = "\0" hence it prints nothing and pointer value is incremented. The second time it prints from x[1] i.e., "ohn" and the third time it prints "hn" and the last time it prints "n" and the loop terminates.

11. **ANSWER :**

Compiler Error : size of v is Unknown.

EXPLANATION :

You can create a variable of type void * but not of type void, since void is an empty data type. In the second line you are creating variable vptr of type void* and v of type void hence an error.

12. **ANSWER :**

2 5 5

EXPLANATION :

The sizeof(str1) is a character pointer so it gives you the size of the pointer variable. The next sizeof(str2) indicates the name of the array whose size is 5 (which includes the '\0' NULL character). The last sizeof("abcd") is similar to the second one, hence you get the above output.

13. **ANSWER :**

10

EXPLANATION :

The variable i is a block level variable and the visibility is inside that block only. But the lifetime of j is lifetime of the function so it lives upto the exit of the main() function. Since i is has its allocated space, *j prints the value stored in i (since j points i), hence you get the above output.

14. **ANSWER :**

0001 - 0002 - 0004

EXPLANATION :

The ++ operator when applied to pointers increments address according to their corresponding data-types.

15. **ANSWER :**

Garbage value.

EXPLANATION :

The pointer ptr is pointing out of array range of 'arr'.

16. **ANSWER :**

300

EXPLANATION :

The pointer points to % since it is incremented twice and again decremented by 2, it points to "%d\n" and 300 is printed.

17. **ANSWER :**

Compiler Error. We cannot apply indirection on type void*.

EXPLANATION :

Void pointer is a generic pointer type. No pointer arithmetic can be done on it.

18. **ANSWER :**

4

EXPLANATION :

The expressions *a and -*a cancels out. The result is as simple as (1+3) = 4.

19. **ANSWER :**

b

EXPLANATION :

The expression (ptr++) assigns the first value to ++*(ptr++) expression, and then gets incremented, the expression ++* increments the value in the address stored pointed by the pointer.

20. ANSWER :

b

EXPLANATION :

There is no difference between the expression ++*(p++) and ++*p++. Note that parenthesis is a visual clue for the reader to see which expression is first evaluated.

21. ANSWER :

Some garbage value
0

EXPLANATION :

The memory space allocated by the malloc() function is uninitialized, whereas the calloc() function returns the allocated memory space initialized to zeros.

22. ANSWER :

16 16

EXPLANATION :

The pointer variables ptr1 and ptr2 both refer to the same memory location a. So changes through ptr1 and ptr2 ultimately affects only the value of a.

23. ANSWER :

2 1 4 5 4

EXPLANATION :

The expression sizeof(ptr) is similar to sizeof(char*), which is 2. The expression sizeof(*ptr) is similar to sizeof(char), which is 1. The expression sizeof(arr) is size of the character array, which is 1. When sizeof() operator is applied to an array it returns the sizeof the array and it is not the same as the sizeof the pointer variable, since the sizeof(arr) where arr is the character array and the size of the array is 5 because the space necessary for the terminating NULL character should also be taken into account.

24. ANSWER :

x = 20 y = 10

EXPLANATION :

This is one way of swapping two values, using pointers.

25. ANSWER :

x = 20 y = 10

EXPLANATION :

Just another way of swapping two values, using bitwise operators.

26. ANSWER :

1 1

EXPLANATION :

The integer value 257 is stored in the memory as, 00000001 00000001 (in 16 bits), so the individual bytes are taken by casting it to char* and gets printed.

27. ANSWER :

2 1

EXPLANATION :

The integer value 258 is stored in the memory as, 00000001 00000010 (in 16 bits), so the individual bytes are taken by casting it to char* and gets printed.

28. ANSWER :

556

EXPLANATION :

The integer value 300 in binary notation is, 00000001 00101100. It is stored in memory as, 00101100 00000001.

Result of the expression *++ptr = 2 makes the memory representation as, 00101100 00000010. So the integer corresponding to it is 00000010 00101100 is 556.

29. **ANSWER :**

0

EXPLANATION :

After 'ptr' reaches the end of the string the value pointed by 'str' is '\0'. So the value of 'str' is less than that of 'ch'. So the value of 'ch' is 0.

30. **Answer & EXPLANATION :**

If the body of the loop never executes ptr is assigned no address so ptr remains NULL. When *ptr = 0, may result in problem (which gives rise to runtime error or NULL pointer assignment and terminate the program).

31. **ANSWER :**

Undefined behavior.

EXPLANATION :

The second statement results in undefined behavior because it points to some location whose value may not be available for modification. This type of pointer in which the non-availability of the implementation of the referenced location is referenced as 'incomplete types'.

32. **ANSWER :**

5

EXPLANATION :

The output is simple, it divides the two integer pointer values, hence you get the above output.

33. **ANSWER :**

Yes.

EXPLANATION :

The pointer ptr will point at the integer in the memory location 0x400.

34. **ANSWER :**

String constant

EXPLANATION :

The program suffers no problem and gives the output correctly because the character constants are stored in code/data area and not allocated in the stack, so this doesn't lead to dangling pointers.

35. **ANSWER :**

Garbage values.

EXPLANATION :

Both the functions suffer from the problem of dangling pointers. In someFun1() temp is a character array and so the space for it is allocated in heap and is initialized with character string "string". This is created dynamically as the function is called, and is also deleted dynamically on exiting the function so the string data is not available in the calling main() function leading to print some garbage values. The function someFun2() also suffers from the same problem but the problem can be easily identified in this case.

STRUCTURES & UNIONS

1. ANSWER :

Compiler Error.

EXPLANATION :

You cannot initialize variables in structure declaration.

2. ANSWER :

Compiler Error.

EXPLANATION :

The structure Y is nested within structure X. Hence, the elements of structure Y are to be accessed through the instance of structure X, which needs an instance of Y to be known. If the instance is created after defining the structure the compiler will not know about the instance relative to X. Hence for nested structure Y a member have to be declared.

3. ANSWER :

Compiler Error.

EXPLANATION :

Initialization should not be done for structure members inside the structure declaration.

4. ANSWER :

Compiler Error.

EXPLANATION :

In the end of nested structure Y a member have to be declared.

5. ANSWER :

2

EXPLANATION :

All the above statements form a circular doubly linked list. The statement, abc.next -> next -> prev -> next -> i; points to "ghi" node, the value at that particular node is 2.

6. ANSWER :

Value of ptr is 0 - 0
Value of ptr is 0 - 0

EXPLANATION :

The variable ptr is a pointer to structure variable. We can access the elements of the structure either with an arrow mark or with indirection operator. Since structure A_A is globally declared, its members x & y are initialized as zeroes by default.

7. ANSWER :

Compiler Error: Undefined structure date

EXPLANATION :

Inside the struct definition of 'student' the member of type struct date is given. The compiler doesn't have the definition of date structure before it is used, hence you get the above error.

8. ANSWER :

Compiler Error: Undefined structure date.

EXPLANATION :

Only declaration of struct date is available inside the structure definition of 'student' but to have a variable of type struct date the definition of the structure is required.

9. **EXPLANATION :**

The fread() function reads 10 records and prints the names successfully. It will return EOF only when the fread() function tries to read another record and fails while reading EOF. So it prints the last record again. After this only the condition feof(fp) becomes false, hence exits from the while loop.

10. **ANSWER :**

No.

EXPLANATION :

Is it not legal for a structure to contain a member of the same type as in this case. Because this will cause the structure declaration to be recursive without end.

11. **ANSWER :**

Yes.

EXPLANATION :

*b is a pointer to type struct a and so is legal. The compiler knows, the size of the pointer to a structure even before the size of the structure is determined (as you know the pointer to any type is of same size). This type of structures is known as self-referencing structure.

12. **ANSWER :**

No.

EXPLANATION :

The typename 'Type' is not known at the point of declaring the structure (i.e., forward references are not made for typedefs).

13. **ANSWER :**

Yes.

EXPLANATION :

The typename Type is known at the point of declaring the structure, because it is already typedefined.

14. **ANSWER :**

No.

EXPLANATION :

When the declaration, (typedef struct a Type;) is encountered body of struct a is not known, these are referred as incomplete types.

15. **ANSWER :**

10   20.5   10   20.5

EXPLANATION :

Structure variable assignments are equivalent to the simple data type variable assignments. So the values of v1.x and v1.y into the v2.x and v2.y.

ANSWERS --- III

1. (c) and (e)
2. (d), (e) and (f)
3. (a) Integer
   (b) Unsigned integer
   (c) Signed integer
   (d) Long integer
   (e) Unsigned short integer
   (f) Unsigned long integer
4. (a) Integer
   (b) Double
   (c) String
   (d) Character
   (e) Character
   (f) String
5. (a) and (d)
6. (a), (c) and (d)
7. (a) 6
   (b) 20
   (c) 8
   (d) -3
   (e) 99
   (f) 4
8. (d)
9. (a) -6
   (b) -3
   (c) 2
   (d) 3
   (e) 1
   (f) 5
10. (a) 1
    (b) 0
    (c) 1
    (d) 0
11. (a) a == 0
    (b) a <= b
    (c) (a == 0) < b
    (d) a == b == 0
12. (a) 0
    (b) 1
    (c) 0
    (d) 0
13. (a) 2
    (b) 2.5
    (c) 1
    (d) Compile Error: Illegal use of floating point
14. (a) -27536
    (b) 38000.000
    (c) -536
    (d) 65000.000
15. (a) 'S'
    (b) 'S'
    (c) 'S'
    (d) 'S'
16. (a), (b) and (d)
17. (a)
18. (b) and (d)
19. (a) size of operator
    (b) Arithmetic operator
    (c) Ternary operator
    (d) Assignment operator
20. (b), (c) and (d)
21. (a), (b) and (c)
22. (a) 5
    (b) 9
    (c) 2
    (d) 10
    (e) 0
    (f) 0
23. (a) 7
    (b) 15
    (c) 7
    (d) 24
24. (a), (b) and (c)
25. (a)
26. (a) Signed integer
    (b) Hexadecimal integer
    (c) Unsigned integer
    (d) Octal integer
    (e) Unsigned long integer
    (f) Signed long integer
27. (a) Floating point value in exponent form
    (b) Float type
    (c) Floating point value in exponent type or float type depending on value
    (d) Double type

28. (a) Pointer to integer
    (b) Unsigned Hexadecimal integer
       (With A, B, C, D, E, F)
    (c) Pointer
    (d) Unsigned octal integer
    (e) Signed decimal integer
    (f) Unsigned Hexadecimal integer
       (With a, b, c, d, e, f)
29. (b)
30. (b)
31. (c)
32. (a), (b), (c) and (e)
33. (a) 32769
    (b) 0
    (c) Infinite Loop
    (d) Infinite Loop
    (e) 1
    (f) Infinite Loop
34. (b) and (c)
35. (a)
36. (b)
37. (b)
38. (b)
39. (b)
40. (a)
41. (a), (c) and (d)
42. (b), (c) and (d)
43. (a), (c), (e) and (f)
44. (a)
45. (d)
46. (a) 5.0
    (b) 5.0
    (c) 5.5
    (d) 5.44
    (e) 0.0 (ANSI C does not support fabsl())
    (f) -0.0 (ANSI C does not support fabsl())
47. (a) 5
    (b) 6
    (c) 5
    (d) 6
    (e) 5
    (f) 6
48. (a) 40.0
    (b) 41
    (c) 0.1
    (d) 0.2
    (e) 200
    (f) 250.00

49. (a)
50. (b)
51. (a)
52. (a) a
    (b) A
    (c) g
    (d) G
    (e) 5
    (f) 5
53. (a), (c) and (d)
54. (a), (b) and (e)
55. (d) and (e)
56. (a)
57. (a) and (d)
58. (a), (c) and (d)
59. (a), (c) and (d)
60. (d)
61. (d)
62. (b) and (d)
63. (d)
64. (b)
65. (a), (b) and (c)
66. (a), (b) and (c)
67. (a), (c) and (d)
68. (d)
69. (a)
70. (a) 1
    (b) 2
    (c) 4
    (d) 8
71. (a) 2
    (b) 2
    (c) 4
    (d) 4
72. (a) and (d)
73. (d)
74. (c)
75. (b)

❖ ❖ ❖ ❖ ❖ ❖ ❖

I. ASCII TABLE

This table lists the ASCII characters and their ASCII codes in decimal. The first 32 ASCII characters and the last character are control characters. These characters are non-printable characters, which are enclosed in parentheses (*e.g.*, (nul)).

Character	ASCII code	Character	ASCII code	Character	ASCII code	Character	ASCII code
(nul)	0	(sp)	32	@	64	'	96
(soh)	1	!	33	A	65	a	97
(stx)	2	"	34	B	66	b	98
(etx)	3	#	35	C	67	c	99
(eot)	4	$	36	D	68	d	100
(enq)	5	%	37	E	69	e	101
(acK)	6	&	38	F	70	f	102
(bel)	7	'	39	G	71	g	103
(bs)	8	(	40	H	72	h	104
(ht)	9	)	41	I	73	i	105
(nl)	10	*	42	J	74	j	106
(vt)	11	+	43	K	75	k	107
(np)	12	,	44	L	76	l	108
(cr)	13	–	45	M	77	m	109
(so)	14	.	46	N	78	n	110
(si)	15	/	47	O	79	o	111
(dle)	16	0	48	P	80	p	112
(dc1)	17	1	49	Q	81	q	113
(dc2)	18	2	50	R	82	r	114
(dc3)	19	3	51	S	83	s	115
(dc4)	20	4	52	T	84	t	116
(nak)	21	5	53	U	85	u	117
(syn)	22	6	54	V	86	v	118
(etb)	23	7	55	W	87	w	119
(can)	24	8	56	X	88	x	120
(em)	25	9	57	Y	89	y	121
(sub)	26	:	58	Z	90	z	122
(esc)	27	;	59	[	91	{	123
(fs)	28	<	60	\	92	|	124
(gs)	29	=	61	]	93	}	125
(rs)	30	>	62	^	94	~	126
(us)	31	?	63	_	95	(del)	127

II. PRECEDENCE TABLE

Description	Operator	Associativity
Function expression	()	Left to right
Array expression	[]	Left to right
Structure operator	–>	Left to right
Structure operator	,	Left to right
Unary minus	–	Right to left
Increment/Decrement	++ ––	Right to left
One's complement	~	Right to left
Negation	!	Right to left
Address of	&	Right to left
Value at address	*	Right to left
Type cast	(type)	Right to left
Size in bytes	sizeof	Right to left
Multiplication	*	Left to right
Division	/	Left to right
Addition	+	Left to right
Subtraction	–	Left to right
Left shift	<<	Left to right
Right shift	>>	Left to right
Less than	<	Left to right
Less than or equal to	<=	Left to right
Greater than	>	Left to right
Greater than or equal to	>=	Left to right
Equal to	==	Left to right
Not equal to	!=	Left to right
Bitwise AND	&	Left to right
Bitwise exclusive OR	^	Left to right
Bitwise inclusive OR	|	Left to right
Logical AND	&&	Left to right
Logical OR	||	Left to right
Conditional	?:	Right to left
Assignment	=	
	*= /= %=	Right to left
	+= –= &=	Right to left
	^= |=	Right to left
	<<= >>=	Right to left
Comma	,	Right to left

III. HEADER FILES

This appendix is a summary of the header files defined by the ANSI (American National Standards Institutions) standard. The header files contain information about various library functions that are functionally same. Header files may be included in any order in the program. A header file must be included outside any external declaration or definition and before the use of library functions present in it.

The library functions, constants, global variables, and macros of the standard library are declared in the following header files.

alloc.h	assert.h	bios.h	conio.h	ctype.h
dir.h	dos.h	errno.h	fcntl.h	float.h
graphics.h	io.h	limits.h	malloc.h	math.h
mem.h	process.h	setjmp.h	share.h	signal.h
stdarg.h	stddef.h	stdio.h	stdlib.h	string.h
time.h	values.h			

Some header files consist only of constants, global variables, and macros, such header files are of less importance. Hence they are not included in the description.

alloc.h

The header <alloc.h> declares functions for dynamic allocation (also reallocation) of memory, and clearing of used memory before the execution of program is over.

Example : calloc(), malloc(), etc.,

assert.h

The assert macro is used to add diagonstics to programs. If NDEBUG is defined at the time of including <assert.h> the assert macro is ignored.

bios.h

The header <bios.h> declares functions for interrupt enabling / disabling functions, which are used for RS-232 communications and bios interrupts.

Example : bioscom(), biostime(), etc.,

conio.h

The header <conio.h> declares functions which deals with the text mode window.

Example : crscr(), clreol(), etc.,

ctype.h

The header <ctype.h> declares functions for testing characters. For each function the argument is an int, whose value must be EOF or representable as an unsigned char, and the return value is an int. These functions return non-zero value, if the argument C satisfies the condition. zero otherwise.

dir.h

This header file <dir.h> defines library functions that are used to do functions with the directories existing in the drive. The functions present in the header file can be used to rename, delete, copy , move a directory from one place to another and so on.

Example : chdir(), rmdir(), etc.,

dos.h

This header file <dos.h> defines library functions that are used to do functions with the operating system. The functions present in the header file can be used to get, set, data, time, and so on. The functions can also be used to suspend execution of a time for some time also.

Example : delay(), gettime(), etc.,

errno.h

Many of the functions in the library set status indicators when error or end of file occurs. These indicators may be set and tested explicitly. The integer expression errno may contain an error number that gives further information about the most recent error.

fcntl.h

This header file < fcntl.h >defines "open flags" for open and similar library functions.

float.h

The subset of the header file <float.h> are constants related to floating-point arithmetic. When a value is given, it represents the minimum magnitude for the corresponding quantity, Each implementation defines appropriate values.

Example : FLI_RADIX, FLT_DIG, etc.,

graphics.h

The header file <graphics.h> consists of library functions used to do all graphics effects in graphical window. This is one of the header files, which has lot of library functions in it.

Example : circle(), detectgraph(), etc.,

io.h

The header file <io.h> defines library functions used for input and output functions that are not present in the stdio.h header file.

Example : chmod(), eof(), etc.,

limits.h

The header file <limits.h> defines constants for the size upto integral types. The values below are acceptable minimum magnitudes. Larger values may also be used.

Example : CHAR_BIT, CHR_MAX, etc.,

math.h

The header file <math.h> declares mathematical functions and macros. All those functions returns a datatype double. Angles for trignometric functions are expressed in radians.

Example : sin, cos, exp, etc.,

setjmp.h

The declarations in <setjmp.h> provide a way to avoid the normal function call and return sequence, typically to permit an immediate return from a deeply nested function call.

Example : longjmp, setjmp, etc.,

signal.h

The header file <signal.h> provides facilities for handling exceptional conditions that arise during execution, such as an interrupt signal from an external source or an error in the execution. The initial state of signals is implementation defined. The group of signal functions have their names beginning with SIG.

Example : SIGABRT, SIGFPE, etc.,

stdarg.h

The header file <stdarg.h> facilitates for stepping through a list of function arguments of unknown number and type. The macro can be called once, after the arguments have been processed.

Example : va_list, va_start, etc.,

stdlib.h

The header file <stdlib.h> declares function for number conversion, storage allocation and similar tasks.

Example : ralloc, malloc, exit, etc.,

stdio.h

The input and output functions, types and macros defined in <stdio.h> represent nearly one third of the library. It is one of the commonly used header file.

Example : scanf, printf, etc.,

string.h

The header file <string.h> is used to perform functions in strings. There are two group of string functions defined in the header file <string.h>. They have names beginning with str and also have names beginning with mem.

Example : strcpy, strcmp, memcpy, etc.,

time.h

The header file <time.h> declares types and functions for manipulating data and time. Some functions process local time, which may differ from calendar time.

Example : fm_sec, fm_min, fm_hour, etc.,

IV. LIBRARY FUNCTIONS

MEMORY MANAGEMENT FUNCTIONS (include file is alloc.h)

Function	Purpose
calloc(n, size)	Allocates n multiple blocks of (n * size) bytes and initializes the memory to 0.
coreleft(void)	Returns a measure of RAM memory not in use.
farcalloc(n, size)	Allocates n multiple blocks of (n * size) bytes larger than 64K.
farcoreleft(void)	Returns a measure of RAM memory not in use beyond the highest allocated block.
farfree(*ptr)	Releases a block of memory previously allocated by farcalloc(), farmalloc(), & farrealloc() pointed by ptr.
farmalloc(size)	Allocates a block of (size) bytes larger than 64K.
farrealloc(*ptr, size)	Reallocates the size of the allocated block to size pointer by ptr previously alocated by farcalloc() / farmalloc(), copying the contents to a new location, if necessary.
free(*ptr)	Releases a block of memory previously allocated by calloc(), malloc(), & realloc() pointed by ptr.
malloc(size)	Allocates a block of (size) bytes.
realloc(*ptr, size)	Reallocates the size of the allocated block to size pointer by ptr previously allocated by calloc() / malloc(), copying the contents to a new location, if necessary.

INTERRUPT ENABLING / DISABLING FUNCTIONS (include file is bios.h)

Function	Purpose
bioscom()	Used for RS-232 communications (serial I/O).
biosdisk()	Used for interrupt 0x13 to issue disk operations directly to the BIOS.
biosequip()	Used for BIOS interrupt 0x11 to return an integer describing the equipment connected to the system.
bioskey()	Performs various keyboard operations using BIOS interrupt 0x16.
biosmemory()	Used for BIOS interrupt 0x12 to return the size of RAM.
biosprint()	Used for BIOS interrupt 0x17 to perform various printer functions on the printer identified by port.
biostime()	Used for BIOS interrupt 0x1A to either read or set the BIOS timer.

TEXT MODE WINDOW FUNCTIONS (include file is conio.h)

Function	Purpose
clrscr()	Clears the text mode window.
clreol()	Clears to end of line in text window.
cgets(char*str)	Reads a string of characters from the console and stores the string (and the string length) in the location *str.

cputs(char*str)	Writes the null-terminated string str to the current text window. It does not append a newline character.
cprintf(..)	Displays formatted output to the text window on the screen.
cscanf(..)	Reads formatted input from the text window.
getch()	Reads a character from console but does not echo to the screen.
getche()	Reads a character from console and echoes to the screen.
gotoxy()	Positions cursor in text window.
movetext()	Copies text on screen from one rectangle to another.
gettext()	Copies text from text-mode screen to memory.
puttext()	Copies text from memory to text-mode screen.
kbhit()	Checks for currently available keystrokes.
putch()	Displays the character to the current text window.
textbackground()	Selects a new text background color.
window()	Defines active text-mode window.

CHARACTER CLASSIFICATION FUNCTIONS (Include file is ctype.h)

isalnum(c)	Determine if argument is alphanumeric. Return non-zero value if true; 0 otherwise.
isalpha(c)	Determine if argument is alphabetic. Return non-zero value if true; 0 otherwise.
isascii(c)	Determine if argument is an ASCII character. Return non-zero value if true; 0 otherwise.
iscntrl(c)	Determine if argument is an ASCII character. Return non-zero value if true; 0 otherwise.
isdigit(c)	Determine if argument is a decimal digit character. Return non-zero value if true; 0 otherwise.
isgraph(c)	Determine if argument is a graphic ASCII character. Return non-zero value if true; 0 otherwise.
islower(c)	Determine if argument is lowercase. Return non-zero value if true; 0 otherwise.
isodigit(c)	Determine if argument is graphic ASCII character. Return non- zero value if true; 0 otherwise.
isprint(c)	Determine if argument is a printing ASCII character. Return non-zero value if true; 0 otherwise.
isspace(c)	Determine if argument is a white space character. Return non -zero value if true; 0 otherwise.
isupper(c)	Determine if argument is uppercase. Return non-zero value if true; 0 otherwise.
isxdigit(c)	Determine if argument is hexadecimal digit. Return non-zero value if true; 0 otherwise.
tolower(c)	Tests the charater and converts to lowercase if uppercase.
toupper(c)	Tests the charater and converts to uppercase if lowercase.

DIRECTORY FUNCTIONS (include file is dir.h)

chdir(char *path)	Causes the directory specified by path to become the current working directory.
findfirst(char *path)	Uses the DOS system call 0x4E to begin a search of a disk directory.
findnext(char *path)	Finds subsequent files that match the pathname argument of findfirst.
getcurdir()	Gets current directory for specified drive.
getcwd()	Gets the current working directory.
mkdir(char *path)	Creates a new directory from the given path.
rmdir(char *path)	Deletes the directory whose path is given by path.
searchpath(char *p)	Searches the DOS path (p) for a file.

DISK OPERATING SYSTEM FUNCTIONS (include file is dos.h)

absread()	Uses DOS interrupt 0x25 to read specific disk sectors.
abswrite()	Uses DOS interrupt 0x26 to write specific disk sectors.
allocmem()	Uses the DOS system call 0x48 to allocate a block of free memory and return the segment address of the allocated block.
delay()	Suspends execution of a program for an interval in milliseconds.
disable()	Used to disable interrupts.
dostounix()	Converts date and time to UNIX time.
enable()	Used to enable interrupts.
freemem()	Frees a previously allocated DOS memory block.
geninterrupt()	Macro that generates a software interrupt.
getdate()	Gets DOS system date.
gettime()	Gets DOS system time.
inport()	Reads a word from a hardware port.
inportb()	Reads a byte from a hardware port.
int86()	Used to execute an 8086 software interrupt.
intdos()	Used to execute DOS interrupt 0x21 to invoke a specified DOS function.
intr()	An alternate interface for executing software interrupts, that generates an 8086 software interrupt.
keep()	Exits the current program and remains resident.
nosound()	Turns the PC speaker off.
outport()	Sends a word to a hardware port.
outportb()	Sends a byte to a hardware port.
setdate()	Sets DOS system date.
settime()	Sets DOS system time.
sleep()	Suspends execution for an interval in milliseconds.
sound()	Turns the PC speaker on at the specified frequency.
unixtodos()	Converts date and time from UNIX to DOS format.

INPUT / OUTPUT FUNCTIONS (include file is io.h)

access()	Determines the accessibility of a file.
chmod()	Sets file access permissions (read, write & execute).
chsize()	Changes the size of the file.
close()	Closes a file previously opened by open().
creat()	Creates a new file or overwrite an existing one.
creatnew()	Creates and opens a new file for reading & writing in binary mode.
eof()	Checks for end-of-file.
filelength()	Gets file size in bytes.
lock()	Sets or resets file-sharing locks.
mktemp()	Makes a unique file name.
open()	Opens a file.
read()	Uses DOS function 0x3F (read system call) to read bytes from a file into a buffer.
remove()	Macro that removes a file.
rename()	Changes the name of a file from oldname to newname.
tell()	Gets current position of file pointer.
write()	Uses DOS function 0x40 to write bytes from a buffer to a file.

ARITHMETIC FUNCTIONS (Include file is math.h)

cos(d)	Returns the cosine value of double d.
cosh(d)	Returns the hyberbolic cosine value of double d.
ceil(d)	Returns a value rounded up to the next higher integer.
acos(d)	Returns the arc cosine of d.
asin(d)	Raises the exponential e to the power d.
exp(d)	Returns the value of power d.
fabs(d)	Returns the absolute value of d.
floor(d)	Returns the value rounded down to the next lower integer.
fmod(d_1,d_2)	Returns the remainder of d_1/d_2.
hypot(d)	Returns the hypotenuse of right triangle.
log(d)	Returns the natural logarithm of d.
log10(d)	Returns the natural logarithm of d.
modf(d)	Returns the argument into integer and fractional parts.
pow(d_1,d_2)	Returns d_1 raised to the d_2 power.
sin(d)	Returns the sine of d.
sinh(d)	Returns the hyperbolic sine of d.
sqrt(d)	Returns the square root of d.
tan(d)	Returns the tangent of d.
tanh(d)	Returns the hyperbolic tangent of d.

MEMORY FUNCTIONS (include file is mem.h)

memccpy()	Copies a block of n bytes from source to destination.
memchr()	Searches for a character in a string of n bytes.
memcmp()	Compares the first n bytes of strings s1 and s2.
memcpy()	Copies a block of n bytes from source to destination.
memicmp()	Compares the first n bytes of strings s1 and s2, ignoring case.
memmove()	Moves a block of n bytes from source to destination.
movmem()	Moves a block of length bytes from source to destination.
setmem()	Sets a block of length bytes in memory.

PROCESS FUNCTIONS (include file is process.h)

abort()	Abnormally terminates a process.
execl()	Enable your program to load and run other files (child processes).
exit()	Terminates the program.
getpid()	Gets the process ID of the program.
spawnl()	Enable your programs to run other files (child processes) and returns control to your program when the child processes finish.
system()	Invokes the DOS command interpreter file from inside an executing C program to execute a DOS command.

JUMP FUCTIONS (include file is setjmp.h)

longjmp()	Performs a nonlocal goto.
setjmp()	Sets up for a nonlocal goto.

SIGNAL RECEIVING / SENDING FUNCTIONS (include file is signal.h)

raise()	Sends a software signal to the executing program.
signal()	Specifies signal-handling actions.

DATA CONVERSION FUNCTIONS (Include file is stdlib.h)

atof(s)	Converts string to float.
atoi(s)	Converts string to int.
atol(s)	Converts string to long.
abs(i)	Returns the absolute value of an integer.
ecvt(d)	Converts double to string.
fcvt(d)	Converts double to string.
gcvt(d)	Converts double to string.
itoa(i)	Converts int to string.
strtod(s)	Converts long to string.
strtal(s)	Converts string to double.
strtoul(s)	Converts string to an unsigned long integer.
ultoa(l)	Converts unsigned long integer to string.

STRING MANIPULATION FUNCTIONS (Include file is string.h)

strcats(s_1, s_2)	Concatenate string s_2 at the end of string s_1 and terminates with '\0' return s_2.
strchr(s_1, c)	Compare characters of s_1 with characters starting from the headofstring s_1. Return pointer to the first occurence of c in s1. If c is not present in s_1 returns NULL.
strcmp(s_1, s_2)	Compares two strings lexicographically with regard to case. Returns a negative value if $s_1 < s_2$, 0 if s_1 and s_2 are identical and a positive value if $s_1 > s_2$.
strcpy(s_1, s_2)	Copies string s_2 to string s_1.
strdup(s)	Duplicates string s.
strcmpi(s_1, s_2)	Same as strcmp.
strlen(s)	Returns the number of characters of strings.
strlwr(s)	Converts a string to lowercase.
strncat(s_1, s_2)	Concatenates string s_2 at the end of string s_1 return s_2 and terminates s_2 with '\0'.
strncmp(s_1, s_2, n)	Same as strcmp but it compares a portion of string s_2 to string s_1 upto position n.
strncpy(s_1, s_2, n)	Same as strcpy but it copies a portion of string s_2 to string s_1 upto position n.
strnicmp(s_1, s_2, n)	Same as strncmp but it compares a portion of string s_1 and string s_2 upto position n.
strrchr(s_1, c)	Compare characters of s_1 with character c starting from the tail of string s_1. Returns pointer to the last occurence of c in s_1. If c is not present in s_1 it returns NULL.
strrev(s)	Reverses the string s.
strset(s_1, s_2)	Set all characters within s_1 to s_2 (excluding the null character).
strstr(s_1, s_2)	Return pointer to first occurence of whole string s_2 in s_1. If string s_2 is not present in s_1 returns NULL.
strupr(s)	Converts a string to uppercase.
strpbrk(s_1, s_2)	Return pointer to first occurence in string s_1 of any character of string s_2 and if not character of s_2 is present return NULL.

STANDARD INPUT/OUTPUT FUNCTIONS (Include file is stdio.h)

fclose(f)	closes a file f, return 0 if file is sucessfully closed.
feof(f)	Determine if and end-of-file condition has been reached. If so, return a non-zero value; 0 otherwise.
fgetc(f)	Reads a single character from file f.
fgetchar(f)	Reads a single character from keyboard.

| fgets(s,n,f) | Reads a string s, containing n characters, from file f. |
| fopen(ft,s) | Opens a file named f of types s. Returns a pointer to the file. |

TIME FUNCTIONS (INCLUDE FILE IS TIME.H)

asctime()	Converts date and time to ASCII.
clock()	Returns number of clock ticks since program start.
ctime()	Converts date and time to a string.
difftime()	Computes difference between two times.
gmtime()	Converts date and time to Greenwich Mean Time (GMT).
localtime()	Converts date and time to a structure.
mktime()	Converts time to calendar format
stime()	Sets system date and time
time()	Get time of the day.

NOTE

*	denotes a pointer.
c	denotes a character-type argument.
d	denotes a double-precision argument.
f	denotes a file argument.
i	denotes an integer argument.
l	denotes a long integer argument.
s	denotes a string argument.

V. COMMON PROGRAMMING ERRORS

This appendix is written for C programmers for finding the bugs (errors) while compiling a program. It is advisable to keep track of such errors and to see that these known errors are not present in the program. I have made a list of more common programming mistakes, which will help you while writing programs. They are not arranged in any particular order.

1.   Forgetting to include stdio.h

Forgetting to include the header file stdio.h in the program, which reads input from the user through the keyboard or displays the output in the screen. In such cases, the compiler issues an error message.

2.   Forgetting to include header files

Forgetting to include the header file in the program, which uses one or more functions from a header file. In such cases, the compiler issues an error message.

3.   Missing semicolons

Every C statement must end with a semicolon. Missing a semicolon may cause confusion to the compiler and results in error messages.

Example : `x = a + b + c`

The above statement should be

`x = a + b + c;`

4.   Using a keyword as an identifier

Another common mistake is to use a keyword as an identifier for naming variables, arrays, functions, structures, or unions, etc., In such cases, the compiler issues an error message.

5.   Placing semicolons at the end of function definitions

It is common error to place a semicolon after the right paranthesis enclosing the argument list of a function definition.

6.   Missing semicolons at the end of function declarations

It is common error to omit a semicolon after the right paranthesis enclosing the argument list of a function declaration (i.e., function prototype).

7.   Ending an if statement with a semicolon

Another common mistake is to put a semicolon at the end of the if statement after the paranthesis. The semicolon may cause the if statement to omit its body, and hence it will not perform any action regardless of whether the condition is true or false.

8.   Ending a loop with a semicolon

Another common mistake is to put a semicolon in a wrong place i.e., in a loop. A semicolon may cause a loop to be an indefinite loop and the programmer may get a different output.

Example :

```
#include<stdio.h>
main()
```

```
    {
        int x = 1;
        while(x<=50);
        {
            printf("ERROR");
            x++;
        }
    }
```

In the above program the value of x will not be incremented and always remains less than 50. Therefore the program segment should be

```
while(x <= 50)
    {
        printf("ERROR");
        x++;
    }
```

9. Improper comment characters

Every comment should start with a /* and end with a */. Anything between them is ignored by the compiler. If we miss out the opening /* or the closing /* then the compiler searches in the program treating all lines as comments. Hence, we will get an error message. One opening /* should be always accompanied with a closing */. Otherwise, an error will be occurred.

10. Undeclared variables

C requires every variable to be declared for its type, before it is used. During the development of a large program, one may use a variable, which has not been declared. Hence, it gives an error.

11. Using spaces in between operators

It is a common error to leave spaces in between operators like ==, !=, >=, <=.

12. Reversing the order of operators

It is a common error to reverse the order of operators like =! , =>, =<.

13. Confusing the precedence of various operators

Expressions are evaluated according to the precedence of operators. It is common among beginners to confuse the precedence of operators.

Example : `while(sum=multiply() <= 50)`
`sub = 5 - sum;`

The function call multiply() returns the product of three numbers, which is compared to 50. If the value is equal to or less than 50, the relational test is true, and 1 is assigned to sum, otherwise 0 will be assigned. But this is not the output the programmer wanted.

The expression should be

```
while(sum=multiply()) <= 50)
        sub = 5 - sum;
```

14.   Omitting the ampersand (&) before the variables used in scanf()

Example :

```
int x;
scanf("%d",x);
```

The statement should be

```
int x;
scanf("%d",&x);
```

15.   Using the operator = instead of operator ==

It is quite possible to forget the use of operator == and use the operator = when we perform a relational test.

Example :

```
#include<stdio.h>
main()
 {
      int x = 1;
      while(x = 5)
      {
         printf("Hello");
          x++;
      }
 }
```

The statement is syntactically valid and the variable x assigns 5 and then, because x = 5 is true, the message is printed once and the control will come out of the loop since x becomes 6. Hence we have fallen in an indefinite loop. Similar mistakes can occur in other control statements such as for and if. Such a mistake in the loop control statements might cause infinite loops.

The statement should be

```
while(x == 5)
```

16.   Omitting the break statement at the end of a case in a switch statement

Example :

```
#include<stdio.h>
main()
 {
      int x;
      printf("ENTER AN INTEGER : ");
      scanf("%d", &x);
      switch(x)
      {
          case 1 :
                  printf("Hello");
```

```
              case 2 :
                        printf ("Welcome");
              case 3 :
                        printf ("Hai");
          }
      }
```

Remember that if a break statement is not included at the end of a case then execution will continue to the next case. Since in the above program we have not used break after the printf() in case1, case2 and case3, the control prints all the messages.

The program segment should be

```
switch (x)

    {
       case 1 :
                printf ("Hello");
                break;
       case 2 :
                printf ("Welcome");
                break;
       case 3 :
                printf ("Hai");
                break;

    }
```

17. Using a continue statement in a switch statement

It is a common error to use the continue statement instead of break statement in a switch statement. Note that the continue statement works only in loops, and never with a switch statement.

18. Crossing the bounds of an array

Example :

```
#include<stdio.h>
main ()
    {
        int x[50], i, sum = 0;
        for (i = 1; i < 100; i++)
          sum += x[i];

    }
```

In the array x there is no such element as x[50], since array counting begins with 0 and not 1. Compiler would give warning if the program exceeds the bounds.

Note that all indices starts from 0 and not 1.

19. Missing braces at the end of a compound statement

It is common error to forget a closing brace when using a loop. It will be usually detected by the compiler because an opening brace should have a closing brace. However, if we put a matching brace in a wrong place, the compiler won't notice the mistake and the program will produce unexpected results.

20.   Inserting a semicolon at the end of macro definition

A macro definition must not end with a semicolon. A semicolon may cause confusion to the compiler and results in error messages.

Example :

```
# define SIZE 40;
```

The above macro definition should be

```
# define SIZE 40
```

21.   Confusing a character constant and a character string

In the statement

```
ch = 'x';
```

a single character is assigned to ch. In the statement

```
str = "x";
```

a pointer to the character string "x" is assigned to str.

Note that in the first case, the declaration of ch would be

```
char ch;
char *str;
```

22.   Forgetting to reserve an extra location in a character array (string) for the null terminator

Remember that each character array ends with a null character ('\0'), therefore its dimension should be declared big enough to hold the characters in the array as well as the null character.

Example : For storing a string "ANITHRA" the dimension of the array should be 8

```
i.e., char str[8] = "ANITHRA";
```

23.   Missing quotes

Every string must be enclosed in double quotes, while a single character constant must be enclosed in single quotes. If we miss the quotes, the string or the character would be referred to as a variable name.

Example :

```
if(output == NO)

mark = B;
```

In the above example NO and B are treated as variables and therefore an error message "undefined variable B", "undefined variable NO" will occur.

24.   Passing the wrong argument type to a function

For example,

```
abc = fleet_sum(5);
```

If the fleet_sum function is expecting a floating-point argument, then the above statement will produce a result with errors, since an integer value is being passed. We can use a typecast operator to explicitly convert a value that is passed to a function.

25.   Omitting return type declarations

Omitting the return type of a function is a syntax error, if the function returns any other value other than int.

For example,

```
abc = sum (a);
```

If the return type for a function is not declared explicitly then the compiler will assume that is function returns a value of type int. Hence, it is a good programming practice to use void as a return type.

26.   Mismatch of arguments in the function definitions and the function call

It's a syntax error to call a function, which doesn't match with the arguments present in function definition or function declaration.

27.   Defining a function inside another function

It's a syntax error to define a function inside another function. However, you can call a function from any other function.

28.   Confusing the operator (->) with the operator(.) when referencing structure variables.

Note that, the dot or period operator (.) is used for structure variables, while the arrow operator -> is used for structure pointer variables. So if **'a'** is a structure variable then the notation **a.b** is used to refer the member **b** of **a**, where as if **'a'** is a pointer to a structure, then the notation **a -> b** is used to refer the member **b** of the structure pointed to by **b**.

29.   Leaving a blank space between the name of a macro and its argument list in the #define statements.

For example,

```
#define    PAY    (m, n)    (30, 80)
```

The above macro definition is incorrect, as the preprocessor considers the first blank space after the defined name as the start of the definition of that name.

The definition should be

```
# define PAY(M, N)       (30, 80)
```

30.   Omitting parenthesis around arguments in macro definition

```
#define SQR(x)    x * x
main()
{
    int y;
    y = 16/SQR(4);
    printf("%d",y);
}
```

In the above example we would expect the value of y to be 1, but the value will be 16. this happens because on preprocessing the arithmetic statements takes the form of

```
y = 16 / 4 * 4 ;
```

the arithmetic statement should be

```
y = 16/(SQR(4));
```

VI. KEYS USED IN C COMPILER

MENU BAR KEYS

Keys used	Menu item	Function
Alt+Spacebar	Menu	Takes you to the (System) menu
Alt+C	Compile menu	Takes you to the Compile menu
Alt+D	Debug menu	Takes you to the Debug menu
Alt+E	Edit menu	Takes you to the Edit menu
Alt+F	File menu	Takes you to the File menu
Alt+H	Help menu	Takes you to the Help menu
Alt+O	Options menu	Takes you to the Options menu
Alt+P	Project menu	Takes you to the Project menu
Alt+R	Run menu	Takes you to the Run menu
Alt+S	Search menu	Takes you to the Search menu
Alt+W	Window menu	Takes you to the Window menu
Alt+F4 (Alt+x)	File quit	Exits C compiler.

GENERAL IDE KEYS

Keys used	Menu item	Function
F1	Help	Displays a help screen.
F2	File-Save	Saves the file that's in the active edit window.
F3	File-Open	Brings up a dialog box so you can open a file.
F4	Run/Go to cursor	Runs your program to the line where the cursor is positioned.
F5	Zoom window	Zooms the active window.
F6 (ctrl+F6)	Next window	Cycles through all open windows.
F7	Run/Trace Into	Runs your program in debug mode, tracing into functions.
F8	Run/Step Over	Runs your program in debug mode, stepping over function calls.
F9	Compile & Make	Invokes the project manager to make an .exe file.
F10	None	Takes you to the menu bar.

EDITING KEYS

Keys used	Menu item	Function
Ctrl+Del	Edit-Clear	Removes selected text from window; doesn't put it in Clipboard
Ctrl+Ins	Edit-Copy	Copies selected text to Clipboard
Shift+Del	Edit-Cut	Places selected text in Clipboard, deletes selection
Shift+Ins	Edit-Paste	Pastes text from Clipboard into the active window
Alt+Bksp	Edit-Undo	Restores text in active window to previous state
Ctrl+L	Search/Search again	Repeats last Find or Replace command.

WINDOW MANAGEMENT KEYS

Keys used	Menu Item	Function
Alt+#		Displays a window, where # is the number of the window you want to view
Alt+0	List All	Displays a list of open windows
Ctrl+F4 (Alt+F3)	Close window	Closes the active window
Shift+F5	Tile window	Tiles all open windows
Alt+F5	Debug/Inspect	Opens an inspector window
Shift+F5	User Screen	Displays user screen
F5	Zoom Window	Zooms/unzooms the active window
Ctrl+F6 (F6)	Window³Next	Switches the active window
Ctrl+F5		Changes size or position of active window.

ONLINE HELP KEYS

Keys used	Menu Item	Function
F1	Help-Contents	Opens a context-sensitive help screen
F1 F1	Help-Using Help	Brings up help on help. (Just press F1 when you're already in the help system.)
Shift+F1	Help-Index	Brings up help index
Alt+F1	Help-Previous Topic	Displays previous help screen
Ctrl+F1	Help-Topic Search	Calls up language-specific help in the active edit window.

DEBUGGING / RUNNING KEYS

Keys used	Menu Item	Function
Alt+F5	Debug/Inspect	Opens an Inspector window
Alt+F7	Search-Previous Error	Takes you to previous error
Alt+F8	Search-Next Error	Takes you to next error
Alt+F9	Compile	Compiles to .obj
Ctrl+F2	Run/Program Reset	Resets running program
Ctrl+F3	Debug/Call Stack	Brings up call stack
Ctrl+F4	Debug/Evaluate/Modify	Evaluates an expression
Ctrl+F5 (ctrl+F7)	Debug/Add Watch	Adds a watch expression
Ctrl+F8	Debug/Toggle Breakpoint	Sets or clears conditional breakpoint
Ctrl+F9	Run	Runs program
F4	Run/Go To Cursor	Runs program to cursor position
F7	Run/Trace Into	Executes tracing into functions
F8	Run/Step Over	Executes skipping function calls
F9	Compile/Make	Makes (compiles/links) program

VII. GLOSSARY

access time	The time taken to retrieve information from memory.
address	It is the value that points to a location in memory.
address bus	Unidirectional line or pathway, which is used to identify the storage location in memory where the next instruction to be executed or the next piece of data will be found.
adjacency matrix	The most frequently used graph representation scheme.
algorithm	It is a step-by-step recipe for solving an instance of a problem.
analog computer	Device that performs operations on data that are represented within the device by continuous variables having a physical resemblance to the dependent quantities being represented by using one kind of physical quantity to represent another.
application software	Software used to accomplish specific tasks other than just running the computer system.
arguments	List of values provided when a function is called. They are specified within paranthesis following the function name.
array	It is a group of elements that share a common name and that are differentiated from one another by their positions within the array.
ASCC	Automatic Sequence Controlled Calculator.
ASCII	American Standard Code for Information Interchange.
Assembler	A translator program that translates the program written in assembly language into machine language.
assignment	It is the process of copying of one variable into another.
associativity	The direction (either left to right or right to left) used to evaluate an expression when a statement contains number of operators.
auto	It is a storage class specifier for local variables.
auto variable	It is visible only in the block or function in which it is declared. All the variables are of type auto by default.
auxiliary memory	See *secondary memory*.
base-10 number system	Also referred as decimal number system since it uses ten separate symbols, 0 to 9 to represent its numbers.
base-16 number system	Also referred as hexadecimal number system since it uses sixteen separate symbols, 0 to 9 and A to F to represent its numbers.
base-2 number system	Also referred as binary number system since it uses only two separate symbols, 0 and 1 to represent its numbers.
base-8 number system	Also referred as octal number system since it uses eight separate symbols, 0 to 7 to represent its numbers.
BCD	Binary-coded decimal.
binary	A numbering system with a base of 2. The binary digits are 0 and 1.

binary-coded decimal	Simplest method used to represent the decimal digits 0 through 9 using binary digits.
binary search	It is a method used to search an ordered list. The search begins in the middle of a table and determines whether the argument is in the upper or lower half of the table, and then continues to divide that portion of the table in which the argument being sought is located until the argument is found.
binary tree	It is a tree that has nodes either empty or not more than two child nodes, each of which may be a leaf node.
bit	Binary digit. It is the basic storage unit of a computer with the capability of storing the values in the form by 0 and 1.
bitwise operator	Operators that operate on individual bits within a word of memory.
Blaise Pascal	A French mathematician who invented the first mechanical calculator.
boolean	It is a variable or an expression that can assume the value of true or false.
branch	A link between a parent node and its child node.
break	It is used to terminate or to exit from a loop or from a switch statement.
bubble sort	Compares the top element of an array with its successor, swapping (interchanging) the two if they are not in proper order.
buffer	A storage location used for temparary storage of data transferred from disk.
bug	It is an error in a program.
bus	Group of lines interconnecting central processing unit and I/O devices.
byte	Eight binary digits (i.e eight bits). A character represented in ASCII requires a byte of storage.
call by reference	It is the process of calling a function using pointers to pass the address of variables.
call by value	It is the process of passing the actual value of variables.
calloc	This function allocates a block of memory (in bytes) dynamically and it returns a pointer variable. The block of memory is initialized with zeroes.
card reader	An input device that uses punched cards to read input information into the computer.
case	It is used to provide labels in a switch statement.
CD-ROM	Compact Disk-Read Only Memory. A common type of portable secondary storage device that can store large volumes of data in the range 700 MB to 1.4 GB.
cell	It is the smallest part of memory that can be accessed by the CPU to store data. Each cell has a capability to store one bit of information. Each cell stores a binary digit referred to as bit.
central processing unit	Heart of the computer system, mounted on the motherboard of every computer, responsible for the interpretation and execution of instructions.
char	It is a primary datatype which is used to declare character variables and arrays.
Charles Babbage	Father of computers, who invented the analytical engine.

Chinese Abacus	First calculating device invented some 2000 years ago in china.
child	*See child node.*
child node	Each link in the root node.
circular queue	It is another form of a linear queue in which the last position is connected to the first position of the list.
comma operator	Operator which connects multiple statements in a single expression.
command	A directive to the operating system to provide a specific function.
command line	The entire command issued to the operating system.
command line arguments	These are arguments that are passed on to main function at the command prompt.
compiler	It is a software program that translates a high-level language program into a machine language program at a stretch.
computing	Study of processes that describe and transform data and instructions. It is a set of techniques to define and solve problems, a way to complete an information-based task adaptable to a specific problem.
computer	A programmable electronic data processing machine, which receives, stores, correlates, performs arithmetic and logical operations & outputs a large volume of data with high speed as per the instruction given.
complete binary tree	It is a binary tree in which every non-leaf node has exactly two children not necessarily to be on the same level.
complete graph	*See strongly connected graph.*
connected graph	It is a graph if there exists a path from any vertex to any other vertex.
constants	It refers to fixed values that does not change during execuetion of a program.
contiguous	A storage characteristic that specifies that the values are stored in consecuetive locations either in memory or on disk.
continue	It is used to transfer the control to the begining of the loop, but does not terminate a loop.
control bus	Bi-directional line or pathway, which is used to pass the controlling signals from control unit to other units in the system and vice versa.
cycle	It is a path containing at least three vertices such that the starting and the ending vertices are the same.
data field	It is a field in the node of a linked list that contains the actual data (i.e., value) of the element to be stored in the list.
data bus	Line or pathway, which is used to transfer data from one unit to another in both directions.
data structure	It defines the way of organizing all data items that includes not only the elements stored, but also stores the relationship between the elements.
data type	It is the named set of values and operations defined to manipulate the character set.
debugging	It is the process of removing errors from the program.

default	It is the default label in the switch statement. The control is transferred to the default statement when none of the case labels match with the expressions in the switch.
dereference operator	It is the asterisk (*) symbol to indicate a pointer's contents (an address).
degree	The number of sub trees in a node.
depth	*See height.*
deque	It is another form of a queue in which insertions and deletions are made at both the front and rear ends of the queue.
dequeue	It is an operation in queue which is used to remove an element from queue at the front end.
derived data type	It is a composite data type constructed from other types, such as array pointer, structure, union,etc.,
digital computer	Device that reads input, stores data, processes and outputs discrete signals.
digraph	*See directed graph.*
directory	The index that stores file locations.
directed cycle	It is the cycle in a digraph.
directed graph	It is a graph in which an edge between any two nodes is directionally oriented.
directed path	In a digraph, all edges are in same direction, which follows a path always moving in the same direction indicated by arrows.
directory	The index that stores file locations.
do	It is a control statement that creates a loop of operations. It is used with while keyword.
double	It is a floating-point datatype specifier, which is used to double the number of digits after decimal point of a floating-point value.
double word	It is a collection of bits on 16-bit boundary.
doubly linked list	It is a linked list containing two pointers, one to its predecessor and another to its successor, thus allowing traversal of the list both backwards and forwards.
dynamic data structure	A data structure formed when the number of data items are not known in advance.
DRAM	Dynamic Random Access Memory. Type of physical read/write memory used in most personal computers and holds data only if it is continuously/ constantly refreshed or reenergized or it will lose its contents.
E²PROM	Electrically Erasable Programmable Read Only Memory.
EAPROM	Electrically Alterable Programmable Read Only Memory.
EDSAC	Electronic Delay Storage Automatic Calculator
EDVAC	Electronic Discrete VAriable Computer
EEPROM	Electrically Erasable Programmable Read Only Memory. Type of ROM that can be erased using electrical pulses and reprogrammed, byte-by-byte, without removing it from the computer system.
edge	It is a connection between two nodes. Also referred as a link.

else	It is used to specify an alternative path in a two-way branch control of execution. It is used with if statement.
ENIAC	Electronic Numeric Integrator And Calculator.
enum	It is used to create a user-defined integer datatype.
enqueue	It is an operation in queue which is used to add a new element in to a queue at the rear end.
EOF	End-Of-File, the condition that occurs when a read operation attempts to read after it has processed the last piece of data.
EPROM	Erasable Programmable Read Only Memory. Type of information in which the information written can be erased by exposing EPROM to high intensity ultraviolet rays for 5 to 10 minutes, and the new information can be written.
expression	It is the sequence of operators and operands that reduces to a single value.
extern	It is a storage class specifier.
extern variable	It is a variable that is visible to all functions and all parts of the program. It is usually declared at the start of the program before main function.
external address	It is the address of the first node in the list, which is stored in the head pointer of the list.
fibonacci numbers	Numbers that are the sum of the preceding two numbers in a sequence. For example : 1 , 1 , 2 , 3 , 5 , 8 and so on.
fibonacci search	A possible improvement in binary search is not to use the middle element at each step, but to guess more precisely a fibonacci number where the key being sought falls within the current interval of interest.
FIFO lists	*see queue.*
file	It is a place in the disk where a group of related data is stored permanently, so that the information is accessed and altered whenever necessary.
file pointer	Pointer to structure that contains information about a file.
float	It is a primary datatype which is used to declare a variable to store a single-point precision value.
for	It is a control statement which is used to create a loop of iterative operations.
free	It deallocates the block of memory already allocated by malloc or calloc.
front end	The end at which deletions are made in a queue.
full binary tree	It is a binary tree in which all the leaves are on the same level and every non-leaf node has exactly two children.
function	It is a self contained program segment (block of statements) that performs some specific well defined task.
function call	It is a statement that invokes another function.
function declaration	It provides the information needed to call a function. This gives information about the name of the function, its return type, and the type of each argument passed in the function.
function prototype	*see function declaration.*
garbage collection	The effective recovery of memory that is no longer in use.

garbage value	It is an unpredictable value which is taken by an auto or register variable when it is not initialized.
getch	It is similar to getchar which reads a single character the instant it is typed without waiting for the ENTER key to be hit. It will not display the character in the screen.
getchar	It is a function which is used for getting a single character from the standard input device. It does not require any arguments.
getche	It is similar to getch which reads a single character the instant it is typed without waiting for the ENTER key to be hit, but it will echo or displays the character that the user have typed, in the screen.
gets	It stands for *"get string"*. This function is used to get a string as input and automatically assigns a null-character to the end of the string.
global variable	*see extern variable.*
goto	It is a transfer statement that enables us to skip a group of statements unconditionally.
graph	It consists of a set of non-empty vertices (referred as nodes in case of trees), together with a set of edges, and each edge joins two different vertices.
graphics tablet	A graphical input device used by graphics designers, which can produce much more accurate drawings on the screen than could do with a mouse or any other pointing device.
gray code	It is a binary code with the property that only one-bit changes between any two consecutive elements.
hard disk	Commonly used secondary storage device made up of a rigid metal disk covered by a magnetic material used to store large volumes of data.
hardware	Various functional units of the computer system.
head pointer	It is a pointer in the linked list, which points to the first node in the list that stores the address of the first node of the list.
header file	It is a file containing the declarations that are to be used in one or more files. This file is normally included in a program with an # include directive.
height	It is the maximum level of any node in the tree.
hybrid computer	Combination of both analog and digital computers, which posses all the good qualities of analog and digital computers.
if	It is a control statement that is used to test an expression and transfer the control to a particular statement or a group of statements depending upon the value of expression.
impact printers	Type of printers that produce their output by making a contact (by using hammers, which strike against a ribbon and paper) to print the text on the paper to be printed.
Input unit	Comprises of various input devices, which helps to read the program, data, information, and various operating commands into the computer.
incidence matrix	*See adjacency matrix.*
indegree	It is the number of edges entering from the vertex in a digraph.

Infix notation	It is the normal way of expressing mathematical expressions. In this notation the operator is present in between the operands.
insertion sort	It is a type of sorting by inserting the i *th* element in the i *th* pass in its correct place.
int	It is a primary data type which is used to declare a variable that stores integer values.
Joseph-Marie Jacquard	Inventor of an automatic loom referred as the **Jacquard loom**, with a punched-card system.
joysticks	Input device used for playing computer games and controlling computer simulations.
keyword	It is a word that has a specific meaning in certain contexts.
Lady Ada Lovelace	First programmer who programmed for computer to run on the Babbage's Analytical Engine.
leaf node	See terminal node.
library	It is a collection of programs or functions that can be utilised by several programmers.
LIFO lists	*see stack.*
linear data structure	A data structure having a linear relation ship between its adjacent elements
linear search	*See sequential search.*
link	*See edge.*
link field	It is a field in the node of a linked list also referred as the next address field that contains the address of the next node in the list.
linked list	It is a linear dynamic data structure that can grow and shrink during its execution time.
left sub trees	All the nodes to the left of a given node in a binary tree.
left-skewed binary tree	It is a binary tree, which has only left child nodes.
long	It is a data type modifier that can be applied to some of the basic data types to increase their size.
LSB	Least Significant Bit. The rightmost bit in a number system with bit position zero.
macro	A statement or series of statements inserted in line within a program in place of a symbol.
mainframe computers	These are computers with large memory capacity and can processes large volumes of data and can solve complicated, scientific and mathematical problems.
magnetic tape	A low cost secondary storage device used for storing data and files.
malloc	It stands for *"memory allocation"*, which allocates a block of memory (in bytes) at run time and it returns a pointer variable. The block of memory is not initialized.
MAR	Memory Address Register.The register, which stores the address of the location from where a word is to be retrieved or to be stored.
Mask-programmed ROM	Type of ROM in which contents are written at the time of its manufacture.
matrix	A two-dimensional array in which the position of a data element must be specified by giving two co-ordinates (i.e., row and column.)

MDR	Memory Data Register. The register, which stores the data retrieved from memory or stored in memory.
microcomputers	These are small computers with built on a single silicon chip (IC/ microprocessor) as its CPU.
merge sort	It is the most commonly used external sorting. A file is divided into two subfiles. These files are compared, one pair of records at a time, and merged by writing them to other files for further comparisons.
Modularity	Process of splitting a large program / project in to smaller modules to perform the operations fast and, which helps in easy error checking.
multidimensional array	It is an array of rank higher than one. Each data element must be specified by giving one co-ordinate for each dimension.
nibble	It is a collection of bits on 4-bit boundary.
next address field	Also referred as the forward link field, which stores the address of its next node.
node	Each data item in a data structure.
non-impact printers	Type of printers that produce their output without making contact (such as electro sensitive, electrostatic, ink jet, and laser for printing) on the paper to be printed.
non-terminal nodes	All intermediate nodes that traversing the given tree from its root node to the terminal nodes.
non-volatile cell	A memory cell, which does not loose the information stored in it when power is switched off.
null address	It is the address stored by the NULL pointer of the last node of the list, which indicates the end of the list.
null character	It is used for terminating strings. It has the ASCII code of zero.
octal	A numbering system with a base of 8. The octal digits are 0 1 2 3 4 5 6 and 7.
OCR	Optical Character Recognition. An input device commonly referred as optical scanner recognizes the printed characters directly from printed documents.
OMR	Optical Mark Reader. Recognizes characters that have been darkened by a dark pencil or ink.
operand	An object in a statement on which an operation is performed.
operating system	Collection of programs that acts as an interface between the user and the computer by coordinating the operations of hardware and software.
outdegree	It is the number of edges exiting from the vertex in a digraph.
output restricted deque	It is another form of a deque which allows deletion at one end (it can be either front / rear) only.
parameter	It is a value or a variable passed to a function.
path (tree)	It is a sequence of distinct nodes in which successive nodes are connected by edges in the tree.
path (graph)	It is a sequence of distinct vertices each adjacent to the next, except possibly the first vertex and last vertex is different in a graph.

piles	see stack.
pointer	It is a variable that represents the location (not the value) of a data item, such as a variable or an array element.
plotter	An output device, which is used to draw graphs and figures using a computer.
pop	It is an operation in stack which is used to delete an existing element from the stack at the top.
postfix notation	Also called as reverse polish notation, in which the operator is represented after its operands.
precedence	It determines the order in which operations are performed.
precision	It specifies the number of meaningful digits in value that must be represented in a fixed number of binary digits.
prefix notation	Also called as polish notation, in which the operator is represented before its operands.
preprocessor	It is the part of the compiler that manipulates the program text before any further compiling is done.
previous address field	Also referred as the backward link field, which stores the address of its previous node.
printf	It stands for *"print function"* or *"print formatted"*. This function is used to output any combination of digits, characters and strings according to the format string on the standard output device.
program	It is the series of instructions provided to the computer that directs the computer in executing a task.
programming	It is the process of preparing and feeding the instructions into the computer for execution.
PROM	Programmable Read Only Memory. Type of memory where the information can be written only once and then onwards it can only be read. Its contents cannot be altered in future.
pseudocode	It is an informal language written in English, particularly used for developing algorithms.
push	It is an operation in stack which is used to add a new element in the stack at the top.
push-down lists	see *stack*.
puts	It stands for *"put string"*. This function is used to output a null-terminated string on the standard output device.
queue	It is an ordered collection of elements in which insertions are made at one end and deletions are made at the other end.
quick sort	This sort divides the initial unsorted list in to two parts, such that every element in the first list is less than all the elements present in the second list. The procedure is then repeated recursively for both the parts, up to relatively short sequences, which can be sorted until the sequences, reduces to length one.

radix sort	It derives its name from the fact that while sorting the data, it considers the radix (digit position) of elements from lower order byte to higher order byte and sorts the data items in the list.
RAM	Random Access Memory. It is a read write memory, in which the contents can be read and can be used to write any information on it. It forms the major part of the main memory.
realloc	It stands for *"re allocation"*. This function increases or decreases the size of dynamically allocated block of memory.
rear end	The end at which insertions are made in a queue.
recursion	It is a process by which a function calls itself repeatedly until some specified condition has been satisfied.
register variable	It is similar to an auto variable which is used to store variables in the CPU register in order to access them as quickly as possible.
register	It is a storage class specifier.
return	It is used to mark the end of a function execuetion and to transfer the control back to the calling function.
return value	It is the value sent by the called function to the calling function.
right sub trees	All the nodes to the right of a given node in a binary tree.
right-skewed binary tree	It is a binary tree, which has only right child nodes.
ROM	Read Only Memory. It is a RAM fabricated with permanently stored information, which cannot be erased. It is a non-volatile memory.
root	See root node.
root node	It is the highest level or the first level in a tree.
sorting	Rearranging a group or sequence of elements or data items in either ascending or descending order depending upon the relationship among the data items present in the group.
scanf	It stands for *"scan function"* or *"scan formatted"* This function is used to get input any combination of digits, characters or strings according to the format string from the standard input device.
searching	It is a programming technique that determines whether an element or a data item is present in the given list or not.
secondary memory	The memory, which is not directly connected to the CPU and stores the data and instructions permanently.
selection sort	Successive elements are selected from a file or from an array and placed in their proper position.
sequential search	The value to be found is searched, from left to right one by one until the element is found or until the end of the list is reached. This search doesn't require that the data items in the list to be in sorted order.
short	It is a data type modifier that can be applied to some of the basic data types to decrease their size.
siblings	The child nodes of a given parent node.

signed	It is a data type modifier used with character and integer data type variables to indicate that the variables are stored with the sign.
singly linked list	It is a linked list in which each node contains only one link field pointing to the next node in the list.
sink vertex	It is a vertex whose outdegree is 0.
sizeof	It is an operator used to get the size of a data type in bytes.
SRAM	Static Random Access Memory. Type of physical read/write memory used in personal computers and holds data, as long as power is supplied to the circuit.
source vertex	It is a vertex whose indegree is 0.
stack	It is an ordered collection of elements in which insertions and deletions are restricted to one end. Stacks are also referred as "piles" and "push-down lists".
static variable	It is a variable whose value persists between different function calls until the end of the program.
static	It is a storage class specifier.
static data structure	A data structure formed when the number of data items are known in advance.
stderr	It is the standard error files operand automatically for displaying the error messages.
stdin	It is the standard input file opened automatically for getting the input for the program.
stdout	It is the standard output file opened automatically for displaying the output of the program.
string	It is an array of characters terminated by a null character.
strongly connected graph	It is a directed graph in which for every pair of distinct vertices their is a **graph** directed path from every vertex to every other vertex.
structure (struct)	It is a collection of one or more variables possibly of different data types, grouped together a single name for convenient handling. They are also used to create user-defined datatypes.
sub tree	A subset of a tree that is itself a tree.
super computers	Large sophisticated, expensive computers, using the latest state-of-the-art technology.
switch	It is a control statement which provides multi-way branching that matches its argument against each of the pattern arguments in order.
syntax	The rules that govern the order of words and relationships in a language.
system software	It is a collection of programs written to service other programs, such as the basic input-output system (bios), device drivers, an operating system, typically a graphical user interface and so on.
terminal node	A node that has no children (i.e., with zero degree).
top	The end from which elements are added and/or removed from a stack.
traverse	Moving through all the nodes in the binary tree, visiting each node in the tree exactly once.

tree	It is a non-linear, two-dimensional data structure, which represents hierarchical relationships between individual data items.
tribonacci numbers	Numbers that are the sum of the preceding three numbers in a sequence. For example : 1 , 1 , 2 , 4 , 7 , 13 , 24...
touch screen	Input device that allows users to operate a computer by simply touching the display screen.
type cast operator	It is the operator that changes the type of an expression.
typedef	It stands for *"type definition"* which allows the user to define new data types that are equivalent to existing data types.
unary minus	It is the operator that complements the value of an expression.
undirected graph	It is a graph in which an edge between any two nodes is not directionally oriented.
union	It is similar to struct in declaration which is used to allocate storage for several data items at the same location.
UNIVAC	UNIVersal Automatic Computer.
unqualified graph	*See undirected graph.*
unsigned	It is a data type modifier used with character and integer data type variables to indicate that the variables are stored without the sign.
User-programmed ROM	Type of ROM introduced before two decades, which are used by users to store their own data / information.
variable	It refers to a quantity which may vary during execuetion of a program
VDU	Visual display unit. Most commonly used output device, which is also referred, as monitor is a device resembling a television that displays what you have typed or otherwise entered in to the computer on the screen in front of you.
void	It is a data type which is used to indicate that the function returns nothing.
volatile	It is a data type modifier used in variable declarations. It indicates that the variable may be modified by factors outside the control of the program.
weakly connected graph	It is a directed graph if any vertex doesn't have a directed path to any other vertices.
weighted graph	It is a graph in which every edge in the graph is assigned some weight or value. The weight of an edge is a positive value that may be representing the distance between the vertices or the weights of the edges along the path.
while	It is a control statement used to execute a set of statements repeatedly depending on the outcome of a test.

INDEX

A

Abstract Data Types 1.2

Access Method 3.90

Actual arguments 2.3

Address field 1.20

Adjacency matrix 4.7

Adjacency list 4.16

Algorithm 1.1

Arrays 1.1

Arguments 2.2

AVL Trees 3.54

Articulation point 4.34

B

Binary search 3.18

Binary search tree 3.18

Binary tree 3.13

    - complete 3.13

    - full 3.13

    - left-skewed 3.13

    - right-skewed 3.13

Binary tree traversal 3.2

    - inorder 3.3

    - level order 3.47

    - postorder 3.3

    - preorder 3.3

Bubble sort 5.6

Bucket 5.23

B Tree 3.71

B+ Tree 3.90

Byte Sort 5.16

C

Child 3.1

Circular Queues 2.37

Child node 3.1

Complete graph 4.1

Conditional expressions 1.37

Connected graph 4.1

Conditional operator 1.37

Conversion of notation 3.45

Conversion specifiers 1.24

Collision 5.24

Cycle 4.1

Cyclic list 1.22

Cut-vertex 4.34

D

Data structure 3.1

    - primary 3.1

    - secondary 3.1

Data types 1.14

    - floating 1.14

    - integer 1.14

    - primary 1.14

Decision making statements 1.29

Declaration part 1.7

Degree 4.2, 4.39

Depth of a tree 4.2

Dequeue 2.37, 3.34

Dereferencing operator 2.15

Digraph 4.38

Directed cycle 4.38

Division method 5.20

Double precision numbers 1.14

Dynamic data structure 3.1

    - linear 3.2

    - non-linear 3.2

E

Edge 4.1

Euler Circuits 4.36

End-order traversal 4.7

End-of-list 1.22

Empty data type 1.16

Empty stack 2.6

Empty deque 2.56

Empty queue 2.43

Enqueue 2.40, 3.12, 3.32

Execution 1.9

Execution part 1.7

Exponential form 1.10

F

First-In-First-Out list 2.36
Fixed size data structure 1.1
Floating point numbers 1.14
Formal arguments 2.3
Forward link field 1.21
Folding method 5.25
Format string 1.24
Fully occupied stack 2.6
Fully occupied queue 2.44
Function 1.5, 2.1
        - library function 2.1
        - user defined function 2.1
Function declaration 2.5
Function prototype 2.5

G

Graph 3.1, 4.1, 4.37
        - directed 4.38
        - undirected 4.37
Graph traversal 4.26
        - breadth first 4.26
        - depth-first 4.26

H

Header file 1.6
Head Pointer 1.20
Height of a tree 4.2
Hash addressing 5.23
Hashing 5.23, 5.24
Hashing function 5.24
Hash table 5.24
Heap sort 5.18
        - max heap
        - min heap
        - ternary heap
Hamilton circuits 4.37

I

Identifier 1.2
if statement 1.29
if-else statement 1.31
        - multiple 1.32

- nested 1.33
Incidence matrix 4.3
Indegree 4.3
Insertion of a node 1.24,1.47
Insert 1.6
Index Node 3.90
Indirection operator 1.22, 2.15
Infix notation 2.21
Input statement 1.5
Inorder traversal 3.3
Insertion sort 5.10
Integers 1.6,1.14
Internal addess 1.20
ISAM 3.90

J

K

Keywords 1.3
Knuth 5.15

L

Leaf 3.2
Left subtree 3.3
Library file 1.4
Linear Queues 2.37
Last-In-First -Out 2.1
Linear linked list 3.19
Linear probing 5.27
Linear search 5.2
Link 3.1
Linked list 1.20
        - circular 1.21
        - doubly 1.21
        - singly 1.21
Linked list application 3.59
Linking 1.8
List 3.1
Load factor 5.24
Looping statements 2.18
        - do-while loop 2.18
        - for loop 2.19
        - while loop 2.20

M

Main function 1.7
Malloc 2.6
Mantissa 1.10
Merge sort 5.2,5.11
Mid-square method 5.26
Mixed-mode arithmetic 1.18

N

Nested structure 2.23
Node 3.1
Non-terminal node 3.2
Null Address 1.20
Null 2.7
Null graph 4.1

O

Operands 2.21
Operator 2.21
          - arithmetic 2.17
          - assignment 2.21
          - ternary 2.21
          - unary 2.21
Open addressing 5.26
Outdegree 4.3
Output statement 1.5
Overflow 5.24
Overflow resolution technique 5.31

P

Parameters 2.2
          - actual 2.3
          - formal 2.3
Partition exchange sort 5.14
Path 3.1, 3.37
Path compression 3.36
Peek operation 2.5, 2.45,
Pendant 4.3
Piles 2.72
Polynomial manipulation 1.122,2.74
Pointer 2.1
          - arithmetic 2.17
          - initialization 2.17
          - operator 2.2
Pop operation 2.3, 2.22

Postfix notation 2.21
Polish notation 2.22
Prefix notation 2.21
Primary data structure 1.1
Pre-processing 1.8
Preprocessor 2.32
Printf function 2.19
Priority 2.67
Push-down lists 2.1
Push operation 2.2, 2.21

Q

Quadratic probing 5.28
Queue 3.2, 2.36
Quick sort 5.2,5.14
Queue size 2.44

R

Recursion 2.1
REAR 2.55
Relational expression 1.19
Rehashing 5.29
Return statemet 2.6
Right subtree 3.13
Root 3.1
Root node 3.1
Radix Sort 5.2,5.16

S

Scanf function 1.34
Scatter table 5.24
Searching 5.1
Separate chaining 5.32
Set 4.33
Sequential search 5.2
Semantics 1.3
Selection sort 5.8
Shell sort 5.8
Siblings 3.1
Single precision numbers 1.14
Sink vertex 4.3
Sinking sort 5.6
Sizeof operator 1.18
Smart union algorithm 4.34
Sorting 5.1
Source vertex 4.3
Static data structure 1.1

Stack 1.2
Strongly connected graph 4.1
Secondary data structure 1.1
Structure 2.18,3.1
            - declaration 2.18
            - defining 2.19
            - initialization 2.21
Structure of C 1.3
Sub graph 4.1
Subtree 3.1, 3.2
Symmetric order 3.3
Switch-case statement 2.8

T

Terminal node 3.2

Threads 3.33
Tokens 1.2
Top pointer 2.1
Topological Sort 4.31
Traversing 3.3
Tree 3.1, 4.1
Truncation method 5.23
Two dimentional data structure 3.1
Towers of Hanoi 2.13

U

Unordered list 1.3
Undirected graph 4.2
Union by height 4.34
Union by size 4.34
Unary operator 2.21
Unqualified graph 4.1
User defined data types 1.15

V

Variables 1.12
            - declaration 1.12
            - initialization 1.13
Variable size data structure 1.2
Vertex 4.4
Void 1.16

W

Weekly connected graph 4.2
Weighted graph 4.3